ALEXANDER CAMPBELL AND
THE DISCIPLES

Alexander Campbell and the Disciples

Lectures delivered in Brite College of the
Bible, Texas Christian University
April and May, 1925

By

JESSE R. KELLEMS

Ph.D. (Edin.), D.D., F.R.G.S.
Evangelist, Churches of Christ

RICHARD R. SMITH, INC.
NEW YORK
1930

Copyright, 1930, by
RICHARD R. SMITH, INC.

PRINTED IN THE UNITED STATES OF AMERICA
BY THE CORNWALL PRESS, INC.

To

DEAN JOHN STRAUB, MA. LITT. D.

FOR FIFTY YEARS PROFESSOR IN THE
UNIVERSITY OF OREGON
TEACHER AND LIFE-LONG FRIEND THIS
BOOK IS LOVINGLY DEDICATED

PREFACE

THE gracious invitation of Dean Colby D. Hall to deliver a course of lectures to the faculty and students of Brite College of the Bible, Texas Christian University provided the urge which resulted in the following study. The substance of the volume was submitted as a successful thesis for the degree of Doctor of Philosophy in the University of Edinburgh under the title "The Theology of Alexander Campbell in its Relation to the Origin of the Disciples." In the subsequent pages this dissertation has been revised and enlarged and much of it rewritten for popular dissemination.

It will be observed that copious quotations from the sources of Disciple history, especially from the writings of the Campbells, abound. Whether or not this be a weakness is, of course, largely a matter of taste. In the present case the realization that the documents of early Disciple days are not readily accessible in attractive form has dictated the method of allowing the Disciple Fathers to tell what they taught in their own words as far as space permits.

The exacting demands upon the time and energy of an evangelist whose field of service takes no account of oceans render consecutive research extremely difficult. Hours for the production of the following chapters have been snatched from a ministry whose behests have called the author from one end of the earth to the other. One was composed in a lovely little university town beside the laughing waters of the bright Willamette amidst the stately blue mountains of Western Oregon; others in the shadow of the grey old Castle Rock in Edinburgh; another in the spray of the "Smoke that Sounds" on the banks of the broad Zambesi. It is hoped that they have suffered no loss of penetration

vii

into the heart of those problems with which the path of
Disciple progress is beset because they have issued from
a vigorous life in which the power of the ground convictions
of Disciple witness has been unsparingly tested in the fires
of evangelistic endeavour. Perhaps they have rather gained
thereby? The conclusions which they embody may at least
lay valid claim to meet the modern demand for a basis in
experience. The author finds himself impelled to agree
with Principle Wheeler Robinson that "important as is the
work of the theologian, it is always subsidiary to that of
the evangelist, the missionary, the preacher and pastor, with
whom lies, under God, the 'Future of Christianity.'" The
one who has put his principles to the test and found them
powerful in committing men to Christ is assuredly as well
prepared to speak with authority in regard to their validity
as he who sees in them only untried theories.

It is to be hoped that an occasional relaxation of that
dispassionate reserve supposedly the concomitant of the
purely historical presentation, or inadvertant indulgences in
seemingly undue enthusiasms or modest eulogistic periods
concerning one for whom the author confesses an ever-
deepening admiration may not receive too ruthless castiga-
tion as being uncritical or as evincing indifference to the
sober facts of Disciple history as they are. Whether such
enthusiasms mar a work of this nature must be purely a
matter of opinion depending largely upon one's theological
predilections. For one whose ancestral roots strike deep
into Disciple soil, whose infancy, childhood, and university
years were lived in an atmosphere surcharged with a militant Disciple conviction and whose manhood has been engaged in an unremitting proclamation of that conviction
upon four continents, a proper scholarly restraint of such
ebullience may be indeed well nigh impossible. It is decidedly difficult for one so sired and for a life time committed to the substantial truth of the chief conclusions of
Disciple teaching to assume that coldly detached attitude

from that which has been the very life blood of his spirit. If that not altogether happy term "propagandist" be justly applied to a work in which the author confesses warmth for conclusions reached, then this study must be so catalogued. I wonder if any book which lives is ever entirely free from this quality?

To the Reverend Professor James Mackinnon, D.D., Ph.D., of the University of Edinburgh, I wish to render heartiest appreciation for his patient guiding of the work through many months. I am also deeply indebted to the Reverend Professor H. R. Mackintosh, D.Phil., D.D., of New College, for numerous helpful suggestions. The connection of the names of these, teachers warmly esteemed, with this book does not in any way commit them to agreement with the conclusions herein set forth. My deepest thanks are also due to my wife, Inez Toledano Kellems without whose inspiration and help the work could not have been published.

JESSE R. KELLEMS.

Manor Croft,
Ratcliffe Road,
Leicester,
September 25th, 1927.

from that which has been the very life-blood of his spirit. If that not altogether happy term "propaganda" be justly applied to a work in which the author confesses warmth for conclusions reached, then this study must be so categologued. I wonder if any book which lives is ever entirely free from this quality.

To the Reverend Professor James Mackinnon, D.D., Ph.D., of the University of Edinburgh, I wish to render heartfelt appreciation for his patient guiding of the work through many months. I am also deeply indebted to the Reverend Professor H. R. Mackintosh, D.Ph., D.D., of New College, for numerous helpful suggestions. The connection of the names of these teachers, warmly esteemed, with this book does not in any way commit them to agreement with the conclusions herein set forth. My deepest thanks are also due to my wife, Idea Tolentino Kullen, without whose inspiration and help the work could not have been published.

JESSE R. KULLEN.

Manor Croft,
Ratcliffe Road,
Leicester.
September 28th, 1927.

CONTENTS

CONTENTS

ALEXANDER CAMPBELL AND
THE DISCIPLES

CHAPTER I

INTRODUCTORY

In his vivid style Professor Streeter calls upon us to consider the spirit of our age. "The Renaissance of the fourteenth and fifteenth centuries reinforced in a new way the backward look of Europe. The Church, to its credit, was to the fore in the revival of learning. But learning meant the study of the Humanities, that is, of the great writers of the classical period of Greece and Rome, and the study of the Humanities again implies a Golden Age in a distant past. Down to very recent times, European education in general has been, and clerical education still is, mainly along Renaissance lines. It has tended to suggest, as the ideal of intellectual attainment, acceptance and imitation rather than invention and experiment.

But today outside the Church men are looking forwards for the Golden Age. The really live intellectual activity of the present age is not so much conservative as adventurous. Its motto is not learning but research, not acceptance but criticism, not imitation but invention. Experiment and fresh construction are the dominating ideas, not only in natural science and engineering, but in economics, in art, in philosophy, and in political and ethical ideals. Outside organized Christianity the motto of the idealist in every department of life is "Behold I make all things new." [1] It would be difficult to dissent from this graphic statement. Men of the twentieth century are pioneers. The inexorable command which throbs through our spiritual blood bids us look up and ahead—"Look not behind thee for thy life" —"Sail on, and on, and on."

[1] "Christ the Constructive Revolutionary" in "The Spirit," 356.

But while we thrill to the behests of this imperious spirit, let us pause ere we unwittingly speak a half truth. Is the backward look reprehensible if through it one draws into his spiritual veins the spicy wine of courage for the adventure of fresh beginnings? Is a classic less a classic because hoary centuries intervene between us and that time, electric with noble thought and instant with rich emotion, when whole it sprang from out some glowing heart? Is the radiance of Shakespeare's name bedimmed because of swift-passing years or do we accord to him a place less exalted than to the poets of our day because of their possession of modernity? The nineteenth century enthusiasm for the philosophical dogmas of evolution and eternal progress has waned, and the shallow method of historical interpretation which glimpses its Golden Ages only in some distant future has been frowned upon by modern men to whom the sobering power of more mature reflection has brought a truer view. Representative of this better tendency, Dean Inge with accustomed vigor reacts against the infection of this, in other fields, discarded surface method which has spread its insidious way through much of the religious literature of the present. "No one treats the history of art and poetry in this way, but the delusion has not been completely abandoned in the case of religion. We have discussions on what is supposed to be a serious difficulty in the way of accepting Christianity—that on the Christian hypothesis the highest revelation came to mankind nearly two thousand years ago. The truth is that the great religions—Buddhism, Christianity, and Islam—date from the millennium which ends with the career of Mohammed; and all of them were at their best when they were fresh from the mint." [2] How utterly abject indeed would be our poverty were there no classics to rivet our admiring gaze, that within us might be provoked that holy awe out of which high resolution rises, to fire our hearts for Golden Ages which shall transcend in wonder those ever farther from us receding into

[2] "Science, Religion, and Reality," 351.

the misty past. Is not the assumption that a classic belongs
only to the past an evacuation of the very meaning of the
term? A classic is of the past, the present, the future—it
is timeless. If we divest the present of what has been,
wherein is there meaning in history?

I

In this conviction that inspiration for future endeavor is
best derived from an immersion in the thought and spirit
of classic epochs, has the present evaluation of the theological and religious contributions of Thomas and Alexander
Campbell been essayed. The time has arrived when the
Disciples should study the works of these doughty fathers
of their communion. It must regretfully be admitted that
for many years the majority of them have not done so.
But few who have espoused Campbellian principles have
perused the pages on which they are inscribed. A generation of splendid men has come to maturity absolutely un-
acquainted with that noble literature which a hundred years
ago profoundly stirred American religious society, engen-
dering a storm the rumbles of which even yet have not
completely died away. Hundreds of these are devout and
earnest ministers in Churches of Christ while hundreds of
others, fellows of their college and university days, with
high courage nurtured by a consuming love of Christ, and
an idealism as pure as the gleaming snow on mountain
crags, have eagerly gone forth into the far places holding
aloft the light of faith to the wandering peoples of the
world. Is it then to be thought strange that among such,
even though their motives be acknowledged pure and good,
there should occasionally be those whose indifference to
teaching and practice in which there lurks the taint of sectarian tendency, bespeaks for them an ignorance of the
foundation principles which alone constitute a reasonable
apologetic for the separate existence of the Churches of
Christ in a world already cursed to the full with belligerent

sects and divisions? With the sturdy independence of their
sires these modern Disciples steadfastly have been disinclined to "glory in men." And after all the Campbells
were but men. We are certainly as free to interpret the
Word of God as were any of the renowned heroes of the
Reformation—a Luther, a Calvin, a Knox or a Wesley—
indeed the basal truth which has ever been the dynamic
urge to ceaseless Disciple progress exactingly demands it.
There is, furthermore, no such thing as a Disciple theology
and any over-stressing of the teaching of one man, even
though that man be Alexander Campbell himself, might con-
ceiveably involve us in the danger of crystallization, combining our plea, thereby, within the immobile confines of a
cast-iron theological system. Like a grim spectre, the haunt-
ing fear of creedalism has dogged the footsteps of Disciple
progress. But such fears are groundless. Having once
breathed the free air of New Testament Christianity the
Disciples are not likely ever again to be enmeshed in the
toils of an effete sectarianism, nor lightly to throw away
noble gains so hardily won. Theological Schools and Colleges of the Bible assuredly have a grave responsibility de-
volving upon them in the obligation which their very
institution entails, to see to it that those who go forth from
their halls as leaders of Disciple thought shall know the
plea for the unity of the people of God upon the basis of
a restored New Testament faith. If they fail in this—if
they are but the poor copies of the great denominational
training centers—the money which has been expended in
their establishment were put to far better use if employed
to send their young men and women to the colleges of their
denominational brethren or to the universities supported by
the state.

In dealing with the origin of the communion variously
known as "The Disciples of Christ," "Christians," or
"Churches of Christ," one instinctively feels that he is considering a movement rather than a church or churches. *In
its beginning* there was no thought among any of those

whose efforts resulted in its ultimate formation, of the organization of a *new Church or religious party*. The high ideal which had been the moving cause of all they thought and did, was diametrically opposed to such a course; indeed, to abolish all divisions and parties was the lofty resolve to which they heartily directed their every energy. At the time of its inception, it profoundly affected the whole of American religious society. Like a new Renaissance or Reformation, it was an imperative call to freedom of thought, freedom of speech, and the right of the individual to interpret the Christian Scriptures. Its first leaders did not hesitate openly to preach its doctrines as calculated to reform the Church, to accomplish a destruction of sectarian walls, and to bring all Christians to a unity upon the truth. For the first period of its existence, it was a movement for Reformation, and those who espoused its principles were known as "Reformers." Gradually recognizing the fact, however, that a new reformation, as such, was seemingly doomed to fail because of the simple fact that those to whom their appeals were addressed and in whose interests the work was being propagated, were treating it all with bland indifference, the movement began to crystallize into an independent organization. Since the reformatory principles would not be received into the Churches, the "Reformers" decided to organize around them, drawing to them christians from the churches, as well as sinners from the world. About the year 1830, therefore, the movement definitely changes its character and becomes a movement for the "Restoration of Primitive Christianity." The great principles forged in the days of Reformation, were now courageously and unshrinkingly put to the acid test of actually trying them out in organizational life. In this period the movement definitely becomes a propagandist organization, tremendously militant and daringly evangelistic. Dr. Moore correctly dates the distinctively Restoration phase from 1830 to 1870. With 1870 began the third great era of Disciple history,—that which may be termed "the period of

Toleration." [3]   Having waged to victory their war against what they considered the despotic reign of priestcraft, and having won a powerful and influential place in the religious life of America, there grew up at the close of the Civil War, a spirit of toleration which manifested itself in a hearty welcome of every opportunity to federate with other communions in furthering the progress of the kingdom of God. Points of agreement were more and more emphasized, while those things which divide were considered less frequently than in the former years.   Our study has to do with the progress of the movement up to the year 1870, since this is the period in which Alexander Campbell did his epochal work.

That Thomas Campbell was the founder of the communion sometimes known as "The Reformation Movement of the Nineteenth Century" is beyond refutation. Its ground principles were all thought out by him, and the work well under way, before his distinguished son left Scotland's shores to take his part in it.   Because of his elevation of intellect, his catholocity of spirit, the incisive accuracy of his scholarship, the burning passion of his soul for truth, and above all, his indomitable courage in the face of determined and at times seemingly over-powering opposition, Alexander became the leader of the movement and, because he was simply a more agressive fighter than his father, has virtually eclipsed him in the place which was by right his own.   The son never failed, however, gratefully to accord him the credit for inaugurating the effort in his composition of the "Declaration and Address" and even in the work which preceded it and out of which it grew.   While, therefore, any historical presentation of the theology of Alexander Campbell in its relation to the origin of the Churches of Christ must take into account the prefatory work of the father, no true disclosure of the inwardness of Disciple spirit is possible without incursion into the genius

[3] "History of the Disciples of Christ," Moore, v, vi.

of the son. The father created the movement; the son made it to live, nor is it too much to say that without his fighting energy it might have died out in defeat amidst its native Pennsylvania hills.

There were some things which Alexander Campbell and his devoted fellow-laborers said better than anyone who had preceded them or any have followed in the path their feet have pioneered. Disciple indifference to the documents in which these pronouncements lie enshrined is censurable not alone for its want of appreciation of the heroic toil and sacrifice out of which the plea was forged, but also of the intellectual and spiritual heights to which their fathers attained. The desponding prattle that the Disciples have really made no worthy contributions to modern Christian life and thought evinces a culpable ignorance, not only of what the early leaders so fearlessly taught, but also of what the brave host who followed in their train have done. There are some things forever settled. Sober, constructive Disciple thought guards jealously the conviction that there is a "faith which was once for all delivered unto the saints." While heartily agreeing with Professor Streeter that it is ours to criticize rather than meekly to accept, to adventure rather than blindly to imitate, they are yet convinced that there is a core of faith which criticism, reverent though it be, cannot whittle away, a precious deposit of divine and saving truth which must be accepted because it is true, a residue for which no amount of adventure or invention, however brave or hopeful, can ever find a substitute. Such was the masculine faith of Campbell and those who so untiringly toiled with him. As one journeys through the pages of the memorable works to which the white heat of his heart and brain gave being, one may once again enter into the thrill of that superb confidence that here was indeed a new reformation —a reformation through a return to the greatest period of the life of Christianity upon the earth, the period of its beginning. A discriminating modern exponent of this age, Dr. Vernon Bartlett, envisages the unity and freedom which characterizes the Church in the days of the apostles of our Master, as the final standard by which our own senseless divisions may some day be healed: "All the more striking, then, is the unity of spirit amid the diversity of thinking. 'In things essential unity, in things secondary, liberty, in all things, charity'; if this be the abiding motto of a true Catholicity, then the Apostolic Age realized it to the full. And its necessary things were few, simple, but radical, reducible in the last resort to one—the heart's devoted faith in one Lord, as pledged in baptism and evinced in obedience of life. But that one thing involved and carried with it all else needful for life and godliness. May the experience of the Apostolic Age, as it becomes better known not only in detail but also in its underlying conception of what Christian religion really is, yet prove the great Eirenicon, harmonizing the distinctions to which its partial rediscovery at the Reformation gave rise under the peculiar political and mental conditions of the sixteenth century." [4]

Perhaps we may feel that here we are in the presence of an over-weening confidence—far too sanguine are these courageous pioneers in their rude, untutored western land. Such hopefulness of an immediate and joyous reception of their audacious appeal for Christian unity by the discordant sects whose bitter party strife made desolate true religion in the world bespeaks for them an immaturity both intellectual and spiritual, difficult to reconcile with truly great leadership. While it must be confessed that all the intricacies with which the problem of Christian unity bristles did not present themselves to their minds in the perspective possible to us, who have so greatly profited because they have gone the way before us, it is abundantly evident that their unquestioned assurance of ultimate success was the child of a mighty conviction that the basis which it had been theirs to discover was divinely true—God's own plan for the reunion of His people. It may be that the antidote for the admittedly

[4] "Apostolic Age," xi, xii.

prevalent pessism of our own time in regard to the ultimate possibility of Christian reunion, will be made apparent as we pilgrimage along the path which their brave feet have beaten out before us, back to the unpolluted source of our faith, there with devout and teachable mind to learn God's way of its accomplishment. Typical of this persistent gloom are the dispirited words of Dr. Gore. "There cannot, I am convinced, be a reunited Church except on the basis of the Catholic Creeds, and the acknowledgment of the sacramental principle as well as the due administration of the sacraments, and the recognition of the episcopal link of connection and continuity in the Catholic body. Here again, then, unity seems a long way off. I do not know if anything can heal the breaches, unless very evil times force us together." "But meanwhile" and assuredly this is language which every Disciple would approve, so distinctively Campbellian is its trend, "the best preparation for future unity lies, I believe, in the detached and disinterested study of our Christian origins and in close fellowship for social service." [5]

It falls not within our purview to prosecute any exhaustive research into the sources of Campbell's theology nor to accord more than passing notice to those influences which the environment of childhood and early manhood exerted upon him. A commendable contribution in this direction has been made by Dean Garrison in his "Alexander Campbell's Theology." In this work he has sought to assemble those sources, political, philosophical and theological out of which, consciously or otherwise, Campbell drew his theological conclusions, and an evaluation of their relations to the theology as such. The province of the present attempt, on the other hand, is restricted to a somewhat critical examination of that theology itself and an estimate of the inter-relation subsisting between it and the viril communion which it admittedly initiated and of which its fundamental conclusions have ever been the inspiration and driving power. Wher-

[5] "The Holy Spirit and the Church," 352.

ever pertinent to this purpose such influences will receive candid attention, but for the inquiry to which we have addressed ourselves they are but secondarily important. I must, however, confess a large measure of debt to Dr. Garrison in the brief outline of such sources which is here included.

II

Thomas Campbell was born in County Down, February 1, 1763. With his brothers, he received an excellent English education at a military regimental school not far distant from Newry. He early experienced a vital spiritual awakening which was the fountain of all his subsequent religious life. The cold formality of the Episcopal ritual, and the apparent lack of a deep and vital piety which he considered to be the essential thing in Christianity, caused him early to lose interest in the faith to which his father belonged, and to seek instead the society of the more rigid and devout Covenanters and Seceders. After attending their meetings for some time, he finally became a regular communicant in the Seceder Church. It was during his attendance upon the Seceder services, that he became deeply concerned about his own salvation, and for some time sought peace in vain. Though aided by the sympathy and prayers of many earnest friends, he could not find the assurance of the foregiveness which he craved with an agony born of a realization of his own exceeding sinfulness and his impotence to do anything for his own redemption. "While in this state, and when his mental distress had reached its highest point, he was one day walking alone in the fields, when, in the midst of his prayerful anxieties and longings, he felt a divine peace suddenly diffuse itself throughout his soul, and the love of God seemed to be shed abroad in his heart as he had never before realized it." [6] All doubt and fear vanished as if by magic, and he knew himself to be a child of God. At this very moment, he felt

[6] "Memoirs of Alexander Campbell," Richardson, I, 23.

himself to be called, and the feelings which he experienced, —the sudden change from doubt and fear to peace,—he regarded as proceeding from a direct divine influence which had miraculously imparted to him a saving or justifying faith.

Filled with an ardent desire to devote himself to the ministry in the Secession Church, but unable to secure the consent of his father, who as a member of the Church of England, looked with no great favor upon his connection with the Seceders, and while a final decision was pending, he engaged in teaching, first in an English Academy which he established in Connaught, and later in a school at Sheepbridge, near Newry. Mr. John Kinley, through whose influence he had obtained his latter position, impressed with his high abilities and the deep piety of his life, urged him to carry out his desire to enter the ministry, and even proffered the means to defray the expenses of his classical and ministerial education. His father's opposition having finally been overcome, he proceeded to Glasgow, where he became a student in the University.

The course prescribed for students in Divinity, at this time extended over three years. It being considered proper for ministers to have some knowledge of medicine, Thomas Campbell, while carrying on his other studies, also attended the medical lectures. At the conclusion of his University career, he entered the Divinity Hall of the Secession or Antiburgher Church, which at this time was at Whitburn. Doctor Archibald Bruce was minister of a Secession church there, and during the week conducted the classes in Divinity.[7] Having completed the five sessions of eight weeks each required by the Synod, he submitted to the usual examination and trials for license before the Presbytery in North Ireland, and became a probationer or preacher, under the direction of the Synod, to such churches as were destitute of a fixed ministry.[8] It was during the vacations between his periods

[7] "Memoirs of Alexander Campbell," Richardson, I, 23, 27.
[8] Ibid., 27.

of study in Scotland, that he became acquainted with the descendents of the Huguenots who had settled on the shores of beautiful Lough Neagh. These deeply religious people had fled from France upon the revocation of the Edict of Nantes by Louis XIV, and had settled first in Scotland, and later in Ireland, where two families, the Bonners and the Corneigles, purchased an entire townland on the shores of Lough Neagh. Here they devoted themselves to agriculture, and established schools in which the Bible was carefully taught, and the forms and practices of the Presbyterian Church were faithfully inculcated.[9] While engaged in teaching school during the vacation periods, Thomas Campbell met Jane, the only daughter of the Corneigles, and in June of his twenty-fifth year he was married to her. To this union, on September 12th, 1788, in Ballymena, about a mile from the silvery waters of Lough Neagh, was born his first child, Alexander Campbell.[10]

After a ministry of several years among various congregations near Sheepbridge and Market Hill in County Armagh, Thomas Campbell was called, in 1798, to a newly established church at Ahorey, about four miles from the town of Armagh, and about ten miles from the flourishing town of Newry. He accepted the call and moved to a farm near Rich-Hill. It was here that most of the boyhood of Alexander was spent, and those early impressions made, which so largely formed the character of his thought in after years.[11] It was here also, during his ministry at the little country church in Ahorey and as master of the academy which he later founded at Rich-Hill, that Thomas Campbell was brought into contact with those influences which bred within his heart that hatred of sectarianism which, in the new world, grew so amazingly into a mighty movement for a return to the pristine unity and purity of the Church.

In order to an understanding of his subsequent course in

9 *Ibid.*, 19, 20.
10 *Ibid.*, 19.
11 "Memoirs of Alexander Campbell," Richardson, I, 28, 30.

America, it is essential that some of these influences be detailed and the impressions made by them evaluated.

(1) The politico-religious distraction of North Ireland at this time was undoubtedly one of the most powerful of these influences directing his mind toward a consideration of the necessity for Christian unity. His ministry was coincident with those travail years which brought forth the rebellion of 1798, and ended with the attempt of Emmet and others in 1803. Intent upon driving the Roman Catholics from North Ireland, the society of Orangemen was formed in County Armagh in 1795. Various contending parties such as the "Defenders," the "Peep-o' day Boys," etc., kept the whole province of Ulster in constant commotion. Under the pretense of searching for arms, many went around by night, and since the doors were generally opened at the first summons, common robbers often took advantage of this excuse to carry out their depradations against the property of the ravaged and distracted people. In the midst of all this anarchy, Theobald Wolfe Tone, a Protestant lawyer of Dublin, organized his secret order, known as the "United Irishmen," purposing through them to launch a rebellion against the government, which would eventuate in an Irish Republic. The Catholics became members of this order that they might secure protection against the Orangemen; the Presbyterians in order to bring about reform in Parliament, through which they hoped for equality in taxation and representation. The organization eventually secured membership of one hundred and fifty thousand men. The Presbyterians of the six Northern Counties formed the major part of it, and the fact that Campbell steadfastly refused to have anything to do with it was calculated to bring him into disfavor with many of his people ardent in its support. He went even to the lengths of denouncing secret societies and secret oaths. There can be no doubt but that all this political and social disorder made a profound impression upon his mind. The firm conviction which followed him, and also his son, through life,

that secret societies were wrong for Christians, can be traced directly to the experience of these chaotic times.

(2) The divisions in his own Presbyterian family were also a source of great sorrow to him. In 1733 had occurred the defection from the National Kirk of Scotland, on the part of Alexander Erskine and his three confederates, under the designation of the "Associate Presbytery," resulting in the organization of the Seceders.[12] This schism extended to Ireland, and as early as 1736 a request was sent to the Synod for ministerial aid. It was not until 1742, however, that this request was complied with and Gavin Beugo was sent over to form churches of the new order. Soon after this first great rent in the body of the National Kirk, Thomas Boston and his coadjutors also seceded and formed the "Presbytery of Relief." [13] This movement differed only from the Seceders in entertaining more liberal views of the communion.

The "Associate" or "Secession" church had but a short period of peace, and then it was disrupted by the question as to the propriety of subscribing to certain oaths, required by the burgesses of the towns, that "they would support the religion presently professed within the realm." To many, this seemed to be a sanction of the very abuses which had caused the first great defection from the National Church. The Secession, therefore, became divided into the Burghers and Antiburghers.[14] A half century later these, in turn, were split into the "Old Light Burghers" and the "New Light Burghers," and in the case of the party to which Thomas Campbell belonged, into the "Old Light Antiburghers," headed by Campbell's former teacher of theology, Dr. Archibald Bruce, who with several others formed a Presbytery known as the "Constitutional Associate Presbytery," and the "New Light Antiburghers." [15] Hence the Secession was it-

[12] "Ecclesiastical History of Scotland," Grub, IV, 61.

[13] "Ecclesiastical History of Scotland," Grub, LV, 79.

[14] Ibid., 74, 76. Also, "Story of the Scottish Church," Ninian Hill, 220, 221.

[15] Ibid., 165.

self divided into four main bodies, not counting several others of minor importance, which, during the heated discussion of Synods and Assemblies, "flew off like sparks from a forge."

The depths of aversion with which Campbell viewed these schisms in his beloved Presbyterian Church is manifest by the fact that he had frequently urged upon all the desirability of a union between the various branches of the Seceders. Largely through his influence, a committee of consultation met in October, 1804, at Rich-Hill, by which a report, with propositions for union, prepared by him, was adopted and forwarded to the Synod at Belfast, where it was very cordially received. In March, 1805, a joint meeting was held at Lurgan, and on each side an earnest desire for union was expressed. The fact that the Burgher oath had never been required in Ireland was evidence that nothing in the state of things existing there warranted a division. The General Associate Synod in Scotland, however, hearing of these growing movements for union, expressed their dissent in advance of any application, and, for a time, put an end to the matter. In the following year, the Provincial Synod made application to the Scottish Synod to consider if it would not be better for the brethren in Ireland to transact their own business wihout being in immediate subordination to that body. Thomas Campbell was sent to Scotland to lay the matter before the General Synod and, although he argued the case with great earnestness and clarity before that body in Glasgow,[16] the Synod decided that the proposal was inexpedient, and accordingly matters remained as they had been before. The efforts were not unavailing, however, for on September 5th, 1820, in the very church in Edinburgh where the division had occurred seventy-three years before, a union of the

[16] While Alexander Campbell was in the University, four years later, a gentleman who heard his father on this occasion, said to him: "I listened to your father in our General Assembly in this city, pleading for a union between the Burghers and Antiburghers. But, Sir, while in my opinion he out-argued them, they out-voted him." "Memoirs of Alexander Campbell," Richardson, I, 58.

Burghers and Antiburghers was consummated amidst great rejoicings and impressive ceremonies.[17]

(3) One other influence which must have impressed the kindly soul of Thomas Campbell during the European period of his life emanated from an earnest body of Independents who had a church at Rich-Hill, and with whose pastor, Mr. Gibson, and the members he was on terms of friendly intercourse. While not permitted to neglect any service of his own communion, a Seceder minister was given the privilege of "occasional hearing," and frequently after his evening services at Ahorey, Thomas Campbell and his son attended the meetings of the Independents. Their people being more liberal than other communions in granting the use of their meeting house to preachers of other churches, opportunity was given to hear some of the most illustrious men of the period. Rowland Hill, one of the most celebrated men of the time, preached here, as did also James Alexander Haldane. John Walker, formerly fellow and teacher at Trinity College, Dublin, and minister of Bethesda Chapel, a man whose great ability and learning made a profound impression upon the young Alexander,[18] preached at Rich-Hill during the time of the Campbell's residence there. It was his custom to invite any who desired to do so, to come to his room and talk with him concerning the things of the kingdom of God. Thomas Campbell and one of his elders accepted this invitation, and enjoyed a long conversation with him. Before the talk was over, Alexander joined the party. The work and teaching of Walker eventually resulted in the organization of the Plymouth Brethren, who, while not according with all his views, really owe their origin to him. Just how far the Campbells were influenced by this one conversation, is not known. Whether the views concerning the ministry which they held in the earlier days of their re-

[17] "Ecclesiastical History of Scotland," Grub, IV, 167, 168. "Memoirs of Alexander Campbell," Richardson, I, 58.
[18] "Memoirs of Alexander Campbell," Richardson, I, 60, 61.

formatory ministry are traceable to this incident cannot be determined with certainty.

The Scottish Independents differed somewhat from the English Congregationalists. Though nominally in connection with the Independents of Scotland, the Rich-Hill people were Haldanean in sentiment. The Scotch branch of the Independent movement had its rise in the eloquent preaching of John Glass,[19] an able minister of the National Church of Scotland, who, influenced by the works of John Owen, seceded from the Church about 1728, giving up his parish of Tealing near Dundee, and began to organize churches in the larger Scottish cities, on Independent lines. The followers of his views were called Glassites.[20] Robert Sandeman, about 1755, developed and sustained the views of Glass, and through his controversy with Hervey concerning the nature of faith, the leading doctrine of his "Theron and Aspasio," became the acknowledged champion of the Scottish Independent movement. His most distinctive doctrines were that faith in Christ is merely an assent to the testimony concerning Him, which was first given by the apostles and preserved for us in the New Testament; it therefore differs not at all from faith in any other fact or truth. He advocated the weekly observance of the Lord's Supper, love feasts, weekly contributions to the poor, mutual edification on the part of members of the Church, a plurality of elders, conditional community of goods, etc. He was also very liberal in his views concerning theatres, public and private amusements when unconnected with influences positively wrong.

The Rich-Hill Independents did not sanction all the views of Sandeman. They observed the Lord's Supper weekly, as they did also their contributions, but were opposed to

---

[19] "Ecclesiastical History of Scotland," Grub, IV, 55.

[20] "He had some followers, but they were neither numerous nor influential. The sect which he founded, continues to exist in Scotland. Its opinions were considerably modified by Robert Sandeman, a son-in-law of its founder, from whom its members received the name Sandemanians." "Ecclesiastical History of Scotland," IV, 55.

theatre-going, feet washing as an ordinance of the Church, community of goods, and some of the other extremes preached and practiced by Sandeman. They were also free from much of the bitterness and the dogmatic and controversial spirit which all too often characterized the work of the distinguished advocate of Scottish Independency.

Just how far the little Independent Church influenced the Campbells cannot be inferred with certainty. If either of them at this time made a study of the Sandemanian views concerning faith, with which at a later date they were assuredly in partial accord, there is no evidence of the fact. It is certain that both father and son carried to America substantially the Presbyterian conception, both as to the nature of saving faith and the manner of its coming. That the great Independent doctrine of private judgement did have some influence, at least upon Alexander, is affirmed by Dr. Richardson. "It was the natural tendency of his mind to seize upon principles, and this doctrine, so consonant with his own native independence of thought, was peculiarly agreeable to him. He does not appear, however, to have fully or practically adopted this principle, so entirely at variance with the denomination to which he belonged and with the religious authority he had been taught to revere." [21]   It is certain, his aversion to the doctrine that the authority to interpret the Scriptures is exclusively confined to the clergy—a doctrine held almost universally by the Churches of the day, with the exception of those who had adopted congregational government—found its beginning in his own experience with the clergy of the Seceder denomination, and the influence of the Rich-Hill Independents. The wrath which later, in the "Christian Baptist," flamed forth with such power against the authority of Presbyteries, Synods, Conventions, Church courts, etc., must have found its first kindling in his resentment toward the

[21] "Memoirs of Alexander Campbell," I, 64.

experiences which he knew his father had gone through with the leaders of his own communion in Ireland.[22]

(4) The movement for a more "evangelical" style in preaching was a further influence exerted upon Thomas Campbell during his last years in the mother country. The great revival under the Wesleys and Whitfield, attended at first with almost fanatical manifestations of excitement, had toward the close of the century given place, in a large degree, to indifference and conformity to worldly pursuits. The influence of skeptical ideas from France, and the general commotion which was everywhere manifest as the result of the French and American wars, had wrought sad havoc in the Church. In order to counteract this spiritual stagnation with its accompanying immorality, numbers of earnest men had resolved themselves into a body for the promotion of field preaching, which was known as the "Evangelical Society." It was not confined to one denomination, and some of its most enthusiastic members were communicants in the Church of England. Thomas Campbell was a member of this Society, and much interested in its mission. Its greatest exponents in Scotland were the Haldanes. The later enthusiasm for evangelism, such a powerful factor in the growth of the Disciples, assuredly owes much to the influence of this early Society in the old world.

In 1807 the health of Thomas Campbell began to fail, and, being advised that a sea voyage would probably benefit him, he decided to go to America. He landed in May, 1807, and finding the Antiburgher Synod of North America in session in Philadelphia, he presented his letters of recommendation, and was cordially received and assigned to the Presbytery of Chartiers in Western Pennsylvania. After a long and wearisome journey, he reached his new field, presented his credentials, and was received into the membership of the Presbytery. A charge was immediately assigned to him and without delay he took up his labors. His liberal

[22] *Ibid.*, 64, 65.

action in allowing members of the various Presbyterian organizations other than his own to come to the communion table, soon involved him in difficulties with the Presbytery. The censure which they imposed caused him to appeal his case to the Associate Synod, which, while reversing the decision of the Presbytery, referred the whole matter to a committee which reported that his utterances and actions were not in accord with Seceder usage and were deserving of censure. While submitting to the disposition of his case on the part of the Synod and the committee, in order that he might not evince a refractory spirit, he attempted to continue his labors. The constant suspicion of the Seceder denomination soon made it clear that he could no longer work in harmony with that body. Though regretting profoundly the necessity for his action, he saw that there was no course but to withdraw from them. He therefore withdrew from the Presbytery, severing all ministerial connection with it. His popularity as a preacher had caused him to be in great demand, so the rupture with the Presbytery did not occasion any diminution in his ministerial services. On September 7th, 1809, the people to whom he had been ministering, resolved to form an association for the promotion of the cause which had now become dear to them all, that of restoration to the Church of God of her original unity and purity. At some time previous to this, a committee of those interested had met with him and had discussed the way to unity. They had also requested him to compose a document setting forth the principles which should best bring the results which they all so ardently desired. This brochure was read by its author on the day of the organization of the "Christian Association of Washington." The events leading up to the publication of this remarkable treatise, and an analysis of its contents, will be given in detail, in consideration of the Campbellian doctrine of Christian Unity.

III

Before noting the part which Alexander played in the plea for christian unity, it will be necessary to consider briefly those influences, exerted upon him before he left the old world, which were so powerful in shaping his theological thought. Some of these are direct, and no difficulty is experienced in discovering what they are and just how far they made their impressions upon him; others, while none the less important, are indirect, from the very air which he breathed. He was accustomed to look with little interest, upon the works of some whom later generations have thought to have exercised strong influence upon him. But he was not a man detached from his time. Consciously or unconsciously, the period in which he lived with its characteristic modes of thought and life, got into his spiritual blood. In addition to those he shared with his father, and which have already been noted, there were some which were peculiarly his own.

1. Among these, first place must be given to his early religious influences. The devout family into which he was born, in addition to the strict observance of religious duties, the custom of Seceders of the period, and especially in the homes of the ministers, constituted a religious and spiritual environment which was calculated to give him a profound respect for divine things. The minister's family was supposed to be a model for all in the parish. To this end, the Synod had prescribed that the minister "should worship God in his family by singing, reading, and prayer, morning and evening; that he should catechize and instruct them at least once a week in religion, endeavoring to cause every member to pray in secret, morning and evening, that he should remember the Lord's day to keep it holy, and should himself maintain a conversation becoming the gospel." Thomas Campbell and his wife were very prompt in the dutiful observance of all these things. It was a rule of the family

that each member should, during the day, commit some passage of Scripture, to be recited at the evening worship. Long sections were frequently quoted by the older members, and on the Lord's day all the verses learned during the week were rehearsed. Faithful observance of the Lord's day was inculcated, each member of the family being expected to attend the services, and to be able, on return, to give the text and the main points discussed in the sermon. During enforced absences of Thomas Campbell the family worship was regularly continued by his wife whose early religious training and thorough knowledge of the great teachings of the Scriptures, made her eminently able to perform this duty with gracious effectiveness. In after years, Alexander, speaking of these very influences so powerful in childhood, paid her a loving tribute: "Having a peculiarly ready and retentive memory, she treasured up the Scriptures in early life, and could quote and apply them with great fluency and pertinency from childhood to old age. She, indeed, also possessed a mental independence which I have rarely seen equaled, and certainly never surpassed, by any woman of my acquaintance. Greatly devoted to her children, and especially to their proper training for public usefulness, and for their own individual and social enjoyment, she was indefatigable in her labors of love, and in her religious training and development." In regard to her influence in stimulating him to a study of the Scriptures, he says; "I can but gratefully add, that to my mother, as well as to my father, I am indebted for having memorized in early life almost all the writings of King Solomon—his Proverbs, his Ecclesiastes—and many of the Psalms of his father David. They have not only been written on the tables of my memory, but incorporated with my modes of thinking and speaking." [23]

The influence upon the son, religiously and spiritually, of such a family life as the Campbells lived, cannot be over-

[23] "Memoirs of Alexander Campbell," Richardson, I, 37.

emphasized. Next to this benign atmosphere of the family life as a whole, must be considered the personal influence and example of Thomas Campbell as a man and a father. Possessed of the warm Irish temperment, essentially social in nature, he was one whose company was always agreeable, and it was the testimony of his son that none was ever a more delightful companion. While he loved the graver topics of conversation, he enjoyed with his family and his parishioners the occasional good times which are so characteristic of the Irish people. In his biography, Alexander says of him: "We only express a prevailing public opinion when we say that he was the most earnest, indefatigable, and devoted minister in the presbytery and synod to which he belonged. In preaching, teaching, and visiting his charge, inculcating personal and family religion, he had certainly no superior; and so far as we could ascertain, no equal. His family training and discipline were peculiarly didactic, biblical, and strict. The Bible, with Brown's Catechism, was, during the minority of his family, a daily study and a daily recitation. He instituted these customs in all the families of his congregation. His congregation at Ahorey, in the County Armagh, was therefore regarded as the best educated community in the Presbytery of Market Hill, to which he belonged." [24]

Nothing in the character of Thomas Campbell is more marked than his supreme reverence for the Bible as the Word of God. It is evident in every thing he wrote, and it was the testimony of his entire family that, during the early days of his ministery in Ireland, this love was manifest in all his teaching and preaching. Probably the greatest impression made upon the mind of the son was this reverence in which his father held the sacred volume. He relates the fact that while the elder Campbell was possessed of a large and well-stocked library, he was wont, upon enter-

[24] "Life of Elder Thomas Campbell," Alexander Campbell, quoted by Kershner, in "Christian Union Overture," 16.

ing that room, to see on the table only his Bible and Concordance, and a simple outfit of pen and ink. Of this custom, he writes: "Whether he had read all these volumes and cared nothing more for them, or whether he regarded them as wholly useless, I presumed not to inquire and dared not decide." [25] Later, during the performance of his duties, finding that the children were confounding the words of the Scriptures with those of the Catechism, he dispensed with the latter, fearing that they might assign to it the same importance as they did to the Holy Word itself. This constant exaltation of the Scriptures above all other books, and the attitude of reverence for its authority in all things divine, was to result in a great distinctively Bible movement when his life should be lived in the new world. The young lad in his own home, who was to be the future leader, was being unconsciously trained by this influence, as well as by the direct inculcations of the divine truth.

2. The moulding influence of the dominant philosophy of the day falls next to be considered. As the intellectual side of Alexander's nature began to display itself in an eager thirst for knowledge, Thomas Campbell assumed his tuition. His studies were such as should anticipate the usual University course. Very early he became proficient in Latin and Greek. It was his custom to commit to memory the select passages of the best authors, both from the desire to please his father and because of his love of them for themselves. His biographer makes a statement about this early education which is of utmost importance in understanding his later thought: "His mind became stored with the finer passages of the British poets, which he was able to retain through life. He was extremely fond of reading, and became gradually quite conversant with many of the standard English authors, especially with such as were of a moral, philosophical, or religious cast. As he advanced in age, he learned greatly to admire the character and works of Locke, whose 'Letters on

[25] "Memoirs of Alexander Campbell," Richardson, I, 39.

Toleration' seem to have made a lasting impression upon him, and to have fixed his ideas of religious and civil liberty. The 'Essay on the Human Understanding' he appears to have thoroughly studied under the direction of his father, who was earnestly desirous that his son should make all possible advancement and preparation, trusting that he would be able, after some time, to send him to the University." [26] The frequent allusions which Campbell makes to Locke and his writings, and their evident influence in the formation of some of his most characteristic positions, will appear as his theology is studied in detail. It is of interest to note, however, that thus early he grasps the only available philosophical instrument.

Anything more than a cursory view of the Lockian system, cannot be attempted in this study. Locke relates, in the preface to his "Essay on the Human Understanding," the circumstances which led him to a consideration of the problems which he attempts to solve. With a party of friends, he had been considering "the principles of morality and revealed religion," [27] when he was suddenly brought to a halt by the question as to the actual constitution and limits of human knowledge. The key note of the philosophy of a century was struck by his inquiry into this problem.

The most outstanding feature of the Lockian philosophy, and that which was of greatest influence on the thought of Alexander Campbell, was his doctrine concerning the source of ideas. Denying the Cartesian doctrine of innate ideas which all men possess in common, he went to the very lengths of philosophical individualism. All ideas are the result of sensation and reflection.[28] The mind of man is like a blank sheet of paper. It is capable of receiving im-

---

[26] "Memoirs of Alexander Campbell," Richardson, I, 33, 34.

[27] Locke himself does not relate the subject which, on this occasion, puzzled the assembled friends, and caused him to make his inquiry. James Tyrrell, a member of the party, recorded it in a note on the margin of his copy, now in the British Museum. "Locke's Essay on the Human Understanding," Fraser, I, XVII.

[28] *Ibid.*, I, 121, 122.

pressions; it may combine and compare these impressions, but it can do no more. Since there are no innate ideas,[29] the idea of God, the law of cause and effect, etc., must be the result of sensation and reflection. All knowledge comes from the impressions which are created upon the mind by external objects. An object, therefore, is known to us only if the impression which we receive of it, corresponds with the external reality of that which has made the impression. The validity of knowledge depends, then, upon one thing only, the trustworthiness of the report which our senses make concerning the objects by which they are stimulated.

Locke, however, acknowledges that the greater part of our sensations are not exact copies of the external objects which stimulate them. They are not absoluetly accurate. There are two classes of qualities which we may know through sensation: primary,[30] such as form, extension, solidity, mobility,—the qualities which necessarily exist in external objects as we perceive them, and are therefore connected with our conception of all external realities; and secondary,[31] those of color, sound, smell, etc., which are only the manner in which objects affect us. Secondary qualities, being subjective, are really nothing more than sensations. In this classification, we see the first gleam of that scepticism which should later find an irremediable weakness here, but it did not so appear to the philosopher. His successors were to ask the perfectly obvious question, "What evidence have you for the actual existence of primary qualities, if your sensations do not tell you the actual truth about those which are secondary?" In the Lockian system there is no answer to this question.

The human mind cannot really know the nature of substance, since substance cannot make any direct impres-

[29] *Ibid.*, I, 37.
[30] "Locke's Essay Concerning the Human Understanding," Fraser I, 169, 170.
[31] *Ibid.*, 170, 173.

sion upon it through sensation.[32]   Only qualities are know-
able; therefore, substance is but the combination of certain
simple ideas which we receive together.[33] When metaphysics
endeavors to get below the primary and secondary qualities,
such as form, hardness, softness, color, smell, etc., it goes
beyond its depths—it transcends the limits of human
knowledge.[34]   Cause and effect are also combinations of
simple ideas.[35]   We observe that one action always follows
another, and therefore reason that one is the cause of the
other.

It is evident that upon a purely sensational theory of
knowledge, such as thus developed, we can have no knowledge save of particular things.   The universal, species,
genus, etc., are but combinations of, and abstractions from,
the simple ideas which have come to us of the individuals.[36]
We assume that our simple ideas have given us a knowledge
of reality, because they are not the products of our own
minds, as are those which are complex.   Since they have
come to us from without, we assume that there is something
which is externally real, but this cannot be proven.

There are four lines of development from the Lockian
basis, of the theory of the source and nature of knowledge.
Berkeley annihilated all reality external to ourselves, by
asking the simple question, "If secondary qualities are only
subjective, why is it not also true of those which are called
primary?   If it is impossible to know substance through
sensation, it will be impossible to know it at all.   If primary
and secondary qualities are only subjective affections, there
is no reality outside of the individual."   Berkeley did retain
the idea of cause since only through cause could the impressions come to us and the simple ideas rise in our minds.

[32] *Ibid.*, 107, 108.

[33] *Ibid.*, 422.

[34] *Ibid.*, 157.

[35] "Locke's Essay concerning the Human Understanding," Fraser, I,
433, 434.

[36] *Ibid.*, II, 63, 64.

God is this cause, and the only external reality. The result of the development of Lockianism through Berkeley, is a system of absolute idealism or spiritual monism.[37]

While Berkeley had destroyed all reality external to the individual, save the Deity himself, Hume attacked the idea of causation, and demonstrated that it had no more validity than the assumed primary or secondary qualities of substance. This conclusion was a logical deduction from the Lockian basis that knowledge can come only through sensation and reflection. If we can have no knowledge except that which comes through sensuous impression, there is no way by which we may know the cause for these impressions, either physical or spiritual.[38]

In the field of natural science, the same principles applied by Berkeley in the development of his system of absolute idealism, and by Hume in his sceptical theory of knowledge, were applied by Newton and Hartley, respectively, resulting in a purely mechanical view of the universe. God created the universe as a perfect machine, and left it to run according to the laws of its own nature. The only place for the Deity, in such a system, was at the beginning. Thus the application of the Lockian principles to religion produced Deism. As a movement, more especially of English thought of the 17th and 18th centuries, it was the chief exponent of the tendency to sacrifice the immanence of God to his transcendence. In this manner the Divine or progressive element is eliminated from history; the only religion which men can believe becomes "the religion of Nature," which is the apprehension of the religious truth inhering in human reason as such. The historical religions are but degenerations of this inherent religious truth through the accretions of superstitions, priestcraft, etc. Deism, therefore, became the religion of reason. Every tenet, dogmatic or historical, which could not stand in the light of reason, was resolutely

[37] *Ibid.*, Prologemena, I, cxxviii, cxxix.

[38] "Locke's Essay concerning the Human Understanding," Fraser, Prolegomena, I, cxxxiv, cxl.

uprooted, until eventually the system had resolved itself
into a purely ethical affair, with one article of faith, "Believe
in God," and one command to the conscience, "Do your
duty." The scepticism of Hume made even this one article
untenable, for by reason alone God could not be known.
On the very principles which Deism had taken for its foundation, it was eventually overthrown. The fourth line of
development proceeded in the realm of Ethics, resulting in
a purely hedonistic theory. The pains and pleasures of
the individual became the ultimate course of ethical control.

The relation of Alexander Campbell to the philosophy of
the eighteenth century,[39] will become evident as his doctrines
are set forth in detail. In the main, it may be said that
while he reacted vigorously against the tendencies which it
developed, he accepted the methods by which it worked.
This double attitude he held with most of the theologians
and apologists of his time who tried to confute the scepticism and infidelity which had come in like a tide with the
development of Deism. This denial of the results is illustrated in his numerous battles with the Deists. Their inconsistency in accepting the principles of Locke's theory of
knowledge while endeavoring through reason alone to
know God, brought down his criticism upon them. Since
they could not know God through reason, and yet the God
idea was in the world, the only conclusion was that it must
have come from God himself,—it must have been a revelation. Writing in the "Christian Baptist," he says: "They
are the poorest driveling philosophers that ever assumed the
name—for they pretend to hold principles which have no
foundation at all, which is sublimated enthusiasm. They
boast of the belief in one God, of the immortality of the soul,
and a future state—but ask them, how they came by it,
and they will tell you, by the use of their reason! Reasoning on what? the things that are made—but who made

[39] For one of the most illuminating discussions of the influence of the
Lockian philosophy on Campbell and the early disciples see Dr. Fortune's
recent work "Origin and Development of the Disciples," 123, 128.

them? Thus it goes in a circle; they prove that there is a creator from the things created; and they prove that things are created, because there is a creator." He states, in a sentence, the dilemma in which the Deists found themselves, and from which, according to him, there was no escape: "Either Athiesm, unqualified Athiesm, or faith in Jesus as the Son of God, are the legitimate stopping places on the principles of sound reason and good logic. All that halt between these extremes are besotted with a brutish stupidity. The ox and the ass are their reprovers." [40]

The studies of the Lockian philosophy, begun in his youth under the direction of his father, seem to have been continued, for as late as 1844 he published, in several numbers of the "Millennial Harbinger," numerous lengthy extracts from the "Essay on Toleration." With all its manifest faults, this system of philosophy was the only one ready to his hand. He found it peculiarly adapted for the work of reformation, which he believed himself called to do.

3. The influence of the Covenant Theology of Cocceius, Witsius, and their associates exercised also a profound influence on Campbells thought. Cocceius was a professor of theology in Leyden, where he died in 1669. There are three high points in the teaching of this school of Dutch theologians which are of interest to the student of Alexander Campbell. The emphasis placed upon these same positions, in his own teaching, is almost conclusive proof that he must have had more than a casual acquaintance with them. The

[40] Christian Baptist, 271. Cf. Dean Paterson's statement: "Turtullian of the Fathers, and Luther among the Reformers, used strong language about the imbecility of reason. Some of the later Scholastics sheltered radical doubts and denials under the formula that what was true in Theology could be false in Philosophy" while "the Ritschilian School, whose contemptuous treatment of Natural Theology is one of its constant marks, must be held to be committed to the view that the light of nature only serves to discover to man that God is unknown and unknowable." "The Nature of Religion," 5. In modern times Dean Mansel has reproduced the position which Campbell here avows. In his "Limits of Religious Thought" he develops the thesis that apart from Christianity Agnosticism would have been the most logical creed.

idea that the plan of salvation has been gradual development, —that it has a very clearly outlined history—was one of the contributions of this school to theological thought. Out of the distinction between the covenants they were also enabled to set forth a more sane and satisfactory method of exegesis than was generally prevalent. The relation between God and man, as that of a covenant, was a third contribution which constituted a decided advance, in that it emphasized man's ability to do something in his own salvation. These doctrines were salutary because they met the three evident defects of the Calvinism of the time. These three defects were as follows: first, a failure to realize that the way of salvation offered by God in the Old Testament and that in the New, is not identical—that the revelation, in a word, has been progressive; secondly, growing out of this, a mechanical use of the Scriptures; and thirdly, a failure to recognize the fact that since salvation is a covenant, there is something which man must do on his own behalf. That the idea foundational to this school of Theology, the distinction which they made between the covenants, may be gathered from the titles of a few of their works:

Cocceius, "Summa Doctrinae de Foedere et Testamentis Dei."

Witsius, "Œconomy of the Covenants between God and Man."

Burmann, "Synopsis Theologiae et Œconomiae Foederum Dei."

Braun, "Doctrina Foederum."

Mona, "De Varia Conditione et Statu Ecclesiae Dei sub Triplici Economia Foederum Dei."

At first the covenant theology openly opposed Calvinism, endeavoring to interpret its doctrines in a more liberal spirit. In the stress of theological controversy, however, the true implications of the system became apparent, and for a time there was grave danger that the Reformed Church in Holland would be divided over its teachings. A timely compromise averted this, and the school continued to exist as a school rather than as a sect. Because of this character, its teachings were widely disseminated among thinkers of all denominations, both upon the continent and later in the British Isles, where its influence colored the theological thought which was to be the heritage of Alexander Campbell. The first influence of this new doctrine is noted in the Church of England after the Synod of Dort. The Westminster Confession distinguished, as Cocceius had done, between the Covenant of Works and the Covenant of Grace, making the dividing line at the Fall. Its doctrine of the atonement was also stated in terms of the covenants. The rise of the controversy between the Antinomians and the Neonomians, inconsequential except for the influence which it exerted upon the Scottish Church, emphasized the two sides of Cocceius' teachings. The Antinomians, perceiving the distinction between the Jewish and Christian dispensations, maintained that the Christian is no longer under the old law, in any sense, but is under grace alone. The Neonomians, on the other hand, declared that while we are not under the old law in the sense that we are required to obey all its commands, we are still under a new law, since in the teaching of Christ and his apostles there are certain commands which must be obeyed in order to salvation.

In the Church of Scotland, the influence of the Covenant Theology was much more marked than it had been in England. The enforced exile of many of the Presbyterians during the period when Episcopacy was enforced in Scotland, was spent in Holland, where, despite its condemnation by the Synod of Dort, Arminianism was prevalent and the Covenant Theology was at the zenith of its influence. Even after Presbyterianism was restored to its rightful place, it was customary to send students to Holland for their theological education. The influence of Arminianism in Scotland continued even after Prelacy was withdrawn, and the battle between the Antinomians and the Neonomians was transplanted from the southern kingdom to the northland. The eighteenth century, the period of division in Presbyterian history, witnessed a growth of more liberal views among many, but, at the same time, it gave rise to a great popular conservative revolt. The Secession, a counter-reformation of Calvinism, vigorously reaffirmed the doctrine of Predestination as it had been interpreted by the English Antinomians. An old book, "The Marrow of Modern Divinity," which ably discussed the points at issue in the controversy, was adopted and widely circulated by the Seceders. This work was written in 1646 by Edward Fisher of the University of Oxford, an English Antinomian.[41] It was resurrected by Thomas Boston, the well known author of "The Fourfold State," and republished in 1718.[42] The whole theology of the Seceders was cast in the mould of the dispensations as representing the various stages of salvation which God has vouchsafed unto men. The "Marrow of Divinity" and the "Fourfold State" were almost universally read by them, both clergy and laity. While toward the close of the century many of the positive virtues of the Covenant Theology, as it had been set forth by its Dutch founders, were lost, the influence of it was still strong, especially as it was embodied in the two books which will forever be associated with the name of Thomas Boston.

That this conception was of profound influence upon the teaching of Alexander Campbell, does not seem to admit of serious doubt. His father was a Secession minister, educated in a Secession Seminary. It is known that Alexander read the "Fourfold State," on his voyage to Scotland.[43] It is not probable that he was ignorant of the "Marrow of Modern Divinity," a book which was as widely circulated among his own people as a popular novel. While there is no direct evidence that he read this work, he casually refers to it in after years,[44] as one might speak of a book with which he

[41] "Church History of Scotland," Cunningham, II, 249, 250.
[42] *Ibid.*, 252, 256.
[43] "Memoirs of Alexander Campbell," Richardson, I, 99.
[44] "Millennial Harbinger," Volume for 1848, 345.

was intimately acquainted. His frequent quotations from the works of Cocceius and Witsius,[45] as well as the fact that his own theology, in so many regards, was similar to theirs, is evidence that he knew their teaching. It is not necessary to prove that he read these in the original, to substantiate the contention that the Covenant Theology influenced him. However, that he was acquainted with the original works is probable.

4. The influence of the Protestant Reformers must be acknowledged. In reply to a letter from Elder William Jones of London, a Scottish Baptist, inquiring as to the sources of his theological thought, he warmly mentions among many others to whom he confesses himself indebted, the great Reformers. "For my own part I am greatly indebted to all Reformers, from Martin Luther down to John Wesley." [46] While he does not tell just when he read the works of Luther, or how extensively he had explored into the voluminous writings of the greatest of the Reformation leaders, his frequent quotations from him,[47] and the admiration in which manifestly he held him, is sufficient testimony to the fact that he was largely influenced by Luther's life and work. Even in a cursory reading of Campbell's works one is constantly reminded both of the language and the thought of the great Reformer. In his reverence for the Scriptures, in his doctrines of their content and authority, and in his insistence upon the right of private judgement, he reflects the great German theologian. Though criticizing Luther's attitude in his dispute with the Swiss reformers, he pays him a high compliment, and thus indirectly shows his admiration for him, referring to him as "the great Luther, so conversant with language, and so just in general in his views of divine truth." [48] Just how early the works of the

[45] "Campbell-Rice Debate," 153, 261; "Christian Baptism," 146.

[46] "Millennial Harbinger," Volume for 1835, 103.

[47] "Christian Baptism," 146; "Campbell-Rice Debate," 460, 461; "Millennial Harbinger," Volume for 1832, 574; 1842, 143; 1854, 635; 1858, 191; etc.

[48] "Millennial Harbinger Abridged," I, 191; V, for 1849.

reformers exerted their influence upon him, there is no way of knowing; but that he studied them early, one may fairly conjecture.

5. Influences during university life.

On October 1st, 1807, Thomas Campbell, having determined to remain in the new world and continue the work of the "Christian Association," the Campbell family set sail for America. On October 7th, their ship was wrecked on the island of Islay, off the Scottish coast. This experience was one of the most important in the life of the younger Campbell. While sitting on the stump of a broken mast, watching the frightened passengers, "he thought of his father's noble life, devoted to God and the salvation of his fellow-beings, and felt that such a calling, consecrated to the salvation and everlasting happiness of mankind, was, indeed, the highest and most worthy sphere of action in which any human being could engage. It was then, in that solemn hour, that he gave himself wholly to God, and resolved that, if saved from the present peril, he would certainly spend his entire life in the ministry of the gospel. It was at this moment that he, for the first time, fully decided to adopt the ministry as his profession." [49] He ever afterward looked back to this experience as the moment of his greatest decision.

The wreck off the coast of Scotland was important, also, in that through this accident, it was decided that he should attend the University of Glasgow. The season being too far advanced for the family to brave the perils of the North Atlantic, they proceeded to Glasgow, where he enrolled as a student. Here he was surrounded by an environment which was to influence his whole future course. In addition to the influence of his university classes,[50] and his outside

[49] "Memoirs of Alexander Campbell," Richardson, I, 101, 103.

[50] He entered the classes of Professor Young, both public and private, in Greek; those of Professor Jardine, both public and private, in Belles Lettres; and that of Dr. Ure in Experimental Philosophy. In addition, he resumed the study of French, and gave much time to English reading and composition. Professors Young and Jardine had been his father's professors, twenty-five years before. They had also been favorite professors of the poet Campbell. "Memoirs," I, 130, 132.

reading in which he seems to have indulged freely,[51] he was thrown into religious circles which were to leave their impressions upon him for life.

Dr. Richardson admits that the religious conditions by which he was surrounded in Glasgow were of such a nature, that, while leaving his main purpose to dedicate his life to the ministry unaffected, he experienced an entire revolution in his views concerning the Seceder church and all the existing denominations. At this time, the work of the Haldane brothers was at the height of its influence. Those two devout men, with their co-laborers, becoming interested in stimulating evangelistic zeal throughout Scotland, had given largely of their means for this purpose. Eventually, they had constituted themselves into a Congregational Church with the purpose of enjoying the benefits of Christian fellowship according to the Scriptural plan, to observe the Christian ordinances, and to avoid a narrow spirit which would exclude from their pulpit any true preacher of the Word. Among the new Congregational Churches which grew up from this movement, James A. Haldane became the first minister. He continued in this capacity until his death, or for a period of fifty-two years. The Haldanes, while admiring many of the teachings of Glass, Sandeman, and Walker, were much opposed to the bitter spirit which their followers manifested. The Sandemanian view of faith—that it is mere assent to testimony—appeared to them cold and frigid. They would add to the credence of testimony, trust in Christ as Saviour and Lord. Their view of faith was adopted by Campbell. The Haldanian conceptions of the independency of the local congregation, the teaching concerning the necessity for a plurality of elders in every church, their constant insistence

[51] In a memorandum of this period, he records that from May 1st, 1809, he read Dr. Beattie's Minstrel, "Life and Poems of James Hay Beattie." In addition, he read Stuart MacKenzie's "Man of Feeling," Buffon's "Natural History," Johnson's "Lives of the Poets," Dr. Beattie's "Ethics." Many passages appear in his notes, from Johnson's "Lives of the Poets," and even more from Beattie's "Ethics." "Memoirs," Richardson, I, 137, 138.

upon the Scriptures as the only authority for Christians, the practice of weekly communion, and the example which they had set before him, of preaching without salary, all impressed him deeply. In regard to the last named item, it is significant that throughout his life, he refused compensation, either for his services or for the expenses incurred in preaching the gospel. The intimate association which he enjoyed with Mr. Greville Ewing, one of the most prominent of the Haldanian ministers, gave him opportunity to know personally many of the leading men in the new communion. Dr. Richardson says that it was from this movement that he "received his first impulse as a religious reformer," and that it "may be justly regarded, indeed, as the first phase of that religious reformation which he subsequently carried out so successfully to its legitimate issues." [52]

On August 5th, 1809, the family again set sail for America, arriving in New York on September 29th. After a short stay, they proceeded directly to Washington, Pennsylvania. The "Declaration and Address" was, at the time of their arrival, on the press, and, finding that its positions were those to which he had himself come in the revolt against creeds and ritualism which had been engendered during his sojourn in Scotland, Alexander immediately decided to cast his lot with the infant movement. Later, he decided, much to the gratification of his father, to enter the ministry and, pursuant to this decision, embarked upon a course of ministerial training under the tuition of the elder Campbell. His marriage to Miss Margaret Brown, March 12th, 1811, determined him to remain in the community in which his father had settled since the farm of his father-in-law passed to his wife, becoming the basis of the substantial fortune which he afterwards amassed through the importation of pure-bred sheep from Scotland. The refusal of the Synod of Pittsburgh to welcome the Christian Association of Washington to its membership hastened the evolution of the little band, which

[52] "Memoirs of Alexander Campbell," Richardson, I, 149.

had been rapidly developing under the weekly ministrations of the Campbells, towards the organization of a Church. The immersion of the Campbells in June 1812, followed by the majority of the members of the Association, made it practically certain that the new communion would become an immersionist body.   After careful consideration and a committal of their position to writing to be presented to the officers, the Brush Run Church decided to accept the importunate invitation of the Redstone Baptist Association to take membership with that body.   Amicable relations were sustained with these people until the delivery of Alexander Campbell's famous "Sermon on the Law," in 1816, when opposition was aroused which continued with increasing bitterness until a complete separation of Baptists and Reformers was accomplished.   On June 19th, and 20th, 1820 Campbell engaged in his first public discussion, that with the Reverend John Walker, and while it was hailed everywhere among the Baptists as a remarkable vindication of their cause and a victory to "the brilliant and versatile young disputant from the Buffalo," it served only to increase the hostility against him in Baptist circles since they did not accord with him in the arguments through which the discomfiture of his opponent had been brought about.   The launching of the "Christian Baptist," July 4th, 1823, was yet another cause of friction, providing as it did an instrument through the columns of which opportunity was afforded for a wide dissemination of Campbell's radical reformatory views.   Availing himself assiduously of the extensive attention which the Walker debate had attracted, he drove home his reformation principles in vitriol-filled pages and with a cold fury which raised a hue and cry throughout the country and prepared the soil for the subsequent evangelistic campaign which swept thousands into the ranks of the so-called "Reformed Baptists."   The debate with McCalla, October 15th, to 23rd, 1823, even more widely enhanced his reputation in that it was held on Kentucky soil and achieved the capitulation to him of practically the whole state, but the arguments by which another crushing defeat was administered only further widened the breach between himself and his reactionary brethren among the Baptists. Finding his position in the Redstone Association intolerable, he, and the members of a number of churches which had been organized upon the same platform as that of the Brush Run congregation, accepted the invitation of the Mahonning Association of Ohio and were heartily received into its fellowship. In August, 1827, under the auspices of this liberal body, evangelism of a very militant nature was initiated under the brilliant leadership of Walter Scott. This grew into a mighty wave, which, led by a score of splendid evangelists, rolled over Ohio, Kentucky and Virginia, demonstrating the practical power of the plea which the Campbells had been making for almost twenty years. The power of the reformatory principles, as thus demonstrated, further incensed the Regular Baptists, with the result that Associations began to exclude those churches committed to the "Ancient Order of Things." By 1832 this exclusion was complete and from that time the Disciples may be said to exist as a separate communion. A great practical example of Christian unity was the amalgamation of these Reformers with the movement from Kentucky under the leadership of Barton W. Stone, in Lexington, January 1st, 1832.

Two streams thus united to form the movement for the Restoration of New Testament Christianity as it exists today; one from Pennsylvania and Virginia on the racial and religious basis of sober Quakerism, leavened with a strong admixture of New England Puritanism from the Western Reserve of Ohio, and the other from the southern Cavalier soil of Kentucky. The followers of the Campbells were mostly of the Separatist Baptist persuasion who had inherited their abhorrence of the extremes of Calvinism from their ancestors, who had come out during the great awakening in New England under the preaching of Whitefield and

Edwards. The Kentucky stream, on the other hand, was almost entirely of Presbyterian extraction. The result of this union of various religious types of mind is of paramount influence in the final formation of distinctively Diciple thought. The product of the union between Puritan and Cavalier in the great midwest states has produced the finest American type and the unprecedented progress of the Disciples in these central western areas has given rise to the opinion that the Churches of Christ are purely American. In view of the rapid progress of the movement in Australia and the recent remarkable success which has attended the proclamation of its message in South Africa as well as the awakening of evangelistic fervor in Great Britain, it is manifest that this opinion must be decidedly revised. Because he was eclipsed by the great man at Bethany in those general qualities which make for leadership, Stone has never fully received the honor which is his due. The early history of the Disciples is the history of two outstanding personalities, the Campbells, father and son, and of the theology which was the creative force of all their labors.

The remaining events of Campbell's life, may be briefly summarized. In 1829, he conducted his world-famous debate with Robert Owen, the communistic infidel of Lanark, Scotland. This was held in the Methodist church at Cincinnati, Ohio. Owen had thrown down the gauntlet to the clergy of America, to discuss the foundations of the Christian Religion, and Campbell accepted it. This discussion was read throughout the English speaking world, and gave him international recognition. In the same year, seeing that the work of destructive criticism was completed, and fearing that the people who had become members of the new movement would be called "Christian Baptists," he discontinued the publication of the paper which he had been editing for seven years. These seven volumes contain some of the finest work of his life. In August, he was elected to the Constitutional Assembly of Virginia, in which body he served with distinction until the following year.[53] The first of the new year, saw the birth of the "Millennial Harbinger," which he edited for thirty-three years. 1836, while in Cincinnati, he met Bishop Purcell, and clashed with him over the use of the Bible in the Public Schools and the general results of the Protestantism in the new world. The Campbell-Purcell debate on the Roman Catholic Religion, arranged at this time, was conducted the following year, January 13th to 17th. In January, 1840, the charter of Bethany College was secured; in May the first meeting of the trustees was held; and in October its doors were opened. At the second meeting of the trustees, Campbell was elected President of the new institution. Beginning on November 15th, 1843, and continuing for sixteen days, he engaged in his last public debate. His opponent was the Rev. N. L. Rice of Paris, Kentucky. The debate was held in the "Reformers" meeting house in Lexington, and was presided over by the eminent statesman, Henry Clay. The whole ground of difference between the Disciples and the Presbyterians was thoroughly canvassed during this discussion. The Presbyterians were so confident that Rice, whose numerous witticisms and facetious handling of great questions brought frequent applause, had won a glorious victory, that they had the debate printed and widely disseminated. It soon became apparent, however, that they had mistaken witty sallies for sound arguments, for the published debate made so many converts to Campbell's cause, that they soon ceased its distribution.

[53] While a member of the Constitutional Assembly of Virginia, Campbell was in close association with some of the great statesmen of America. Ex-President Madison was a member of this convention, as were also Ex-President Monroe, Chief-Justice Marshall, John Randolph, and many others of distinction. Campbell spoke every Sunday on the great things of the primitive Gospel, to large audiences. At this convention Ex-President Madison, after speaking in highest terms of his political ability, said to Mr. Pendleton, "But it is as a theologian that Mr. Campbell must be known. It was my pleasure to hear him very often, as a preacher of the gospel, and I regard him as the ablest and most original expounder of the Scriptures I have ever heard." "Memoirs of Alexander Campbell," Richardson, II, 312, 313.

It is now owned and sold by the Disciples. In 1847 Campbell made a tour of the British Isles, speaking to crowded houses in all the larger cities of England and Scotland.[54] In 1849, the question as to missionary cooperation having been long discussed, the Disciples took a forward step in the organization of the American Christian Missionary Society, and the election of Campbell as its first President. In the following year, while on a trip to Baltimore, he received a pressing invitation to address both houses of the United States Congress. On June 2nd, he preached from John 3:17, to the Senate and the House, in the hall of the Representatives. In 1852, he made a visit to the state of Missouri, and at the urgent invitation of the Legislature, addressed that body on two occasions before his return to Bethany. Thomas Campbell, the father, passed away January 4th, 1854, at the advanced age of ninety-one. In 1863 Alexander Campbell delivered the president's address on the occasion of the fifteenth anniversary of the American Christian Missionary Society. The following year he attended the general convention for the last time. At 11:45, the

[54] The following letter, forwarded to Campbell by Henry Clay, on hearing of his contemplated European journey, is of interest. "The Rev. Dr. A. Campbell, the bearer hereof, a citizen of the United States of America, residing in the Commonwealth of Virginia, being about to make a voyage to Europe and to travel particularly in Great Britain, Ireland and France, I take great satisfaction in strongly recommending him to the kind offices and friendly reception of all persons with whom he may meet and wherever he may go. Dr. Campbell is among the most eminent citizens of the United States, distinguished for his great learning and ability, for his successful devotion to the education of youth, for his piety, and as head and founder of one of the most important and respectable communities in the United States. Nor have his great talents been exclusively confined to the religious and literary walks in which he has principally moved; he was a distinguished member, about twenty years ago, of the convention called in the State of Virginia to remodel its civil constitution, in which, besides other eminent men, were Ex-Presidents Madison and Monroe, and John Marshall, the late Chief-Justice of the United States. Dr. Campbell, whom I have the honor to regard personally as my friend, carries with him many wishes and prayers for his health and happiness whilst abroad, and for his safe return to his country, which justly appreciates him so highly. H. Clay, Ashland, Kentucky, May 1847." Quoted in "Alexander Campbell's Tour in Scotland," Chalmers, 30. "Memoirs," Richardson, II, 548.

night of March 4th, 1866, after an illness of a few days, he finished his life work, sincerely mourned around the world, by a communion of more than a half million members.

In addition to his work as President of Bethany College, editor of the "Christian Baptist" and the "Millennial Harbinger," and President of the American Christian Missionary Society, Campbell made scores of trips in which he touched almost every part of the eastern, middle-western, and southern sections of the United States. Many of these journeys were for the purpose of collecting funds for Bethany College; others in order that he might more widely disseminate the principles of the Restoration Movement. As a lecturer on political, economic, and literary subjects, he was very popular, being invited frequently to address various learned societies, as well as the colleges and universities of the young republic. In such pursuits, his influence was widened, and it is significant that many of the leaders in university life, especially in Kentucky and the middle west, came into the Disciple movement largely through the personal influence exerted in these various visits.

Campbell was a voluminous writer. In addition to the seven volumes of the "Christian Baptist," 1823 to 1830, and the thirty-four volumes of the "Millennial Harbinger," 1830 to 1863, there are extant six volumes of his published debates. That with Walker appeared in 1820; that with McCalla in 1823; and that with Owen in 1829. The discussion with Purcell appeared in 1837 and was read throughout the country, and also in Europe. The Rice debate, the largest volume of all his works, was published in 1843. The debate with Skinner on Universalism, ran for two years in the Harbinger, and was later published by Skinner. In addition to his debates, the works in which his doctrinal system is best set forth are the "Christian System" 1835, and "Christian Baptism—Its Antecedents and Consequents" 1852. In 1827 he published the translation of the New Testament by Doctors George Campbell, Dodridge and Macknight, with notes and annotations: this work he called "The Living Oracles." The year 1828 saw the publication of his first hymn-book, which was later revised and enlarged. In 1855 he finished his revision of the book of Acts, with critical notes: this task he had accepted at the request of the Bible Union of New York. Many requests having been made for his popular addresses, a large edition of these appeared in 1861, under the title "Popular Lectures and Addresses." The same year he published a biography of his father, entitled "The Life of Elder Thomas Campbell," but it by "no means met public expectations; for, though it contained many interesting facts and documents worthy of preservation, it was scanty in its details and defective in its arrangements." [55] One other work, the "Christian Preacher's Companion, or Infidelity Refuted by Infidels," should be mentioned, although it does not rank with his primary works. A volume of the morning lectures which President Campbell was accustomed to deliver before the students of Bethany College, was edited by Dr. W. T. Moore, in 1881. They are entitled "Lectures on the Pentateuch." They were not corrected or revised by Campbell personally. In all, however, he was the editor or author of about sixty volumes.

The late Archibald McLean, at one time President of Bethany College, and at the time of his death President of the Foreign Christian Missionary Society of the Disciples of Christ, in his "Alexander Campbell, Master of Assemblies," quotes an interesting statement from General Robert E. Lee, Commander of the Confederate Armies in the American Civil War. "Referring to Campbell, General Lee quoted the words of Dr. Symonds, spoken about Milton: 'He was a man in whom were illustriously combined all the qualities which could adorn or elevate the nature to which he belonged; knowledge the most various and extended, virtue that never loitered in her career nor deviated from her course. A man who, if he had been delegated as a representative of his species to one of the many superior world, would have suggested a grand idea of the human race.' " [56]

---

[55] "Memoirs of Alexander Campbell," Richardson, II, 645.
[56] "Millennial Harbinger Abridged," II, 629.

CHAPTER II

THE PLEA FOR CHRISTIAN UNITY

An understanding of the plea for the unity of the Church, advocated by Alexander Campbell with such ardour and success, presupposes acquaintance with the events leading up to the publication of the "Declaration and Address" of the "Christian Association of Washington," and a knowledge of the contents of that remarkable document itself. These events, with the publications to which they gave rise, form the logical introduction to the ground which finally came to be occupied by the Disciples, as their distinctive platform. The events in which the principles of the Restoration Movement of the Nineteenth Century were wrought out, may be grouped into three periods: first, the conflict of Thomas Campbell with the Presbytery of Chartiers and the Associate Synod of North America; second, the meeting of brethren to whom the call of Christian unity made special appeal, in which the foundational principle of the coming movement was announced; and third, the organization of the "Christian Association of Washington" and the issuance of the "Declaration and Address." These three important periods will be considered with their relation to the growing clarity of understanding concerning the basis upon which an enduring unity might be consumated.

I

1. The conflict with the Seceders on the question of Christian Communion brought the necessity for Christian unity forcibly to Thomas Campbell's mind and furnished the driving motive for his mighty plea. One of the first duties

47

which devolved upon him, after his assignment to the Presbytery of Chartiers, took the form of a visit to scattered members of his flock, who lived some distance up the Alleghany River, above Pittsburgh, to conduct among them a communion service, or as it was then called, a "sacramental celebration." He was accompanied on this mission by a Mr. Wilson who acted as his assistant.[1] The thinly-settled condition of the country made frequent visits for instruction in the Scriptures and celebration of the Lord's Supper impossible. This destitution of religious services was rendered even more accute by the almost infinite variety of religious views entertained by the population, drawn from various parts of the old world, with the resulting sectarian strife and party bickerings. Such schism, in the old world, had already sadly rent the Presbyterian family, in the bosom of which Thomas Campbell found his labors. Deeply touched by the paucity of religious opportunity everywhere evidenced among the new settlements which had been thrown up by an ever-increasing tide of immigration from Europe, and especially by the evident destitute condition of the divided members of his own religious communion, many of whom had not had the opportunity to partake of the Lord's Supper for years, Thomas Campbell boldly launched out on a program which was to eventuate in an entirely new movement. In his sermon, in preparation for the communion, he lamented in vigorous terms the existing divisions, and invited all who loved the Lord, without respect to party affiliations, to enjoy the privileges of the communion season which his visit had so providentially provided.[2]

Wilson did not, at the time, openly oppose this action which was so manifestly out of line with the usage of the Seceders, but learning in many conversations with Campbell, of the light estimate in which he held party walls and religious distinctions, he deemed it his duty to lay the whole

[1] "Memoirs of Alexander Campbell," Richardson, I, 223, 224.
[2] *Ibid.*, I, 225.

case before the next meeting of the Presbytery. His chief charge against Campbell was "that he had failed to inculcate strict adherance to the Church standard and usages, and had even expressed his disapproval of some things in said standard and of the usages made of them." [3] When asked certain questions by the Presbytery, Campbell, desirous to continue his labors among the friends whom he loved, made guarded replies, appealing the while to the Scriptures, and against the sad divisions which had rent the body of Christ into so many unhappy sects. His plea fell upon deaf ears, however, for the Presbytery found him deserving of censure for failing to adhere to the "Secession Testimony." Campbell protested against the decision, which action automatically brought the case before the next meeting of the Synod. Desiring to be understood, and realizing that a tide of opinion against him, was steadily rising, he addressed a very earnest written defense to the Synod. He clearly foresaw that should this body uphold the decision of the Presbytery, his connection with the Seceder communion must cease. As the defense contains the germs of the "Declaration and Address," and also gives a faithful reproduction of his mind on the whole question of Christian unity at the time, liberal quotations from it are given here.[4]

After addressing the brethren with his accustomed courtesy, he calls their attention to the gravity of an act of expulsion against one who has sinned only in advocating the pure word of God. "How great the injustice, how highly aggravated the injury will appear, to thrust out from communion a Christian brother, a fellow-minister, for saying and doing none other things than those which our Divine Lord and his holy apostles have taught and enjoined to be spoken and done by his ministering servants, and to be received and observed by all his people." [5] Humbly disclaiming any desire to be considered infallible, and heartily prom-

[3] "Memoirs of Alexander Campbell," 225.
[4] *Ibid.*, I, 225, 226.
[5] "Memoirs of Alexander Campbell," I, 226.

ising to relinquish any position shown to be out of line with Scriptural teaching, he continues: "So far am I from this, that I dare not venture to trust my own understanding so far as to take upon me to teach as a matter of faith or duty, but what is already expressly taught and enjoined by Divine authority; and I hope it is no presumption to believe that saying and doing the very same things that are said and done before our eyes on the sacred page, is infallibly right, as well as all-sufficient for the edification of the Church, whose duty and perfection is to be in all things conformed to the original standard.[6] It is, therefore, because I have no confidence, either in my own infallibility or that of others, that I absolutely refuse, as inadmissible and schismatic, the introduction of human opinions and human inventions into the faith and worship of the Church. Is it, therefore, because I plead the cause of scriptural and apostolic worship of the Church, in opposition to the various errors and schisms which have so awfully corrupted and divided it, that the brethren of the Union should feel it so difficult to admit me as their fellow-laborer in that blessed work."[7]

Having no desire to dictate to others as to the manner in which they feel impelled to advance in the noble cause of restoring unity to the distracted Church of God, he yet claims the right to go forward in his own way, so long as his efforts do not contravene the express teaching of the Divine standard. "Nor do I presume to dictate to them or to others as to how they should proceed for the glorious purpose of promoting the unity and purity of the Church; but only beg leave, for my own part, to walk upon such sure and peaceable ground that I may have nothing to do with human controversy, about the right or wrong side of any opinion whatsoever, by simply acquiescing in what is written, as quite sufficient for every purpose of faith and duty; and thereby to influence as many as possible to de-

[6] "Comprehensive History of the Disciples of Christ," 100, 102.
[7] "Memoirs of Alexander Campbell," Richardson, I, 226, 227.

part from human controversy, to betake themselves to the
Scriptures, and, in so doing, to the study and practice of
faith, holiness and love." [8]   A distinction which later was
to become so powerful in shaping all the plans of Alexander
Campbell for Christian unity, the distinction between faith
and opinions, is here clearly set forth. Continuing his plea,
Thomas Campbell asks to be informed as to the nature of
his offense. "All this, without any intention on my part
to judge or despise my Christian brethren who may not see
with my eyes in those things which, to me, appear indespon-
sibly necessary to promote and secure the unity, peace and
purity of the Church. Say, brethren, what is my offense,
that I should be thrust out from the heritage of the Lord,
or in serving him in that good work to which he has been
graciously pleased to call me? For what error or immortality ought I to be rejected, except it be that I refuse to acknowledge as obligatory upon myself, or to impose upon
others, anything as of Divine obligation, for which I cannot
produce a 'Thus sayeth the Lord'?"[9]   His sincere desire
to labour with the brethren of the Synod, even though not
agreeing with them in all things, was manifest in his voluntary application for membership in their body. "Surely,
brethren, from my steadfast adherance to the Divine
standard—my absolute and entire rejection of human authority in matters of religion—my professed and sincere
willingness to walk in all good understanding, communion,
and fellowship with sincere and humble Christian brethren,
who may not see with me in these things—and permit me
to add, my sincere desire to unite with you, in carrying forward that blessed work in which you have set out, and
from which you take your name—you will do me the justice
to believe, that if I did not sincerely desire a union with
you, I would not have once and again made application for
that purpose." [10]   While perfectly willing to accord to others

[8] "Memoirs of Alexander Campbell," Richardson, I, 227.
[9] "Memoirs of Alexander Campbell," Richardson, I, 227.
[10] *Ibid.*, 227, 228.

the right to be judged by the standards which they have embraced, he reserves to himself the same right, to be judged only by the Divine standard as it is revealed in the Sacred Writings.

After reading his defense and hearing the case before the Synod, it was decided by that body "that there were such informalities in the proceedings of the Presbytery in the trial of the case as to afford sufficient reason to the Synod to set aside their judgment and decision and to release the protestor from the censure inflicted by the Presbytery." [11] This was accordingly done, but all the documents in the case were referred to a committee, which, after deliberation, reported that since Campbell's replies were evasive, and since it was evident that he had expressed views very different from the Seceder articles of faith, such utterances constituted sufficient grounds to infer censure. The hopes of Thomas Campbell for further amicable relations with the Seceder brethren, were thus dashed to the ground. He submitted to the disposition of his case on the part of the Synod, serving notice that he did so only that he might not give offense to his brethren "by manifesting a refractory spirit." It was soon apparent, however, that he would no longer be able to work in peace and harmony with them. His every movement was watched, misrepresentations and calumnies were constantly employed to detract from his influence, until he at last, reluctantly realized that only one course was left to him—separation. Accordingly he presented to the Synod a formal renunciation of its authority, announcing that he had severed "all ministerial connection" with it, and would hold himself thenceforth "utterly unaffected by its decisions." [12] Though he certainly had no realization of it at the time, this break was fraught with momentous consequences to his own life.[13]

[11] *Ibid.*, 229.
[12] "Memoirs of Alexander Campbell," Richardson, I, 230.
[13] "Comprehensive History of the Disciples of Christ," 103.

2. The severance of his relations with the Seceders, occasioned no relaxation in his ministerial services.[14] His large personal influence, the friendships he had formed in Ireland with many of the new settlers before their emigration to America, his learning and talents, conspicuous in a pioneer country, and, above all, the novelty and force of his plea for Christian unity and liberality, upon the basis of the holy scriptures, continued to draw large numbers to his ministry, whenever it was possible for him to hold meetings. Sometimes, when the weather was favorable, such services were held in the deep shade of a maple grove, but more often in the homes of his Irish neighbors whom he had known in the days of his early ministry. Observing that many continued to come week after week, and that they were representative not only of his own former communion, but of many others as well; persuaded, also, that many, especially among the Seceders, were convinced of the correctness of the principles which he taught, and were anxious for the success of his efforts for Christian unity upon the Bible alone, Campbell finally proposed to some of the leading attendants upon his ministrations, that a meeting be held in which the whole question as to the future of the work should be considered. So far, they had been cooperating without any formal arrangement or definite organization. His proposal receiving the immediate and hearty approbation of these leaders, such a meeting was announced to be held at the home of Abraham Altars, who lived between Mount Pleasant and Washington, and who, though a member of no church, was very much interested in the new movement.

Up to the time of this epochal assembly, meetings under the leadership of Thomas Campbell had been held solely for the purpose of edification and worship. While in his earnest messages, he had insisted upon the Bible as the all-sufficient guide to faith, as yet no definite plan had evolved, nor was there any apparent desire to formulate a platform

[14] "Memoirs of Alexander Campbell," Richardson, I, 234, 238.

for carrying out the reformation for which all felt a crying need. No desire for separation from the existing parties was contemplated, no bond of union had been forged to hold together those who were one in their desire for the unity and purity of the Church. The little band was held together "by a vague sentiment for Christian Union, and by the personal influence and character of Thomas Campbell."[15] Campbell himself had no wish to form a new denomination. His whole desire was to put an end to partyism, and, if possible, to induce the denominations to unite upon the basis of the Holy Scriptures, and to desist from their controversies about those things which were purely matters of opinion and expediency. He wished not to do away with the creeds, for at this time, he had no objection to them as such. There was nothing in the Westminister Confession which he felt called upon to renounce nor with which he found himself at variance, save possibly its teaching concerning the position and authority of the clergy, an "authority which he felt unauthorized, and which he had found by experience, could be readily abused."[16]   Dr. Richardson, speaking of his mind at this period, says: "He was well aware that it was already conceded, in the Protestant formularies, that the Bible was the only rule of faith and practice; he felt that he had the right to urge upon all parties the practical adoption of this concession, and the pressing need there was that it should be at once cordially accepted as the only true basis of Christian union."[17]   He was urged further by the immediate success he had experienced on his withdrawal from the Seceders, in surrounding himself with many from the several denominations, who were like-minded with him in their dissatisfaction with the strife and partyism of the time.

On the day appointed for the meeting, a large assembly congregated at the place designated. It was indeed, a

[15] "Memoirs of Alexander Campbell," Richardson, I, 231.
[16] *Ibid.*, I, 231, 232.
[17] *Ibid.*, I, 235, 236.

unique group. Here were men and women still holding connection with their denominations, and having no desire to dissociate themselves from such communions, yet, sick and tired of party strife, and anxious for a unity which would make possible the preaching of the Gospel to the farthermost reaches of the earth, met together to discover a common ground upon which all could unite without sacrifice of opinions which, though dear, were not necessary to salvation. "A deep feeling of solemnity prevaded the assembly when Thomas Campbell, having opened the meeting in the usual manner, and, in earnest prayer, specially invoked the Divine guidance, proceeded to rehearse the matter from the beginning, and to dwell with unusual force upon the manifold evils resulting from the divisions in religious society—divisions which, he urged, were as unnecessary as they were injurious, since God had provided in his sacred Word an infallible standard, which was all-sufficient and alone sufficient as a basis of union and Christian cooperation." [18] Showing that men had not been satisfied with the plain revelations of the Scriptures, but had gone outside these to manufacture opinions and speculations which were the real occasions of the unhappy strifes and controversies which had so long desolated the Christian world, he earnestly urged a return to the Divine standard, casting out from religion everything for which there could be found no Divine warrant.[19] He then proceeded to announce the dictum which was destined to be quoted more by future Disciples than any other statement of the movement, the great rule or principle by which he trusted they would continue to act consistently and perseveringly, to the end. "That rule, my highly respected hearers," said he, in conclusion, "is this, that where the Scriptures speak, we speak; and where the Scriptures are silent, we are silent." [20]

[18] "Memoirs of Alexander Campbell," Richardson, I, 235, 236.

[19] "Comprehensive History of the Disciples of Christ," Moore, 104, 105.

[20] "Memoirs of Alexander Campbell," Richardson, I, 236.

The impression created by the reading of this apothegm, was immediate and profound. Never before had religious duty been presented in such simple language and yet fraught with such far-reaching results. The Word of God was thenceforth to be their only guide in matters pertaining to life and salvation. Its silences were to be respected as well as its express statements. Dr. Richardson refers to this statement and the meeting out of which it grew, as the true beginning of the Disciple movement. "It was from the moment when these significant words were uttered and accepted, that the more intelligent ever afterward dated the formal and actual commencement of the Reformation which was subsequently carried on with so much success, and which has already produced such important changes in the religious society over a large portion of the world." [21]   A considerable time elapsed after Thomas Campbell had announced the guiding principle of the new Reformation, before anyone attempted to speak. Finally, a shrewd Scotch Seceder, Andrew Munro, a bookseller and the postmaster at Canonsburg, arose and said: "Mr. Campbell, if we adopt that as a basis, there is an end of infant baptism." [22]   A profound sensation was produced by this statement, carrying with it as it did, a seemingly immediate conviction. Campbell replied by saying that if infant baptism conflicted with the Scriptures, "of course, we must have nothing to do with it." Upon hearing this, Thomas Acheson of Washington, a man of very warm impulses, arose and advancing a short distance, placing his hand on his heart, said: "I hope I may never see the day when my heart will renounce that blessed saying of the Scripture, 'Suffer the little ones to come unto me, and forbid them not, for of such is the kingdom of heaven.' " Much affected after saying this, he was about to retire to an adjoining room, weeping the while, when James Foster, unwilling that what he considered a misapplication of the Scripture should go unchallenged, exclaimed: "Mr. Acheson, I would remark

[21] *Ibid.*, I, 237.
[22] *Ibid.*, I, 237, 238.

that in the portion of the Scripture you have quoted, there is no reference, whatever, to infant baptism." Acheson passed out of the room to weep alone. This one incident but foreshadowed the many trials which were before those who, without knowing the far-reaching implications of the principle they had adopted, were now embarking upon a course which was to produce the Disciple communion.[23]

One immediate result of the meeting at the home of Abraham Altars, was that several, seeing the direction in which the new movement was tending, ceased their attendance upon the meetings. These defections, and the discussions which frequently brought them about, caused some concern among those who were to carry on the work to its conclusion. However, they had set their faces toward the unity of the household of faith, and they were not to be deterred, even though loved friends walked no more with them. James Foster, having given the question of infant baptism exhaustive study, became convinced of its unscriptural character, and frequently urged his views upon Thomas Campbell. While admitting that there was no express command on the subject, nor any definite statements in the New Testament which seemed to warrant its practice, he was reluctant to renounce what he considered could be substantiated upon other than scriptural grounds.[24] So ardent was he for Christian unity that he felt this question, as well as that concerning the so-called mode of baptism, should be left to the individual conscience. One day while riding with James Foster, the question of infant baptism came up for discussion. Foster urged his position with more than usual warmth. At length, turning to Campbell, he said with great emphasis; "Father Campbell, how could you, in the absence of authority in the Word of God, baptize a child in the name of the Father, and of the Son, and of the Holy Spirit?"[25] Campbell, not a little confounded at this ques-

---

[23] "Memoirs of Alexander Campbell," Richardson, I, 237, 238.
[24] "Memoirs of Alexander Campbell," Richardson, I, 238, 239.
[25] *Ibid.*, I, 240, 241.

tion, colouring, said in a somewhat irritated tone: "Sir, you are the most intractable person I have ever met." [26]

3. On the 17th of August, 1809, at a meeting held on the headwaters of Buffalo Creek, it was resolved to organize those who still persisted in their belief in the principle announced at the meeting in the home of Abraham Altars, into an association under the name of "The Christian Association of Washington." The purpose of this organization should be to carry on the work of bringing about Christian unity. A committee of twenty-seven of their number was appointed to confer with Thomas Campbell as to the most effective means to forward the work of the Association. Not being satisfied with meeting in the various homes, or in the groves in the summer season, it was decided to build a meeting house. Accordingly, the neighbors assembled, and in a short time "erected a log building on the Sinclair farm, about three miles from Mount Pleasant, on the road leading from Washington to that place, at a point where it was crossed by the road from Middletown to Canonsburg. This building was designed, also, for the purpose of a common school, which was much desired in that neighborhood." [27] In this new house of God, Thomas Campbell continued to meet his brethren regularly. Since he was accustomed to go, after each meeting, to the home of Mr. Welch, who lived nearby, a little room was fixed up specially for him and was considered thereafter his apartment. Here he lived during the week, and in the quiet retirement which it afforded, wrote the "Declaration and Address." When the document was completed, he called a meeting of the members of the Association, and read it to them. It was received with hearty approval, and was at once ordered to be printed. This meeting, September 7th, 1809, is most frequently alluded to by Disciple writers as the actual beginning of the Disciple movement. In order to introduce the work of Alexander

26 *Ibid.*, I, 240.
27 "Memoirs of Alexander Campbell," Richardson, I, 241, 242.

Campbell, a rather careful analysis of this historic monograph must be given.[28]

II

The "Declaration and Address" has already been casually
noted, but an exhaustive analysis of it must be made in order
to reach an understanding of Alexander Campbell's final
position on the question of the unity of the Church. The
great principles of the movement, which afterwards became
so distinguished because of its plea for Christian unity, are
all to be found in this epochal document. The work of the
son was simply to elaborate, clarify, and follow to the logical
conclusions, the fundamental principles enunciated by his
father, in the now, among the Disciples at least, immortal
brochure. Reference has been made to the fact that Alexander, on his arrival from Scotland, read the proof sheets
of the document, which at that time were in his father's
hands for correction. A study of the positions advocated
evidently brought to definite focus his past inclinations and
caused him to resolve to make the ministry and the propa-
gation of the plea for Christian unity his life calling. His
biographer speaks of this high moment. "To all the propositions and reasonings of the Address, Alexander Campbell
gave at once his hearty approbation, as they expressed most
clearly the convictions to which he had himself been brought
by his experience and observation in Scotland, and his
reflections upon the state of religious society at large. Captivated by its clear and decisive presentations of duty, and
the noble Christian enterprise to which it invited, he at once,
though unprovided with worldly property, and aware that
the proposed reformation would, in all probability, provoke
the hostility of the religious parties, resolved to consecrate
his life to the advocacy of the principles which it presented." [29] Soon afterward, when asked by his father as to his

[28] "History of the Disciples of Christ," Moore, 109, 110.
[29] "Memoirs of Alexander Campbell," Richardson, I, 273, 274.

life's work, Alexander replied that he had firmly resolved to enter the ministry and to devote his life to the reformation which must assuredly result from the publication of the "Declaration and Address." [30]

It is of interest to every student of the Campbellian movement, to note this incident as the changing point in the life of Alexander Campbell, and the reason for the change. At the present time it is being debated in some Disciple quarters as to just what was the actuating motive in the work of the Campbells. There can be no doubt that from the time of his reading the "Declaration and Address" until the very day of his death, the great motive in all Alexander Campbell did and said, was the desire to see the Church reunited. Even in the heat and fire of those days, which may be most fitly denominated "the days of Restoration," when the communion which was to be known as the "Disciples of Christ" was being forged, he never forgot the primary motive which had urged him to the great undertaking. In the brief historical statement with which he prefaces the "Christian System," he refers to this motive. "Next to our personal salvation, two objects constituted the *summum bonum*, the supreme good, worthy of all the sacrifice of all temporalities. The first was the union, peace, purity, and harmonious cooperation of Christians, guided by an understanding enlightened by the Holy Scriptures; the other, the conversion of sinners to God. Our predilections and antipathies on all religious questions arose from, and were controlled by, those all-absorbing interests. From these, commenced our campaign against creeds. We had not at first, and we have not now, a favorite opinion or speculation which we would offer as a substitute for any human creed or constitution in Christendom." [31] In an article in the "Harbin-

[30] A lawyer of Pittsburgh about this time made him a flattering offer of a thousand dollars a year to take charge of an academy of which he was the principal trustee. He gave as his reason for rejecting this offer his determination to devote himself to the new Reformation. Richardson, I, 274.

[31] "Christian System," 9.

ger" entitled "Our Mission," [32] written in the later years of his life, he affirms that the earlier passion which inspired him has not become less, but still remains the paramount object of his every effort. Discussing his life's plea for unity, he says; "The realization of this object should be, and, indeed, is, the sole purpose and intent of the present Reformation; the realization of the desire of Jesus Christ in his ever memorable prayer to His Father, in behalf of those who should believe on Him upon the principles there laid down. This I understand to be the whole gist of this effort; for this done, all that God or man desires is accomplished. All else is false, deceptive, and useless; all else burlesque and nonsense, futile and contemptible. It is this alone that can make a man a fit associate of God and angels; this union alone that will preserve him from eternal ruin; He the only Ark in which we may safely ride the billows of life and death." [33] The supreme object of the Campbellian movement is clear, and without it no plausible explanation can be given of its unprecedented growth in power and influence. It is manifest, also, that its foundational document is the "Declaration and Address," and this must be considered in order to comprehend the course followed by the movement after its publication.[34]

1. The introductory statement of the Declaration is important in its announcement of four fundamental propositions.

(1) The familiar Protestant principle of the Right of Private Judgement is boldly asserted. From the situation as it exists in the Western country among the various churches, and from the widely known condition of the religious world every where, "we are persuaded that it is high time for us not only to think, but to act, for ourselves;

[32] This article was written in 1854 when Mr. Campbell was sixty-seven years of age.

[33] "Millennial Harbinger," 1854, 373, 374.

[34] The best critical edition of the "Declaration and Address" is that by Dean Frederick Kershner of Butler University, entitled, "The Christian Union Overture." This is the edition employed in the present analysis.

to see with our own eyes, and to take all our measures directly and immediately from the Divine standard." [35]   No man has the right to judge his brother, and no one can be judged for his brother.   Each must give his own account to God.   The stern Puritanical background of Thomas Campbell's theology, shows itself in his assertion of this principle which has ever been the very core of the Protestant Gospel, this right of private judgement for which Luther so grandly battled.[36]   In almost prophetic language, Thomas Campbell urges his readers not only to think for themselves as a duty, but also to act.

(2) The Protestant principle of the authority of the Scriptures, as the court of final appeal in things pertaining to the kingdom of Christ, is firmly maintained. "We are also of the opinion, that as the Divine word is equally binding upon all, so all lie under the obligation to be found by it, and it alone; and not by any human interpretation of it." [37]   For this reason, no man has any right to judge his brother "except in so far as he manifestly violates the express letter of the law."   Any such judgement would be itself a violation of the law of Christ, a daring usurpation of His throne, and the gravest sort of intrusion upon the rights and privileges of those who belong to Him.   This second principle, so fundamental to Protestantism, was basic in everything Thomas Campbell taught, as it was, also, to the development of his positions in the later teachings of his illustrious son.   The Scriptures, freely interpreted in accordance with the individual conscience and judgement, "furnishes the religious standard of the Declaration." [38]   The seemingly implicit contradiction between these two principles will be considered later; it is sufficient here to note Thomas Campbell's confident affirmation of them.

(3) The sad divisions among the people of God are bit-

---

[35] "Overture," Kershner, 32.
[36] "Luther's Primary Works," Wace and Buchheim, 170, 171.
[37] "Overture," Kershner, 32.
[38] Comment by Dean Kershner, "Overture," 41.

terly deplored. Being aware of the terrible consequences of religious controversy among those who love the same Lord and even wear his name, "tired and sick of the bitter jarrings and janglings of a party spirit, we would desire to be at rest; and, were it possible, we would also desire to adopt and recommend such measures as would give rest to our brethren throughout all the Churches, as would restore unity, peace, and purity to the whole Church of God." [39]

(4) The only way to that unity which would bring the desired peace and purity, is pointed out. The rest so earnestly wished for "we utterly despair either to find for ourselves, or to be able to recommend to our brethren, by continuing amid the diversity and rancor of party contentions, the veering uncertainty and clashings of human opinions; nor, indeed, can we reasonably expect to find it anywhere but in Christ and His simple word, which is the same yesterday, today, and forever. Our desire, therefore, for ourselves and our brethren, would be, that, rejecting human opinions and the inventions of men as of any authority, or as having any place in the Church of God, we might forever cease from further contentions about such things; returning to, and holding fast by the original standard; taking the Divine word alone for our rule; and the Holy Spirit for our teacher and guide to lead us into all truth; and Christ alone, as exhibited in the word, for our salvation; that, by so doing, we may be at peace among ourselves, follow peace with all men, and holiness, without which no man shall see the Lord." [40]   In reality, this paragraph contains the whole plea and plan for the consummation of the unity and peace which the gentle soul of Thomas Campbell longed so fervently to see established. On almost every one of the fifty-four pages of his epoch-making monograph, he evidences the pain which the divided and distracted state of the Church of his time, gave him.

[39] "Overture," Kershner, 32.
[40] Ibid., 32, 33.

The resolutions which form a part of the introductory statement, are of no concern in the present analysis, save the one in which any intention to form a new church or party, is vehemently denied. "This society by no means, considers itself a Church, nor does it assume to itself the powers peculiar to such a society; nor do the members, as such, consider themselves as standing connected in that relation; nor as at all associated for the peculiar purposes of Church associations; but merely as voluntary advocates of Church reformation; and as possessing the powers common to all individuals who may please to associate in a peaceable and orderly manner for any lawful purpose." [41] This, and the other resolutions of which it is a part, evidences the fact that at this period, one of the most abhorrent of possibilities, to the mind of Thomas Campbell, would be that of adding another sect to the already great number of those whose wars and bitter backbitings were such a source of anguish to his soul. These resolutions have to do only with the formation of an association for the promotion of Christian unity.[42] The colossal task which such principles involved, apparently did not manifest itself to the author of the "Declaration," and to his earnest associates at the time.

2. The clamant necessity for unity is manifest.

(1) Since love is the foundational principle of the Christian religion—since its first aim is to reconcile man to God and man to his brother man—it will be to the glory of the everlasting Father if Christians in the present sad state of affairs do all within their power to heal the schisms which have rent the Church asunder.[43]

(2) That awful and distressing effects have been produced by divisions among God's people, is patent to all. "What dreary effects of those cursed divisions are to be seen, even in this highly favored country, where the sword of the

[41] "Overture," Kershner, 33.
[42] *Ibid.*, 33, 34.
[43] "Overture," Kershner, 51, 52.

civil magistrate has not yet learned to serve at the altar. Have we not seen congregations broken to pieces, neighborhoods of professing Christians first thrown into confusion by party contentions, and, in the end, entirely deprived of Gospel ordinances; while, in the meantime, large settlements and tracts of our country remain to this day entirely destitute of a Gospel ministry, many of them in little better than a state of heathenism, the Churches being either so weakened with divisions that they cannot send them ministers, or the people so divided among themselves that they will not receive them." [44] One of the dread results of such a state of affairs is that some who live next door to a brother in Christ dare not worship with him or commune with him lest they bring upon themselves the displeasure and censure of others of the same faith. Discipline is relaxed to such an extent that if one be excommunicated from one communion for gross immortality, he can find no difficulty in eventually securing shelter in the fold of some rival denomination. Upon all this, there is evidence of the Divine displeasure in that such schismatics are given up to all manner of grevious scandals and are visited by Divine judgements." [45]

(3) Upon the Church in America rests a special responsibility because of her freedom from the awful judgements which at the moment, are being heaped upon the devoted nations "that have given their strength and power unto the beast; in which, of course, no adequate reformation can be accomplished, until the Word of God be fulfilled, and the vials of his wrath be poured out upon them." [46] Freed

[44] *Ibid.*, 52.

[45] "Overture," Kershner, 52, 53.

[46] There can be no doubt that in his appeal for the unity of the Church, Thomas Campbell squints somewhat in the direction of premillenarianism. At the time of the writing of the "Declaration and Address" Napoleon was at the zenith of his power. In 1807 the treaty of Tilsit, which probably marks the loftiest point in his career, had been signed. The few years immediately following saw him the undisputed sovereign of Europe. In the thought of many devout Christians of the time, he was identified with the beast of Revelation. It is practically certain that Campbell held this view. "Overture," 53.

from the baneful influences of any civil establishment in matters of religion, the hope for a reformation eventuating in Christian unity, lies in America.[47] While the task is a heavy one and the discouragements many, yet, if ever such an enterprise can succeed, it must be in a land favoured as America is favoured.[48] Therefore, "with such encouragements as these, what should deter us from the heavenly enterprise, or render hopeless the attempt of accomplishing, in due time, an entire union of the churches in faith and practice, according to the Word of God? Not that we judge ourselves competent to effect such a thing; we utterly disclaim the thought; but we judge it to be our bounden duty to make the attempt by using all due means in our power to promote it; and also, that we have sufficient reason to rest assured that our humble and well-meant endeavours shall not be in vain in the Lord." [49] The cause is not that of one man, or of one party; it ought to be the cause of all who love the Lord Jesus "to forever put an end to our hapless divisions, and restore to the Church its primitive unity, purity, and prosperity." [50]

(4) The basis of the proposed unity can be found only in the Church as it is described in the New Testament. That there is such a Church is clearly manifest, and a return to it surely ought not to be a thought incredible. "Or, is there anything that can justly be deemed necessary for this desirable purpose, but to conform to the model and adopt the practice of the primitive Church, expressly exhibited in the New Testament?" [51] Even were this to necessitate alterations in the present churches we ought to be happy to make them for the unity which would result, and the glory that such unity would bring to the cause of Christ. Were we, then, "in our Church constitution and managements, to

[47] "Overture," Kershner, 53, 54.
[48] Ibid., 54.
[49] Ibid., 55.
[50] "Overture," Kershner, 59.
[51] Ibid., 59.

exhibit a complete conformity to the apostolic Church, would we not be, in that respect, as perfect as Christ intended we should be?" [52]   In this position, namely, that Christian unity can be brought to pass only by a return to the model of the New Testament Church, is the germ of the whole future movement as a distinct communion for the restoration of primitive Christianity as the New Testament declares it.

(5) A survey of modern Christianity enforces the fact that the communions are not divided over essential things. There is a ground which all hold in common. "It is, to us, a pleasing consideration that all the Churches of Christ which mutually acknowledge each other as such, are not only one in the great doctrines of faith and holiness, but are also materially agreed as to the positive ordinances of the Gospel institution; so that our differences at most, are about the things in which the kingdom of God does not consist, that is, in matters of private opinion or human invention." [53] Christian unity, then, may be stated at its lowest terms.[54] "With you all, we desire to unite in the bonds of entire Christian unity—Christ alone being the head, the center, his word the rule, an implicit belief of and manifest conformity to it, in all things, the terms." [55] Such a union is reasonable and timely.[56] There can be no decline of bigotry under the divided conditions which obtain; it will only be as those who love the Lord make an honest effort to return to the New Testament basis, that the discordant notes will gradually die away. Such a unity can be accomplished by a return to the platform universally acknowledged to be Divine. The general plea, here made, assuredly cannot hurt the feelings or excite the jealousy of any party, "on the contrary, every effort toward a permanent Scriptural unity among the Churches, upon the solid basis of universally acknowledged

[52] *Ibid.,* 59.
[53] "Overture," Kreshner, 60.
[54] *Ibid.,* 60, 61.
[55] *Ibid.,* 61.
[56] *Ibid.,* 61, 62.

and self-evident truths, must have the happiest tendency to enlighten and conciliate." [57] If there be no such Divine and universally acknowledged platform, it is difficult to see how any unity of God's divided people is possible. "Indeed, if no such Divine and adequate basis of union can be fairly exhibited as will meet the approbation of every upright and intelligent Christian, nor such mode of procedure adopted in favour of the weak as will oppress their consciences, then the accomplishment of this grand object upon principle must be forever impossible." [58]

(6) The plea for Christian unity which composes this section of the "Declaration and Address" includes just here, an earnest appeal to the ministry of the time, as leaders of the flock of God to take the lead in this reform which cries out so insistently for attention, throughout the land.[59] Since Christians are to be united in the great hereafter, since there are to be no divisions in the grave, why not be united here.[60] The glorious result can be furthered by fraternal association, by prayer together in all things as far as possible. Following this plan, God's people in the various communions will come to know each other, and this is assuredly a necessary requisite to the healing of divisions.[61] The plea for unity is not one which would be content that the freedom so dearly bought in the long and bloody struggle with the Roman Church, should be now lightly cast aside. Far from it! It is rather a plea to stand fast in that liberty in which Christ has made his people free, a plea to hold precious that "liberty from subjection to any authority but His own in matters of religion."[62]

(7) In the closing paragraphs of this section, Thomas Campbell introduces plainly his proposed patform for unity,

[57] *Ibid.*, 61.
[58] *Ibid.*, 62.
[59] "Overture," Kreshner, 70.
[60] *Ibid.*, 70, 71.
[61] *Ibid.*, 70.
[62] *Ibid.*, 72.

and definitely denominates it as such.[63] The thirteen propositions which he sets forth are not in any way to be considered as a final program for unity; they are rather, merely
to "serve as a preliminary, to open up the way to a permanent Scriptural unity among the friends and lovers of truth
and peace throughout the Churches."[64] The devout mind of
the whole Church should consider a matter so fundamentally
important as that of its own unity. That all men who love
the Master will immediately and heartily concur in this
effort, can be confidently expected.[65]

The modesty which is evinced in these paragraphs, was
characteristic of Thomas Campbell in all his handling of
the subject of the unity of the Church. He felt himself but
one man, humble but courageous and above all reverently
desirous forever to put an end to the dreadful state of the
Church of his time, resultant from her shameful divisions.[66]
That his hopes for a ready and whole-souled response to his
"Declaration and Address" were far too sanguine, was soon
apparent. Its reception at the hands of his own time
brought sad disillusionment to his benevolent heart.

(8) Before introducing his basis for unity positively,
he once more carefully guards against any possible mis-
apprehensions as to the purpose he has in mind, by an out
and out denial that he intends to form a new party on the
basis of his brochure as a creed or term of communion. "Let
none imagine that the subjoined propositions are at all intended as an overture toward a new creed or standard for
the Church, or as in any wise designed to be made a term
of communion; nothing can be further from our intention.
They are merely designed for opening up the way, that we
may come fairly and firmly to the original ground upon
clear and certain premises, and take up things just as the
apostles left them; and thus disentangled from the accruing

[63] *Ibid.*, 72, 73.
[64] *Ibid.*, 72.
[65] "Overture," Kreshner, 72, 73.
[66] *Ibid.*, 73.

embarrassments of intervening ages, we may stand with
evidence upon the same ground on which the Church stood
at the beginning." [67] The daring of this position, even at
this day when for more than a hundred years the Campbellian principles have been taught, arrests the reader.
None of the Protestant reformers had presumed to take such
a position, passing over so lightly as it does, the authorities,
usages, and decisions of so many intervening ages. The
words of one who perhaps better than anyone save his own
son, knew his mind, clearly and succinctly set forth his
whole purpose. "Here, indeed, was the startling proposition
to begin anew—to begin at the beginning; to ascend at once
to the pure fountain of truth, and to neglect and disregard,
as though they had never been, the decrees of Popes, Councils, Synods and Assemblies, and all the traditions and corruptions of an apostate Church. Here was an effort not
so much for the reformation of the Church, as was that of
Luther and Calvin, and to a certain extent even that of the
Haldanes, but for its complete restoration at once to its
pristine purity and perfection. By coming at once to the
primitive model and rejecting all human imitations; by submitting implicitly to the Divine authority as plainly expressed in the Scriptures, and by disregarding all the
assumptions and dictations of fallible men, it was proposed
to form a union upon a basis to which no valid objection
could possibly be offered. By this summary method, the
Church was to be at once released from the controversies
of eighteen centuries, and from the conflicting claims of all
pretenders to apostolic thrones, and the primitive gospel
of salvation was to be disentangled and disembarrassed
from all those corruptions and perversions which had here-
tofore delayed or arrested its progress." [68] The principles
by which this restoration of New Testament Christianity,
with its consequent reunion of the divided Church of God

[67] *Ibid.*, 73.
[68] "Memoirs of Alexander Campbell," Richardson, I, 257, 258.

may be accomplished, form the next section of the "Declaration and Address."

3. The basis of Christian unity is discussed in thirteen propositions.

(1) Proposition one is an affirmation of the unity of the Church of Christ, and defines clearly who are members of that Church. "That the Church of Christ upon earth is essentially, intentionally, and constitutionally one; consisting of all those in every place that profess their faith in Christ and obedience to Him in all things according to the Scriptures, and that manifest the same by their tempers and conduct, and of none else; as none else can be truly and properly called Christians." [69] There is probably no statement in all the vast round of Christian Union literature which has come into being during the last hundred years, more justly famous than the statement of Thomas Campbell "that the Church of Christ on earth is essentially, intentionally, and constitutionally one." Dean Kershner calls attention to the fact that the emphatic and comprehensive nature of Campbell's definition is indicated by the three adverbs which he uses. The word "essentially" caries with it the idea that the Church possesses a unity which is not extraneous or insignificant, but that it is of its very essence or nature. It belongs there inherently, so that a divided Church is a contradiction in itself. The whole denominational theory of the Church is, therefore, absolutely without foundation. In this attitude Thomas Campbell is decidedly at one with the High Church view. As "intentionally" one, the Church possesses a norm or standard, one given to it by its author. Unity is one of the distinguishing characteristics of the Church as the Divine founder conceived it. To divide it is to commit one of the gravest sins against it and the purpose which it has for the salvation of the world. As "constitutionally" one, the Church possesses a political organization; it is structurally one. "The underlying philoso-

[69] "Overture," Kreshner, 81.

phy involved in Christian union is brought out in the word
'essentially.' The mystical and sacramental feature is embodied in the word 'intentionally,' and the political and
organizational elements in the word 'constitutionally.' The
Church of Christ has a constitution, a definite structure, an
organization which it must maintain in the world. It belongs to the very warp and woof of the organization that it
should be unitary. The idea of a federation of churches for
example, violates the constitutional unity of the body of
Christ. There is no place in the political framework of the
ecclesia for separate denominations or sects. The Church
is a seamless robe and not a Joseph's coat of many colored
patches." [70]

(2) In the second proposition the province of the local
church is defined.[71] It must be understood in connection
with number one. While the church of God must exist in
many separate congregations, yet there must be no schism
in the body; it must remain one. It must be a unity in
which there is congruity, samness of mind and word.

(3) Propositions three, four and five will be quoted in
toto in the consideration of the Campbellian conception of
the Rule of Faith.[72] They affirm the authority of the Scriptures,[73] the proper distinction which ought to be made between the Old and New Testaments as constitutions respectively of the Old Testament Church and that of our Lord in
the new dispensation, and the proper attitude which should
be observed toward the New Testament ordinances.[74] In
proposition five occurs the famous statement which defines
the limits of the Campbellian movement in its backward
journey to discover the pure source of Christianity, "Nothing ought to be received into the faith or worship of the

[70] "Overture," Kershner, 82, 83.
[71] Ibid., 83, 84.
[72] See page
[73] "Overture," 84, 85.
[74] Ibid., 85.

church, or be made a term of communion among Christians, which is not as old as the New Testament." [75]

(4) The place of inferential truth is clearly set forth in the sixth proposition. Theology has a very definite place, but not in the confession of the Church. "That although inferences and deductions from scripture premises, when fairly inferred, may be truly called the doctrine of God's holy word; yet they are not formally binding upon the consciences of Christians farther than to perceive the connection, and evidently see that they are so; for their faith must not stand in the wisdom of men; but in the power and veracity of God—therefore no such deductions can be made terms of communion, but do properly belong to the after and progressive edification of the church. Hence it is evident that no such deductions or inferential truth ought to have any place in the church's confession." [76] In these words Thomas Campbell prepares for that fuller discussion of the whole question of the distinction between faith and opinions, which was to be made by his son, and which was to become so foundational in all the Disciple conceptions of the way to Christian unity.

(5) In proposition seven, the futility of human creeds is considered. It is of interest to compare the father's handling of the question with the later vigorous denunciation of these human documents, by the son. "That although doctrinal exhibitions of the great system of divine truths, and defensive testimonies in opposition to prevailing errors, be highly expedient; and the more full and explicit they be, for these purposes, the better; yet as these must be in a great measure the effect of human reasoning, and of course must contain many inferential truths, they ought not to be made terms of Christian communion: unless we suppose, what is contrary to fact, that none have a right to the communion of the church, but such as possess a very clear and decisive judgement; whereas the church from the beginning did, and ever

[75] "Overture," Kershner, 86.
[76] *Ibid.*, 87.

will, consist of little children and young men, as well as fathers." [77] This proposition is really but a continuation of the one preceding. It has to do, however, with those opinions and speculations as they become crystallized into creedal form.

(6) In proposition eight, the subject of terms of admission into the church is considered. Assuredly all Protestant bodies could give unqualified assent to the position here advocated by Campbell, for there has never really been any division on those things essential to the appropriation of the salvation in Christ. "That as it is not necessary that persons have a particular knowledge or distinct apprehension of all divinely revealed truths in order to entitle them to a place in the Church; neither should they, for this purpose, be required to make a profession more extensive than their knowledge; but that, on the contrary, they having a due measure of self-knowledge respecting their lost and perishing condition by nature and practice, and of the way of salvation through Jesus Christ, accompanied with a profession of their faith in and obedience to him, in all things, according to his word, is all that is absolutely necessary to qualify them for admission into his Church." [78] There is one position hinted at in the foregoing statement, which Thomas Campbell later gave up, that referring to original sin, in the words "by nature and practice." This can only be understood in reference to the current distinction between "original" and "positive" sin. Otherwise the position here set forth is in agreement with the terms of salvation; repentance, faith and obedience, as universally accepted by the leaders of the Church in all ages.

(7) Propositions nine and ten have respect to the necessity for love [79] to obtain among the people of God if any agreement is to be reached, and also continue the denunciation of divisions in the body of Christ. Such divisions are anti-chris-

[77] "Overture," Kershner, 88.
[78] *Ibid.*, 89.
[79] "Overture," Kershner, 90.

tian, anti-scriptural, and anti-natural, resulting in confusion and every evil work.[80]

(8) The eleventh proposition considers the causes which have operated to divide the Church of God. "That (in some instances) a partial neglect of the expressly revealed will of God, and (in others) an assumed authority for making the approbation of human opinions and human inventions a term of communion, by introducing them into the constitution, faith, or worship of the Church, are, and have been, the immediate, obvious, and universally acknowledged causes, of all the corruptions and divisions that ever have taken place in the Church of God." [81]   It is evident that the language of Campbell in this paragraph is not entirely free from exaggeration.   In his own time these two causes, the neglect of the word and the introduction of human innovations and human speculations into the constitution and worship of the Church, were doubtless the paramount causes of the divisions which everywhere existed.   They would be true today but they would not explain all the reasons underlying the perpetuation of that divided state which is even now the sorrow of all devout Christians.   Division is a far more complex affair than Thomas Campbell, environed as he was, could see.   It is obvious that Dean Kershner is right when he opines, "We question whether Mr. Campbell, if he were alive today and were rewriting his platform, would use precisely the same language in Proposition eleven which he used in 1809." [82]

(9) Proposition twelve is really a summary of the program for the Church as it is given in the "Declaration and Address." "That all that is necessary to the highest state of perfection and purity of the Church upon earth, is, first, that none be received as members but such as having that due measure of scriptural self-knowledge described above, do profess their faith in Christ and obedience to Him in all

[80] *Ibid.*, 91, 92.
[81] *Ibid.*, 93.
[82] "Overture," Kreshner, 93.

things according to the scriptures; nor, secondly, that nay be retained in her communion longer than they continue to manifest the reality of their profession by their temper and conduct. Thirdly, that her ministers, duly and scripturally qualified, inculcate none other things than those very articles of faith and holiness expressly revealed and enjoined in the word of God. Lastly, that in all their administrations they keep close by the observance of all divine ordinances, after the example of the primitive Church, exhibited in the New Testament; without any additions whatsoever of human opinions or inventions of man." [83]

(10) In the thirteenth proposition, Campbell makes a somewhat hesitant pronouncement concerning the law of expediency. His son, later, was to make this a fundamental in the accomplishment of unity. Thomas Campbell, however, because he realized so keenly the tremendous part purely human considerations had played in the division of the Church, was somewhat reluctant to admit too much for expediency. "Lastly: That if any circumstantials indispensably necessary to the observance of divine ordinances be not found upon the page of express revelation, such, and such only, as are absolutely necessary for this purpose should be adopted under the title of human expedients, without any pretense to a more sacred origin, so that any subsequent alteration or difference in the observance of these things might produce no contention nor division in the Church." [84]   In strong contrast to this somewhat timorous handling of the subject is the clear and vigorous manner in which Alexander later faced the whole issue which necessarily rises when differentition is made between those things which are matters of commandment and those which are left to the good sense of the people of God.

4. The Method and Purpose of the Platform occupys the last portion of the Declaration.[85]   It reads almost like a

[83] *Ibid.*, 94, 95.
[84] "Overture," Kershner, 95.
[85] *Ibid.*, 96-99.

sermon, so filled is it with exhortation to those who ought, as God's children, to heed it with utmost reverance. Thomas Campbell appeals to the common enlightened mind and affirms, in essence, that this is the same in its pronouncements as though such pronouncements had come from a general council. Yet, though such decisions be slow in coming, they will come eventually, and it behooves those who see the truth, to act upon it. "It is not the voice of the multitude, but the voice of truth that has power with the conscience; that can produce rational conviction and acceptable obedience." [86]

The motto of the Association under whose direction the "Declaration and Address" was sent out and that which later was to become the motto of the whole Campbellian movement, is declared in significant words. Continuing his discussion of the courage necessary if the work for reunion is abundantly to succeed, he says: "Union in truth has been and must ever be, the desire and prayer of all such; Union in truth is our motto. The Divine word is our standard; in the Lord's name do we display our banners." [87] Certainly this is about the last word that can be said in relation to the whole mooted question of the basis of unity. The manner of discovering what that truth is, how it may be disentangled from the admixture of error which has accrued through the ages, was another problem, one which was left for the son to solve.

5. The "Declaration and Address" closes with the Appendix which constitutes about three-fifths of the document.[88] While containing some very valuable passages, it is in the main identical with the position of the "Declaration" proper. It is really a commentary on the positions already advanced. Two important facts Campbell stresses with great earnestness; first, that it is not intended to "proselyte" or by endeavoring to erect Churches out of

[86] *Ibid.*, 97.
[87] "Overture," Kershner, 97.
[88] *Ibid.*, Dean Kershner's edition gives thirty-two pages to the Appendix.

Churches, to distract and divide congregations; [89] and, secondly, that the unity desired can be brought about only by a return to the faith, to that for which a 'thus sayeth the Lord' can be given, and not to opinions. It will never be possible for God's people to see alike on all things, nor is it necessary that they should to do so on those things which are non-essentials.[90] He is firm in his belief that there is a core of assured Divine revelation which is so obviously Divine and so clearly set forth that there is universal agreement upon it. This, and this alone, is essential as a basis or system upon which unity may become a fact. Alexander Campbell clarified this position; he preached and defended it; beyond its foundational content he does not go. It is not too much to say that every basic thing in the whole Disciple plea for unity is found in the now immortal document of which, without a doubt, Thomas Campbell was the sole author.

[89] *Ibid.*, 98.
[90] *Ibid.*, 131, 132.

CHAPTER III

THE BASIS OF CHRISTIAN UNITY

WHETHER or not the earnest plea of Thomas Campbell and his devoted fellow-members in the Christian Association would ever have resulted in more than the slight stir which created the few churches to which he ministered for ten years, is very seriously to be doubted. Thomas Campbell was a man of peace. Nothing so filled his gentle soul with anguish as the thought that he might wound a brother or sister in the Lord. At the very moment of the publication of the "Declaration and Address," another type of leader was needed, one who could through courage and untiring energy, put the great principles enunciated with such clarity and persuasiveness in the immortal document, to the test. The leader was discovered in the son. The ministers to whom Thomas Campbell sent the Declaration with such eager expectation of an immediate and glorious reformation, were not excited about it at all; they did not even read it, or, if they did, they said nothing about it. Had the plan been followed to its conclusion under the continued leadership of the senior Campbell, it must be acknowledged that it would simply have died out. From this period onward the amazing success of the movement must be attributed to the energy, the fighting spirit, and the unflagging zeal of Alexander Campbell.

While every principle discoverable in Campbell's final position is to be found in the "Declaration and Address," these principles are resolutely pushed to their logical conclusions in the years of conflict which their active proclamation engendered. Realizing that such revolutionary positions could not be advocated in the churches of the day,

79

Alexander Campbell, determining that they should not be thrust aside to die out in defeat, decided to organize upon them and thus to stand as a witness for them before the religious world. While reluctant to form a party—shrinking from the anomaly of advocating union, yet creating another division—he saw that this was the only way, unless the plea for Christian unity was to be forgotten. He, and those who labored so valiantly with him, determined that the principles of the plea should be put to the test as a basis. They resolved to try it out in practice, and with what astonishing results, is evidenced in the fact that before Campbell's death, five hundred thousand converts had been won to his cause.

I

1. In 1824, in the second volume of the "Christian Baptist," Campbell published the first of a series of thirty-two articles, entitled "The Restoration of the Ancient Order of Things." [1] In these essays he developed the principles set forth in the "Declaration and Address" with special emphasis upon just what the Ancient Order was, meaning by this the Church as described in the New Testament. The thesis of the whole series is stated: "A restoration of the ancient order of things is all that is necessary to the happiness and usefulness of christians." [2] Following the negative method which characterized his work in the "Christian Baptist," he devoted three articles [3] to a vigorous denunciation of creeds as bonds of union and communion. Reformations have not been reformations of religion but of creeds and clergy.[4] Creeds are condemned because they have perpetuated the theologies of men and thus have caused divisions in the Church.[5] They are not plainer than the Scriptures, else the

---

[1] "Christian Baptist," 126.
[2] *Ibid.*, 126-128; 133-136; 139-142.
[3] *Ibid.*, 127.
[4] *Ibid.*, 127.
[5] "Christian Baptist," 140.

Scriptures have failed in the very purpose for which they were written.[6] They fail, also, in the very purpose for which they their protagonists avow their creation—as bonds of union.[7] They have been responsible for division in that they have always excluded every one who has held opinions contrary to them.[8] In doing this, they have often excommunicated the very best minds of the Church. Since they are composed of the inferences of human minds, they cannot be made tests of fellowship for the Church, nor can they be thus placed upon the same plane as the assured revelation in the word.[9] In the remainder of the series he devotes two essays to "Purity of Speech," [10] one to the New Testament "Order of Worship," [11] four to the "Breaking of the Loaf," [12] one each to the "Fellowship" [13] and "The Washing of Feet," [14] three to the "Bishop's Office," [15] one each to "Love Feasts" [16] and "The Spirit of Ancient Christians," [17] one to a refutation of "Arguments against the Ancient Order," [18] one each to "Devotion" [19] and "The Deacon's Office," [20] two to "Singing," [21] one to "The Church," [22] eight to "Discipline," [23] and one to "Official Names and Titles." [24] From this list it will be seen that he dealt with the whole question

[6] *Ibid.*, 133.
[7] *Ibid.*, 134.
[8] *Ibid.*, 140.
[9] *Ibid.*, 134.
[10] *Ibid.*, 158, 160, 312, 314.
[11] *Ibid.*, 165, 166.
[12] *Ibid.*, 174, 176, 180, 182, 188, 189, 194, 195.
[13] *Ibid.*, 209, 211.
[14] *Ibid.*, 222, 223.
[15] *Ibid.*, 231, 233, 242, 243, 260, 261.
[16] *Ibid.*, 282, 285.
[17] *Ibid.*, 294, 296.
[18] *Ibid.*, 322, 323.
[19] *Ibid.*, 335, 336.
[20] *Ibid.*, 362, 363.
[21] *Ibid.*, 395, 396, 406, 407.
[22] *Ibid.*, 428, 429.
[23] *Ibid.*, 440, 442, 467, 468, 471, 473, 485, 487, 500, 501, 510, 530, 531, 549, 550.
[24] *Ibid.*, 585, 586.

of the life and worship of the ancient Church. These essays formed an outline of the writings which were to follow. They belong to the immature stage of his theological thought and are noted here only because they occupy a certain place in the journey toward his final position. That position may be found in his writings in the "Harbinger," "The Christian System," "Christian Baptism," and "The Campbell-Rice Debate."

2. To the very last he decried division among God's people, considering it the grossest evil of his time. Among the scores of eloquent and sometimes vitriolic paragraphs which might be quoted, two are here given as indicative of the intensity of his hatred of schism in the body of Christ. If it be true that in the beginning Christ's followers were united, "and true it is, if Jesus be the Messiah, in what moral desolation is the kingdom of Jesus Christ! Was there at any time, or is there now, in all the earth, a kingdom more convulsed by internal broils and dissensions, than what is commonly called the church of Jesus Christ? Should any one think it lawful to paganize both the Greek and Latin churches—to eject one hundred millions of members of the Greek and Roman communions from the visible and invisible precincts of the Christian family or kingdom of Jesus Christ, and regard the Protestant faith and people as the only true faith and the only true citizens of the kingdom of Jesus; what then shall we say of them, contemplated as the visible kingdom over which Jesus presides as Prophet, Priest, and King? Of forty millions of Protestants shall we constitute the visible kingdom of the Prince of Peace? Be it so for the sake of argument; and what then? The Christian army is forty millions strong; how do they muster? Under forty ensigns? Under forty antagonistic leaders? Would to God there were but forty! In the Geneva department alone there is almost that number of petty chiefs. My soul sickens at the details!" [25]   In one of the sweeping

[25] "Christian System," 105.

summaries of his whole program, which appear so often in his writings, near the close of his great debate with Rice, he says: "If the sects would sheathe forever the sword of partizan strife; if they would make one *auto da fe* of all their creeds and shibboleths; if they would make one grand burnt-offering of their schismatical constitutions, and cast forever to the moles and bats their ancient and apocryphal traditions, and then unite on the apostolic and divine institutions, the Christian religion might be sent to the farthest domicile of man in less than a single age—in less than the life of one man." [26] These words are almost like a thousand others which we are hearing today. In earnest Christian minds everywhere there is the conviction that were we truly united as followers of Christ, the gospel could be preached to the whole world in this generation. Campbell continues in the same vein: "Protestant England and Protestant America have, at their disposal, all the means necessary to send the gospel from pole to pole, and from the Thames or the Euphrates to the ends of the earth. They have men enough; genius, learning, talent, books, money, enterprize, zeal, adequate to such a splendid scheme; if they would, in Christian faith and purity, unite in one holy effort, on the book of God, to humanize, civilize, and evangelize all the brotherhood of man. The unholy warfare of this age is international, inter-sectional, interpartizan. All the artillery —intellectual, moral, physical—is expended upon the little citadels, fortifications, and towers of partyism. It is a barbarous, incivil, savage warfare against our own religion, against ourselves, against the common Saviour, against the whole family of man." [27] In a brief, comprehensive statement he bespeaks the reason for his whole life's work and the plan by which this condition of affairs so faithfully described as it existed in his day, and so utterly abhorrent to him, might be remedied. "For all these reasons, I pray for the annihilation of partyism, and of everything that, directly or in-

[26] "Campbell-Rice Debate," 903.
[27] "Campbell-Rice Debate," 903.

directly, tends to keep it up; and instead of these human devices, of which I have so often spoken, these ordinances and traditions of men, I plead for the Bible, and nothing but the Bible, as the standard and rule of all the personal and social duties; our bond of union, our terms of communion, the directory and formulary of our whole church relations— faith, discipline and government." [28]

II

The causes of division among God's people are considered, since an understanding of what divides must necessarily precede the formulation of any acceptable platform for unity. In the main, he agrees with the father's position in the "Declaration and Address"; as regards items he goes farther. There are four great causes of a divided church; others might be enumerated, but these are comprehended in the four which he names. They are considered generally in the following order.

1. Division is due, first of all, to incomplete efforts at reformation. "A reformation of Papacy was attempted in Europe full three centuries ago. It ended in a Protestant hierarchy, and swarms of dissenters. Protestantism has been reformed into Presbyterianism—that into Congregationalism—and that into Baptistism, etc. Methodism has attempted to reform all, but has reformed itself into many forms of Wesleyism." [29] He does not mean to be understood as denouncing these laudable attempts at reformation. Not at all. His own work, he well understood, was based upon what these men who had preceded him, had so gloriously accomplished. The incompleteness of their reformatory efforts, however, coupled with the fact that they began at the wrong place, has resulted in an almost ceaseless multiplication of sects and parties. The denominations have done well as far as they have gone, but no one of them "has

[28] *Ibid.*, 903.
[29] "Christian Baptism," 15.

begun in the right place. All of them retain in their bosoms, in their ecclesiastic organizations, worship, doctrines, and observances, various relics of Popery." [30]   Here was a favorite Campbellian objection to the whole denominational system. The church is not divided now, and has never been divided, upon the divine revelation, but by her inheritances from the Roman Church, in her human names, human creeds and formularies of belief, human substitutions for the baptism taught in the New Testament, human innovations in Church government—these and many others which are direct "relics of popery" divide the Church into warring sects and parties. His whole program as he conceived it, was to de-Romanize the Church of his day by a return to that Church which existed as the creation of the Apostles.

Because of the admixture of distinctively Roman elements with those which were originally Christian, in the church of his time, Campbell did not consider it to be the Church of Christ as exhibited in the New Testament writings. "Having long reflected upon these premises—these creeds, schisms, and parties—as well as on the sacred writings of Apostles and Prophets, and the primitive communities founded on them, we are fully convinced that neither Popery, nor any of its Protestant reformations, is the Christian Institution delivered to us in the Holy Scriptures. What is Popery but the extreme of defection and apostasy? What is prelacy but a reformed modification of Popery? What is Presbyterianism but a reform of Prelacy? What is Congregationalism or independency but a reform of Presbyterianism? And what is Wesleyan Methodism but a popular emendation of English Episcopacy, combined with the enthusiasm of ancient Quakerism? Amongst them all, we thank the grace of God that there are many who believe in, and love the Saviour, and that, though we may not have many Christian churches, we have many Christians." [31]

The divisions which have resulted from the incompleteness

[30] "Christian Baptism," 15.
[31] "Christian Baptism," 15.

of attempted reformation, in that they have retained in their various organizations the inheritances from Romanism, have eventuated in almost disastrous consequences. The great denominations have, because of their disunity, impaired their efficiency for the extension of the kingdom. "The doctrines and traditions of men yet impair the power and progress of the gospel in their hands; and, therefore, as communities, they are not distinguished by the ancient piety, zeal, and humanity, nor for their efforts and success in evangelizing the world at home or abroad. It is probable that as many of their own offspring are converted to the world, or to infidelity, as they have reclaimed from the world and the various forms of infidelity, during any given period of years. Most of the Socialists, Agrarians, Fourierists, Owenists, Rationalists, Puseytsts, etc., now in Protestant countries, are of Protestant ancestry. Our missionary gains from heathen lands do not more at most than fill up the apostasies from Protestant households to the numerous and various forms of infidelity." [32]   These words would doubtless be an exaggeration if applied to conditions of our day; they were not in the day in which they were written. It is probably true that defections from Protestant ranks in our time are due to causes other than those Campbell mentioned, but in his own hour nothing contributed more to apostasy from the Christian faith than the very causes which he delineates in such vigorous and pointed language.

2. A second cause of division, he found in the emphasis of peculiarities rather than that common ground of faith which is the possession of all evangelical bodies. In those things which are matters of faith, there has always been universal agreement; in the circumstantials of the gospel only, has there been division. "Protestant parties are all founded upon Protestant peculiarities. Indeed, there is but one radical and distinctive plea in any of them. That is their centre of attraction and of radiation. They baptize them-

[32] "Christian Baptism," 15.

selves at the laver of that idea, and assume the name of it, whatever it may be, Episcopalian, Presbyterian, or Methodist, etc., etc. They build on what is peculiar, and thus, in effect, undervalue that which is common to them all. And yet, themselves being judges, that which is common is much more valuable than that which is peculiar. The sub-basis of all parties is the tenet which is their cognomen." [33]

He proceeds to illustrate the difference between that which is foundational to faith and that which is a peculiarity. The difference between a Churchman and a Presbyterian is neither Calvinism nor Arminianism, faith nor repentence, righteousness nor holiness, baptism nor the eucharist, but the politics of ecclesiastical organization—the policy called Episcopacy or Presbytery—the idea of a Bishop, or two Bishops in one church, a Prelate or a Presbytery. Every other peculiarity is but the coloring, modification or development of this idea. This consecrates the sacramental table." [34] The fact that there is a common ground held by all evangelical Christians, was a favorite topic with him. The Church is not divided by essential things but by those which are peripheral—the circumstances of the Gospel. Those things most commonly believed are assuredly far more valuable than those which are but the peculiarities, dividing their devotees from all other Christians.[35] If these peculiarities were to be given up and a union consummated upon the commonly-held ground, it would be Scriptural and enduring. "We conclude, then, that a party founded on all that is commonly received by Romanists, Greeks, and Protestants, and nothing more, would not only be a new party, one entirely new, but incomparably more rational, and certainly more spiritual than any of them." [36] Speaking of a division which he would make of the whole Christian Institution, were he to follow the schools of his day, into Christian faith, Christian worship,

[33] *Ibid.*, 17.
[34] "Christian Baptism," 17.
[35] *Ibid.*, 17.
[36] *Ibid.*, 17.

and Christian morality, he makes reference once again to the commonly-accepted belief upon which Christian unity, if it ever comes, must be established. "Now, in the first chapter, we and all Christians are agreed; for as Christian faith has respect to the matter of fact recorded—to the direct testimony of God found in the New Testament concerning Himself—concerning His Son and Spirit—concerning mankind—what he has done and what he will do—on it there is no debate. I find all confessions of faith, properly so-called, like the four Gospels, tell the same story as far as matters of fact or faith are concerned." [37]

In a somewhat caustic paragraph at the close of the Rice debate, he sums up his position as regards the difference between that which is essential and commonly-held, and that which is peculiar, dividing God's people. "No man thinks that the world will ever be converted to Episcopalianism, Presbyterianism, Methodism, etc. All these denominations are creatures of the apostacy. Christianity was before them all, and will survive them all. They must all perish. Take from each of them its peculiarites, and Christianity remains, so far as they possess parts of it. What all sects have in common may be Christianity; but what they have in particular most certainly is not." [38] The progress of a divided Church as represented by these denominations, has been most discouraging. In their divided state they will never be able to bear a united testimony to the Lord whom they claim to love and serve. "They are not suited to the genius of human nature and must give place to something that is. That popular something is the pure and uncorrupted catholicity of original Christianity, in letter and spirit, as inscribed upon these pages. These partizan institutions, built upon peculiar phrenological developments of human nature, must give way to the whole genius of human nature. We want a broader, higher, deeper, purer Christianity than any of them. The world wants it, and Chris-

[37] "Christian System," 124.
[38] "Campbell-Rice Debate," 903.

tians pray for it." [39] While not many modern Disciples
would follow Campbell in his phraseology, his main thesis,
that Christians are united in belief upon essentials and divided only by those peculiarities in which the kingdom of
God does not consist, would find among them almost universal acceptance. Christian unity is not impossible; the
difficulties in its way are not at all insurmountable.

3. A third cause of division among Christians, according
to the Campbellian view, is to be found in the attachment
of men to great personalities and the doctrines propounded
by them. This was the fruitful cause of division in the
primitive church, as illustrated in the attachment of the
Corinthian Christians to Paul, or Apollos, or Cephas, or
Christ. Paul warns against such attachments for in them
he saw the dissolution of the Church.[40] Such attachments
which result in drawing away members from the body of
Christ, is heresy in the true meaning of the term. "The
whole philosophy of the matter, then, is that separation is
the effect of alienation of heart, alienation the fruit of rival
attachments which in the church generally begin in personal sympathies or personal antipathies, and end in de-
taching the subjects of them from the body of Christ." [41]
To prefer the works of Calvin, or Wesley, or Luther, to
Christ is to be sectary. No man really can love any one of
these or others in the kingdom more than Christ, without
first losing some of his love for Christ.[42] Thus it is true
"that all strifes, contentions, parties and sects grew out of
corruption. Sects are the egress of corruptions. The approved hold to Christ, and thus become manifest; the disapproved follow human leaders, and are also made manifest.
There appears to be no other cure for a corrupt and mixed
community than heresies or sects." [43] The majority of

[39] *Ibid.*, 903.
[40] "Christian System," 95.
[41] *Ibid.*, 98.
[42] *Ibid.*, 99.
[43] *Ibid.*, 99.

these, even in the various divisions of the Church, imagine that they are following the Lord when they really are but following the words of men.[44] In their desire to advance the kingdom of the Lord, they are not sectarian. The true sectarian is that one who deliberately endeavors to keep alive a sect or fleshy division, relegating the true Gospel of Christ to the background while slavishly following the teaching of some man.[45]

4. A fourth cause of division, and one which he condemned most untiringly, Campbell discovered in human speculation, philosophy, and tradition, crystallized into creedal formularies. For this reason we find him insisting that human traditions or speculations should never be made tests of fellowship. "We think we have discovered that all the divisions in Protestant Christendom—that all the partyism, vain jangling, and heresies which have disgraced the Christian profession, have emanated from human philosophy and human tradition. It is not faith, nor piety, nor morality, but philosophy and tradition, that alienated and estranged Christians, and prevented the conversion of the world. Socrates, Plato, and Aristotle deserved not the reputation of philosophers, if Calvin, Arminius, and Wesley were not worthy of it. The former philosophized on nature and ancient tradition—the latter, on the Bible and human society." [46] He harks back constantly to his ground position, that division is not caused by diversity on essential things, but on those in which the kingdom of God has never consisted. This is true as regards speculation.[47] On the great facts of the Gospel the Church is united in faith; she is divided concerning her speculations on the meaning of the facts. "It requires but little reflection to discover that the fiercest disputes about religion are about what the Bible does not say, rather than about what it does say—about words

44 *Ibid.*, 100.
45 *Ibid.*, 101.
46 "Christian System," 124.
47 *Ibid.*, 125.

and phrases coined in the mint of speculative theology. Of these the homoousios and homoousios of the ever-memorable Council of Nice, are a fair sample. Men are neither wiser, more intelligent, nor better after, than before, they know the meaning of these words. As far as known on earth, there is not, in the 'Book of Life of the Lamb slain from the foundation of the world,' the name of any person who was ever converted or santified to God by any of these controversies about human dogmas, nor by anything learned by the cannons or creeds of all the Councils, from that of Nice to the last Methodistic Conference." [48] This seemingly exaggerated statement shows the depth of aversion in Campbell's soul towards what he perhaps considered the most fruitful cause of schism in the body of Christ,—speculations in which salvation does not consist at all.

Had speculations and traditions never been made tests of membership in the Church by being written out in the form of creeds, they would not have outlived their own time. When formulated into a creed, however, they have come down to modern generations, as the fruitful and perpetuating cause of continued divisions. For these reasons, as well as others, they are supremely iniquitous. "All creeds are mere theories of Christian doctrine, discipline, and government, exhibited as a basis of church union. Being speculative, they have always proved themselves to be 'apples of discord' or 'roots of bitterness' among the Christian profession. They have, in days of yore, erected pillories, founded prisons, provoked wars, kindled fires, consecrated *autos da fe,* instituted star-chambers, courts of high commission and horrible tribunals of Papal inquisition. Exile, banishment, and confiscation of goods, lands, and tenements, and martyrdom, have been their convincing logic, their persuasive rhetoric, and their tender mercies." [49] These crystallized traditions of men "are easily distinguished from the Apostle's traditions.

[48] "Christian System," 126.
[49] "Christian Baptism," 16.

Those of the Apostles are found in their writings, as those of men are found in their books." [50]

Now these inherited speculations formulated into the creeds of the various divisions of the Church, are a perpetuating cause of such divisions. In reply to Rice who had accused him of affirming that creeds had been the originating cause of divisions, he says: "I teach that parties are older than written creeds; that there were persons who had made divisions, before there were written creeds. Satan was the first secretary that ever lived. He made a party. He is the prime heresiarch, and the author of the oldest schism in the universe. I could trace through two centuries before Arius and the Council of Nice, other causes for parties than creeds. But it is important to know, that whatever causes operated to produce divisions, the great source of all ecclesiastical division was the dogmatical opinions of churches and synods. These preserved the strife; consolidated and perpetuated the enterprise, which, but for them, had spent its strength and given up the ghost!" [51] The basic reason for the Campbellian opposition to creeds, will be considered in another connection; it is sufficient to note here that, to him, speculations and traditions are preserved in the creeds, and that divisions are caused, not by truth which all the creeds contain and which is the very ground work of them, but by such speculations which may or may not be true. He clearly sets forth his own attitude toward all such speculative theories and doctrines, and the attitude which he believes every Christian should hold. "Concerning these and all such doctrines, and all the speculations to which they have given rise, we have the privilege neither to affirm nor deny —neither to believe nor doubt; because God has not proposed them to us in his word, and there is no command to believe them. If they are deduced from the Scriptures, we have them in the facts and declarations of God's Spirit; if

[50] "Christian System," 126.
[51] "Campbell-Rice Debate," 796.

they are not deduced from the Bible, we are free from all the difficulties and strifes which they have engendered and created." [52] This is but to say, as he does so frequently and vigorously elsewhere, that these things cannot be made tests of fellowship in the creeds and result in union among God's people. There must be a commonly-acknowledged foundation which shall be considered by all as the irreducible minimum of faith; on this, and on this alone, can there be hope for reunion.

III

1. In considering the basis for Christian unity, Campbell was very careful to make it clear that it was original and not merely ancient Christianity, which he wished to restore. "The plea of ancient tradition is the strength of Popery and the weakness of Protestantism. We advocate not ancient but original Christianity. The plea of high antiquity or tradition has long been the bulwark of error. It cleaves to its beloved mother, Tradition, hoary Tradition, with an affection that increases as she becomes old and feeble." [53] The whole method through which he hopes to accomplish the great purpose of bringing about an enduring unity, is succinctly set forth in a kindred statement. "From a full survey of the premises of ecclesiastical history, of human creeds and sects—and especially from a profound regard for the wisdom and knowledge that guided, and the Spirit that inspired the Apostles of Jesus Christ, and that qualified them to do His will—we have proposed an Evangelical Reformation—or rather, a return to the faith and manners anciently delivered to the saints—a restoration of original Christianity both in theory and practice." [54] The title of the "Christian System" is significant as suggestive of the great Campbellian ideal—"The Christian System, in Refer-

[52] "Christian System," 125.
[53] "Christian Baptism," 233.
[54] "Christian Baptism," 18.

ence to the Union of Christians, and a Restoration of Primitive Christianity, as plead in the Current Reformation." [55] In his introduction to this work, he elaborates the meaning of the title and sets forth in unmistakable language, the method by which he hopes to bring about the results so ardently desired. "Tired of new creeds and new parties in religion, and of the numerous abortive efforts to reform the reformation; convinced from the Holy Scriptures, from observation and experience, that the union of the disciples of Christ is essential to the conversion of the world, and that the correction and improvement of no creed, or partizan establishment in Christendom, could ever become the basis of such a union, communion, and cooperation, as would restore peace to a church militant against itself, or triumph to the common salvation; a few individuals, about the beginning of the present century, began to reflect upon the ways and means to restore primitive Christianity." [56] In a passage in the debate with Rice, widely known and much quoted in Disciple ranks, he affirms that the only way to the pristine unity of the Church is to return to the basis upon which that unity was formerly enjoyed. "The fact that all synods, councils, and convocations are, by Protestants, acknowledged to have erred, will forever stain the pride of their boasted glory, impair their authority and convert their wisdom into folly. Whenever the time comes for the one fold, the one shepherd, and the one holy and beloved brotherhood, to combine all their energies in the holy cause, they will as certainly reprobate all human devices, and rally on the identical ground originally consecrated by the feet of the apostles. If, then, there is to be any millenium, any thousand years of triumphant Christianity before the Lord comes, these systems must all be abjured, and men must place the church exactly on the ground, the identical ground, on which she stood at the beginning." [57]

[55] "Christian System," Title Page.
[56] *Ibid.*, 5.
[57] "Campbell-Rice Debate," 878.

It is evident that Campbell would have but scant interest in some of the modern schemes for Christian unity which propose a return to the Council of Nicea and the creed which it gave to the world. His plan is to go back of all councils and creeds to the ground on which the Church stood at the death of the last of the Apostles. The passages in which this position is affirmed are so plain that they need no expounding.

2. In placing his feet firmly upon the position which has been outlined, he made two assumptions. Upon these assumptions all for which he contended rests; without them his plea falls to the ground. He assumes first that there was a consistent New Testament Christianity. It was united in its faith in Jesus as uniquely the Son of the Living God. "Kindred drops do not more readily mingle into one mass, than flowed the souls of primitive Christians together in all their aspirations, loves, delights, and interests." [58] It has been noted that Thomas Campbell before him, had assumed the essential, intentional, and constitutional unity of this New Testament Christianity. [59] In the second place, he assumes that there is a self-consistent New Testament which attests this Christianity. It is difficult to see how there could be any place for such a plea as the Campbells make, apart from these assumptions. That the Disciples, even with the critical attitude which most of them are free to take and willing to take, believe these assumptions to be fundamentally sound, is evidenced by their influential and rapidly growing communion. While it is obvious that modern men do not have the reverence for the New Testament which manifests itself everywhere in the "Declaration and Address" and which is so conspicuous in the writings of Alexander Campbell, yet it is impossible to explain the growth and influence of the Disciples on the position of the Campbells, on other ground than that they too, have accepted these two assumptions as self-evident.

[58] "Christian System," 95.
[59] "Overture," 81.

IV

The principles underlying his plea for Christian unity on the basis of a restored New Testament Christianity, according to Campbell's own outline, are five. The first of these must be a return to the "Christian Scriptures, the only rule of Christian faith and learning." [60] It has already been noted that he speaks of unity as to be consummated on the "Bible alone." [61] In the study of the Rule of Faith, his qualifications of this term will be pointed out. All denominations profess to go by the Bible alone. If on the whole Bible in every jot and tittle, such unity is proposed, immediate and determined objection would be found from many quarters. In numerous statements, therefore, Campbell declares his meaning when he contends that unity must be on the "Bible alone." After allowing for these qualifications, his proposal for unity really resolves itself into a contention that unity can only come upon the great saving facts of the Divine revelation. It is the peculiar Campbellian doctrine that revelation has to do wholly with facts and upon these facts which are universally accepted, is unity to be consummated. "All the modes of faith and worship are based upon a mistake of the true character of revelation, which has long been our effort to correct. With us, revelation has nothing to do with opinions or abstract reasonings: for it is founded wholly and entirely upon facts. There is not one abstract opinion, not one speculative view, asserted or communicated in Old Testament or New. Moses begins by asserting facts that have transpired in creation and providence; and John ends by asserting prophetic or prospective facts in the future displays of providence and redemption. Facts, then, are the *alpha* and *omega* of both Jewish and Christian revelations." [62] The manifest unsoundness of this

[60] "Christian Baptism," 18.
[61] "Campbell-Rice Debate," 903.
[62] "Christian System," 109, 110.

statement in the light of our modern attitudes on Biblical criticism, does not impair its fundamental meaning, namely that revelation really has to do with great facts and not with abstractions. Were Campbell re-writing this in our own time, he would doubtless emphasize this point more and generalize in his statement less. A fact is something done.[63] In Jesus Christ, God has wrought mightily in the world for the redemption of men. The power of the gospel is the power of its facts which constitute the greatest series of moral deeds on the part of heaven, that the world has ever seen.[64] Testimony brings to us these facts. The testimony was first given by the apostles and confirmed by the Holy Spirit which gave unto them the power to work miracles.[65] Hence, "when the confirmation of the gospel is spoken of in the apostolic writings, it is resolved into the doings or works of the Holy Spirit." [66] To enumerate all the gospel facts, would be to narrate all that Jesus did from His birth until His ascension. These may be concentrated into a few prominent ones: that He died for our sins; that He was buried in the new tomb; that He was raised on the third day by the power of God; and that He ascended to Heaven where He sits on the right hand of the Father.[67]

The revelation of God in the mighty acts of the life, death, resurrection, and ascension of His Son, is made known to the soul in all its saving power when these facts are presented to the mind through the preaching of the gospel. In a word, they evoke faith. "When these facts are understood, or brought into immediate contact with the mind of man, as a moral seal or archetype, they delineate the image of God upon the human soul. All the means of grace are, therefore, only the means of impressing this seal upon the heart—of bringing these moral facts to make their

[63] *Ibid.*, 110, 111.
[64] "Christian System," 110, 111.
[65] *Ibid.*, 117, 119.
[66] *Ibid.*, 120.
[67] "Christian System," 111.

full impression on the soul of man. Testimony and faith are but the channel through which these facts, or the hand of God, draws the image on the heart and character of man. If, then, the fact and testimony are both the gift of God, we may well say that faith and eternal life are also the gift of God, through Jesus Christ our Lord." [68]   Now all that is necessary to become a Christian, is that one should believe these facts, or rather the one great proposition for the proof of which they have been revealed, that Jesus is the Christ, the Son of the Living God. The belief of this "one fact, and that upon the best evidence in the world, is all that is requisite, as far as faith goes, to salvation. The belief of this one fact, and submission to one institution expressive of it, is all that is required of Heaven to admission into the Church." [69]   Every such person "is a disciple in the fullest sense of the word, the moment he has believed this one fact, upon the evidence, and has submitted to the above-mentioned institution." [70]   There is nothing upon which there is more universal agreement among Christians, than upon these conditions necessary to admission into the Church of Christ, for all agree "that whosoever confesses that Jesus is the Christ, and is baptized, should be received into the Church; and not an instance can be produced of any person being asked for any other faith, in order to admission, in the whole New Testament." [71]   Now since this cardinal matter—the steps necessary to salvation—is so uniformly accepted as the very essence and heart of the Christian revelation, this ground about which there is no controversy should form the basis for Christian unity. "The point is proved that we have assumed; and this proved, everything is established requisite to the union of all Christians upon a proper basis." [72]

[68] *Ibid.*, 111.
[69] *Ibid.*, 122.
[70] "Christian System," 122.
[71] *Ibid.*, 122.
[72] *Ibid.*, 122, 123.

A summary of this important point in the Campbellian theology should here be given. The unity of the Church can never be consummated upon any system of Biblical or dogmatic theology, nor upon any source of authority which is to be found in the individual himself, but rather upon the authority of Christ and the terms of salvation as laid down by Him. This precisely, is what is meant by union upon the "Bible alone." He does not mean, certainly, that this union is to be upon his own theology or his interpretation of the Bible. This would have been a return to the position that "the Bible and the Bible alone, is the religion of Protestants." The Campbellian idea, without a doubt, is that the Scriptures are to be taken as the authority, determining what is essential in Christianity. It is clear that the Bible as a whole is not concerned about setting forth such essentials. Therefore, it is not upon the whole Bible, concerning many parts of which there would be diverse opinions and interpretations, but rather the example of the early Church under the guidance of the apostles, through whom the Holy Spirit directed, as representing the authority of Christ. The question then would be, "What did Christ and the apostles taught by Him consider the essentials in salvation and in the form, worship, and government of the Church?" Dean Garrison has so clearly expressed this Campbellian distinction that he is quoted liberally here. "The distinction between union on the Bible in the sense of union on all the doctrines which each individual conceives to be taught in the Bible, and union on the Bible in the sense of union on Biblical statements regarding the essentials of Christianity, is an important one to bear in mind, as it helps to define the position which Mr. Campbell's theology occupied in his general scheme of thought. His theology was his interpretation of the teaching of Scripture on a great many points, and it shows the influence of some contemporary systems of theology and philosophy. But he did not make his theology his basis for union. For example, he conceived that faith, repentance, and baptism were essentials of Christianity, and were therefore included in the basis of union. But his interpretation of the nature of faith, the manner in which the Holy Spirit operates in conversion, and the design of baptism in the scheme of redemption, were parts of this theology which he taught as truths but did not erect into tests of fellowship." [73] This distinction will appear even more clearly in our discussion of the difference between faith and opinion.

V

The second principle necessary to a restoration of primitive Christianity, is a return to "the Christian confession" as "the foundation of Christian union and communion." [74] Under this general division may be considered Campbell's opposition to human creeds. This aversion has already been casually noted from time to time; in this connection it is essential that it be considered exhaustively. He defines, in unmistakable terms, what he means when he discusses "creed" and "creeds," and gives the reason for his opposition to them. In the Rice debate he says: "Ecclesiastic creeds and the faith apostolic are just as diverse as inference and premise, as fallibility and infallibility, as human reason and divine wisdom. When, then, we use the word creed in this discussion, we do not mean the truth nor the faith, the law nor the gospel, the apostles' writings, or those of the prophets. Nor do we mean our simple belief of the testimony of God. We all have a belief and a knowledge of Christian doctrine; but this belief or knowledge is not what is indicated by a creed. A creed or confession of faith is an ecclesiastic document—the mind and will of some synod or council possessing authority—as a term of communion, by which persons or opinions are to be tested, approbated, or reprobated." [75] Defending himself against the accusation

[73] "Alexander Campbell's Theology," 70, 71.
[74] "Christian Baptism," 18.
[75] "Campbell-Rice Debate," 762.

of Rice, that his "Christian System" is the creed or statement of belief of the Disciples, he observes that there is a
great difference between one man's views on theological
themes contained in a book and "a creed, a test by which
to try the principles of men, in order to church or ministerial
fellowship." [76] He allows every man to have a statement
of belief if he desires—he may write it out and have it
printed if he wishes; it is the making of any such creedal
statement a test of membership in Christ's Church, to which
he objects. He concludes another eloquent answer to Rice,
with an invective against the delusive nature of creeds.
"We all see, that Christendom is, at present, in a disturbed,
agitated, dislocated, condition—cut up, or fritted down into
sects and parties innumerable, wholly unwarranted by right
reason, pure religion, the Bible, the God of the Bible. Before the high, and holy, and puissant intelligences of earth
and heaven, this state of things is most intolerable. I have,
for some five and twenty years, regarded human creeds as
both the cause and the effect of partyism, and the main perpetuating causes of schism, and, therefore, have remon-
strated and inveighed against them." [77]

In his memorable debate with Rice, he affirmed as his
sixth proposition, that "human creeds, as bonds of union
and communion, are necessarily heretical and schismatical." [78] It is impossible in this connection even to summar-
ize the thirteen arguments by which he sought to
substantiate his proposition.[79] His objection to these documents as disturbing the peace of Zion, is that which con-
cerns the present inquiry. As a matter of fact, all of his
other objections may be engrossed into this one.[80] For this
reason, through a lifetime, he fought against them. "Not
like many who oppose creeds, because they first opposed
their peculiar tenets; we opposed them on their own de-

[76] *Ibid.*, 782.
[77] "Campbell-Rice Debate," 783, 784.
[78] *Ibid.*, 759.
[79] For summary of his arguments, see "Debate," 901, 903.
[80] "Campbell-Rice Debate," 796, 799. "Christian Baptism," 16.

merits, not because they opposed us. In this particular at least, if not on other accounts, we differ from the majority of those who oppose them—because old parties were sustained by them, because they made new parties, and because they were roots of bitterness and apples of discord, we opposed them." [81] In the "Christian System" he makes the somewhat startling declaration: "It were useless to furnish other evidence in proof that human opinions, inferential reasonings, and deductions from the Bible, exhibited in the form of creeds, can never unite Christians; as all their fruits are alienation, repulsion, bickering and schism. No human creed in Protestant Christendom can be found that has not made a division for every generation of its existence. And I may add, the more thinking, inquisitive, and intelligent the community which owns a creed, the more frequent their debates and schisms." [82] His main reason for such unremitting opposition to all creeds, is summed up in one trenchant sentence.[83] "Our opposition to creeds arose from a conviction that, whether the opinions in them were true or false, they were hostile to the union, peace, harmony, purity, and joy of Christians, and adverse to the conversion of the world to Jesus Christ." [84]

As a solution of the whole knotty problem presented by the creeds, he proposed a return to the baptismal confession of the primitive church. Since faith is personal, a personal trust in Jesus Christ as the Son of God, it can be expressed in the simple words of the confession which was manifestly made by all who became members of the New Testament church. To the objection that such a confession is too narrow, Campbell would reply that all the gospel is implicit in

[81] "Campbell-Rice Debate," 784.

[82] "Christian System," 109.

[83] In the debate with Rice (page 760), he makes an interesting distinction between Grecian symbols and Roman creeds. Grecian symbols are "compounds of Christian truths," summaries of prominent facts, "of which the document called the apostles' creed is a fair specimen." Roman creeds, however, are records of "opinions and inferences concerning them."

[84] "Christian System," 9.

it. If one believes that Jesus is the Christ, uniquely the Son of God, he believes all that is essential to his salvation. "Here, then, is the whole revelation of the mystery of the Christian institution—the full confession of the Christian faith. All that is peculiar to Christianity is found in these words; not merely in embryo, but clearly expressed in outline. A clear perception, and a cordial belief of these two facts (that Jesus is the Messiah and uniquely the Son of God) will make any man a Christian." [85] "On that simple confession with the lips, that he believes in his heart this glorious truth, he is, by the authority of the heavens, constituted a Christian." [86] Any party building on a foundation other than this one on which the New Testament believing community was builded, will eventually perish from the earth. "I again say, that every denomination built on any other foundation than this rock—on this simple confession of faith, in the fair, just, and well-defined meaning of its words, will as certainly perish from the earth as man does." [87] He does not mean here that they shall cease as organizations in so far as they are Christian, but only as sects and parties. "They may have much truth in their systems, but they have so much mortality with it, that perish they must, as sects, parties, and denominations." [88] This will be brought to pass by a gradual change in the attitudes of these bodies, and in a few years or generations they will be found to be standing upon the truth and that only. It is remarkable how largely this prediction has already been fulfilled.

That unity of Christians upon this great confession is possible, he claims to have demonstrated in the movement of which he was the acknowledged leader. "We have made an experiment under conditions not the most propitious, in the midst of many conflicting and rival institutions, to lay again

[85] "Campbell-Rice Debate," 822.
[86] *Ibid.*, 823.
[87] *Ibid.*, 823.
[88] *Ibid.*, 823.

the same well-tried cornerstone—the primitive confession on which the church was built—the stone which the Master laid at Caesarea Phillippi, on which to build His church, in first commending it to the notice of the world, promising most solemnly to build His church of all nations and ages upon it. The experiment for the time has been most successful. Probably not less than two hundred thousand persons of all creeds, and parties, and various associations around us; persons of all sorts and varieties of mind, education, and circumstances in Christendom, as well as those from the ranks of scepticism in various forms, have united in making the same confession, and have associated upon the same grand fundamental and constitutional principles." [89] From the acknowledged success of this movement on the simple New Testament institution alone, he argues that it is possible as a foundation for the unity of the whole Christian world. "Now, we argue, that if so many persons of all these varieties, before mentioned, can meet, unite and cooperate in faith, hope, and love, on this foundation, under the new constitution; all the world—all who know, believe, and love the same Saviour, might. It is broad enough and strong enough for them all." [90] If asked how can this be, the answer is to be found in the foundation, "the charter, the confession of our faith, the creed, the constitution if you please, under which we are incorporated." [91] The strength of the whole edifice is in the foundation and that foundation is Jesus Christ in His unique character as God's Son.

Here we find Campbell once more upon his true basis for the unity of the Church upon those things essential to salvation and universally acknowledged by Christians. For the more than one hundred years of their history, the Disciples have had no written creed, and yet they have given to the world a demonstration of unity which has never before been

[89] "Campbell-Rice Debate," 820, 821.
[90] *Ibid.*, 821.
[91] *Ibid.*, 821.

equaled in the modern Christian era.   One of their mottoes expressing what we have found Campbell teaching in this connection, is "No creed but Christ; no book but the Bible."

VI

A third principle upon which the success of the Campbellian program for Christian unity rests, is that a return must be made to "the Christian ordinances—baptism, the Lord's Day, and the Lord's Supper, as taught and observed by the Apostles." [92]   The Campbellian teaching regarding the ordinances of Christ as observed by His Church in primitive days, will later be considered at length.   In the teaching of Paul, the ordinances were regarded as acts "monumental to the Christian facts, Christ's death, burial and resurrection (Rom. 6:4, 5)." [93]   They were symbols of the unity of the Church.   In the great experiences of baptism and the Lord's Supper, into which the Christian entered, he was definitely at one with all others who shared with him these experiences.   Principal Robinson has well stated the Pauline conception, and also that of the New Testament Church, when he says, "we have seen how in St. Paul's Christianity, unity was centered in these two institutions, how they stood as barriers to division.   Sacramental Christianity is essentially corporate as opposed to more individual types, whether mystical or otherwise.   Sacraments stand as a witness to the fact that 'God is no respector of persons.' What is the possession of one may be the possession of all." [94]

Campbell contended that only a return to what he believed to be the uncontested position of the New Testament Church in the manner of observance of these unifying ordinances

[92] "Christian Baptism," 18.
[93] *Ibid.*, 19.
[94] "Essays on Christian Unity," 177, 178.

of the Lord, could Christian unity ever be brought about. This conviction is the foundation of all the voluminous writing which he did on this subject.

VII

A fourth principle which is absolutely essential in a return to primitive Christianity that the Church may be reunited, is "that instead of the modern ecclesiastic and sectarian terminology, or technical style, we adopt Bible names for Bible things." [95]   To Campbell, this was one of the most necessary requisites. "There is nothing more essential to the union of the disciples of Christ than purity of speech." [96] "If we could, by any means, restore a pure speech to the present church militant, we might have some hope of an evangelical union, communion, and cooperation in Protestantdom—that would give an impetus to the Apostolic Gospel, adequate to the wants of distracted Christendom; and to the prevention of the daily accumulating influence of infidelity and practical atheism, within the territory which we rather, as now existing, ironically call Christendom." [97]

Campbell objected to the theological terminology of his day because he was certain that there lurked in it the speculation of the various schools. "I object to much of the nomenclature of modern theology. We have drawn too much on the paganized vocabulary of Rome. Neither Jewish, Christian, nor Pagan, but a mongrel dialect is the jargon of the present age." [98]   He frequently illustrated his meaning on this point, by substituting the words used in the Sacred Writings in place of those which were current. "Instead of 'sacraments,' we prefer 'ordinances'; for 'the Eucharist,' the Lord's Supper; for 'covenant of works,' the law; for 'covenant of grace,' the gospel; for 'Testament,' Institution or

[95] "Christian Baptism," 20.
[96] "Christian System," 125.
[97] "Millennial Harbinger Abridged," II, 33.
[98] "Campbell-Rice Debate," 709, 710.

Covenant; for 'Trinity,' Godhead; for 'first, second, and third person,' the Father, the Son, and the Holy Spirit; for 'Eternal Son,' the Son of God; for 'original sin,' the fall or offense; for 'Christian Sabbath,' the Lord's Day or First Day; for 'effectual calling,' calling or obedience; for 'merits of Christ,' righteousness or sacrifice of Christ; for 'general atonement,' ransom for all; for 'free grace,' grace; for 'free will,' will; etc., etc." [99]   A study of these terms and many others which will readily come to mind, must assuredly bear out the Campbellian contention that the terminology of modern theology contains many speculations which may or may not be Christian. Campbell believed that if the Christian world could get behind all this phraseology which had grown up through the centuries of speculation, to the original text and speak in the language employed during the days of the New Testament community, a great stride toward unity would be made. He states clearly his own reason for using Bible names for Bible things. "We choose to speak of Bible things by Bible words, because we are always suspicious that if the word is not in the Bible, the idea which it represents is not there; and always confident that the things taught by God are better taught in the words and under the names which the Holy Spirit has chosen and appropriated, than in the words which man's wisdom teaches." [100]   He relates his own experience in attempting reformation in this regard, and confesses that it has been only with the greatest difficulty that this necessary principle has been applied, and that even up to the time of his writing he had not been absolutely successful. "The Bible alone is the Bible only, in word and deed, in profession and practice; and this alone can reform the world and save the Church. Judging others as we once judged ourselves, there are not a few who are advocating the Bible alone and preaching their own opinions. Before we applied the Bible alone to our views, or brought our views or religious practices to the Bible, we plead the

[99] "Christian Baptism," 20.
[100] "Christian System," 125.

old theme. 'The Bible alone is the religion of Protestants.' But we found it an arduous task, and one of twenty year's labor, to correct our diction and purify our speech according to the Bible alone; and even yet we have not fully repudiated the language of Ashdod. We only profess to work and walk by rules which will inevitably issue in a pure speech, and in right conceptions of that pure, and holy, and celestial thing called Christianity—in faith, in sentiment, and in practice." [101]

The Campbellian principle of purity of speech has been rigidly applied by the Disciples, especially in the matter of names which should be worn by the Church as an organization, and individuals as members of it. Very early in the movement the question as to just what name should be worn, agitated the leaders. The discussion began in the days of the "Christian Baptist." It appears in a very interesting form in the "Harbinger" for 1839. The determining reason, Campbell tells us, for his change in the name of the "Christian Baptist" to that of the "Millennial Harbinger" was that those who were following his views were being called "Christian Baptists." [102] Because of the position which they advocated, nicknames were peculiarly odious to the Disciples. Campbell himself was constantly busied in trying to make his opponents see that his co-laborers resented being called by any human name. "We do protest against christening the gospel of Jesus and the Christian religion, by the name of any mortal man. To carry the principle out, we ought to call every man's sentiments by his name. Because we have disclaimed creeds, names, and sects, our adversaries seem to take a pleasure in designating our writings and speeches by the name creed, Campbellite theory, system, etc. This is both unmanly and unchristian. Men, fond of nicknaming, are generally weak in reason, argument, and proof." [103] In another connection, he states the founda-

[101] "Christian System," 6.
[102] "Millennial Harbinger," Volume for 1839, 337, 338.
[103] "Millennial Harbinger," Volume for 1830, 118.

tional position upon which he has stood from the very beginning of his work, in regard to the whole, much-discussed
question of a name. "Call no man on earth Father, or
Leader, or Master, is a positive precept. Under that flag
we put forth to sea when we set sail from the moorings
of sectarianism for the haven of ancient and primitive
Christianity." [104] In almost sarcastic language he strikes
back at those of his day whom he believed were endeavoring
to sectarianize his movement. "The Lutherans, Calvinists,
Arminians, judging us according to their standard, and
weighing us in their balances, have nicknamed us 'Camp-
bellites.' They wish us to take no precedence of them. They
are very proud of the livery they wear, and would have us
to be like themselves—the followers of an earthly fallible
leader. But our Master forbids us to assume any such
designation as derogatory to Him and to ourselves, and
tending to schism." [105]

The name above all other, preferred by Campbell, was
"Disciple." The names "Reformers" and "Bible Christians"
receive severe treatment at his hands. Of the former he
says; "Some would have us call ourselves Reformers, as if
this word were specific of anything. Like the word Protestant, it means nothing definite, either in principle or in
practice. There have been protestants and reformers, political, economical, ecclesiastic, and sacerdotal, times and ways
without number. We are not reformed Baptists, or Methodists, or Presbyterians, or any such things. Why, then,
misrepresent ourselves? We may be reformed Baptists or
reformed sinners, and yet a great way off Christians." [106]
Of the suggested name "Bible Christians," he writes in the
same style: "Some like the name 'Bible Christians,' as if
there were Christians without the Bible; or Bible, and not
Bible Christians. There are no Koran Christians. Hence
Bible before Christian is like human before man, or female

[104] *Ibid.*, Volume for 1839, 338.
[105] *Ibid.*, Volume for 1839, 337, 338.
[106] "Millennial Harbinger," Volume for 1839, 338.

before woman. A human man, a female woman, and a
Bible Christian are creatures of the same parentage." [107]

He presents four arguments in favor of the name Disciple. (1) It is more ancient.[108] The followers of Christ
were called Disciples before they received the name Christian
in Antioch. "Disciples of Christ, is, then, a more ancient
title than Christian, while it fully includes the whole idea.
It is, then, as divine, as authoritative, as the name Christian,
and more ancient." (2) It is more descriptive.[109] Christian, as a name, may be confusing. It may be that some one
would confound it with a title of citizenship in a country,
like that of an American, a Roman, etc. Disciple is more
descriptive in that it indicates the relation of the follower
to his Lord, as that of a learner or scholar. (3) It is more
scriptural.[110] Luke wrote his Acts some thirty years after
Jesus had ascended to Heaven. In his writings, which relate
at least thirty years of the history of the primitive church,
the word Christian is used but twice—once by the people
of Antioch (Acts 11:26), and once by King Agrippa; "but
no disciple, as far as Luke relates, ever spoke of himself or
brethren after that designation. More than thirty times
they are called disciples in the Acts of the Apostles. Luke
and other intelligent men call them 'brethren' and 'disciples,'
but never Christians. Again we have the word Christian
but once in the epistles, and then in circumstances which
make it pretty evident that it was used by the enemies rather
than by the friends of the brotherhood." [111] (4) As it distinctly regards our own communion, it is a name unappropri-
ated at the present time. In New England and in other
sections of the country, there are those who are Unitarians
yet they wear the name Christian. Those who believe in

107 *Ibid.*, 338.
108 *Ibid.*, 338, 339.
109 *Ibid.*, 339.
110 *Ibid.*, 339, 340.
111 "Millennial Harbinger," Volume of 1839, 339.

the restoration of primitive Christianity, do not wish to be confused with Arians and Unitarians.[112]

Thomas Campbell contended for the name Christian (1) "because of the radical and comprehensive import of its appelative signification," and (2) "because of its Scriptural Consistency with the intention of the proposed reformation." [113] With regard to the former, it is evident that

[112] *Ibid.*, 337. Also, see 339. In his very interesting discussion of the "Names of Christian Believers" Harnack points out the fact that while the term μαθηταί was employed during the lifetime of Jesus to designate the relation between Himself and His disciples the growing conception of the Messianic dignity of the Master caused the name gradually to be discarded. The resurrection of Jesus caused the followers of the Lord to witness confidently to His Messiahship and even though the name had, strictly speaking, "ceased to be applicable, it was retained by Christians for one or two decades as a designation of themselves, especially by the Christians of Palestine. Paul never employed it, however, and gradually one observes, the name of οἱμαθηταί (with the addition of τοῦ κυρίου) came to be exclusively applied to personal disciples of Jesus, i.e., in the first instance to the twelve, and thereafter to others also, as in Papias, Irenaeus, etc. In this way it became a title of honour for those who had themselves seen the Lord (and also for Palestinian Christians of the primitive age in general?), and who could therefore serve as evidence against heretics who subjected the person of Jesus to a docetic decomposition. Confessors and martyrs during the second and third centuries were also honoured with this high title of 'disciples of the Lord.' They too became, that is to say, personal disciples of the Lord. Inasmuch as they attached themselves to Him by their confession as He to them (Matt. 10:32), they were promoted to the same rank as the primitive personal disciples of Jesus, being as near the Lord in glory as were the latter to Him during His earthly sojourn." Expension of Christianity, II, 2, 3. In regard to the gradual disuse into which the name fell Harnack further remarks "During the period subsequent to Acts it is no longer possible, so far as I know, to prove the use of μαθηταί (without the addition of τοῦ κυρίου or χριστοῦ) as a term used by all adherents of Jesus to designate themselves; that is, if we leave out of account, of course, all the passages— and they are not altogether infrequent—in which the word is not technical. Even with the addition of τοῦ κυρίου, the term ceases to be a title for Christians in general by the second century." Footnote, page 3. As to the reason for the gradual disappearance of the name he says, "The term 'disciples' fell into disuse, because it no longer expressed the relationship in which Christians now found themselves placed. It meant at once too little and too much. Consequently other terms arose, although these did not in every instance pass into technical titles." Page 4.

[113] "Millennial Harbinger," Volume 1840, 21, 22.

the name means one who is a disciple and follower of Christ. From Him it receives all is significance. All of the titles used by the early followers of the Lord, are comprehended in this one. As regards the second argument, it must be evident that such a name is more in harmony with the reformation, the fundamental principle of which, has been a return to the foundational things of the Christian religion. For this reformation "some of us have been laboring both by tongue and pen, by pulpit and press, for, at least, thirty years. The professed object is, and has been, from our commencement the restoration of pure, primitive, apostolic Christianity in letter and spirit, in principle and practice; witness our "Declaration and Address," published at Washington, Pennsylvania, in the fall of 1809." [114] This name which was given at Antioch, the name which we have the right to wear because we have been baptized into Christ (Gal. 3:27), because the Church is the bride of Christ, and ought to wear her husband's name—what more suitable or Scriptural name or one more in harmony with all we have taught, can be found! "Surely, no name can possibly combine in it so many interesting considerations to excite us to everything that is good, honorable, and praiseworthy, as the name Christian. It is, without exception, the most exalting, the most honorable, and distinguishing title under heaven." [115]

In reply to his father, Alexander Campbell, beginning with an affirmation that enough has already been said on the matter, since we cannot help what the outside world may call us anyhow, affirms that there is but one question in his own mind regarding the name Christian. Have we really any divine authority for the title at all? [116] Was the

---

[114] "Millennial Harbinger," Volume of 1840, 22.

[115] *Ibid.*, 22.

[116] *Ibid.*, 24, 25. See discussion of χριστιανοί in my book, "The Resurrection Gospel," 244, 268. Harnack agrees with Thomas Campbell as against his son in regard to the position of the name χριϛτιανοί. He speaks of it as "the cardinal title of the faith." In regard to its origin he agrees

name first given by heaven or earth? Was it recommended first by human authority, and finally adopted by divine authority? For three reasons, he believes that the name does not come to us by direct divine authority. (1) The arguments for its divine character from the days of John Newton until his own time, based upon the term χρηματίσαι, in Acts 11:26, are inconclusive. It has never been clearly proven that the word means "divinely called." Those who have contended that it is the "new name" referred to in Isaiah 60:3, are employing a type of argument which ought to be discredited. In this connection, he shows the critical attitude of his own mind and gives us a hint at least, of what his posture on the Biblical criticism of our own time, might be. Speaking of the method by which those substantiate their position who hold the view that Isaiah had in mind the name Christian, he says: "But that was in the

---

with Alexander. "Luke has told us where this name arose. After describing the foundation of the (Gentile Christian) church at Antioch, he proceeds (XI:26): "χρηματίσαι ηρώτως ἐν Αντιοχεία τους μαθητὰς Χριστιονούς [Χρηοτιανούς]·" It is not necessary to suppose that the name was given immediately after the establishment of the church, but we need not assume that any considerable interval elapsed between the one fact and the other. Luke does not tell us who gave the name but he indicates it clearly enough. It was not the Christians (otherwise he would not have written χρηματίσαι), for they simply could not have given it to themselves. The essentially inexact nature of the verbal form precludes any such idea. And for the same reason it could not have originated with the Jews. It was among the pagans that the title arose, among pagans who heard that a man called 'Christ' (Chrestus) was the lord and master of a new sect. Accordingly they struck out the name of 'Christians,' as though 'Christ' were a proper name, just as they spoke of 'Herodiani,' 'Marciani,' etc. At first, of course, Christians did not adopt the title. It does not occur in Paul or anywhere in the New Testament as a designation applied by Christians to themselves, for in the only two passages where it does occur it is quoted from the lips of an opponent, and even in the apostolic fathers (so-called) we seek it in vain. The sole exception is Ignatius, who employs it quite frequently; a fact which serves admirably to corroborate the narrative of Acts, for Ignatius belonged to Antioch. Thus the name not only originated in Antioch, but, so far as we know, it was there that it first became used by Christians as a title." Expansion of Christianity, II, 15, 16. See also Weizsäcker's discussion of Χριστιανοί. Apostolic Age, I, 47; 108.

days of text-preaching, when the context had little or nothing to do with the interpretation of any passage; for now all are satisfied that the new name there spoken of is Hepzibah—'the delight of the Lord,' or 'My delight is in her.'" (2) A second argument which seems to indicate that the name Christian has no directly derived divine authority, is to be found in the very fact that it was not given at Jerusalem but at Antioch.[117] "From Jerusalem went forth the law and the word of God. Since the Holy Spirit was then fully communicated to the Apostles, and they had a full revelation of the whole institution and of the Master's will, whatever name they gave to the followers of Christ was of divine authority, and no other." [118] Now it is certain that they were not then called Christians, for that was not done until the name was given at Antioch. Unless the Apostles received a new revelation on the subject some fourteen years after Pentecost, we cannot say that it was given by direct divine authority. (3) In the third place, Luke must have been an ungodly man, if during the twenty-one years after they were called Christians first at Antioch and the fourteen years before that time, he refused to call them by this divinely-given title.[119] Instead of doing so, he constantly calls them disciples. "Unless, then, we suppose this man Luke to have been a bold and daring offender against a divine revelation, it is infallibly certain that he and his companions, the Apostles, did not receive the name Christian as coming from Heaven, but from the rude and profane Antiochans." [120] (4) The reference to the name in I Peter 4:16 is not conclusive as an argument for the divine source of derivation. The writer is but exhorting those who are suffering fiery trials in His name which is to the pagans one of reproach and derision, not only to deport themselves honorably, but in their suffering, to even glorify God in this

---

[117] "Millennial Harbinger," Volume of 1840, 25.
[118] *Ibid.*, 24, 25.
[119] *Ibid.*, 25.
[120] "Millennial Harbinger," Volume of 1840, 25.

name.[121] While Peter uses this term in his exhortation, at the same time "the saints called themselves brethren and disciples." "For A.D. 60, Luke says 'the disciples' came together to break the loaf at Troas; while Peter spoke of their persecution under the title of Christians in the same year, and not far from the same place. The world, then, it seems called them Christians while they called themselves disciples and brethren, etc., down to A.D. 64." [122]

While believing it to be of humble origin, Campbell evidently became convinced that the name Christian had been adopted by the early disciples, and that it was therefore divinely approved, for his final position is that any and all New Testament names should be worn by Christ's followers. While his own preference was expressed for Disciples, any name which had the sanction of the New Testament, was permissible. "The brethren all have a vote in this matter; and among the candidates for public favor, I give my vote for 'The Disciples' or for 'Disciples of Christ.' This is, for the reasons now given, my choice; but I will not contend with any man for a mere name, especially when they are all good." [123] It is interesting to note how the Disciples have followed Campbell in this regard. In the eastern part of the United States, they are generally known as "Disciples of Christ." In the middle west and south, due largely to the influence of those who had composed the movement under Barton W. Stone, they are called "Christian Churches," while in the far west of the continent they are more frequently known as "Churches of Christ." The latter name is employed exclusively by the churches in Great Britian and Ireland, and in Australasia. The "Year Book" of the United Christian Missionary Society, which officially tabulates the membership of the churches, and records their missionary and benevolent gifts, is entitled,

[121] *Ibid.*, 26.

[122] Campbell believed Acts to have been written in 64 A.D. and I Peter in 60 A.D. See Harbinger, Volume of 1840, 26.

[123] "Millennial Harbinger," Volume of 1839, 536.

"Year Book, Disciples of Christ." [124]   To Campbell, however, the thing was so much more important than the name, that he refused to contend about one designation more than another. In the closing paragraph of his article against the direct divine authenticity of the name Christian, he writes: "But let all remember that those who were first called Christians in Antioch, were persons who had first believed the gospel preached by the Apostles—had then repented of their sins—were then immersed into the name of the Father, the Son, and the Holy Spirit—met the first day of the week— showed forth the Lord's death—contributed freely to the necessities of the saints, and kept the apostolic ordinances. Will those who contend for this name do the same things, and exhibit the same moral excellencies! If so, I will call them Christians, if that will please them better than Disciples, or any other name; so far superior, in my judgement, is the thing to the name—the fruit to the blossom—the living man to the inanimate statue—the character to the profession. It will be remembered that I have used almost indiscriminately sundry names, and will likely continue to do so; for where the Lord has made me free, I cannot, without good cause, agree to bind myself." [125]

[124] Year Book for 1925.

[125] "Millennial Harbinger," Volume of 1840, 26. If the position of Harnack in regard to the gradual disuse of the name Disciple is correct, the contention of Thomas Campbell and thousands of members of Churches of Christ after him that the name "Christian" is more significant seems to be justified. Since it cannot be demonstrated that either of these names was divinely given the name "Christian" has far greater claims since it was the one adopted by the followers of Christ as best expressing their relationship to Him. When the Church became an organization distinct from Judaism the new name expressive of this uniqueness was adopted. Concerning this change Harnack writes: "At any rate a church was founded at Antioch which consisted for the most part of uncircumcized persons. For this church the designation of Χριστιανοί ('Christians,' Acts xi:26) came into vogue, a name coined by their heathen opponents. This title is itself a proof that the new community in Antioch stood out in bold relief from Judaism. The name of Christian was the title of Gentile Christians; neither at first nor for a long while to come, were Jewish Christians designated by this name." Expansion of Christianity, I, 60.

VIII

The fifth "grand proposition essential to the evangelical reformation—to Christian union and cooperation in the kingdom of Christ is, that unity of faith, and not unity of opinions, must be publicly and privately taught and advocated as prerequisite to the communion of the children of God." [126] Conscious that they were attacking the knotty question of how an enduring unity could be preserved with the greatest degree of liberty of opinion,[127] the Campbells, and practically every one of their fellow-disciples wrote largely upon this angle of the unity issue. Alexander Campbell often and clearly states the distinction. In the Rice debate, he makes a very clear pronouncement concerning it. "With us, then, faith is testimony believed; knowledge is our own experience; and opinion is probable inference. Whenever we have clear, well authenticated testimony, we have faith, and this faith is always in the ratio of the testimony we have, or in the apprehension of its truth and certainty. Our personal acquaintance with men and things constitutes our knowledge; of which, different individuals, according to their discrimination and capacity, have various proportions. But, in the absence of our own personal acquaintance, observation and experience, and in the absence of good and well authenticated testimony, we have mere opinion." [128] Illustrating this definition, he says, "I believe

[126] "Christian Baptism," 21.

[127] A paragraph from Chillingsworth, often quoted by Disciples, discusses this distinction. "Let all men believe the Scripture, and that only, and endeavor to believe in the true sense, and require no more of others, and they shall find this not only a better, but the only means to suppress heresy and restore unity. For he that believes the Scripture sincerely, and endeavors to believe it in the true sense, cannot possibly be a heretic. And if no more than this be required of any man to make him capable of the Church's communion, then all men, so qualified, though they were different in opinion, notwithstanding any such difference, must be of necessity one in communion." "The Religion of Protestants a Safe Way to Salvation," 23. Bohn edition.

[128] "Campbell-Rice Debate," 835, 836.

that Julius Cæsar was assassinated in the Roman senate-house, at the statue of Pompey; I know that the sun is the source of our light and heat; and I am of the opinion that Saturn is inhabited." [129]

But where does faith cease and opinion begin? How are we going to discover that which is the basic foundation upon which we may all be one? This question was repeatedly asked by Dr. Rice.[130] In answer to it, Campbell defines the difference between "faith" and "the faith." This distinction is essential to a further elucidation of the domains of faith and opinion. " 'Faith' and 'the faith' are not identical. They are never used as synonyms; consequently they represent two distinct ideas." [131] "Christians have faith in the faith originally delivered to the saints." [132] Faith, according to the writer of the Hebrew letter, is the ἔλεγχος, the conviction or persuasion of things not seen. It is of the nature of a proof, a conclusive argument, a demonstration. It is clear that the writer, in this word, means that central body of assured, saving truth which the early Christians believed to their salvation. "Faith, therefore, has nothing to do with opinions, theories, or speculative reasonings, of any sort whatever. Its field is facts reported, well authenticated, and nothing else." [133] While in modern times, we have many "Faiths, falsely so called," the plain and definite statements of St. Paul indicate that there was in the primitive Church but "one evangelical faith—as there is but one God and Father of all, one Lord and Saviour of all, and one Holy Spirit—the Holy Guest of all who receive Jesus as the Christ of God." [134] This faith, this body of assured divine truth, which they believed unto their salvation, is contained in the New Testament. "The primitive Christians had one, and but one faith, written out for them by apostles and proph-

[129] "Campbell-Rice Debate," 835, 836. "Harbinger Abridged," II, 39.
[130] Ibid., 775, 780, 818.
[131] "Millennial Harbinger Abridged," II, 32.
[132] Ibid., 32.
[133] Ibid., 32, 33.
[134] Ibid., 33.

ets; we have it in the one volume, usually called the New Testament." [135] Now it is also indisputable that this body of truth was called by different names. "In the days of the apostles, there was something called 'the faith,' 'the form of sound words,' 'the truth,' 'the gospel,' which was to them something more than our summaries, called creeds and confessions of faith." [136] The faith, then, is the gospel, the divinely authenticated deposit of revelation enshrined within the New Testament Scriptures. Such a revelation is made known to us through the words or testimony of the apostles. " 'Contend earnestly for the faith once delivered to the saints.' Jude wrote his short and comprehensive epistle near the close of the apostolic age. He saw an approaching defection and enjoined, in these words, an antidote against the early workings of the mystery of iniquity. He saw efforts to introduce new things by the converted Jews and Pagans incorporated in the Christian family, and in the midst of these efforts wrote his epistle. Such a precept, emanating from such circumstances, is equivalent to a positive prohibition of everything but the faith, the truth, the identical words, commanded by apostles and prophets, as the foundation of the Christian temple, and the constitution of the Christian Church." [137] Campbell does not mean to take a legalistic turn in this affirmation; his thought is rather that in the express words of the apostles, we have the revelation vouchsafed to us. In his identification of the faith with the Divine revelation, we have an echo of the words of Thomas Campbell in the "Declaration and Address." He appeals to the ministry of his day "to remove human opinions and inventions of men out of the way, by carefully separating this chaff from the pure wheat of primary and authentic revelation." [138]

But just what is this "primary and authentic revelation?"

[135] "Campbell-Rice Debate," 759.
[136] *Ibid.*, 759.
[137] *Ibid.*, 819.
[138] "Overture," 70.

Of what elements is it composed? Campbell answers with an exposition of I Tim. 3:16. The six items related in this passage concerning the life, work, and person of the Christ, form the summary of "the faith. God manifest in the flesh, justified in the Spirit, seen or attended upon by Angels, announced or preached to the Gentiles, believed on in the world, taken up into glory—these are the great facts of the good news that God has granted salvation to men." [139] "This is the most splendid summary of the faith; not of faith alone; but of the transcendent facts of the peerless majesty, the more than regal glory, honor, and official grandeur of Jesus Christ, culminating in his absolute Lordship, constituting him the anointed High Priest, the glorified King, the Oracle of the Absolute Jehovah." [139] "This is the faith, the hope, the rejoicing of the regenerate." [140]

There is another approach to an explication of the nature of "the faith." It is to be found in Paul's definition of the gospel (I Cor. 15:1-5). Campbell once more identifies the gospel with "the faith." "Now the question, the great question, with many of our contemporaries is, what was the gospel which Paul preached—or in other words, what was the faith, the gospel faith which Paul preached to the Gentiles?" Paul, himself, tells us. "Now I make known unto you, brethren, the gospel which I preached unto you, which also ye received, wherein also ye stand, by which also ye are saved, if ye hold fast the word which I preached unto you, except ye believed in vain. For I delivered unto you first of all that which also I received: that Christ died for our sins according to the scriptures; that he was buried; and that he hath been raised on the third day according to the scriptures." Here are the facts that constitute the gospel —without which there would be no gospel. The Apostle does not state them merely as interesting facts, but with the statement includes their gospel interpretation, and declares that these words are not inventions of his own; this is the

[139] "Millennial Harbinger Abridged," 34.
[140] Ibid., II, 34.

authentic tradition which he has received. The Apostles, doubtless, did have their various theologies—this we now know to be a fact established beyond the region of controversy, but in these great foundational facts and their meaning for salvation and the future life, they were at one.[141] "These, then, are the saving, soul-redeeming elements, or the principles—the life-giving principles, of the faith then delivered to the saints in Corinth."[142] No man of discernment and culture, with the New Testament in his hand— even without that spiritual culture which is so essential to the truest interpretation of things Divine, "can for a moment doubt that this is the kernel of the tree of life eternal."[143]

From the definition which Campbell gives of "the faith," there appears a further reason for his continued opposition to partyism in the Church. While holding to the same fundamental faith, the various denominations stand apart from each other, divided, not by what is essential to the very life of Christianity—the common faith, but by their opinions and speculations. "Now these sects are all founded on opinions and not on faith. Every society in Christendom admits the same faith, or builds on the same grand evangelical facts; though, indeed, by their opinions and traditions, some of them have made the faith of God of none effect."[144] The error which has made Protestantism into a horde of warring sects, increasing in numbers year by year, is the failure to differentiate between faith—that which must be held by all and without which there can be no salvation on Gospel terms, and opinions—speculations which, though they may be in themselves interesting, are not essential to salvation. The making of such opinions into tests of fellowship by reducing them to creedal formularies, has held followers of the same Lord, in various and rival camps. The "grand error" of Protestant Christianity, then, "is, that it seems

[141] "Millennial Harbinger Abridged," II, 35.
[142] Ibid., 35, 36.
[143] Ibid., 36.
[144] "Campbell-Rice Debate," 835.

never to recognize where faith ends, and where opinion begins; nay, it very often confounds faith and opinions, and lays full as much emphasis upon right opinions, as upon right faith; and, in some instances, places opinions above faith. Our faith, then, and our opinions, do not clash for we can never have both faith and opinion on the same subject." [145]

In the light of the above definitions and distinctions, the way to unity, as Campbell conceived it, is obvious. The Christian world must cease making opinions, those positions which are not clearly matters of Divine revelation, tests of membership in Christ's Church; but allowing each man to think as he pleases on such things, to unite upon that great common faith, the gospel of the Lord and Saviour Jesus Christ. It is evident that men can never give up their opinions. Think, we must! Think, we ought! But should the fact that men must have opinions on Divine things, and that they cannot give them up, stand in the way of the unity of Christians? Not at all, answers Campbell, for "we do not ask them to give up their opinions—we ask them only not to impose them upon others. Let them hold their opinions; but let them hold them as private property." [146] It is only as we try to measure all Christians by the standard of opinion, that we divide. "Men have foolishly attempted to make the deductions of some great minds, the common measure of all Christians. Hence the deductions of a Luther, and a Calvin, and a Wesley, have been the rule and measure of all who coalesce under the names of the leaders." [147] Unity in the faith is not incompatible with diversity in opinions. Only as this basic fact is appreciated by the Churches, can there ever be any hope of reunion. "In religion we have one Lord, one faith, one baptism, one body, one spirit, one hope, and one God and Father. The Church, then, may have opinions by the thousands, while her faith is limited to the inspired testimony of apostles and prophets; where that

[145] "Campbell-Rice Debate," 835.
[146] "Millennial Harbinger Abridged," II, 37.
[147] "Millennial Harbinger Abridged," II, 37.

testimony begins and ends, faith begins and ends. In faith, then, all Christians may be one, though of diverse knowledge and of numerous opinions. In faith we must be one, for there is but one Christian faith; while, in opinions, we may differ. Hence we are commanded to receive one another without regard to differences of opinion, Romans 15:1, 2." [148]

The relation of unity in the faith, with liberty of opinions, to the problem of the conversion of the world, receives careful attention.[149] In the "Christian System," he states it in two syllogistic sentences. (1) "Nothing is essential to the conversion of the world, but the union and cooperation of Christians. (2) Nothing is essential to the union of Christians but the Apostolic testimony." To arrange it in another order: "(1) The testimony of the Apostles is the only self-sufficient means of uniting all Christians. (2) The union of Christians with the Apostles' testimony is all-sufficient and alone sufficient to the conversion of the world." [150] In His so-called intercessory prayer, Jesus definitely associates unity, the words or testimony of His apostles, and the salvation of the world.[151] "Neither for these only do I pray, but for them also that believe on me through their word; that they may all be one; even as thou, Father, art in me, and I in thee, that they may also be in us: that the world may believe that thou didst send me." [152] "Who does not see in this position, that the words or testimony of the apostles, the unity of the disciples, and the conversion of the world, are bound together by the wisdom and love of the Father, by the devotion and philanthropy of the Son." [153] "The words of the apostles are laid as the basis, the unity of the disciples the glorious result, and the only successful means of converting the world to the ac-

[148] "Campbell-Rice Debate," 836.
[149] "Christian Baptist," II, 66, 67. See, also, "Essays on the Westminster Creed," II. Note "Review of Dr. Noel's Circular," V.
[150] "Christian System," 107.
[151] "Christian Baptist," 135, 136, 139.
[152] John 17:20, 21.
[153] "Christian Baptist," 135.

knowledgment that Jesus of Nazareth is the Messiah or the Son of the Blessed, the only Saviour of men." [154] The historical fact that the primitive church was firmly united on the faith as expressed in the testimony of the apostles, though free to hold and express such opinions as they pleased on those matters not clearly revealed [155]—the further fact that through many years, Campbell and his colleagues had been trying this plan out to the very letter, made him believe implicitly that such a basis is possible for all the numerous sects of the Christian world. Referring to the Church in its pristine unity, he says: "When they came to baptism, they all made the same confession, and were builded together upon the same foundation; and having only the apostolic writings, easily maintained the unity of the spirit in the bonds of peace. They had no formula of doctrine as yet, other than the apostolic formula which we still have in the living oracles of the New Testament. I presume that it is always a safe argument, that the same cause will always produce the same effect. If, then, we take the divinely authenticated and authorized creed of the sacred writings, and allow for differences of opinion, not properly called the faith, we might all unite on the same foundation and enjoy the same peace and harmony. We are making the same experiment now, and so far, it proves to be divinely effectual as in the first and second centuries. It has been tried in different nations, and works well both in the old world and the new. From the history of former times, and from our own experience, as well as from doctrines delivered in the

[154] *Ibid.*, 135.

[155] Campbell instances the fact that in the time of Paul, while united in the faith, the early Christians hesitated not to hold and even preach, and express in other ways, their various opinions. Some taught that the world was coming to an end very soon, others that the law of Moses was still binding on those who had become Christians, while others preached that the resurrection was already passed. Much of Paul's writings are taken up with earnest and firm refutations of erroneous opinions. We need not be troubled, then, today when these opinions are expressed within the church. We have the right to differ, but not to divide. "Campbell-Rice Debate," 810, 811.

book, we have the fullest assurance of its adaptation to society, and of its ultimate triumph over all rival systems in the world. The church was once united and happy on the apostolic writings, and it will be so again." [156]

Casual reference has been made to the success of the experiment for unity upon the basis of "the faith," allowing liberty of opinions. A further study of its success, considered from Campbell's own standpoint, is of interest. In giving emphasis to the distinction, and in defining so explicitly the sphere of each, he believed he had discovered the solution to the problem of how to obtain enduring unity, with the largest liberty of opinion—how to retain an authority in which there could be unity, with the right of private judgement. "We have long since learned the lesson, to draw a well-defined boundary between faith and opinion, and while we earnestly contend for the faith, to allow perfect freedom of opinion, and of the expression of opinion, is the true philosophy of church union, and the sovereign antidote against heresy. Hence in our communion at this moment, we have as strong Calvinists and as strong Arminians, as any, I presume in this house—certainly many that have been such. Yet we go hand in hand, in one faith, one hope, and in all Christian union and cooperation in the great cause of personal sanctification and human redemption.[157] Much of the undeniable success of the Campbellian experiment was due, he believed, not only to the rigid distinction made between the provinces of faith and opinion, but to the further fact that when erroneous opinions are let alone, they die out of themselves. "It is not the object of our efforts to make men think alike on a thousand themes. Let men think as they please on any matters of human opinion, and upon 'doctrines of religion,' provided only they hold the head Christ, and keep his commandments. I have learned, not only the theory, but the fact—that if you wish opinionism to cease or subside, you must not call up and

[156] "Campbell-Rice Debate," 838.
[157] "Campbell-Rice Debate," 733.

debate every thing that men think or say. You may debate anything into consequence, or you may, by a dignified silence, waste it into oblivion." [158] He gives further testimony to the fact that the principle has worked in effective fashion, although those who have accepted his position represent almost every conceivable shade of theological opinion. "On this ground"—the faith once for all delivered—"many of us have stood for years. We have fully tested this principle. Men, formerly of all persuasions, and of all denominations and prejudices, have been baptized on this good confession, and have united in one community. Among them are found those who have been Romanists, Episcopalians, Presbyterians, Methodists, Baptists, Restorationists, Quakers, Arians, Unitarians, etc., etc. We have one faith, one Lord, one baptism, but various opinions. These, when left to vegetate, without annoyance, if erroneous, wither and die." [159] "We indeed receive to our communion persons of other denominations who will take upon them the responsibility of their partaking with us. We do, indeed, in our affections and in our practice, receive all Christians, all who give evidence of their faith in the Messiah, and of their attachment to his person, character, and will." [160]

Because he considered it of such fundamental importance in the whole scheme for Christian unity, he gave great prominence in his writings to the method by which opinions of men ought to be received. It was his firm belief that had the case of Arius been let ecclesiastically alone, the heresy which gave it birth would not have outlived its generation.[161] The most certain way to cause a false view of divine things to live, is to get up a debate, call a council, and the work is done.[162] In reply to an accusation of Rice, that his policy would tend to a light treatment of errors, he says,

[158] *Ibid.*, 797.
[159] "Campbell-Rice Debate," 785.
[160] *Ibid.*, 785.
[161] *Ibid.*, 796.
[162] *Ibid.*, 809, 811.

"It is opinions, and not ordinances nor faith, I let alone." [163]
If this is done, false theories will not live, lacking that vitality which is the power of truth.   "I have known innumerable instances of persons outliving their opinions, and
erroneous reasonings, and even sometimes forgetting the
modes of reasoning by which they had embraced and maintained them.   This was the natural result of the philosophy
of letting them alone.   In this way, they came to be of one
mind in all points in which unity of thought is desirable, in
order to unity of worship and action.   We have had as much
experience in the operation of these principles, having observed them longer than perhaps any of our contemporaries,
I feel myself authorized to say, that there are many persons
in our communion who, within ten or fifteen years have attained to more unanimity and uniformity of thinking, speaking and acting upon all the great elements of Christianity,
than is usually found in the members of any other community in the country.   I do not think, after all, that you,
sir, could find so much uniformity of sentiment, covering
so many former opinions and doctrines, in so many degrees
of latitude, and amongst so many persons, as already are
united in the ranks of reformation.   This we regard as a
matter so well proved and documented amongst us, that it
has already the certainty of a moral demonstration." [164]

There are two classic cases in Disciple history, in which
the principle so strongly advocated by the first leaders of
the movement was tested to the extreme.   The first was the
case of Aylette Raines,[165] a Restorationist preacher, who in
1828, during the great evangelistic wave in Ohio became a
convert to the movement.   Some of the members of the
Mahoning Association, being suspicious of Raines, since so
recently he had with power proclaimed his Universalist doctrines, demanded that he make a statement before the Association, of his opinions on the whole Restoration scheme.

[163] *Ibid.*, 809.
[164] "Campbell-Rice Debate," 797, 798.
[165] "Memoirs of Alexander Campbell," Richardson, II, 243, 247.

Aylette Raines clearly stated in the meeting, that when he became a member of the movement for Christian unity, he had renounced all sectarianism, and felt now that he should not be judged for opinions which he held as private property only. Thomas Campbell, as did also his son, defended him on the ground that he had a right to hold such opinions. Alexander Campbell argued that since Raines actually believed in the reality of the punishment of the wicked but held it as an opinion that God would eventually eliminate from the universe all traces of sin, its punishment included, he was in agreement with them on things fundamental.[166] He "considered this to be the substance of the divine communications on the subject, and that conjectures or theories as to anything beyond this, were mere opinions or speculations."[167] Raines, agreeing to hold such opinions privately and not to teach or preach them as a part of the gospel, was cordially received, and became one of the outstandingly faithful and successful ministers of the Disciples. Thomas Campbell expressed his position in defending him, when he said: "He is philosophically a Restorationist and I am a Calvanist, but notwithstanding this difference of opinion between us, I would put my right hand into the fire and have it burned off, before I would hold up my hands against him."[168] The wisdom of this, at that time daring course, was demonstrated, not only in the fact that Aylette Raines became later one of the great leaders of the movement, but also in the further fact that in his attention to the fundamentals of the gospel, he gradually outgrew his Restorationist principles. In 1830, he wrote to Campbell that "my 'restorationist' sentiments have been slowly and imperceptibly erased from my mind by the ministry of Paul and Peter and some other illustrious preachers."[169]

The second case in which the principle was tested, was

---

[166] "Millennial Harbinger Abridged," II, 37, 38.
[167] "Memoirs of Alexander Campbell," II, 246, 247.
[168] *Ibid.*, 245.
[169] *Ibid.*, 247, 248.

that of Barton W. Stone.[170] Stone held views which differed from many, even of his own brethern, on the subject of the atonement and the trinity.[171] His position on the atonement was in reality, similar to the modern widely accepted "moral influence theory." While not agreeing with the orthodox as regards the nature of the trinity, he was certainly not a Unitarian as he was so frequently accused of being.[172] Had he been, it is beyond dispute that Campbell and his colleagues would not have received him. Since, however, he believed in the Christ as uniquely God's Son, and since he repeatedly avowed this faith, he was fellowshiped by the Disciples, holding his views of the atonement and the trinity as private opinions. Campbell, discussing this case and others, in the Rice debate, once more affirms his unswerving faith in the foundational correctness of a unity based upon faith and allowing the largest possible liberty of opinions. "In this sectarian age, good men are found labeled with these symbols of human weakness and human folly. We can neither justify nor condemn a man for his unfortunate education, for his peculiar organization, or his eccentric opinions. Treat him rationally, treat him humanely, and in a Christian-like manner, and all these opinions will evaporate, or die within him. Receive him not as a Calvinist, a Papist, a Baptist, or a Universalist; receive him as a man and as a Christian. Show him that you receive him in the name of the Lord, and upon his faith, his love, his hope, and you will soon allure him from his false opinions, if he have any. But repudiate and excommunicate him for an opinion, you wed him to it; he feels the attachment of a martyr to that in which there is no value, but in his suffering for it. It has cost him something and he will not part with it for nothing." [173]

[170] *Ibid.*, 370, 375.

[171] "Campbell-Rice Debate," 853.

[172] Letter to Mr. A. Kendrick, Mays Lick, Ky., 1843, quoted by Moore in "History of the Disciples of Christ," 396, 400.

[173] "Campbell-Rice Debate," 811.

In the conclusion of his great sixteen days debate with Rice, Campbell makes an appeal which is classic among Disciples for the beauty and power of its impassioned utterance. It will be well to close the present chapter with this stirring plea. "But, my fellow-citizens, there is one point that cannot be too deeply impressed upon your minds—that the union of Christians is essential to the conversion of the world, both at home and abroad. Now, as creeds foster and keep alive, and transmit these parties, on this single account alone, they seem to me altogether worthy of a cordial reprobation. Where there is no contention, the fire of strife goeth out; and where there is nothing to content about, contention itself ceases. Remove, then, these causes of contention; take God's own book; bear with diversities of opinion in things not revealed; and as Paul says, 'Let us walk by the same rule, let us mind the same thing'; and, to paraphase his words, 'if in anything you be of different opinions, God will reveal this unto you': for in this way only, could he invoke peace on them, and on the Israel of God.

"You might, methinks, infer the utter impossibility of either converting or improving the world under the present aspects of Christianity. I have known Lexington and its vicinity for twenty years, and am of opinion that it was as nearly converted then as now. The same may be said of this whole commonwealth. You have been praying for union, and the conversion of the world, and have been putting up all manner of excitements for this purpose, during this period. Something is radically wrong. Why have not your prayers been answered, and your efforts blessed? Does not the Lord say that he desires all men to come to repentance and to acknowledgment of the truth, and to be saved? You are straitened and restrained in yourselves and not by the Lord. He promises to open the heavens, and to pour out a blessing large as your desire, provided only you will obey him. Let us unite upon the ancient foundation. Let us cast away our idols, our human inventions, and meet around the common altar, and there bow our knees together in cordial union and cooperation; then the gospel will resume its ancient spirit and power, spread its holy influence far and wide, and bless your children's children, through many generations." [174]

In a final paragraph, he draws the picture of the sad state of the country because of unchristian strife among brethren in the faith. "The land is full of infidelity. Your schools, your colleges, are full of scepticism. The great majority of your educated men are infidels; some open and acknowledged—many only show it by keeping out of your churches. The reason is, the gospel is blasphemed by the discords, the variance, the hatred, and the strife engendered by your partyism. Abandon your sectarianism, meet on the holy Scriptures, and bear with one another's infirmities, and then pray for a blessing upon your offspring; and you 'shall grow up as among the grass, and as willows by the watercourses.' " [175]

[174] "Campbell-Rice Debate," 904.
[175] Ibid., 905.

CHAPTER IV

THE RULE OF FAITH

A CRITICAL study of the distinctively Campbellian theology should begin with the Rule of Faith. The reform which the Campbells inaugurated, and of which Alexander became the acknowledged leader, makes large claims to be a Scriptural movement in doctrine, ordinances, discipline and life. The movement can be appreciated only as the Campbellian conception of the term "Scripture" is understood.

The watchwords of the Disciples have always exalted the Scriptures to a position of final authority in all things Christian. For more than a hundred years of their history, it has been deeply felt and confidently affirmed that, in their communion, practical application has been given to the dictum attributed to Chillingsworth: "The Bible and the Bible alone, is the religion of Protestants." But it is historically certain that none of the Protestant reformers, nor any of the Protestant denominations, have ever actually used the whole Bible as the Rule of Faith. Of no communion is this more true than the Disciples. They have employed the term "Bible" as though it were synonymous with the Rule of Faith; but in practical usage, it has not been so accepted. A second watchword, one classic with all Disciple writers— "In things essential, unity; in non-essentials, liberty; in all things, charity"—a statement supposed to have been uttered by Rupertus Meldenius, certainly limits their conception of the scope and authority of the Sacred record. Certain parts of the Bible are essential; others are not.

The theological positions of Alexander Campbell are the result of his unflinching application of the central principle

132

of his father's address at the house of Abraham Altars, expressed in the apothem, "where the Scriptures speak, we speak; and where the Scriptures are silent, we are silent." The meaning of this statement to him, was Campbell's conception of the Rule of Faith.

I

1. The basis of authority in the Scripture is to be found in the fact that it comes from God who is its author—it is a divine revelation. That which is contained in the Bible, and which is binding upon the member of Christ's church, has all the qualities of such an assured divine origin. The Bible of itself, however, has been erroneously denominated a divine revelation. It would be far more accurate to say that it contains a divine revelation. "I do not believe, then, that the book commonly called the Bible, is properly denominated a divine revelation, or communication from the Deity to man." [1] In another connection, he states this conception: "That the Bible contains a revelation from God, is susceptible of every variety and degree of evidence which guides men in the affairs of this life." [2]

Having located the revelation as being intrabiblical, he then proceeds to define his acceptation of the term. "Revelation, properly so called, is an exhibit of supernatural things, a disclosure of things unknowable by any other means in the reach of mortals. Whatever can be known by reason, or the exercise of our five senses, is not a subject of revelation at all." [3] "To constitute a divine revelation, in our sense of the term, it is not only necessary that God be the author of it, but that the things exhibited be supernatural, and beyond the reach of our five senses." [4] There are

[1] "Christian Baptist," 344.
[2] "Christian Baptism," 36.
[3] "Christian Baptist," 344.
[4] "Christian Baptist," 344. Cf. Emmet's discussion of "Revelation and revelation." Campbell would not have agreed with the following statement: "The idea of the verbal infallibility of Scripture is dead, not so its

thousands of things in the Bible which of themselves are true, but they cannot be revelations of God because they could have been known by the power of reason unaided by the divine Spirit. "For example; that God is a Spirit, is beyond the reach of our reasoning powers to discover, and could not be known by any human means. That a Spirit created matter, or that God made the earth, is a truth which no man could, from his five senses or his reasoning powers, discover. It is, therefore, a revealed truth. That man will live again, and be either happy or miserable in a future state, is another supernatural truth. That God so loved the world as to send His only begotten Son to enlighten, purify, and happify men, is a supernatural truth." [5] But in addition to these truths which man's reason alone could never know, there are a thousand things and more, which are not of this class. These surroundings of revelation in the Bible are, however, the means through which the revelation is made intelligible to men. There are many historic facts or incidents which the Old Testament writers knew without divine aid. The facts themselves, thus known, were not of supernatural character; hence, they are not divine revelations.

In his debate with Owen, he further elaborates this definition of revelation as contained in the Bible. "But I must tell you, while speaking of revelation, that perhaps I

chief presupposition, that somehow revelation must be the imparting of correct information, and inspiration the power of receiving it. And so attempts are still made, even by those who claim to accept the modern view of inspiration, to vindicate a special position and authority for the Bible, based not on its inherent truth and intrinsic appeal, but on something which can be regarded as unique in the manner of its composition." Revelation with the large "R" according to the view of Dr. Hamilton in his book "The People of God" is the knowledge of God which God directly reveals to man; "revelation" is that knowledge about Him which man discovers through the exercise of his own reasoning faculties. This distinction, however, is hard to define for "As we have already suggested, all discovery is in the end revelation. Man is seeking, God is revealing always and by many channels." "The Psychology of Inspiration" in "The Spirit," 203, 206.

[5] "Christian Baptist," 344.

am misunderstood; and certainly I am, if I am supposed to use this term in the vulgar sense. For now it is usual to call the whole Bible a revelation from God. I must explain myself here. There are a thousand historic facts narrated in the Bible, which it would be absurd to regard as immediate and direct revelations from the Almighty. Paine defines revelation very accurately, although he did not believe we had any, properly so called. He says, page 14, 'Age of Reason'—'Revelation cannot be applied to anything done upon earth. It is a communication of something which the person to whom the thing is revealed did not know before' —and I add, could not otherwise know. (That intelligence which could never have been derived to us through the agency of our senses.) 'Consequently all the historical and anecdotal part of the Bible is not within the compass and meaning of the word revelation.' Revelation, from the import of the term, must be supernatural.[6] But the historic parts of both testaments, present a great variety of typographical and historic facts and incidents; colloquies between friends and enemies, of apostles, prophets, and patriarchs, and of distinguished persons, good and evil; wars, intrigues, amours, and crimes of every dye. Now it would be neither philosophical nor rational to dignify these colloquies, narratives, geographical and biographical notices, etc., by the

[6] Cf. here the position of Robertson Smith: "The Bible is not revelation but the record of divine revelation—the record of those historical facts in which God has revealed Himself to man. That God has really revealed Himself to man—not that we possess an inspired record of this revelation is the point on which Christianity stands or falls. Of course of this view we can no longer speak of revelation as a revelation of truths. The knowledge given in revelation is not the knowledge of facts but the knowledge of a Person. What God reveals is simply Himself—His own character and His disposition towards men. Thus the death of our Lord is not a fact of revelation. The Apostles believed it on the evidence of their senses; we believe it on their testimony accredited to us by their known character. But in this historical fact God revealed Himself as the God who so loved the world, that He gave His only begotten Son, that whosoever believeth in Him should not perish but have everlasting life." "Lectures and Essays," 123. Campbell did not go as far as this but he was driving in this direction.

term revelation. The term revelation in its strict acceptation among intelligent christians, means nothing more or
less than a divine communication concerning spiritual and
eternal things, a knowledge of which man could never have
attained by the exercise of his reason upon material and
sensible objects; for as Paul says, 'Things which the eye
has not seen, nor ear heard, neither has it entered into the
heart of man to conceive, has God revealed to us apostles,
and we declare them to you.' Now the corollary is, that,
to a man to whom this divine revelation has never been
made, it is as impossible to acquire ideas of spiritual and
eternal things, as for a blind man to admire the colors in a
prism." [7]

One of the most characteristically Lockian conceptions of
Campbell, is that of the absolute dependence of man upon
the divine revelation in the Scriptures, for all his knowledge
of God and the spiritual life.[8] Since knowledge comes to
him only through the five senses, the revelations must be
made in such a manner as would be cognizable by him
through these means.[9] This has been done in and through
the Scriptures which are addressed to his intellect and
through the intellect to the heart. "There is not a spiritual
idea in the whole human race which is not drawn from the
Bible." [10] This astonishing statement reveals his utter dependence upon the Scripture for his knowledge of the Divine being and His will towards man. In his discussion of
the work of the Holy Spirit, he says: "To the Spirit of God
we are immediately indebted for all that is known, or know-
able of God, of the invisible world, and of the ultimate
destinies of man. All the ancient pagans and modern skeptics pretend to have known of these sublime topics, was
either borrowed from the oracles of the Revealer of secrets,
or were more uncertain conceits or conjectures of their own.

[7] "Evidences of Christianity," 146. See also 352, 353.
[8] "Christian Baptism," 53, 54.
[9] "Christian Baptist," 344.
[10] "Christian System," 15.

Were it our design, we could easily prove, upon the principles of the modern skeptics, upon their own philosophical notions, that unaided by the oracles of the Spirit, they could never have known that there is a God, that there was a creation or a Creator, or that there is within them a spark of life superior to that of a brute." [11] On the acknowledged principles of John Locke, "the Christian philosopher," and of Hume, the subtile sceptic, all that the Deistical world claims to know about Divine things is a "plagiarism from the oracles of the Divine One." [12] If we could trace the history back step by step, we would find that all the knowledge in the world, of supernatural things, has come from the Bible. The amazing historical assumption which such statements involve, was made without hesitation because he was convinced of the absolute finality of the Lockian position on the limitation of natural knowledge to the five senses. To him, and to his time, such a limitation was considered an exaltation of the Bible, and as magnifying its authority.

A study of the origin of the idea of God further reveals the Campbellian conception of the nature of revelation. He uses with force, the Lockian argument that the natural man can never by his reason know God, or have any idea whatsoever, of His existence.[13] Children are not born with an idea of God; the idea therefore, is not innate.[14] This is illustrated in the cases of many who have been born deaf and dumb. They have testified that they knew nothing of the idea of God until they were taught that He is.[15] The idea cannot come by imagination. Nature cries out everywhere that there is a God, the heavens declare themselves to be the work of His hands; but such declarations are made only to those who are already in possession of the idea of His existence.[16] Nature does not originate the idea of God. The

[11] "Christian Baptist," 82.
[12] "Christian Baptist," 82.
[13] "Evidences of Christianity," 165.
[14] *Ibid.*, 166.
[15] *Ibid.*, 99, 119, 122.
[16] *Ibid.*, 138.

reply of the editors of the *New Harmony Gazette,* a paper published at New Harmony, Indiana, in the interest of Robert Owen's colony of communistic infidels, to Campbell's three questions regarding God, the soul, and immortality, brought instant commendation from him. The reply was agnostic in nature; we can never know anything of such existences, because they are not cognizable by the senses of man. He congratulated the editors upon their answer; they were correct, for there is "no stopping place between deism and atheism." They could not know God, or the soul, or immortality, by reason.[17]

But the idea of God is in the world and has been here for many centuries. How came this idea of a first cause, uncaused? If it came not by reason; if nature has never originated it, but has only declared its implications to the man who already possessed it; if no man was ever born with it, and none could by the power of imagination, bring it into being; how came it to be in the world? The only answer to this question is that God has revealed Himself.[18] "I boldly assert here, and I court objection to the assertion, that every principle of sound reasoning, and all facts and documents in the annals of time, compel us to the conclusion that the idea and name of God first entered the human family by revelation."[19]

The revelation of God in history and through His word, is a progessive revelation.[20] It is suited to man at the various stages of his career; it takes into account his mental development and his capacity to receive it. "So much of the universe, its author, and plan, as man can understand and

---

[17] "Evidences of Christianity," 120. "Christian Baptist," 345.

[18] *Ibid.,* 148, 168, 169.

[19] *Ibid.,* 159.

[20] Cf. the statement of Principal E. Griffith-Jones: "God made Himself known to this people as they were capable of receiving the message; the light was tempered to the vision; not till the fullness of time Christ came and brought the perfect revelation of the Fatherhood do we arrive at the teaching which superceded all the earlier standards and gave us a law of conduct applicable to all times and peoples, and which has even yet been nowhere fully realized." "Peake's Commentary on the Bible," 12.

enjoy, as he 'is now constituted, God has kindly opened to his contemplation and apprehension. All beyond this is designed for future development, or for other ranks of intelligence above us. Meantime, a volume has been kindly presented to man, containing an account of himself, his origin, present condition, and future destiny. It is such a revelation of God and man, such a record of the past, and such an anticipation of the future, as meets all the intellectual wants and moral exigencies of the human race." [21] There is a hint here that Campbell might believe a future revelation possible when man had grown beyond his present mental capacity. It is only a hint, but it is significant.

The human race had had an infancy, a childhood, a manhood, and an old age; the revelation of the Father suits itself each time to the age in which the race finds itself. Were it to go beyond the race, using terminology for an advanced period, it would cease to be a revelation, for it

[21] "Christian Baptism," 89, 90. It is evident that while he recognized the final revelation of God in Christ, Campbell did not see a clearly modern scholarship the fact the divine self-disclosure has always been made in life and action and not merely in a "volume handed down or presented to man." Cf. Reissmann's eloquent statement: "A book from the ancient East, and lit up by the light of the dawn,—a book breathing the fragrance of the Galilean spring, and anon swept by the ship-wrecking north-east tempest from the Mediterranean,—a book of peasants, fishermen, artisans, travelers by land and sea, fighters and martyrs,—a book in cosmopolitan Greek with marks of Semitic origin, a book of the Imperial age, written at Antioch, Ephesus, Corinth, Rome,—a book of pictures, miracles and visions,—a book of the village and the town, book of the people and the peoples,—the New Testament, if regard be had to the inward side of things, is the great book, chief and singular, of human souls. Because of its psychic depth and breadth this book of the East, is a book for both East and West, a book for humanity: a book ancient but eternal. And because of the figure that emerges from the book—the Redeemer, accompanied by the multitude of the redeemed, blessing and consoling, exhorting and renewing, revealing Himself anew to every generation of the weary and heavy laden, and growing from century to century more great—the New Testament is the Book of Life." "Light From the Ancient East," 392. Cf. also the splendid exposition of this truth that God reveals Himself through "Life and Action," by Peake. "The Nature and Authority of Scripture" in "The Future of Christianity," Sir James Marchant, 164, 185.

would not disclose the will of God. "We have the bud and
the blossom, the green and the ripe fruit of humanity, as we
have them in other departments of nature."[22] It is for this
manifest reason that "the divinely inspired volume proceeds
upon the plan of a gradual and progressive development,
adapting itself to all the conditions of human existence."[23]
Various are the revelations through the centuries, but the plan
is always the same—to bring salvation to the sons of men—
eventually to "sum up all things in Christ." "It is the same
great mind, the same supreme intelligence, the same active
benevolence, working everywhere and at all times in the
communication of Himself to his intelligent and moral offspring."

It is in the light of the progressive nature of revelation
that we are to understand the reasons for the employment in
the Scriptures, of the crude and incorrect terminology of impossible conceptions of the physical universe. The inspired
writers used the conceptions of astronomy and physical
science which generally obtained in their time.[24] These
conceptions of science are not in themselves the revelation
from the Father—they are but the channels through which
the true spiritual disclosures are vouchsafed unto men. The
very fact that they used terms intelligible to their time, witnesses to their credibility. Had they spoken in the scientific language of our day, they would not have been understood by their own. The Bible is not a textbook on Science.
Its purpose is to reveal spiritual realities. "Christianity does
not pretend to be a treatise on chemistry, or botany, or
mathematics; but it makes demand upon our faith, and is
simply belief predicated upon testimony." The whole question is out of the realm of Science altogether, and we should
leave to Science those things which belong to her sphere,
and to revelation those which are included in its purpose.
"I am not afraid that if all the lights of Science were rad-

[22] "Christian Baptism," 90.
[23] *Ibid.*, 90.
[24] "Christian Baptist," 358.

iated upon Christianity, that any fallacy could be detected; but I contend this is no scientific question for scientific men to differ and speculate upon.[25] Only as we understand the meaning of revelation, the purpose God had in view in making Himself known through human means, can we come to the proper appreciation of its beauty and power. The Bible is the most wonderful book of knowledge in the moral and spiritual realm, that man has even known. "Though it teaches us not astronomy, medicine, chemistry, mathematics, architecture, it gives us all that knowledge which adorns and dignifies our moral nature, and fits us for happiness." [26]

2. Growing out of the fact of revelation, is the necessity for a consideration of the channel or means through which that revelation comes. With all the older Protestant theologians, Campbell believed that since God is the author of revelation, He would "create an instrument which is sufficient and reliable for the function which it was intended to discharge." [27] If there is a message which brings to salvation, the repository of that message will be of such a nature that it will adequately conserve the revelation, and will hand it without mutilation, to the generations to come.

It is impossible to combine all of Campbell's statements on the subject of inspiration, into a systematic view. Many of them undoubtedly squint in the direction of the verbal theory. He refers to the Scriptures as having been "dictated" [28] by the Holy Spirit. "Thus, the Spirit is the author of the written Word, as much as Jesus Christ is the author of the blood of the atonement. The atoning blood of the everlasting covenant, is not more peculiarly the blood of Jesus Christ, than is the Bible the immediate work of the Holy Spirit, inspired and dictated by Him." [29] "All that is done to us before regeneration, God, our Father, effects by

[25] "Evidences of Christianity," 200.
[26] "Millennial Harbinger Abridged," Smith, I, 476.
[27] "The Rule of Faith," Paterson, 65.
[28] "Campbell-Rice Debate," 616. "Christian Baptism," 290.
[29] *Ibid.*, 711.

his Holy Spirit." [30]   He speaks of the writers of the Scriptures as the "penmen."   God's first method of revealing himself to man was to speak *vive voce* to Adam in the garden, and with Moses on Sinai.[31]   Speech was thus taught to man by the Father through audible conversation with him.   He quotes the words of Newton with approval, "God gave man reason and religion by giving him the use of words." [32]   "When God spoke to man in his own language, he spoke as one person converses with another—in the fair, stipulated and well established meaning of the terms." [33] Campbell held tenaciously to the Lockian position that word and idea are inseparable; hence, the statement about the necessity of words being spoken to man if a revelation was anciently to be made.   Such passages certainly look in the direction of the dead level theory of inspiration, if they do not expressly affirm it.

It would be unfair to him, however, in the light of his numerous utterances on the question, to say that he held to the verbal theory.   In the references which have already been made to his definitions of revelation as being contained within the Scriptures,[34] evidence has been adduced to show that he did not consider the writings as being of uniform level in their inspiration.   The distinction made between those disclosures which are purely supernatural, and the recording of the historical, biographical, and geographical facts which were already known to the writers, absolves him from the accusation of believing in the theory as it was held by the scholastic theology of the seventeenth century.[35]

[30] "Christian Baptist," 200.

[31] *Ibid.*, 37. "Evidences of Christianity," 155, 159.

[32] "Christian System," 16.

[33] *Ibid.*, 23.

[34] "Christian Baptism," 51. "Evidences of Christianity," 146.

[35] Dr. Paterson very clearly defines the verbal theory as held by the seventeenth century scholastics. "The theory is described as mechanical, in that it was supposed that the Holy Spirit completely controlled the action of the inspired subject, and employed him as a penman; and it was described as plenary in that the divine communication was believed to have included the impulse to write the suggestion of the matter and also

While with this theology, he refers to the writers of the Scriptures as "penmen," he did not mean at all what they meant by the term.

It was peculiar to Campbell's thought that the method of inspiration seemingly presented no difficulties to his mind. He classifies Scripture in a twofold manner:[36] first, there is that which is revelation—those things which are purely supernatural and which man by the use of his reason could never discover. In this class, the communications of the Spirit were made in words. In the second place, there are historical, biographical and geographical incidents, accounts of wars, etc., which the writers could know from reason. In this class of testimony, the Spirit simply strengthened the memories of the writers so that their record of them would be accurate to the purpose of the revelation.[37]   Dean Garrison says of this division, that it was "convenient as affording a way of maintaining the complete inerrancy of the Bible in all its parts, without holding the implausible theory that the Holy Spirit dictated accounts of events which men could write about quite accurately on the basis of their own recollections and available historical documents." [38]   It is evident that all Campbell considered inspiration to be, is comprehended in this twofold division. "Revelation and inspiration, properly so called, have to do only with such subjects as are supernatural or beyond the reach of human intellect in its most cultivated and elevated state. In this sense 'holy men of God spoke as they were moved by the Holy Spirit.' But besides this inspiration of original and supernatural ideas, there was another species of supernatural aid afforded to the saints who wrote the historical parts of the sacred scriptures. There was a revival in their

---

the suggestion of the words. The consequences which these definitions carried with them, was the absolute inerrancy of Scripture on all points on which it was its design to teach—historical, geographical and chronological, as well as doctrinal and ethical." "The Rule of Faith," 64.

[36] "Christian Baptism," 51, 53.
[37] "Christian Baptist," 82, 83.
[38] "Alexander Campbell's Theology," 201.

minds of what they themselves had seen and heard; and in reference to traditions handed down, such a superintendency of the Spirit of wisdom and knowledge as excluded the possibility of mistake in the matters of fact which they recorded. The promise of 'leading into all truth,' and the promise of 'bringing all things before known, to remembrance,' by the Holy Spirit, include all that we understand by inspiration in its primary and secondary import." [39]   Here is unmistakable evidence that he did not consider the second class of recorded incidents to be as fully inspired as the first one, the revelation itself.   In recording those things which he calls "secondary," the writers were guided only to the extent that matters of "fact" which had vitally to do with the central message of revelation itself, should be accurate.

In the acknowledgment of the influence of the Spirit in reviving in the minds of the writers [40] "what they themselves had seen and heard," we have another deliberate and definite break with Lockian sensationalism.   On the basis of this theory, it is impossible for the spirit to exercise any general "superintendency" such as "reviving in the memory" those traditions, etc., which had been known before by the writers, without giving them a verbal communication.   The writer could use his own words rather than those which the Spirit gave to him, if he desired, but strictly, this is not

---

[39] "Christian Baptism," 51, 52.

[40] Cf. the beautiful statement by Marcus Dods concerning the Spirit's influence: "It cannot be summarily argued that because God dwells in a man, all that the man speaks partakes of the Divine omniscience.   Inspiration operates as any newborn passion, such as maternal love, operates.   It does not lift the person out of all limitations, but it seizes upon and uses all the faculties, elevating, refining, and directing to one purpose.   It illuminates the mind as enthusiasm does, by stimulating and elevating it; it enriches the memory as love does, by intensifying the interest in a certain object, and by making the mind sensitive to its impressions and retentive of them.   It brings light to the understanding and wisdom to the spirit, as purity of intention or a high aim in life does.   It brings a man into sympathy with the nature and purposes of God where others do not see Him, and to interpret His revelations in the same Spirit in which they are given."   Marcus Dods, "Inspiration" in "Dictionary of Christ and the Gospels," Hastings, I, 835.

according to the Lockian theory. It is certain that Campbell did not believe that the Spirit gave verbal messages to the writers for transmission to the sacred volume, but rather that he exercised some strengthening and superintending influence, which is not defined. Deliberately abandoning his too rigid and manifestly implausible philosophical basis, he adopts one which has far more to commend it, in that it is more in harmony with the Master's promise to the apostles.

While the writers were under the superintendency of the Holy Spirit in reducing the revelation to written form, it is clear that they used their own words. This is probably a contradiction of the former position in which he affirmed that the Holy Spirit gave them the words. The view expressed here, however, is his matured thought on the whole question. "We regard the Apostles of Jesus Christ as gifted with a full and perfect knowledge of the Christian institution; which entitled them, without the possibility of error, to open to mankind the whole will of their Master, whether in form of fact, precept, promise or threatening; and as furnished with such a knowledge of the signs of those ideas in human language as to express this knowledge clearly, accurately, and infallibly to mankind. But from what they have spoken and written, we are authorized to think that they were as free in the selection of words and phrases as I am in endeavoring to communicate my views of their inspiration." [41] The differences in words used by Apostles and Prophets on the same subject, the variations in style between the different writers, numerous scriptural passages in which such differences are expressly stated, all prove that the writers did not use words furnished by the Spirit, but employed their own. "Paul, as an illustration, wrote 'according to the wisdom given him.' Thus 'it was God's Spirit speaking in them, through such words as were natural to them from education and habit.'" [42]

[41] "Christian Baptism," 52.
[42] Ibid., 53.

The whole purpose of inspiration is to give us an accurate and dependable record of the saving Gospel facts. The facts transpired before the record of them was committed to writing. They were true before it, and without it. Inspiration guarantees us a correct record of what happened, and the apostolic interpretation of the facts as they came to pass. "We have a written revelation—this revelation was first spoken, then written." [43] The province of inspiration is to make it absolutely certain that the record of these facts shall be infallible. The authority is not in the record, but in the saving facts which it infallibly attests. Through inspiration, therefore, "the persons who are employed to make these communications are so supernaturally guided as to make them infallible witnesses in all the facts they attest, as well as all the communications concerning supernatural things." [44]

The result of such inspiration is to produce a testimony which is sufficient or adequate to the accomplishment of the object for which it was brought into being. The central assured content of revelation is thus unaffected by any admixture of error in unimportant details. In his debate with Owen, he propounds a query concerning interpolations in the Scriptures, and answers it with a quotation from "Internal Evidences" by the one-time sceptic, Soame Jenyns. His only remark concerning the, at that time radical state-

---

[43] "Christian Baptism," 51.

[44] "Evidences of Christianity," 147. Without the Spirit-revealed meaning of the Christian facts the gospel would have been incomplete. Cf. Dr. W. T. Davidson's illuminating paragraph: "The disciples, during the short period of His ministry, were slow and dull scholars; only after the outpouring of the Spirit were they able to understand who their Master was and what He had done. Hence the Church with true instinct included the Acts and the Epistles in the Canon, as well as the Gospels, and to the whole of these documents we must turn if we would understand what 'Christianity' meant to the Apostles and the first generation or two of those who followed Christ." "Christianity" in Dictionary of Christ and the Gospels, Hastings, I, 319. See also a very clear exposition of the Spirit-guided Apostolic reflection on the Christian facts with its significance for the wholeness of the gospel in Dean Matthew's "The Gospel and the Modern Mind," 61, 75.

ment, is that "some might think this bold assertion is going too far." "For I will venture to affirm that if any one could prove what is impossible to be proved because it is not true, that there are errors in geography, chronology, and philosophy, in every page of the Bible; that the prophecies therein delivered are all but fortunate guesses, or artful applications, and the miracles therein recorded, no better than legendary tales; if any man could show that these books were never written by their pretended authors, but were the posterior impositions on illiterate and credulous ages, all these wonderful discoveries would prove no more than this, that God, for reasons to us unknown, had thought proper to permit a revelation by him communicated to mankind, to be mixed with their ignorance, and corrupted by their frauds from its earliest infancy, in the same manner in which he has visibly permitted it to be mixed and corrupted from that period to the present hour. If, in these books, a religion superior to all human imagination, actually exists, it is of no consequence to the proof of its divine origin, by what means it was here produced, or with what human errors or imperfections it is blended. A diamond, though found in a bed of mud, is still a diamond, nor can the dirt which surrounds it, depreciate its value, or destroy its luster." [45]

The comment which he makes in the same connection with this passage, is of interest as showing his own decided inclination to the view that there may have been errors in the record, which, being on minor matters, affects not the main purpose of the work at all. "All the interpolations and different readings, though numerous as Michaelis, a very learned German professor makes them, counting all the minutiae of letters and points, do not affect the character of a single fact recorded in the whole New Testament. Indeed, men have been so much more concerned about the doctrines than the facts of the Scriptures, that they are much

[45] "Evidences of Christianity," 355, 356.

more alarmed about the omission or change of a term affecting some favorite conclusion to which they have come,
than about the evidence upon which the great salutary facts
are established." [46] Discussing the possibility that Matthew
might have used the name of Jeremiah when he should have
used that of Zechariah, he says, "But whether or not it
affects no more the credibility of the testimony of Matthew
concerning Jesus Christ, than the fact of Paul's forgetting
how many he had baptized in Corinth, proves that he was
not inspired with infallible knowledge of the gospel." [47]

These passages are deeply significant of the slant of
Campbell's mind in the direction of the modern Protestant
view. There is in Scripture an authoritative message. The
witnesses to the facts upon which this message is founded,
have been so supernaturally guided in their work of committing it to writing, that we have a message now in the
form which is sufficient to make men wise unto salvation
which is in Christ Jesus. Even though error in unessential
details be discovered, it cannot make a difference in the
sufficiency or perspicuity [48] of the assured deposit of revelation. "The Bible is the Word of God, not because He
brought it into being by unqualified miracle, but because as
it now stands, it is His gift, and is perfectly suited for doing
the work to which he designed it, in the economy of salvation. It may be added that a demonstration that it contains
a human element of ignorance and error, can no more

---

[46] *Ibid.*, 356.

[47] "Evidences of Christianity," 358.

[48] In reference to the perspicuity of Scripture, Campbell quotes approvingly, an admired teacher, Professor Beattie of Glasgow. "The Christian Religion, according to my creed, is a very simple thing, intelligent to
the meanest capacity. . . . I wonder to see so many men, eminent both
for their piety and for their capacity, laboring to make a mystery of the
divine institution. If God vouchsafe to reveal Himself to mankind, can
we suppose that he chooses to do it in such a manner that none but the
learned and contemplative can understand Him? I am perfectly convinced
that an intimate acquaintance with the Scripture, particularly the Gospels,
is all that is necessary to the accomplishment of true Christian knowledge."
"Christian Baptist," 10.

prejudice its claims to be the Word of God than a residuum
of sin in his character deprives a believer of the title to be
called a child of God." [49]   Campbell must thus be counted
as agreeing with the theologians of the Reformation, in
insisting upon the perfections of Scripture, and upon the
truth that the channel through which the saving message
comes to us, has been divinely guaranteed. [50]

II

The nature and seat of Christian doctrine falls next to
be considered. What then is the Campbellian definition
of the seat of doctrine? What is the revelation? What is
the Word of God? As has already been pointed out, the
answer to these questions is basic to an understanding of
the whole Campbellian theology. In the preceding discussion of revelation and inspiration, frequent hints have been
made as to the nature of this foundational conception; it
remains to develop it more exhaustively. Though there is
no apparent effort to do so, and nowhere any avowed purpose in this direction, the conception of the Campbellian
Rule of Faith is progressively and lucidly set forth in passages so abundant that we are embarrassed by the wealth
of material.

The aphorism first pronounced by Thomas Campbell, in
the meeting at the home of Abraham Altars, and later enthusiastically adopted by Alexander on his arrival from
Scotland, sets forth the general position on the whole ques-

[49] "The Rule of Faith," Paterson, 67.
[50] "The Rule of Faith," Paterson, 67. It is clear that Campbell would
have agreed with Griffith-Jones in his definition of the relation between
Revelation and Inspiration. "Revelation and inspiration are coordinate
terms. The former denotes the unfolding knowledge of God's nature and
saving purpose; the latter, the means and methods by which the knowledge has been achieved. . . . As regards the Bible, the deposit of spiritual
truth which it contains, constitutes its revelation; the characteristic spiritual
quality of the writers and secondarily, the literature through which it has
come to us we call their inspiration." "The Bible: Its Meaning and Aim"
in "Peake's Commentary on the Bible," 4.

tion of the seat of authority: "Where the Scriptures speak, we speak; and where the Scriptures are silent, we are silent." Here is an unmistakable pronouncement that the Scriptures only shall be the Rule of Faith. But what is meant by "the Scriptures"? or is there in the Bible an authority to which all the rest must come, and by which all that remains, besides itself, must be judged? What is meant by the silences of the Scripture, which must be rigidly respected? To answer these inquiries, is to unfold the Campbellian conception of the Rule of Faith.

1. It has already been established that Alexander Campbell did not consider the whole Bible to be a divine revelation, but rather that the revelation which has proceeded from God as its author, is contained in the Bible.[51] He distinguishes very carefully between that which is supernatural and that which man can know by his own intellectual powers, referring to the first as "of primary import" and to the latter as "secondary." What he means by the dictum, "Where the Scriptures speak," then, is some self-authenticating message of divine and saving truth which is contained in the Bible, or that book, the whole of which, is popularly denominated "Scripture."

2. The general definition of the Rule of Faith must again be modified by the conceptions which grew out of his Covenant theology. Nothing has more distinguished Campbell and the Disciples as a communion, than their unfaltering application of the fundamental principles of this theology to Biblical exegesis. In his epochal "Sermon on the Law," Campbell, after defining the law as the whole Mosaic institution, sets forth the things which the law could not accomplish. One of these was "that it could not be a suitable rule of life for mankind in this imperfect state." He proceeds, then, to show how God had remedied the defects of the law, in the Gospel. The conclusion arrived at is that the disciples of Christ are no longer under the law but under

[51] "Christian Baptist," 344.

the new dispensation, the Gospel of Christ. "What a pity that modern teachers should have added to, and clogged the words of inspiration, by such unauthorized sentences as the following: 'Ye are not under the law' as a covenant of works, but as a rule of life. Who ever read one word of the 'covenant of works' in the Bible? or of the Jewish law being a rule of life to the disciples of Christ? Of these you hear no more from the Bible than of the 'Solemn League' or St. Giles Day." [52] The moral law, so called, or that which is eternally right, underlies both the Mosaic dispensation and the Christian. The great commandments of the old law are not binding upon Christians because they are contained in the law, but because they are right. As a whole, with the exception of the fourth—"remember the Sabbath day to keep it holy"—they are incorporated in the law of Christ, and there are amplified and set forth in their truly Christian meaning. The old dispensation is but a portico to the new; "still, we must enter the sanctuary of the Lord through its own porticos. The new covenant always presupposes the knowledge of the old. The reader of the apostolic writings is supposed to have read or learned from Moses and the Prophets. The gospel presupposes the law. It was a school-master to introduce the Messiah to our acquaintance. It is all letter and type; but we receive the spirit through the letter, and the reality through the type. 'The law was given by Moses, but the grace and the reality, or the truth, came by Jesus Christ.' " [53] But we are today under the reality, the truth. This, and not that which contains it, is the rule and guide to faith.[54] "As a body to the Spirit, so stood the Jewish to the Christian institution, in many prominent points of view. As the spirit dwells in the body, so the gospel dwelt in the Levitical institution. When

[52] "Lectures on the Pentateuch," 286.
[53] *Ibid.*, 273.
[54] "Christian Baptism," 105. See also 89, 115.

that died, the spirit, or that indicated by all its ordinances, alone survived." [55]

Applying the Covenant Theology in this manner, it becomes evident that the seat of doctrine is not only to be found in the Bible, but in one section or division of it, the New Testament. And this was exactly the conclusion to which Campbell came. It was stated by his father in another passage, classic among the Disciples. Three of his thirteen propositions are here given in their entirety, as most fully setting forth the Campbellian conception of the seat of Christian doctrine.

(1) "Nothing ought to be inculcated upon Christians as articles of faith, nor required of them as terms of communion, but what is expressly taught and enjoined upon them in the word of God. Nor ought anything to be admitted as of divine obligation in their Church constitution and managements, but what is expressly enjoined by the authority of our Lord Jesus Christ and His apostles upon the New Testament Church, either in express terms or by approved precedent." [56] The rule of faith is enjoined in the word of God, but it is further limited to that which comes from Him who has all authority in heaven and on earth, Jesus Himself, and those to whom He gave power to establish His Church.

(2) "That although the Scriptures of the Old and New Testaments are inseparably connected, making together but one perfect and entire revelation of the Divine will for the edification and salvation of the Church, and, therefore, in that respect cannot be separated; yet, as to what directly and properly belongs to their immediate object, the New Testament is as perfect a constitution for the worship, discipline, and government of the New Testament Church, and as perfect a rule for the particular duties of its members, as the Old Testament was for the worship, discipline, and

[55] *Ibid.*, 105.
[56] "The Declaration and Address, Memoirs of Alexander Campbell," Richardson, 258, 259. "Overture," 84.

government of the Old Testament Church, and the particular duties of its members." [57]   This statement is so clear that no comment is needed.   The rule of faith is identified with the New Testament.   This part of the Scripture and this alone, is "perfect" or sufficient for the purpose for which it was brought into existence.   The New Testament is sufficient for every phase of Christian activity and experience to which a rule of faith could apply.   The Old Testament was a sufficient rule for the old dispensation; the New Will alone is perfect for the new.

(3) "With respect to the commands and ordinances of our Lord Jesus Christ, where the Scriptures are silent as to the express time or manner of performance, if any such there be, no human authority has power to interfere in order to supply the supposed deficiency by making laws for the Church, nor can anything more be required of Christians in such cases but only that they so observe these commands and ordinances as will evidently answer the declared and obvious end of their institution.   Much less has any human authority power to impose new commands and ordinances upon the Church, which our Lord Jesus Christ has not enjoined.   Nothing ought to be received into the faith or worship of the Church, or made a term of communion among Christians, that is not as old as the New Testament." [58]   This powerful handling of the whole question as to the distinct location of that which shall be finally authoritative in the Christian institution, gave direction to the whole Disciple movement.   It was a plea to go behind the creeds and confessions of faith, back to Christ and his apostles.   "Back of Philadelphia, back of Oxford, back of Westminster, back of Augsburg, back of Nicea," back to "those things which are old as the New Testament."   It has been noted before that Alexander enthusiastically adopted these principles of his father.   The father furnished the

[57] "The Declaration and Address, Memoirs of Alexander Campbell," Richardson, 259. "Overture," 85.
[58] *Ibid.*, I, 259. "Overture," 86.

ammunition which the son used so mightily in the later formation of the movement.

3. The definition of the dictum—"Where the Scriptures speak, we speak; and where the Scriptures are silent, we are silent"—is still further narrowed, and its significance more exactly expressed, in the Campbellian distinction between "faith" and "opinion." In no position were the Campbells more unbending than in their insistence upon the foundational importance of this distinction. To the present hour, it is a cardinal principle among the Disciples, and an understanding of it lies at the very root of all they believe and teach regarding the Rule of Faith. Thomas Campbell first speaks of it in his Declaration. Regarding the proposal to form an association for the purpose of promoting Christian unity, he says: "That this society, formed for the sole purpose of promoting simple evangelical Christianity, shall, to the utmost of its power, countenance and support such ministers, and such only, as exhibit a manifest conformity to the original standard in conversation and doctrine, in zeal and diligence; only such as reduce to practice that simple, original form of Christianity expressly exhibited upon the sacred page; without attempting to inculcate anything of human authority, of private opinion, or inventions of men, as having any place in the constitution, faith, or worship of the Christian Church, or anything as matter of Christian faith or duty, for which there cannot be expressly produced a 'Thus sayeth the Lord,' either in express terms, or by approved precedent." [59] That which is to be imposed as a rule of faith must be an unmistakable message from the Lord; it must be a divine revelation. Matters of faith are direct revelations of God; opinions are inferences and deductions from them.[60] The former is based upon clear and divinely authenticated testimony, the latter upon the insufficient and uncertain premises of human

[59] "Declaration and Address," "Thomas Campbell, quoted by Richardson in 'Memoirs of Alexander Campbell,'" I, 244. "Overture," 33, 34.

[60] "History of the Disciples of Christ," Moore, 496, 499.

reason. Matters of faith, those which have been divinely revealed, constitute the rule of faith—that which is binding upon the souls of Christians; those of opinion have no authority whatsoever. "Although inferences and deductions from Scripture premises, when fairly inferred, may be truly called the doctrine of God's holy word, yet they are not formally binding upon the consciences of Christians farther than they perceive the connection, and evidently see that they are so, for their faith must not stand in the wisdom of men, but in the power and veracity of God. Therefore no such deductions can be made terms of communion, but do properly belong to the after and progressive edification of the church. Hence it is evident that no such deductions or inferential truths ought to have any place in the Church's confession." [61]

The Rule of Faith,[62] then, has to do only with those doctrines which are clearly revealed, for which there is incontrovertible Scriptural evidence; those for which no such evidence exists, must be treated as matters of opinion which are of no authority as terms of communion and fellowship.[63] Matters of faith have to do with the Christian facts, and the apostolic or gospel explanation of them, and these facts are revealed for the purpose of making men wise unto salvation. "The measure of faith, then, is precisely the amount of Scripture testimony, neither more or less." [64]

4. Having located the seat of Christian doctrine in the

[61] "Memoirs of Alexander Campbell," Richardson, I, 259. Overture, 87.

[62] "The Message of the Disciples for the Union of the Church," Peter Ainslie, 161, 162.

[63] "Evidences of Christianity," 189, 228, 242, 246, 251, 321.

[64] "History of the Disciples," Moore, 497. Cf. Dr. Hodge: "Christianity, therefore, consists in facts which have a meaning, or in the meaning of the facts, whichever way we choose to put it. Take away either the facts or their authoritative interpretation, and we have no Christianity left. The mere external facts apart from their meaning are, of course, meaningless, and therefore do not constitute Christianity; while the abandonment of the facts no less destroys the Christian religion, reducing it to a mere natural religion, or religious philosophy." "Fact and Theory" in "Dictionary of Christ and the Gospels," Hastings, I, 562.

New Testament, and having differentiated between faith and opinion, the Campbellian Rule of Faith defines the content of the assured message of God, from another standpoint. In the New Testament itself, there is a touchstone from which all the rest of the Scripture is viewed, and in the light of which its value is determined. In his discussion with the New Harmony infidels, Alexander Campbell discloses the nature of this touchstone. "It is not the patriarchal, nor the Jewish, nor the Christian Revelation in piecemeal, that I am about to defend against the querulous, captious Sceptic—it is the consummation of all the ancient revelations in the mission of the Son of God. In reference to this, I view the whole volume; for this is the *alpha* and *omega* of the whole. The Christian religion is the corn in the ear. It germinated in the patriarchal; it shot forth in the Jewish, and ripened in the Christian era." [65] The intrascriptural norm [66] by which he determines that which is of authority and that which is not binding, is the revelation of God as it finds its summation in the work and teaching of Christ and His apostles. A further development of his position will make this even more evident.

The message of God as vouchsafed through Christ and His apostles, is the Gospel. "In the New Testament the phrase 'The Word,' or 'The Word of the Lord,' or 'The Truth,' is almost exclusively appropriated to the testimony which God gave concerning the person and mission of Jesus Christ." [67] "That which is emphatically called the Word of God, the Word of the Lord, or the Word, in the New Testament, is generally, if not exclusively, the Gospel, or Good News concerning Jesus Christ." [68] The mission, the death, burial and resurrection of Jesus, and all other facts which in the Gospel are related to the salvation granted by God through his Son, constitute the word of God—that through

[65] "Christian Baptist," 345.
[66] "The Rule of Faith," Paterson, 21.
[67] "Evidences of Christianity," 374.
[68] "Evidences of Christianity," 402.

which God speaks to our redemption. But the facts alone
are not the Gospel. It is necessary that we have the gospel
interpretation of them as given by the Spirit-led apostles, in
order to have the Word of God in its completeness. Guided
by the Holy Spirit, the apostles revealed the gospel meaning
of the facts, and this revelation is the doctrine of Christ.
"We sometimes read of the doctrines of demons; but it is
only the doctrine of Christ. When this term does not mean
teaching, which it often does, it simply denotes the meaning
of the facts. Hence the meaning of any fact, such as the
death or burial of Jesus Christ, is the doctrine of the death
or burial of Christ. As is the moral to the tale, so is the
doctrine to the fact. Hence all who believe the facts and
understand the meaning of them, have the sound or whole-
some doctrine of Christ." [69] "The apostolic epistles, so far
as doctrinal, are expressive of the meaning of the gospel
facts. They taught the new converts the legitimate bearing
and results of the facts believed. The other parts of these
letters were exhortatory, or deductions from the facts, calculated to direct and comfort christians. But all the doctrine of Christ grew out of the facts, just as all christian
faith is founded upon the testimony concerning them." [70]

He sums up the purpose of the New Testament writings
in one short paragraph: "Two sentences found in John's
writings, explain the whole design of both the historical and
the epistolary parts of the apostle's writings. The design
of the historical books is thus expressed by John: 'Many
other signs, truly, did Jesus, in the presence of his disciples,

[69] *Ibid.*, 374.

[70] *Ibid.*, 374. Dr. Hodge's discussion of this point is pertinent: "The
question of an external authority in religious knowledge cannot be evaded
by saying that the Bible contains no explanation of these great facts. Whatever may be said as to the authority of the Scripture, it is evident that
the Bible does contain an interpretation of the great facts of Christ's life.
And whatever interpretation be put upon the language of Christ and His
Apostles, it is plain that they had definite ideas as to who Christ was,
why and how He came into this world, why He died, and what His death
means." "Fact and Theory" in Hastings, "Dictionary of Christ and the
Gospels," I, 563.

which are not written in this book; but these that are written, are written that you might believe that Jesus is the
Messiah, the Son of God; and that believing you might
have life through His name.' The design of the epistolary
part, he has clearly expressed: 'These things do we write
to you, brethren, that your joy may be complete,' or that
you may know the things that have been gifted to you from
God." [71]

Concerning the province of reason in the rule of faith, he
makes one striking statement. "We have the right to sit in
judgement over the credentials of Heaven's ambassador, but
we have no right to sit in judgement over the information he
gives us." [72] It is the right of reason to determine whether
or not that which claims to be revelation has the marks of
genuineness which commends it to us. If it has the marks
of divine origin, we must accept it as true. Our own spirit,
therefore, bears witness with the message of the Spirit of
God.

In a quotation from his favorite philosopher, approvingly
made, he sums up his own doctrine of the Rule of Faith.
"I will read from this little book, a few sentences confirma-
tory of our views, written by the greatest patron and advocate of civil and religious liberty in the world! The author
of the essay on toleration; the immortal philosopher and
Christian, John Locke, the author of the first American constitution ever ferried over the waves that part us from the
fatherland.[73] 'But since men are solicitous about the true

[71] "Evidences of Christianity," 374.

[72] "Christian Baptist," 546. Cf. Emmet's statement, "The test whether a
writer is inspired is simply whether his message is true. The criterion of truth
is indeed a much vexed question of philosophy, but no system makes truth,
or the highest truth, dependent on the special channel through which it
comes. . . . All revelation must be judged by its inherent truth, by its
power of finding us and appealing to our conscience, by the degree in
which it calls out the best in us and awakens the response of the highest
part of our being. . . . We cannot escape the responsibility of judging
for ourselves by throwing ourselves in blind faith upon the method of
revelation and finding in that a guarantee of divine truth." "The Spirit,"
215, 216.

[73] "Campbell-Rice Debate," 795.

church, I would only ask them, here by the way, if it be not more agreeable to the church of Christ, to make the conditions of her communion to consist in such things, and such things only, as the Holy Spirit has in the Holy Scriptures declared, in express words, to be necessary for salvation; I ask, I say, whether this be not more agreeable to the church of Christ, than for men to impose their own inventions and interpretations upon others, as if they were of divine authority; and to establish by ecclesiastical laws as absolutely necessary to the profession of Christianity, such things as the Holy Scriptures do either not mention, or at least not expressly command? Whosoever requires those things in order to ecclesiastical communion, which Christ does not require in order to life eternal, he may perhaps indeed, constitute a society accommodated to his own opinions and his own advantage; but how that can be called the church of Christ, which is established upon laws that are not his, and which excludes such persons from his communion as he will one day receive into the kingdom of heaven, I understand not.' " [74] Those things necessary to salvation, those essential to eternal life, such comprise the Rule of Faith—such constitute the divine, saving, revelation.

III

If asked to vindicate his belief in the Bible as containing a message so unique and salutary that it is worthy of the exalted title of a revelation from God,[75] Campbell would meet the challenge with a two-fold reply, the first being an argument essentially in line with the method employed by the old Apologists, the second having a decided slant in the direction of the method of the new school.

1. The Christian religion is based upon facts of which the New Testament is an accurate and trustworthy record. These Christian facts, with their gospel interpretation, when

---

[74] "Campbell-Rice Debate," 795.
[75] "The Rule of Faith," Paterson, 7.

presented to the receptive mind, evoke faith in the great
saving proposition that Jesus is the Christ, uniquely the
Son of the Living God. "Christianity is a positive institution—an institution built upon facts. So was Judaism. The
Christian facts are all matters of record. The record of
testimony is the object of faith. Hence faith requires testimony, testimony concerning facts and facts require a witness.
The historian records facts. The philosopher speculates upon
opinions and abstract truths." [76] "We have asserted that
Judaism and Christianity were founded upon matters of
fact—upon things done by the divine power; that these
facts, in the first instance, were attested by the most competent and credible witnesses; that their testimony was delivered to the people orally, and that millions believed upon
their oral testimony; that this testimony was afterward put
into a written form, and that in this shape it has come down
to us; and that upon this kind of testimony our faith in
Christianity chiefly rests." [77]

Christianity, thus, is not something which is distinct from
and above the historical.[78] It is not, so to speak, a religion
which is up in the air and divorced from the actualities of
life. This is an oriental conception; it can never be occi-
dental. History is not merely a picture of reality; it is a
field on which God is actually bringing wondrous things to
pass. Christianity is not based upon philosophical speculation; it is a revelation of God through the lives of men whose
battles, trials, victories and defeats, in the aggregate, make
up what we call history. God reveals himself through personality; and the Scripture is one vast library of biography.

[76] "Evidences of Christianity," 228.

[77] Ibid., 251. See also 321.

[78] See an exhaustive discussion of this point in Professor Mackintosh's
"Aspects of Christian Belief," Chapter I. Cf. also the remark of Griffith-
Jones: "Christianity is a historical religion, i.e., it is based on the validity
and spiritual significance of a series of facts without which it could never
have arisen at all, and with the discredit of which it would speedily and
finally lose its influence." "Peake's Commentary on the Bible," 14.

It is the record of what God has done in and through men.[79]
Hence Campbell insisted always upon facts of God's working in the world, and the interpretation of those facts as the
gospel which makes our salvation actual.

Now the facts of Christianity are triable by legal and
historic criteria. "I aver that the Christian religion is
founded upon facts, upon veritable, historical, incontrovertible facts—facts triable by all the criteria known to the
courts of law, in the ascertainment of what is and what is
not established in evidence—facts triable by all the historic
criteria which any respectable historian of ancient or modern times, has ever had for his pilots." [80]   While it is evident that such facts are triable by scientific criteria, yet
there must be the will to believe, if faith is to be produced.
Man must be willing to examine the evidence with an open
mind, with an honest desire to know, or all the evidence in
the world, no matter how conclusive it may be, will never
evoke faith.

2. In agreement with the modern school of apologetics,
he also saw that Christianity "shines by its own light and
prevails by its own might, and that its best defense consists
in a believing exposition of its inspiring and energizing
truths." [81]   He freely and frankly acknowledges that this
type of evidence is not the best to strike with convincing
force, the mind hardened in doubt or disinclined to give
honest heed to truth.   To the unregenerate, determined in
his unregeneracy, it may not come with force at all, but to
the man whose heart is honest, and who loves the good, this
is the most powerful of all the arguments for the genuineness of the self-disclosure of the Father.   "There is a species
of evidence, sometimes called the internal evidence of Chris-

[79] "Christianity is not bound up with the infallibility of the Church,
whether in Pope or Councils, nor with the inerrancy of the letter of Scripture: it stands or falls with the reality of the facts of the gospel, with
the risen life of Christ and His presence in the Spirit amongst men." "The
Epistle to the Ephesians," Findlay, 85.

[80] "Evidences of Christianity," 35. See also 190, 191.

[81] "The Rule of Faith," Paterson, 8.

tianity. This is made up from the character of the writers, the particulars of style exhibited, and also from the nature, object, and tendency of the doctrine taught, or the communications made. This is what is sometimes called the critical internal evidence; and the moral internal evidence. I am not, however, going into this matter at present. I only remark, that, although the internal evidence found within the volume, is not supposed the best calculated to arrest the attention of the bold, declaiming infidel, or the curious, speculating sceptic; yet this is the evidence which has ever made the deepest impression upon the mind of the honest inquirer; and affords a much greater assurance to the believer, of the certainty of the foundation of his faith, than all the external proofs which have ever been adduced. The moral internal evidence of Christianity, is that which takes hold of the great mass of mankind, because it seizes the soul of man; it adapts itself to the whole man. It speaks to the understanding, to the conscience, to the affections, to the passions, to the circumstances of man in a way which needs no translation—no comment. It pierces the soul of man, dividing even the animal life from our intellectual nature, and developing the thoughts and intents of the heart. There is an internal sense to which it addresses itself, which can feel, examine, weigh, and decide upon its pretensions without pronouncing a word." [82] This argument from the exalted

[82] "Evidences of Christianity," 283. Cf. Dr. Dale's position that in reading the New Testament itself "the idea of the authority of the Book as a book is hardly ever thought of. The Book—explain it how we may—vanishes. The truth read there shines in its own light. I forget Matthew and Mark and Luke and John. I see Christ face to face; I hear His voice; I am filled with wonder and joy. I forget St. Paul and am filled with gratitude for the infinite mercy which justifies me freely for Christ's sake, and for His sake grants me the free gift of eternal life. I forget St. James and think only of the authority of the Divine Law. I forget St. John in the division of the Divine Love. The infallibility of the Council, or of the Pope, recurs to me constantly when I am considering their definitions of truth; it comes between me and the truth itself. Whether the writers of the New Testament are infallible or not is a question which rarely occurs to me. Somehow when they tell me a truth, I come to know it for myself: the truth is mine and not merely theirs. Practically the Bible does not come between me and God." "Protestantism: Its Ultimate Principle," 41, 42.

nature of the content of revelation itself, was a favorite one with Campbell. Had he strictly adhered to his Lockian philosophical foundation, he could not have made it; that he does not, is evidence of his habit, when he found it inadequate to explain the facts, of abandoning it without scruple. To him, even were there no other reason for believing the revelation to have proceeded from God, the divinity of its nature was sufficient ground for relying implicitly upon it. "If we had no other proof of the scriptures being divine oracles than just the contents of the book that alone would warrant us in the conclusion, for we see the hand writing of the Almighty indelibly inscribed in the pages of this volume." [83] "The author is known in his works. God's book is full of divinity." [84]

Christianity has been experimentally proved to be divine, to every man who has cordially embraced it, and has been saved by it. No argument in the world could destroy within him the conviction that the revelation is from God. "The Bible has been proved to be a divine revelation, as many millions of times as there are individuals who have believed it to the salvation of their souls. But it never has been proved to be false to a single individual of the human race." [85] Every man who has received the Christian facts, to the saving of his soul, is an unanswerable argument for the divinity of the message which has brought about so glorious a result.

In the introduction to his debate with Owen he eloquently sums up this mighty argument from the spiritual quality of the gospel revelation. Because this type of apologetic is so congenial to the mind of our own time, the Campbellian appreciation of its significance should be somewhat exhaustively considered. His thesis in the summary is stated

[83] "Evidences of Christianity," 189.

[84] "Christian Baptism," 31.

[85] *Ibid.*, 35. See also 31 and 48. Cf. the remark of Griffith-Jones: "But of the literature as a whole we may say that it is governed by one general and quite unconscious but commanding motive. Everywhere in these glowing pages we meet the living God in His revealing and redeeming agency." "Peake's Commentary on the Bible," 13.

in a sentence. "In defending Christianity, or in proving that it is a veritable, benevolent, and Divine institution, we have nothing to do but to develop it—to show what it is, and, perhaps, what it is not. This can be done with most effect by showing what it has done when perspicuously and faithfully propounded, and sincerely and cordially embraced." [86] What are its fruits? Christianity and infidelity cannot be compared. The former is a positive institution; it has facts and documents, and it has been in the world as an actuality for more than eighteen hundred years. The latter has no facts and no documents; it is a state of mind only. It assails the revelation in the Bible, for it offers nothing in its place; it blandly assumes that nothing in place of it is necessary. "Jesus Christ was, and is, a person; not a thing, not a doctrine, not a theory. Infidelity is not a thing, not a doctrine, not a theory. It is a state of mind, an intellectual or moral imbecility. It is a spiritual jaundice, sometimes green, sometimes black." [87] The two, then, cannot be in any manner compared; one is positive, the other is mere negation. The infidel stands to Christianity as darkness is related to light. Unbelief is the repudiation of evidence; it is spiritual blindness, it is the choosing to live in the darkness when one might live in the light.

"Jesus Christ was a real person, and had personal, positive attributes. He had a real and positive character, unique, original, transcendent. It was as fixed, as positive, and as radiating, as the sun in heaven. The originality and unity of His character is all-sufficient, in the eye of educated reason, to claim for Him a cordial welcome into our world, and to hail Him as the supreme benefactor of our race." [88] To any implication that Campbell was a legalist, external in his conceptions of Christianity and of the manner it is proved to us to be from God, the following exalted utterance ought to be a convincing answer. It is beyond the

---

[86] "Evidences of Christianity," Introduction page III.
[87] *Ibid.*, Introduction page IV.
[88] "Evidences of Christianity," Introduction page IV.

shadow of a doubt that in his age, which was itself external and legal to the extreme, he believed that the most powerful evidences for the divine origin of the Rule of Faith, the revelation of the Bible, were those from the lofty spiritual nature of its content. "To my mind, it has long been a moral demonstration, clear as the sun, that no one could have drawn a character, such as that of Jesus Christ, from all the stores of human learning, from all the resources of human imagination. The simple character of Jesus Christ weighs more in the eyes of cultivated reason than all the miracles He ever wrought. No greater truth was ever uttered than these words: 'He that has seen me has seen the Father also.' No mortal ever could have said so. The wisdom, and science, and learning of the world, compared with His, was, and is, and evermore shall be, as a glimmering spark to a radiant star, as a glow-worm of the twilight in contrast with the splendors of a meridian sun. It is only in the dark we can admire a glow-worm. We cannot see it when the sun shines. But we might as hopefully lecture to a blind man on the philosophy of light, as address the mere sensualist, the visionary, or the dogmatic simpleton, on the originality, unity, transparency, beauty, grandeur, of the character of Jesus Christ. An animal man will not look, and, therefore, he cannot see the light, the true light which shines in the face of the Lord Jesus Christ. He affirms that he sees, but he sees not what he affirms." [89]

It is interesting, as shedding light on his doctrine of the Holy Spirit, that Campbell nowhere teaches that the inner conviction of the truth of the Word of God is wrought be the Holy Spirit. This is the affirmation of the modern school of Apologetics. It was the position of the Protestant reformers. But when it is remembered that he considered the Scriptures to be the work of the Holy Spirit, the organ through which the Holy Spirit actually speaks to the heart and conscience, it is evident that any conviction wrought in

[89] "Evidences of Christianity," Introduction IV, V.

the heart by their inner quality, must be wholly the work of the Spirit. In the fact that the Spirit is the author of the conviction, he agrees with the Reformers and with the modern Apologists; in the manner in which the Holy Spirit works this result, he is in disagreement with them. He contended that the Spirit works instrumentally only through the word of truth; that there is any abstract contact of Spirit with naked spirit, he denied. Consistent with his doctrine of the nature of the Word of God, he did not believe that the Spirit bears witness to the divine origin of every part of Scripture, for this would be an "assumption that the Scripture is a single work, and that if the hand and mind of God are discernible in anything, they must be supposed to have given us everything which it contains." [90] This we know he did not hold. The Spirit bears witness to the divine authenticity of the message which speaks to us of the salvation which is in Christ Jesus; this is the Word of God.

IV

The Campbellian conception of the Rule of Faith includes some very strict rules for the interpretation of scripture. It will be necessary to state these rules, commonplace and obvious as they now are, in order to understand the significance of the influence which created them.

Rule 1. "On opening any book in the sacred Scriptures, consider first the historical circumstances of the book. These are the order, the title, the author, the date, the place, and the occasion of it."

[90] "The Rule of Faith," Paterson, 70. Cf. Robertson Smith, quoted by Denney: "If I am asked why I receive the Scripture as the Word of God, and as the only perfect rule of faith and life, I answer with all the Fathers of the Protestant Church, because the Bible is the only record of the redeeming love of God, because in the Bible alone I find God drawing near to man in Christ Jesus, and declaring to us in Him His will for our salvation. And this record I know to be true by the witness of His Spirit in my heart, whereby I am assured that none other than God Himself is able to speak such words to my soul." "Studies in Theology," Lecture IX.

Rule 2. "In examining the contents of any book, as respects precepts, promises, exhortations, etc., observe who it is that speaks, and under what dispensation he officiates. Is he a Patriarch, a Jew, or a Christian? Consider also the persons addressed, their prejudices, characters, and religious relations. Are they Jews or Christians, believers or unbelievers, approved or disapproved? This rule is essential to the proper application of every command, promise, threatening, admonition, or exhortation, in the Old Testament or New."

Rule 3. "To understand the meaning of what is commanded, promised, taught, etc., the same philological principles, deduced from the nature of language, or the same laws of interpretation which are applied to the language of other books, are to be applied to the language of the Bible."

Rule 4. "Common usage, which can only be ascertained by testimony, must always decide the meaning of any word which has but one signification; but when words have, according to testimony—(i.e., the dictionary)—more meanings than one, whether literal or figurative, the scope, the context, or parallel passages must decide the meaning; for if common usage fail, there can be no certainty in the interpretation of language."

Rule 5. "In all tropical language, ascertain the point of resemblance, and judge of the nature of the trope, and its kind, from the point of resemblance."

Rule 6. "In the interpretation of symbols, types, allegories, and parables, this rule is supreme. Ascertain the point to be illustrated; for comparison is never to be extended beyond the point, to all the attributes, qualities, or circumstances of the symbol, type, allegory, or parable."

Rule 7. "For the salutary and sanctifying intelligence of the oracles of God, the following rule is indispensable:—We must come within understanding distance." [91]

These rules, so widely accepted now, were very daring in

[91] "Christian Baptism," 61.

Campbell's day, and provoked much discussion and opposition. Other men had thought of the necessity for such laws in order to an understanding of the Scripture; Campbell dared to give them practical application in all his teaching and work.[92] His writings give large space to the discussion of these fundamental laws through which the correct knowledge of what the Scripture teaches, is made known to the mind.

The rules of interpretation exhibit two powerful influences. First, there is the influence of the Covenant Theology resulting in a different use of the documents from that which was then current.[93] Since we are not under the law, but under the Gospel of Christ, the New Testament is of far greater importance to us, and should accordingly be studied with more care than the Old." [94] The authority for Christians is to be found in the book of the new dispensation and not in that which belonged exclusively to the Old. There can be no doubt that this distinction between the covenants was the most important of the Campbellian exegetical principles.[95] The debt which he owed to the Covenant Theologians in this regard, has already been considered.

The second influence, clearly evident in all Campbell's writings on the subject of the rules of interpretation, is that of the Baconian empiricism. An interesting statement occurs in the Owen debate, in which this influence is frankly acknowledged. "The principles of investigation on which the inductive philosophy of Lord Bacon is founded, and those adopted by the Christian philosopher, Sir Isaac Newton, are those which should govern us on this occasion. 'Everything,'

[92] "Alexander Campbell, in particular, was the first of the great Bible students of the 19th century to sanctify by actual employment, the historical and literary canons and rules of criticism and laws of language, in the investigation of the problem of Holy Scripture, which have been in vogue ever since, except among reactionary denominationalists, including some of the Disciples." "Debates that made History," Haley, 50.

[93] "Christian System," 16, 17.

[94] "The Living Oracles," pages XX, XXV.

[95] "Christian Baptist," 463, 470, 484, 494.

says this great teacher, 'is to be submitted to minute observation—no conclusions are to be drawn from guesses or conjectures. We are to keep within the certain limits of experimental truth. We first ascertain the facts, then group them together, and after the classification and comparison of them, draw the conclusion. There are generic heads or chapters in every department of physical or moral science. We are never to shrink from the test of these principles.' Any arguments, therefore, which we may offer, we wish to be examined by the improved principles of the inductive philosophy, by those very principles which right reason and sound experimental philosophy have sanctioned as their appropriate tests. But questions of fact are not to be tried by mathematical evidence. It has been well observed that the sciences are of a social disposition, and flourish best in the neighborhood of each other; nevertheless each of them claims to be governed by laws which are perfectly *sui generis;* and none of them can be constrained to agree to an intercommunity of jurisdiction with the rest: it is held essential to the truth and dignity of each of them, that it is to be tried only by its own laws.' When we enter into an examination of the testimony on which religion is founded, we have no other scientific rules to resort to, than those which regulate and govern us in ascertaining the weight of all historic evidence." [96]

The rules which look to the meaning of each word, the noting of time, place and circumstances, and the purpose of each utterance, clearly reflect this common-sense method of Bacon, the method of observation and deduction. They simply apply the Baconian principles to Scriptural interpretation. This is illustrated in the laws of conversion. All the cases of conversion in the New Testament times are studied; the actions of all parties in the conversion process carefully noted, and the laws resulting are deduced. In the same manner, the general principles of religion and the laws

[96] "Evidences of Christianity," 262, 263.

resulting for the Church of Christ, are discovered. Every verse and every fact in the Biblical record is to be treated as so much scientific phenomena.

"God has spoken for men, by men." [97] The language of the Bible is human language, and all the rules which govern the understanding of human language must be applied to it. If the language of the Scriptures is not understandable by these means, then the Bible cannot be said to contain a revelation from God. The fact, however, that God has clothed His revelation in language through which men converse with each other, is evidence of the fact that we are to consider His word as being of the nature of a conversation; it is in language which man can understand, and the same method he would employ in comprehending a message from a human being, must be used in understanding God's message to him.

These rules of interpretation, upon which the Disciples have insisted with such vigor, only throw more strongly into light, the Campbellian conception of the nature of the Rule of Faith. God speaks through the Bible, to man, on the subject of salvation. When He thus speaks, a revelation has been made. This revelation is alone authoritative, as it alone contains the terms of union and communion. It is a matter of faith; other things, not so clearly revealed, belong to the realm of opinions, and opinions are not authoritative. The message of revelation is to be apprehended by the mind, which must of necessity, pronounce upon the authority of those purporting to be the bringers of the divine and saving truth. To the spiritual man—the man whose eye is single and whose will is submissive—will the revelation be made. He, in a word, who has the will to believe, to him will the glorious truth come with saving power. "Everyone, then, who opens the book of God with one aim, with one ardent desire, intent only to know the will of God—to such a person, the knowledge of God is easy; for the Bible is framed to illuminate such, and only such, with the salutary knowledge

[97] "Christian Baptism," 54, 55.

of things spiritual and divine." [98]   He, then, that would interpret the oracles of God to the salvation of his soul, must
approach this volume with the humility and docility of a
child, and meditate upon it day and night. Like Mary, he
must sit at the Master's feet, and listen to the words which
fall from His lips. To such a one, there is an assurance of
understanding, a certainty of knowledge, to which the man of
letters alone, never attained, and which the mere critic never
felt. The seat of authority is not in the saving revelation
alone; it is in the humble, spiritual mind which discriminates,
and in faith receives the truth.

V

The relation to the Rule of Faith of the Campbellian
conception of faith as personal rather than doctrinal is of
cardinal importance in understanding the much discussed
question of authority in Christianity. What then is that
relation? The only religious authority to which the Christian is bound, is Christ Himself. The true Christian is
possessed of one desire—to know the will of Christ. The
Christian Scriptures are authoritative in Christianity only in
so far as they conduct us into the mind and spirit and will
of the Master. The authority of the New Testament is
really but a secondary authority. All authority has been
given unto Him. We know what that authority is, however,
only through the Sacred Writings which reveal Him to us.

To Campbell, there was but one big question regarding
the mediation of the authority of Jesus, through the Word:
Does that Word correctly represent the mind of Christ?
Is it infallible, in that it gives us an accurate picture of
Him, and a true setting forth of His will towards us?   In
company with all devout men of his day, he answered this
question in the affirmative. There can be no doubt that he
believed in the absolute inerrancy of the Christian Scriptures.

[98] "Christian Baptism," 62.

Even with all the qualifications which we have found him making concerning the Word as the Rule of Faith, it is yet undeniable that he believed the Scriptures to be inerrant in what they have been brought into existence to accomplish, "To the Book of God there can never attach aught of uncertainty or delusion. Its teachings are above all suspicion. Hence there are no false facts; no sophisms; no mere rhetorical devices." [99] "It is a delightful reflection that we have thus no fallacy to fear in the Book of God, as we have ever in the books of man." [100] "The Word of God, being inspired, is, of course, infallible as its Author. He who 'cannot lie' dictated it, and it cannot deceive us." [101] Very few Disciples would go this far with him, and from the tenor of his writings and the methods which he employed, it is improbable that he would make these statements himself were he living today.

The deep reverence in which the Campbells held the Bible, is certainly not shared by modern men. It is not probable that Christians will ever again think of the Book as devout souls considered it, during the first half of the nineteenth century. Campbell did his work in the years just preceding the discovery of the linguistic, scientific, and historical apparatus which has revolutionized Biblical study. The critical facilities which were to his hand, were used by him with a courage and resolution which can leave no doubt in the minds of those who best know his work, regarding what his own attitude would have been toward modern Biblical

[99] "Christian Baptism," 63. "Millennial Harbinger Abridged," I, 191; Cf. "Overture," 27. Cf. also the position of Principal E. Griffith-Jones: "Now when pushed to its ultimate conclusion there can be but one clear and self-evident answer to the question—what is the ultimate seat of authority in religion? That authority can be found only in the revealed will of God. He alone who created us and sustains us, and Who has made us for Himself has the right to our entire and unquestioning obedience. The very word 'authority' (like 'religion') implies a personal relation, and this relation can only be that between God and the soul." "Peake's Commentary on the Bible," 7.

[100] "Millennial Harbinger Abridged," I, 192.

[101] *Ibid.*, 195.

Criticism. That all the subjects which in any way help to make the Scriptures clear, must be ransacked by the Biblical scholar, was his firm belief. As early as 1840, he approvingly quotes Ernesti, in support of this view: "While it is of prime importance for the interpreter of Scripture to form a just estimate of his natural faculties, and never to attribute supremacy to his own understanding, or the judgement of any mere man, it is obviously his duty to apply those faculties in the use of the various means with which he is furnished for understanding the Scriptures. Subject to those restrictions, which a sense of the supreme authority of the oracles of God, and the natural darkness of the mind cannot but inspire, human reason and science may, without hesitation, be allowed their full share in the interpretation of those oracles. Though incompetent themselves to the discovery of spiritual knowledge, yet, when discovered, they are competent to discern, to examine, to compare, to illustrate, and to confirm it by means similar to those which, in every other pursuit, lead most certainly to improvement and perfection. Not only must the interpreter render himself familiar with the contents of the sacred volume, by a constant and unremitting reading; but he must spare no pains in finding out, and appropriating to his use, all the accessory means by which his acquaintance with it may be facilitated and advanced; endeavoring to make himself master of every subject in any way connected with the work in which he is engaged; and guarding against every temptation to precipitation and rashness in drawing conclusions on matters of such." [102] That Campbell did use every critical means at his disposal, is certainly evident from his works; that he would continue to do so were he living today, is beyond question. Though unpossessed of the scientific equipment which Biblical scholars now have, his spirit and method were scientific. The same attitude of mind which must characterize the scientist, he thought should also be that of the student of

[102] "Millennial Harbinger Abridged," I, 200.

the Scriptures. "There is required, then, in the student of the Scriptures, the same condition of mind necessary to the successful student of Nature. Both must have a just reverence for the common Author, and an unwavering confidence in the reality and genuineness of the things whether of Nature or Religion. Both should have the same freedom from prejudice and prepossession, and both exercise the same care in observation, and observe the same justness and accuracy in their conclusions. With such prerequisites, there could be no fear of the results. Truth, thus diligently sought, would always be found; and new discoveries would constantly reward pursuit." [103] The discovery of truth was Campbell's only aim. With unsurpassed fearlessness, he followed its leading, never hesitating to discard old beliefs when proved to be unsound, or to act when new light demanded. If he did not go as far as modern men have gone, it was only because he had not the means to do so.

VI

Not only did Campbell cordially accept the formal principle of the Reformation, the supreme authority of the Scriptures; but he was as emphatically in accord with the other distinguishing Protestant principle, the right of private judgement. He frequently states his reliance upon it as basic to the success of the reformation in which he believed himself to be engaged. "In attempting to restore the ancient order of things, the right of private interpretation is of the highest importance. It is the exercise of this right which has elicited and maintained the present effort at Reformation, and this alone which can carry it forward to its legitimate results." [104] Emphasizing the impossibility of scriptural interpretation without a suitable preparation of the mind, he continues: "One of the prerequisites to which we have already adverted, is the conviction that we have a right to

[103] "Millennial Harbinger Abridged," I, 192; cf. 195.
[104] *Ibid.*, 190.

search and interpret the Scriptures for ourselves. A firm conviction that we possess this right is essential to our success. If we doubt our authority to search the Scriptures, we will scarce venture to consult them; or if we do, we will hardly trust ourselves to the conclusions to which they seem to lead us." [105] Like his father in the "Declaration and Address," he contends that the right of private judgement is not only a precious right, but a solemn duty to be most faithfully performed. "In the pursuit of divine knowledge, we must neither doubt nor tamely surrender our right to examine and judge for ourselves. On the contrary, we must fully realize our true position in respect to the divine communications, and not only feel perfectly assured of our right to hear and consider them, but regard this as an imperative duty and a most precious privilege." [106]

It is perenially asserted that the two great Protestant principles upon which the Campbells relied with such confidence, are diametrically opposed to each other. Both the Scripture text and the personal judgement of the individual interpreter, cannot be authoritative, for the perfectly obvious reason that one contradicts the other. Since each man must interpret the Scripture for himself, only his interpretation can be authority for him. Each individual, therefore, has his own Bible which, though authoritative for him, is not so far anyone else, as long as all have the right to interpret it for themselves. We are thus driven back upon the fact that the only authority is within; the inner consciousness must speak the final word. The conclusion, then, seems to be that we must frankly give up one or the other of these principles, if we affirm the right of private judgement, we must renounce the authority of the Scriptures; if we adhere to the authority of the Scriptures, the right of private judgement cannot be granted.

Dean Kershner interestingly discusses the earliest method by which Protestantism endeavored to escape from the di-

[105] *Ibid.*, 190.
[106] "Millennial Harbinger Abridged," I, 191.

lemma created by the apparent antagonism between her two fundamental principles.[107]   It may be called the symbolical —the attempt to resolve Scripture interpretation into harmony, through creedal formulas and confessions of faith. In opposition to the Roman Catholic dogma of the supremacy of the Church, the Reformers had asserted that the Scriptures alone are the infallible authority, but, at the same time, each individual has the right to interpret them for himself.   Very soon aware of the contradiction thus created, they sought to bring about reconciliation by a return to the ancient Greaco-Christian method of formulating a Creed.   This was the actuating reason why the period of the Protestant Reformation became the most prolific creed-making epoch in Christian history.   Through this method the primacy of private judgement was thought to be guarded and retained, in that the creed was supposed to set forth the consensus of the private judgement concerning the authoritative truths of Scripture, for those who subscribed to it. Thus the creed as the written constitution or foundation of the Church, was defiantly opposed to the Roman Catholic dogma of ecclesiastical supremacy.   As a practical theory, however, there can be no doubt that the Roman Catholic solution was superior to that of the Protestant churches. The adaptability, at least in theory, of Papal infallibility, made far better provision for the changes which time brings than that provided by crystallized dogma in the form of a static and absolutely authoritative creed.   The Protestant theory of authority was, therefore, far less workable and efficient than that of Rome.

What had been asserted in theory, with such confidence by the Protestants, was immediately repudiated in practice. The method which had been employed upon the Scriptures, was now turned upon the Creeds.   The members of the various denominations, while subscribing to the creeds, exercised the right of private judgement, and interpreted these

[107] See Overture, 44, ff.   I have practically reproduced Dr. Kershner's argument in this section.

documents for themselves. The effort to establish a uniform method of interpretation was thus proved to be valueless. exercising, upon the Scriptures and the Creeds alike, the right of private judgement, Protestants were consequently brought back to the place from which they had started— the position that there can be no external authority, but that the last word lies with the judgement of the individual.

The solution of this problem, offered by the Campbells, was unique. It lies at the very heart of their program for Christian unity through a return to New Testament Christianity as best expressive of what was in the mind of Christ. That they did hold to the authority of the Scriptures with the right and duty of every individual to interpret them for himself, we have seen. It is evident, also, that they were seemingly unaware of any antagnoism between these principles. By what means did they bring them into harmony? The answer to this question is that both Thomas and Alexander Campbell believed in the substantial accuracy of "the common mind." They believed in unity of thought on the part of the individuals, through universal reason, which is always ultimately correct in its conclusions. While repudiating any one man's interpretation as binding, they were willing unhesitatingly to accept the pronouncements of the intellectual or learned majority, for they were convinced that the universal reason or common mind could not be mistaken. If asked how this common mind is to be known, they would reply that it is composed of those in each sphere, who are best prepared to know on any given subject. In a word, it might be defined in the modern academic phrase, "the concensus of scholarship." Dean Kershner, concerning this important Campbellian doctrine, thoughtfully says: "Whatever the great bulk of thoughtful men agree upon as touching the interpretation of Scripture, is doubtless an expression of the common mind upon the subject. Alexander Campbell was rather addicted to quoting the expression *vox populi vox dei* in his debates and public addresses. What he meant by this quotation was simply that the voice of human intelligence as a whole, expresses the voice of universal reason, and, therefore, the voice of God. It was to this common mind that the Campbells always made their appeal with regard to the various theological positions which they occupied." [108] It may be summed up in a sentence: Reason is from God, and when given a free field and a fair opportunity, it expresses the divine nature in one of its highest forms. Dr. Kershner points out that while the individual reason is often obscured and distorted by individual passions and prejudices, so that it is circumscribed and hemmed in by petty and local considerations, the common mind of the larger group is not subject to these limitations. When the larger group is taken into account, the petty particularities of the individuals which constitute it, drop out of sight or negate each other, and the conclusions of the common mind stand out with clear unanimity.[109] Since the Scriptures are God's word given by revelation, they can be interpreted correctly, only by the universal reason which is God's gift to humanity for guidance through the world. The conclusions of this reason, as reached by the reverent common mind in its interpretations of the Scripture, constitute, therefore, the highest possible standard of accuracy.

VII

It is important to note that the position here advocated, is practically the scientific spirit at its best in the realm of religion. While it cannot be denied that the Disciples have not emphasized the mystical elements in Christian experience as they may do in the future, it is also true that no modern Church "in its fundamental genius and character, is more closely allied to the scientific spirit." [110] Scientific materialism run riot on one side, and legalistic, externalistic, traditionalism on the other, cannot cope with the problems

[108] "Overture," Kershner, 44, 45.
[109] *Ibid.*, 45.
[110] "Overture," Kershner, 100.

of the age. They are both doomed to destruction. But the
great devout common mind, the consensus of enlightened,
thoughtful piety, in the spirit of the true scientist, following
truth for truth's sake, will hold the longing soul of our own
strenuous time, to that light and freedom which belongs to
the sons of God. It can be affirmed without contradiction,
that this was the ideal of the Campbells and those who followed them. "Union in the truth" has ever been the motto
displayed upon their banners. The application of this underlying philosophy of the substantial inerrancy of the common mind, to the program which the Disciples have
espoused, will be noted in another connection; it is sufficient
to observe it here as the fundamental principle by which
they worked in their effort to solve the knotty problem of
authority in Christianity. This spirit of the scientist, the
honest searcher after truth, is manifested by Thomas Campbell, when after submitting this program for unity in the
"Declaration and Address," he asks his readers that his
propositions shall be "examined with rigor, with all the
rigor that justice, candor, and charity, will admit." [111]

In his very lucid discussion of this problem Kershner
further points out that the Campbellian philosophy as to
the question of authority, is closely akin to the conception of
infallibility, as held by the Roman Catholic Modernists.
These, Modernists, notably Father Tyrell, in his "Letters,"
repeatedly made the claim that the Protestant and Roman
Catholic conceptions are identical. The Pope, according to
this interpretation, is simply the spokesman of the united
Church. Since it is not merely his own sentiments as one individual, but the faith of united Catholicism, which he voices,
his decisions are as nearly infallible as it is possible for any
decision to be. If this were true, we could not ask for
greater infallibility. Such a position is exactly that of the
Campbells, except, of course, they would not have agreed
that the Pope should be the mouthpiece of the Church. The
weakness of Father Tyrell's view, and one which he is forced

[111] *Ibid.*, 97.

to admit, is the fact that the Pope does not represent a united Catholicism. The irrefutable evidence of this was the excommunication of the Modernists by the Vatican's own decree. It is a very significant tendency, however, that such brilliant protagonists of more liberal things, as were Tyrell and Loisy, should have confirmed the basic philosophy of the Campbells, even in the face of ecclesiastical autocracy. If the time ever comes that the Papal power shall take a position on infallibility, such as that advocated by the Modernists, whom they have so determinedly thrust out from themselves, a basis of unity will be provided, which will at least evoke sympathetic interest from the Christian world. Basically, the Campbellian philosophy of the infallibility of the common mind is just about the same, also, as the conception that authority rests with a General Council of the Church. Before this authority was transferred from the General Council to the Pope, the belief that the Council represented the common mind of Christendom was almost universally held. However, the weakness of the view consisted in the fact that all too often the best representatives of the common mind were not admitted to the Council. There can be no doubt that, at bottom, the idea that the conclusions of the reverent common mind are final, is relatively sound. The Campbells would not have agreed with Carlyle that history is made up of the biographies of a few mighty personalities. Their faith in democracy was unshakable. It is rather the voice of collective reason, the voice of the common mind as thus expressed, which must be heard. The progress so conceived is slower, but it is sure.

If the underlying philosophy of the Campbells, the principle which history must proclaim as that for which they were most distinguished, is conceded, there is no reason why the authority of the Scriptures and the right of private judgement should not be compatible. That the Campbells so held them, we have seen; indeed, upon this principle one is but the necessary corollary of the other. Dean Kershner makes a pertinent comment upon this point: "If the doctrine of the universal reason is accepted, there is no reason why the Scriptures, as interpreted by this principle, should not be regarded as the ultimate authority in religion. Such a viewpoint means something far more than simply the assertion of the infallibility of private judgement. It rises from the separateness and particularity of the 'inner consciousness' theory to the broad field of prophetic revelation interpreted and made clear from age to age by the ever living and universal reason which guarantees all civilization and progress. That reason itself is, indeed, not the last word. The last word is revelation interpreted by reason." [112] If Roman Catholicism failed to apprehend the significance of the theory set forth by their own Modernists, it is clear that Protestantism as a whole has equally failed to understand its meaning. It is just as certain that many of the Disciples have never truly understood the implications of these very foundational conceptions through which their fathers came to their distinguishing theological positions. Truth is truth, however, and the time will come when this great philosophy, that the common mind—the universal reason, in its searchings, must eventually discover those basic positions upon which alone God's people can find reunion, will be recognized. Through this principle only will it be possible for Christianity and Science to walk hand in hand to the making of a better and a nobler world.

VIII

The application of the Campbellian philosophy of the substantial inerrancy of the common mind, to the problem of Christian unity, resulted in the method, so often discussed, and expressed in the words, "unity in the faith with liberty of opinions." While we have elsewhere considered this principle, a study of its relation to the common mind is of vital importance. The Campbells believed that the

[112] "Overture," Kershner, 47.

common mind had spoken, and that from the very beginning
to the present time, all evangelical Christians have been one
in their acceptance of the essential things, or "the faith."
This unity in the faith already possessed by all was a
favorite topic with both Thomas Campbell and his son.
The Christian world, therefore, is not divided over those
things which, from the first, have been considered essential
to salvation, but concerning opinions, speculations, explanations of the divine facts—those things "in which the kingdom of God does not consist." [113]   Dr. Richardson sets forth
the Disciple's position in a pointed paragraph. "It is, indeed, this simple faith in Christ, accompanied by its
appropriate fruits, which constitutes that 'common Christianity' which is admitted to exist in all parties, independent
of party peculiarities; an admission, by the way, which at
once assigns to these peculiarities their true character, as
mere excrescences upon Christianity; as having no power
to save, and as the very means of perpetuating divisions.
Happy would it be for the world, if all could be induced to
rest content with that 'common Christianity,' which is the
very object of the present Reformation to present the religious community as the only means of securing unity and
peace." [114]   There is, in Disciple literature, no more comprehensive paragraph, as regards the real purpose of the movement.   Those things which divide have nothing to do with
the Christian salvation.   One may be a Christain and never
subscribe to anything which differentiates a member of one
Christian denomination from another.   That alone which
has saving power is that "common Christianity" which,
through the Christian centuries, has been determined to be
essential, by the common thoughtful mind of the Church.
This is precisely the thing which Dr. Denney contends for,
all through his epochal book, "Jesus and the Gospel."   It is
the message of that brilliant Christian scholar, Robert Flint,

[113] "Overture," Kershner, 60.
[114] "Millennial Harbinger Abridged," II, 336.

when he says: "We ought to distinguish between those eternal verities, a realization of which is directly and immediately necessary to the welfare of our spirits, and all questions regarding religion, which may be interesting, but the solution of which is not indispensable." [115]   Professor Curtis recognizes this great fact, so essential if Christian unity is ever to become an actuality: "Under all the diversities of faith and government, which divide the surface of Christendom, and sometimes seem to strike down to the very foundations, there is a common basis of believing loyalty, a common intent to obey and serve the same Lord according to the dictates of His Spirit, whose gifts have always been manifold." [116]

Now, since there is a ground of belief, "the faith," which all Christians hold in common, and without which there would be no Christianity as it has been known through the centuries, and since division has been occasioned not by this faith, but by the explanations of it—the theologies which have grown out of it—the way to reunion lies in the recognition of this faith as alone essential to membership in the Church, allowing every man to have his own opinions, so long as these are held as private property. This is what Campbell meant by unity upon the facts with liberty of opinion regarding their explanation.[117] It is the position, also, which he took in the debate with Rice, in his continual reaffirmations that the plea he advocated was catholic: "Indeed, there is nothing strictly sectarian in our views. There is no opinionism in our system of operations. The facts we believe are admitted; the ordinances we practice are admitted; the piety and morality we inculcate are admitted —universally admitted by all Christendom. There are none excluded from our communities but those who deny the faith, those immoral or unrighteous, and those who are schismatics. These three are by divine authority to be

[115] "Agnosticism," 456.
[116] "History of Creeds and Confessions of Faith," 401.
[117] "Christian System," 124.

severed from the faithful. The schismitic is excluded, not
for his opinion, but for the unrighteous use he makes of
it." [118] Dr. Richardson contended that while unity in the
faith is essential, unity in opinions is neither possible nor
desirable. "It is preposterous to except that men will ever
agree in their religious opinions. It is neither necessary nor
desirable that they should do so." "As well expect to conform the features of the human face to a single standard,
as to secure a perfect agreement of men's minds. Hence
there can be no peace, unless there be liberty of opinions.
Each individual must have the perfect right to entertain
what opinions he pleases, but he must not attempt to enforce
them upon others, or to make them a term of communion
or religious fellowship. They can do no harm, so long as
they are private property, and are regarded in their true
light, as human opinions possessed of no divine authority
or infallibility." [119] The Christian faith alone is essential,
that faith which has been universally recognized by the common Christian mind through the years. "Everyone will agree,
that the true basis of Christian union is the Christian faith.
All parties assert this, but, unfortunately, each one adds to
that faith, or, rather, substitutes for it, human opinions, and
matters of doctrinal knowledge not immediately connected
with salvation; and they refuse to receive each other, because they do not happen to agree in these opinions and
doctrines, while, at the same time, they may hold in common what really constitutes the Christian faith. This Christian faith, as we have seen, is simply belief in Christ, as he
is presented in the gospel, and is concisely engrossed in
the great proposition that Jesus Christ is the Son of
God." [120] Only that which the common Christian mind has
decreed to be the Scriptural requirements for salvation, can
be bound upon the souls of men; this is "the faith" and
the only basis of Christian unity.

[118] "Campbell-Rice Debate," 798, 799; see also 784, 785, 808, 809.
[119] "Millennial Harbinger Abridged," II, 327.
[120] *Ibid.*, 341.

In the light of the application of the principle of the substantial infallibility of the common mind to the problem of Christian reunion, it is evident that two modern objections are answered.

(1) The first one may be stated in a question: "It is all very well to talk about unity in the faith, but how are you going to determine what the faith is?" The Disciples would answer that there is to be but one way—the answer which is given by the universal Christian reason applied to a study of the Scriptures. As has already been stated, they believe that the common mind has expressed itself, and is a unit in declaring what "the faith" is, as opposed to theological and philosophical explanations of it.

(2) The Disciples also agree that the second objection is answered by the same principle. It has been stated in a sentence: "The division between faith and knowledge about Jesus is arbitrary. It is impossible to have a saving faith in Christ without holding some very definite convictions about Him." To this the Disciples agree. Faith and knowledge are not unrelated. That faith, however, which is evoked by the revelation of Christ in the New Testament, leads to a body of convictions about Him, in which the Christian is one with all others who, through the same faith, have been inducted into the same experiences. This is exactly what the Campbells meant by their contentions that, in the fundamentals of Christianity, Christians are one. Every doctrinal position which they embraced, was determined by this unwavering conviction. In a word, they tried to hold only those things which the common mind had held as indisputable, from the beginning. The faith evoked by Jesus himself is not mere assent to the fact of His unique relation to God; it is trust, it is obedience. Professor Mackintosh has well stated it: "When I see Jesus Christ—living, dying, and risen—as the revelation of God, then I know that I have found my Master. I cannot set my faith upon Him without being thereby aware that I

must obey Him unconditionally." [121]　　Those who have such faith in Christ, have never been far apart in the convictions which they have held concerning Him.

That the general position of Campbell and his fellow-Reformers of the nineteenth century in regard to the Rule of Faith is increasingly being vindicated in modern theological tendency there can be no doubt. The chorus of modern approval is continually growing, though generations must pass by before the full scope of early Disciple contributions in this field will be fully appreciated. The New Testiment, interpreted by the great reverent mind of the Church of God will some day bring the discordant sects of Christendom into that unity which was the passion of our Master's heart, and then may we confidently expect to see the saving purpose for which he sacrificed His life gloriously accomplished. While gratefully acknowledging our undoubted obligation to Biblical and Historical Criticism for the colossal task it has fearlessly essayed in clearing away the accumulated theological lumber of days that are gone, I think we must frankly confess that the big things of the Christian faith remain as they were. From the fiery furnace, seven times heated, they have come forth unscathed. And assuredly among these big things is the faith of the militant Church from the day of its birth until now that in its primitive documents there is faithfully guarded a precious deposit which has meaning only as the Great God, who is in and yet above this universe, is acknowledged to be its author, and that, therefore, in this sense they are truly "Spirit breathed." [122]　　There can be but little doubt

---

[121] "The Divine Initiative," Mackintosh, 66.

[122] Cf. the statement of Duchesne: "These books, whatever was their circulation and authority, have this in common, that they were all written for the Church, and that the Church recognized in them the inspiration from which she herself proceeds. They are all esoteric books, spiritual books, fitted to strengthen faith, and to keep alive Christian devotion." . . . "Very early, before the end of the 1st century, the Church possessed a certain number of books of its own, not inherited from the Synagogue, setting forth its special traditions, its principal claims and its fundamental

that sober Christian thought must approve the position of Dr. Gore when he writes: "We must welcome all the conclusions which are apparently assured, and when we have done so we find that a certain kind of belief about the effect of inspiration which was possible to our forefathers has become impossible for us. We must admit more of gradualness, more of fallibility and individuality in the human instruments, than used to be admitted. But when all this has been done, we dare to maintain that the grounds for believing in a real inspiration by the Holy Spirit of God not only of the prophets and apostles, but also of the writers generally of the Old and New Testaments, are not less strong than before. We have been led by the evidence to limit the scope of the inspiration to 'the things of faith and morals'; and we have been led to recognize degrees of inspiration. We do not find nearly so much of the inspiration of God in Chronicles or Ecclesiastes or Esther as in the prophets. But we do find the movement of the same spirit in all the books. And the longer we put ourselves to school in the books of the Bible the more sure do we feel about the inspiration of their writers." [123]

The seat of authority then in Christianity is two-fold— it is in the New Testament; it is in the Church. It is to be found in the New Testament not because it is a volume which has been miraculously handed down to us from heaven but because it is the only standard or norm for the Christian faith. Without this collection of documents which had its birth out of the heart and life of the Church of Christ in the apostolic age we could not know what Christianity is. Inspired by the Holy Spirit of God and by His guidance, collected into what we today revere as the New Testament, they must forever be the rule and guide to faith.

assumptions, and disclosing the essential lines of its doctrinal development, and of its institutions. This fact is of highest importance; and whatever view we take of controverted details, it is a fact beyond dispute." Duchesne, "The Early History of the Church," I, 110, 111.

[123] "The Holy Spirit and the Church," 267, 268.

The New Testament is authority in Christianity because it alone impresses upon the heart of man the saving revelation of God in Christ. Wernle's trenchant words here come to mind; "The significance of the New Testament consists essentially in this, that it alone hands down to us the words of Jesus and His apostle—from where else could we obtain them? and secures them for all times and so still for us." [124] Would we enter into the mind of Jesus? how else save through those documents which thrill with the glowing life, which flame with the startingly vivid experiences into which those who penned them entered through their communion with Him? Would we be faithful to the voice of the Spirit? "the touchstone of fidelity to the Spirit, the touchstone for true discrimination, is—boldly be it said—in the New Testament and nowhere else." [125] The New Testament is authority also in that it alone tells us what the Church in the apostolic age was, both in form and spirit, and therefore what it ought now to be. Interpreted in the true spirit of history it must ever be the touchstone to which all future supposed developments in doctrine and organization shall be brought to account, because it alone can reveal to us what the Christian faith was in its primitive purity and power.

But the Church too is authority—not as a Hierarchy but as the community of believers, as the body in which the

---

[124] "Beginnings of Christianity," II, 296.

[125] "The Holy Spirit and the Church," Gore, 225. The Roman Catholic argument that the Church created the Bible is clearly refuted by Principal E. Griffith-Jones: "The Church did not create the Bible, any more than the Bible the Church; they were both derived from a common source— the experience of these who came into personal contact with Jesus Christ, and felt the inspiration of His saving personality and work. The Gospels are the memorials of His life and teachings which took shape within the early Church, but were not created by it; the epistles are the literary deposit of the experience of those who were filled with the power of His Holy Spirit, and who, living under the quickening influence of His grace, founded the Church. This reciprocal relation between Church and Bible thus invalidates the claim of the Church to superiority over the Bible as the ultimate revelation of God, and the authentic interpreter of His will. They are coordinates." "Peake's Commentary on the Bible," 7, 8.

Spirit of God abides. It was of authority in the apostolic age in that, under the leading of the Spirit, it unerringly collected those books of the New Testament which were indisputably right—it is of authority today in that, under the leading of the same Spirit, it continues its reverent discrimination. No one now denies that "very early, before the end of the 1st century, the Church possessed a certain number of books of its own, not inherited from the Synagogue, setting forth its special traditions, its principal claims and its fundamental assumptions, and disclosing the essential lines of its doctrinal development, and of its institutions. This fact is of highest importance; and whatever view we take of controverted details, it is a fact beyond dispute." In another connection Duchesne continues, "These books, whatever was their circulation and authority, have this in common, that they were all written for the Church, and that the Church recognized in them the inspiration from which she herself proceeds. They are all esoteric books, spiritual books, fitted to strengthen faith, and to keep alive Christian devotion." [126] It is just in this reverent selection under the continual leading of the Holy Spirit which indwells the Church that the inner consciousness asserts itself—not as individual or isolated but as corporate, the sanctified consciousness of the whole Church, the entire body of believers. The words of Emmet strikingly set forth the modern position and show us how closely to it Campbell, and those who so devotedly labored with him, approximated. "But though it is true that each of us must take the responsibility of forming his own judgement, yet it is equally important to insist that ultimately the individual does not stand alone. The organ which decides on truth is in the last resort the community of which he is a member, the *communis sensus fidelium,* by which we mean agreement of the highest and best trained minds in any field, working over the generations. A decision so reached is slow, and it is

[126] "The Early History of the Church," I, 110, 111.

not at any given moment, or in respect to any given point, infallible, but, in the long run, *securus judicat orbis terrarum.*" This is precisely what we have found Campbell saying. His unswerving confidence in the decisions of the devout mind of the people of God, his unshakable faith that in the positions ultimately reached by this method unity would be secured are but echoed in this noble statement. But Emmet continues; "And it is to this general instinct of the religious community that we owe the Bible. By a gradual and unconscious process of selection, this instinct picked out the best books from their competitors—the best Psalms, for instance, from the Jewish sacred poetry of many centuries, the best Gospels from the various lives of Jesus. When we are able to compare, as we can to some extent in this latter case, or in the case of the Jewish literature which arose subsequently to the Old Testament, we see clearly that this instinct, though not beyond mistake or question, did on the whole work out right. The official stamping of books as canonical was simply the formal endorsement of this instinctive selection. And it is worth noting that the process still goes on, as the Bible is used. The pages of St. John or the Epistle to the Philippians are thumbed, while Chronicles or Esther remain untouched. Whatever be the official rules as to the use of the Psalms, those who are free to choose unconsciously select their favorites, and, within limits, the selection is much the same in all ages and in all classes. It is further of the highest significance that the verdict of the simple devotional reader of the Bible agrees on the whole with the verdict of the professed student, and even of the advanced critic, as to the books and the passages which stand on the highest level of inspiration. The more we abandon external tests of inspiration, the more impressive becomes the fact of the universal appeal of the noblest parts of the Bible to the religious instinct of mankind. It is the same general method that we see at work in the selection of the highest achievements of art or literature, no less than in the sifting of truth from

error. As the mills of judgement grind slowly, so does this
process of testing and sifting. The Spirit of God gives us
no clear-cut information as to what we are to approve or
value most highly. He places no external hall-mark of authenticity on His revelation, yet gradually, but surely, He
trains the divine faculty in man by which he may respond
to the true and beautiful, and sift the gold from the
dross." [127]

[127] "The Psychology of Inspiration" in "The Spirit," 216, 217.

CHAPTER V

THE WAY OF SALVATION

In no phase of their teaching have the Disciples been more justly distinguished than in that which deals with the appropriation of the divine salvation. That which man does in order to enjoy the blessing of foregiveness, they have generally styled, in their literature, "The Plan of Salvation." [1] It is certain that they have made no more permanent contribution to modern Christianity than their clear Scriptural exposition of man's part in his own redemption. Dr. Moore, the best known of modern Disciple historians, agrees with this assertion, when he says: "It is probable that the Disciple advocacy has been more satisfactory at this point than at any other in all their contentions. They certainly have taught the way of salvation from a Scriptural point of view, as no other religious people have done." [2]

It has been customary for Disciple preachers and teachers to arrange the salient points of the Gospel in a series of triads. There are three great facts; the death, the burial, and the resurrection of Christ. There are three great commands; believe in Christ, repent toward Him, be baptized into Him. There are three great promises; the forgiveness of sins, the gift of the Holy Spirit, eternal life. The alien sinner, to inherit the promises, must believe these facts and obey the commands.

[1] Several Disciple teachers have written books in which the appropriation of salvation has been the theme. Some of these works are: "The Gospel Plan of Salvation," T. W. Brents; "The Plan of Salvation," E. V. Zollars; etc. Other such books could be mentioned, but these are sufficient to show that the older Disciples were accustomed to refer to man's part in coming to God as "The Plan of Salvation."

[2] "Comprehensive History of the Disciples of Christ," 65.

The foundation for this analysis of the Gospel plan is to be discovered in the arrangement first made by Walter Scott. After the Campbells, Scott was probably the most scholarly man of the early Disciple movement. Being analytically-minded, he thought much, in the first part of his brilliant evangelistic career, upon the consecutive order appropriate to the various items of the Gospel. The result of this pondering eventually manifested itself in the following arrangements; (1) faith, (2) repentance, (3) baptism, (4) remission of sins, (5) gift of the Holy Spirit. This view of the divine way immediately relieved him of his previous perplexities, and the Gospel appeared to him like a new revelation. He now believed that he had a clue which would extricate the minds of men from the labyrinth in which they were involved in their mystical speculations regarding the subject of conversion. From this time forward, he felt he could proclaim the Gospel message in all its primitive simplicity.[3]

The result of Scott's arrangement of the Gospel items was immediately manifest in the unprecedented success of his evangelistic efforts. The whole Western Reserve was tremendously affected by the new movement. Converts were made by the thousands. The Mahoning Baptist Association came over to the new position with practical unanimity. Abandoning their articles of faith, they agreed to take the Scriptures only as their rule of faith and practice. The reason for such interest can be found only in the simplicity and power of the new message so eloquently preached by Scott.[4] The whole subject of conversion at this time was much befogged by the prevalent mysticism. Man of himself could do nothing. The Holy Spirit worked where he would, and if one were fortunate enough to be in his path, conversion might be the result. Among the Baptists, "Christian Experience" was generally accepted as the only valid evidence of conversion. Thus, the message of Walter Scott

<hr />

[3] "Memoirs of Alexander Campbell," Richardson, II, 208.
[4] "Comprehensive History of the Disciples," Moore, 184, 185.

came like new light from Heaven. He insisted that faith was not doctrinal, but personal—a hearty belief in Jesus Christ as the Son of God. The sinner was called upon to look to Christ alone for salvation, to believe the facts concerning Him as they were recorded in the Apostolic testimony, to obey the commands which were so plainly written, and to enjoy the promises. In an age in which there was so much indefiniteness as to the time when, and the place where, the pentinent believer could be assured of pardon, this clear exposition of the Scriptural way came with convincing power.

There has sometimes been an undeniable tendency among Disciple leaders and probably because of this early influence of Walter Scott, to distinguish sharply between the various steps in the conversion process. This has been done when these steps have been isolated for analysis and exposition. While substantially agreeing with Scott as to the arrangement of the various points in the Gospel plan, Alexander Campbell was wont to consider conversion as one process. The whole process as such, comprehending the various steps, or items, or points—however they may be designated, was in his thinking, faith. The tendency among modern Disciples to think of it in this manner is a reaction from Scott to the position of Campbell.

I

It will be impossible to appreciate the position of Campbell on the "Way of Salvation" without an understanding of the attitudes of Protestants of his own day on the question of conversion, and the background of that attitude. The origin of it is to be found in the notable controversy in regard to the nature of faith, which, during the eighteenth century, had agitated England. A member of John Wesley's famous "Godly Club" at Oxford, James Hervey by name, wrote the "Dialogues between Theron and Aspasic," in which he set forth the Methodist-Moravian conception of faith. As defined by him, "saving faith" is purely an emotional experience in which the "sense of adoption" is brought clearly to the soul of the one seeking salvation. This work also expounded the experimental processes through which the emotional experiences, which he identified with saving faith, were brought about. There are two elements which stand out strikingly in this view: (1) It makes faith solely a state of feeling, rather than an act of the intellect; and (2) it places it at the end of the process of conversion—in reality, makes it an effect of conversion.

There were many replies and vigorous objections to the thesis of Hervey. The opponents of his view may be divided into two classes; those who opposed one, and those who opposed both positions. Robert Sandeman, from whom the well-known Scotch sect of the period derived its name, replied to the work of Hervey, opposing with vigor both parts of his thesis. He maintained that faith is an act of the intellect, and that the assurance of salvation is something distinct from it in consciousness, though depending upon it. The change of heart and feeling which constitutes the "sense of adoption" or the assurance of salvation, is produced by this act through which the truth is comprehended as the belief of testimony. In the order of salvation, therefore, faith is given first place. The position here advocated was adopted also by Archibald McLean, a prominent Scotch Baptist.

The acknowledged leader of the English Baptists of the progressive school, was Andrew Fuller. In his work, "The Gospel Worthy of all Acceptation," he endeavors to present a mediating view between these two positions. Faith is simply the belief of what God has said—a cordial reception as true of what has been revealed to us in the Gospel. The assurance of salvation which comes as an emotional experience, is something quite different from faith, and distinct from it.[5] Thus far, Fuller was in agreement with Sandeman

[5] "The Gospel Worthy of all Acceptation," Sixth American Edition, Cincinnati, 1832; Appendix, 214, 215.

and McLean, but in another and fundamentally important particular, he differed from them. Like Hervey, he believed that regeneration preceded faith.

The mediating position of Andrew Fuller found but few supporters as the controversy went on. The rise and influence of the great Wesleyan revival, emphasizing in a mighty evangelistic wave the Methodist-Moravian position, gradually gave currency to Hervey's position, until the Baptists, abandoning their own Fuller, were found, in the time of Campbell, occupying the Methodist-Moravian ground, both as to the nature and place of faith. Longan states their position: "Like Wesley, they regarded an emotional consciousness of pardon as the very essence of true faith. The point ever more insisted upon, in judging conversion, is the feeling testimony of the forgiveness of sins. 'Do you, my brother or sister, feel that God, for Christ's sake, has pardoned you?,' is a question never omitted. It is not the consciousness of faith, so much as the mystic sense of salvation, which is the uniform criterion of judgement, when the church with open doors, sits for reception of converts into its pale." [6] Such was the Protestant mysticism developed as a reaction against a cold formalism which gave inadequate recognition to the importance of the change of heart, prevailing almost universally at the time Campbell began his work.[7]

Campbell read the leading works of this controversy and acquainted himself thoroughly with the foundational principles of each of the disputants. He succintly relates his experience with the literature of the whole mooted question. "I was once puzzled on the subject of Hervey's dialogues; I mean his Theron and Aspasio. I appropriated one winter season for examining this subject. I assembled all the leading writers of that day on these subjects. I laid before me, Robert Sandeman, Hervey, Marshall, Bellamy, Glass, Cudworth, and others of minor fame in this controversy. I

---

[6] "Origin of the Disciples of Christ," Longan, 61, 62.
[7] "Alexander Campbell's Theology," Dean Garrison, 213, 215.

not only read, but studied and wrote off in miniature their respective views. I had Paul and Peter, and James and John, on the same table; I took nothing on trust. I do not care for the authority, reputation, or standing of one of the systems, a grain of sand. I never weighed the consequences of embracing any one of the systems as affecting my standing or reputation in the world. Truth—not who says so— was my sole object. I found much entertainment in the investigation. And I will not blush, nor do I fear, to say, that in the controversy, Sandeman was like a giant among dwarfs. He was like Sampson with the gates and posts of Gaza upon his shoulders. I was the most prejudiced against him, and the most in favor of Hervey, when I commenced this course of reading. Yet I now believe that not one of them was exactly on the track of the apostles." [8]

Campbell's affinities with, and antipithies to, the positions of the various British divines, will become appearent as a study is made of his own writings on the "way of salvation." That, in certain of their features, his views were similar to those of McLean and the Haldanes, rather than those of Fuller and the school of which he was in reality the founder, is evident. "Regarding the nature of faith, as then debated, he agreed with Sandeman, McLean and Fuller, as they confessedly agreed with each other." [9] As regards the prior relation of regeneration to faith, he was in accord with McLean and the Scotch Baptists, and opposed to Fuller and his followers both in England and America.

With one question he is engrossed in all his writings on the subject of man's appropriation of salvation; when and how does salvation come? Is it before faith, or through faith? Does the grace of God win men through the truth believed? Or, is a regenerating influence necessary before the Gospel is believed, and entirely independent of it? Must a man be regenerated in order to believe, or is it possible for him to

[8] "Christian Baptist," 228.
[9] "Origin of the Disciples of Christ," Longan, 67.

believe without such a miracle being performed? These are
the questions in which the whole battle with the prevalent
Protestant mysticism centered.

II

In endeavoring to give a reasoned exposition of what
Campbell taught regarding the way of salvation, the student
is embarrassed by a wealth of material. On no other phase
of the Christian Revelation did he write so voluminously.
In these herculean efforts to clear up the whole question from
its environing fog, one can understand how illogical, unscriptural, and confusing the prevailing mystical explanations were to his mind.

To this current Protestant mysticism, he opposed what he
considered to be a rational and Scriptural anthropology and
soteriology. One of the glaring weaknesses of the Calvinistic Theology was the fact that some of its most essential
doctrines were based upon a conception of man which was
being constantly weakened by the growing appreciation of
the dignity of the individual. From the time of the Reformation onward, the sense of race unity became weaker while
the worth and dignity of the individual was constantly being
affirmed. With the growth of individualism, such doctrines
as that of inherited original sin, in all its Calvinistic rigors,
became increasingly difficult to explain. Those who were
imbued with the modern idea of the freedom and responsibility of the individual, while they might not categorically
deny the far reaching consequences of Adam's sin, yet found
themselves having little time in their thinking for the fall
and the inherited sin of the race.[10] There was, in a word, a
demand for an anthropology and a soteriology which would
leave a man room to work out his own salvation, and this
demand Campbell met. The influence of the Covenant
Theology on this important Campbellian position, should be
noted in passing. The very fact that salvation is conceived

[10] "Alexander Campbell's Theology," Dean Garrison, 127, 128.

as something in which man himself has a part, was a fundamental idea in the positions of the Covenant Theologians. For the idea of absolute divine grace operating on a man who is entirely impotent either to accept or repel its advances, they substituted the conception of salvation as a covenant. A covenant involves the thought that man has a part to perform in the relationship—that he can, therefore, make a difference in his own salvation.[11]

When we turn more directly to the teaching of Campbell on the way of salvation, we are struck by the fact that the so-called steps in conversion form one unbroken process. This is clearly set forth in his teaching concerning the nature of faith. Man is capable of believing the Gospel. His whole conception of the method by which man appropriates the divine blessing of foregiveness, rests upon this anthropology. With clarity he states his position: "The Book of God is addressed to the human understanding. It assumes that man, though fallen and depraved, is yet an intelligent being—that he has certain faculties or powers of ascertaining truth, of perceiving and receiving evidence. It does not, indeed, inform him that he has the faculty of seeing, hearing, speaking, or believing. It does not explain to him that the possession of a faculty or power to do anything, makes it his duty to employ that faculty or power in any way his Creator may require. But it addresses him as though these were matters perfectly understood and agreed upon between his Creator and himself."[12] Squarely he takes issue with the current mysticism in another unmistakable pronouncement. "We, therefore, conclude that God never would have spoken to man, if man could not hear him. The fact, then, that God has given to the world a revelation, is, with me, a demonstration that man has the power to believe it—provided only, his heart and attention are devoted to it."[13]

---

[11] *Ibid.*, 136, 137.

[12] "Christian Baptism," 63.

[13] *Ibid.*, 64. Heaven takes the initiative in our salvation. Compare Otto's eloquent statement: "Whoever sinks in contemplation of that great

Resting confidently upon such an anthropology, he proceeds to define the nature of faith. He begins by calling attention to the meaning of Fact. A fact is something done. "The work of redemption is a system of works, or deeds, on the part of Heaven, which constitute the most splendid series of moral facts which man or angel ever saw. And they are the proof, the argument, or the demonstration, of that regenerating proposition which presents God and Love as two names for the same idea." [14] The facts of the life, death, resurrection, and ascension of Jesus, and the Apostolic interpretation of these facts, while at first presented in oral testimony, are now mediated to us through the written word, the New Testament. Faith consists in crediting these facts: "To admit the testimony to be true, is, in the sacred style, equivalent to believing it; for he that believeth the testimony of God has simply 'set to his seal that God is true.' Faith, indeed, is always but the conviction of the truth of testimony, whether that testimony be human or divine. To be convinced that any testimony or report is true, is to believe it; to be convinced that it is not true, is to disbelieve it; not to be able to decide, is to doubt. Hence there are but three states of mind as regards testimony. We believe, disbelieve, or doubt it." [15] After a vigorous discussion of the power of testimony as residing in the power of the facts narrated, he

---

connected development of the Judaic religion which we speak of as 'the old covenant up to Christ' must feel the stirrings of an intimation that something Eternal is there, directing and sustaining it and urging it to its consummation. The impression is simply irresistible. And whoever then goes on to consider how greatly the scene is set for the completion of the whole story and the mighty stature of the personality that is its fulfillment, his firm, unfaltering hold upon God, his unfailing, unwavering righteousness, his certitude of conviction and assurance in action so mysterious and profound, his spiritual fervour and beatitude, the struggles and trustfulness, self-surrender and suffering, and finally the conqueror's death that were his—whoever goes on to consider all this must inevitably conclude: 'That is god-like and divine; that is verily Holiness. If there is a God and if He chose to reveal Himself, He could do it no otherwise than thus.' " "The Idea of the Holy," 174.

[14] "Christian System," 111.
[15] "Christian Baptism," 64, 65.

concludes: "No testimony; no faith; for faith is only the belief of testimony, or confidence in testimony as true. To believe without testimony is just as impossible as to see without light. The measure, quality, and power of faith are always found in the testimony believed. Where testimony begins, faith begins; where testimony ends, faith ends." [16]

His Lockianism shows itself clearly in this position. Since we receive all our knowledge of the external world, through the five senses, so we derive all our acquaintance with other facts through testimony. Faith, then, in its beginnings, is really equivalent to an extension of sense perception. It will be shown later, however, that his Lockianism applies only to the beginnings of faith. It is not fair to him to say he held to this as a comprehensive definition.

Since faith is the credence of testimony concerning historical facts, there can be but one kind of faith—historical faith. The definitions of faith by the speculative theologians, into "saving faith, historical faith, the faith of miracles, the faith of devils," etc., are but the conceits of such theologians. "There is no faith worth anything that is not historical; for all our religion is based upon history." [17]

The power of faith is not to be found in the manner of believing, nor in the sincerity of the acceptance of the facts. It is not in the act of believing, but in the proposition believed, that the power to save resides. It is not eating that saves the life, but that which is eaten. Some eat and live, while others eat and die. So it is with faith. Its power or efficacy does not "depend upon the act or manner of believ-

---

[16] "Christian System," 113. Cf. Professor Flint's statement: "Nothing, then is to be received as true without sufficient evidence. The great and comprehensive duty of man as to belief is to believe and disbelieve according to evidence and neither to believe nor disbelieve when evidence fails him." "Agnosticism," 426, "All belief ought to be reasonable. We have no right to believe what we do not know to be true. Evidence should be the measure of assent. Assent should be in proportion to evidence," 456.

[17] "Christian Baptism," 70.

ing, nor upon the certainty of the evidence, nor even upon the assurance of its truth, as upon the nature or value of the thing that is believed. The power of faith is in the truth believed. The power of faith is in the power of truth." [18] The saving proposition is that Jesus is the Christ, the Son of the living God. Through him we know that the Father is love and that He desires us to be His. The belief of this proposition and the hearty obedience to what it implies, will make a man a Christian.

Faith is not a shrewd transaction by which we merit forgiveness. It is not by accepting as true the testimony regarding the Christ, that we earn salvation. If this were true, faith would itself become a work. And this is exactly the case when men rely upon the manner of believing, for their acceptance with God. It is for this reason that Campbell constantly sets forth the fact that it is in what we believe, that we appropriate the gracious salvation which the Father has made possible for us. "It is through faith, and not on account of faith, as though there was in faith some intrinsic merit." [19]

Since the beginning of faith is the beginning of testimony, it is generated in a very natural manner. Here, once more, he comes to grips with the mysticism of his day. Men were taught that faith is a gift of God in a miraculous sense. Hence, they could pray for it, or agonize about it, until some glad hour came in which God vouchsafed unto them a glorious religious experience. The recitals of some of these so-called religious experiences were not only absurd in the extreme, but positively disgusting. One of the most potent causes of the wide-spread unbelief of the time, was this iron-clad requirement for an emotional "Christian experience" and the relating of such, many times ridiculous experiences,

---

[18] *Ibid.*, 71. This is a favorite doctrine of Herrmann. He speaks of the "fact that in the Christ of history God so touches each one of us that we may apprehend His reality and comprehend His love." "Communion With God," 197, 198. See also page 97.

[19] "Christian Baptism," 279.

in congregational meetings.[20] In opposition to this prevalent
error, Campbell affirmed that faith comes by hearing the
word of God. If a man wants faith, he must put aside his
blinding prejudices and attend with open mind to the divine
testimony. If the testimony is sufficient, one will believe—
he cannot help but believe. "No person can help believing
when sufficient evidence is presented, and no man can believe without evidence. Such is the constitution of the human mind that a man is as passive in believing as he was in
receiving his name, or as the eye in receiving the rays of
light that fall upon it from the sun; consequently no man
can help believing when the evidence of truth arrests his
attention." [21]   This is an extreme statement, but he was
driven to it in his combat with the extreme views of the day.
It was intended to emphasize the fact that there is no need
of an exercise of divine power in order to create faith within
the heart, nor was any such interposition to be expected. It
was, therefore, useless to pray for faith. The fact that one
prayed for faith, was itself evidence of some faith on the
part of the one offering the prayer. Such was the importance
of a correct understanding of the manner of faith's coming,
in the thinking of Campbell, that we quote him liberally,
once more, on this point. "So true it is, that all our ideas
of the sensible universe are the result of sensation and reflection. All the knowledge we have of material nature has
been acquired by the exercise of our senses and our reason
upon these discoveries. With regard to the supernatural
knowledge, or the knowledge of God, that comes wholly 'by
faith,' and 'faith' itself 'comes by hearing!' This aphorism
is divine. Faith is, therefore, a consequence of hearing, and
hearing is an effect of speaking; for, hearing comes by the
Word of God spoken, as much as faith itself comes by hearing. The intellectual and moral arrangement is, therefore—

[20] Williams describes some of these experiences, and relates the de-
pressing effect of them on John Smith, who was earnestly "seeking salvation." Smith became one of the outstanding Disciple evangelists in Kentucky. "Life of Elder John Smith," 63, 54.
[21] "Christian Baptist," 142, 143.

1. The Word spoken; 2. Hearing; 3. Believing; 4. Feeling; 5. Doing. Such is the constitution of the human mind—a constitution divine and excellent, adapted to man's position in the universe. It is never violated in the moral government of God. Religious action is uniformly the effect of religious feeling; that is the effect of faith; that of hearing; and that of something spoken by God." [22] Here his familiar Lockianism once more asserts itself, not only as the foundation of the meaning of faith as the belief of testimony, but as to the manner of its coming, as well.

We have already hinted at the fact, that in his practical application of it to the religious life, faith was far more to him than the mere credence of testimony. The strictures which have sometimes been directed at him, on the score that his definition is incomplete, have failed to take into account a mode of thought, peculiar to him, in which he frequently includes effects with causes, in a manner not conducive to preciseness of definition. When he speaks of faith as the credence of testimony, he really means belief. Modern theologians have recognized the difference between belief and faith; they are not synonymous. [23] Practically, Camp-

---

[22] "Christian Baptism," 293.

[23] See, Clarke "An Outline of Christian Theology," 403. Dean Paterson recognizes this difference when he says in his Gifford Lectures, "It is the general doctrine of the New Testament that faith is the primary condition of the Christian salvation. This faith involves belief, or the assent of the mind, but it was essentially trust in the gracious God who was revealed by Christ, or in the Christ in whom God was revealed." "The Nature of Religion," 408. Professor Flint also writes of this distinction. Christian faith "is not mere belief, nor mere belief in religious truth, nor even mere belief in Christian truth. It is a self-surrendering acceptance of Christ as of God made wisdom, righteousness, sanctification, and redemption unto us; a supreme trust in Christ based on a distinctive conviction as to His character and His relation alike to God and man. Mere belief is, indeed, sometimes spoken of in the New Testament by the same name as faith but it is always in such cases so spoken of as to indicate that it is not the faith which the Gospel demands but a dead and unprofitable faith such as even the most wicked of beings may have. Faith in its distinctively Christian sense implies the action of all the fundamental powers and affections of the human spirit. It contains in germ the whole Christian life, being a turning away from darkness to life, from sin to righteousness, from self to God manifested in and through Christ." "Agnosticism," 431, 432. See also, 435, 436.

bell also realized this difference and frequently speaks of it.
"Faith in Christ is the effect of belief. Belief is the cause;
and trust, confidence, or faith in Christ, the effect." [24] The
acceptance of the Gospel as true is belief, the beginning of
that whole process of trusting obedience to Christ, of that
whole attitude of the soul to Christ, which is faith. "And
what is Christian faith? It is a belief of testimony. It is a
persuasion that God is true; that the Gospel is divine; that
God is love; that Christ's death is the sinner's life. It is
trust in God. It is a reliance upon His truth, His faithful-
ness, His power. It is not merely a cold assent to truth, to
testimony; but a cordial, joyful consent to it, and reception
of it." [25] In this passage he speaks of both belief and faith,
though he engrosses it all under the latter designation. It
is the belief of testimony which eventuates in that life of
moral unity with Christ, which is the life of faith. Since it
is trust, it is personal, and not alone intellectual or doctrinal.
"Now the belief of what Christ says of Himself, terminates
in confidence or trust in Him; and as the Christian religion
is a personal thing, both as respects subject and object, that
faith in Christ which is essential to salvation, is not the
belief of any doctrine, testimony, or truth, abstractly, but
belief in Christ; trust or confidence in Him as a person, not
a thing." [26] Such statements as the foregoing ought forever
to absolve Campbell of the charge of being purely an intel-
lectualist, as regards faith. In his conception of faith as
comprehending the whole conversion process, he rises definitely above his philosophical foundation. His Lockianism
was insufficient here, and, as he frequently does in other
positions, he deliberately forsakes it for loftier heights.
Dean Garrison's appreciation of his attitude is pertinent:
"When faith is isolated for definition, it is conceived in
purely an intellectual form as the acquisition of information
through testimony, the acceptance of certain propositions as
true. Applying strictly this theological definition, the ob-

[24] "Christian System," 52.
[25] "Christian Baptism," 293.
[26] "Christian System," 53.

ject of faith is certainly not a person but statements about a person. Campbell's Lockian conception of faith stopped here. But he saw at once that, considering faith not as an isolated mental act, but as the first step in the change of the whole man, the acceptance of a certain proposition about Jesus led immediately to a certain attitude of the person toward him as a person. For religious purposes, the object of faith is the person of Jesus in whom the believer is to trust as Saviour. But the theological definition seldom gets beyond the assertion that faith in Jesus is the acceptance of a certain proposition about him. It can be said, therefore, that, as regards the conception of faith, his theological position was a thorough intellectualism, but the practical application of that intellectualism was to counteract a deteriorated Protestant mysticism, and in its highest religious uses it issues in a lofty conception of faith as trust in a person." [27]

As a further illustration of the manner in which he transcends his Lockian intellectualism, we may note two passages, beautiful in their spiritual insight and power. "Faith indeed is but the hand that apprehends and appropriates Christ as revealed to us by the Holy Spirit sent down from heaven. Salvation, then, is of faith, that it might be by grace. For as the hand that plucks the fruit is not the fruit, is not that which either creates or sustains life, but only that which ministers to its development and preservation— so faith's sublime efficacy is not in itself, but in that which it receives and appropriates to the soul of man, in which alone is the spring and fountain of eternal life." [28] Faith is an attitude of the whole man. It is the reliance of a sinner upon the divine person, for all that is salvation. "The head, the heart, the will, the conscience are all simultaneously exercised in the act of believing in order to justification. The head alone believes nothing. Nor does the heart, the will, the conscience alone believe anything. The

[27] "Alexander Campbell's Theology," Dean Garrison, 225, 226.
[28] "Christian Baptist," 73.

understanding simply discerns truth, the conscience recognizes authority, the heart feels love, the will yields to requisition. The Gospel engages, interests, allures, captivates, the enlightened sinner. So that 'with his heart,' his whole soul, 'he believeth unto righteousness, and with his mouth he confesses to salvation.' " [29] There is nothing finer in the theology of Alexander Campbell, than his insistence upon faith as personal rather than doctrinal. Salvation can never be by faith in Christologies; it must be in Him as personal Redeemer and Saviour.

III

The position accorded by Campbell to repentance, in the scheme of redemption, is unique. Not only in his definition of it, but also in the relationship it sustains to faith, did he differ radically from the theologians of his time. It was customary to think of repentance as the first step in conversion. It must be confessed that Campbell is not a follower of Schleiermacher. He is more a disciple of Abelard than of Anslem or Bernard. More strikingly still he is pre-Ritschlian. There are some truly startling affinities between these two men who lived almost at the same period, although Ritschl's work was done a few years later than that of Campbell. With him Ritschl believed (*Justification and Reconciliation*) that repentance is the result of faith, it is included in faith, it is faith itself turning to God (166, 167). The heart of faith is love (591, 593). They were in cordial agreement in regard to the manner of faith's coming. It is evoked by the Gospel, and does not depend upon a preceding "conflict of penitence," which the sinner experiences as he realizes his condemnation under the law (110; 164, 165). The sinner, stirred to contrition by the preaching of the Gospel, experienced an emotional change which was called a change of heart. After this he threw himself into the loving arms of divine mercy, in faith. As we have al-

[29] *Ibid.*, 69.

ready noted, faith was thus placed at the end of the conversion process. But, to Campbell, this arrangement was arbitrary and illogical. Viewed from the standpoint, of the mysticism of his day, which made faith a state of feeling at the end of that whole process which was called conversion, and something for which the sinner must wait, often through a long period of fear and agonizing, until it should please God graciously to grant it to him, repentence was a sorrow which could find no immediate issues in reformation of life. This attitude of his day must be kept in mind, if one would understand his continual insistence upon the importance of the relation of repentance to faith. It also underlies his sometimes questionable rendering of μετανοέω "to reform," and that repentance is, therefore, a reformation of life.

Repentance is related to faith as fruit to the tree which bears it. He writes of that " 'repentance unto life' which God has granted unto the nations as the fruit of their faith in the divinely authenticated proposition that 'Jesus is the Messiah, the Son of God.' " [30] In one connection he speaks of the "necessity of faith as 'the foundation of repentance from dead works.' " [31] Here the metaphor is changed a little, but the meaning of the relation remains the same. In another unmistakable passage, he even more forcibly employs the same illustration. "Still it is needful to press still farther upon the attention of the reader that faith is truly 'the foundation of repentance from dead works,' as testimony is the foundation of faith." [32] "Repentance is an effect of faith: for who that believes not that God exists, can have 'repentance toward God.' " [33] "Repentance, indeed, antecedent to faith, to me, appears impossible; for how could anyone repent of sin against God, if he did not believe that he had sinned against God! And how could the mercy of God afford any encouragement to repentance unless that

[30] "Christian Baptism," 76.
[31] *Ibid.*, 80.
[32] "Christian Baptism," 84.
[33] "Christian System," 53.

mercy is reported to us and believed! So, then, repentance comes by faith, as faith by hearing, as hearing by the Word of God. As no one could hear God unless God had first spoken, and as no one could believe a message which he had never heard, so no one could repent of sin, as respects God, who has not first believed in his mercy." [34] Such statements as these are self-explanatory. It is interesting to note, in passing, how he connects up the whole plan into a process in which it is almost impossible to isolate, for analysis, one step from the rest. In his debate with Rice, he speaks of the relation under another figure, and also emphasizes the continuity and oneness of the various items of the whole Gospel plan. "Repentance is, however, but the adjunct of faith, as the remission of sins is of baptism. In preaching repentance and remission, according to Luke, the apostle must therefore have preached faith, repentance, baptism, and remission; for all these terms, or their equivalents, are found in the three versions of the commission now quoted." [35] Repentance is of faith; it is faith turning away from sin to accept all that the love of God as given in Christ and uniquely in His death upon the cross, means. It is faith in action. It cannot be divorced from faith and set off by itself; its very essence is faith, and the essence of faith is love. As love is the moving power of faith, so faith, thus constituted, is the motive power of that turning away from unrighteousness to God and His way of life.

With the relationship between faith and repentance thus defined, it is evident that a reformation of life could immediately follow. When we come, then, to his definition of the nature of repentance, and knowing his liability to an inclusion of effects with causes, in many of his definitions, we are not surprised to find him speaking of it as "reformation of life." The etymological foundation for his position is to be found in the meaning of the two Greek words which in our English versions, are translated "repent." One,

[34] "Christian Baptism," 80, 81.
[35] "Campbell-Rice Debate," 432.

μετανοέω [36] means a "change of mind or will which eventuates in reformation." The other, μεταμέλομαι means "a sorrow or regret for sin," but "without respect to a change of affections or conduct of an individual," and "is never found in connection with faith, or any of the Gospel facts reported in the Christian records." [37] The proper use of this word is found in the case of Judas who is said to have repented. But his repentance had no respect to any change in his life. God never uses this word in any of his commands requiring repentance. No one is ever commanded to repent in the style of Judas. "Repentance is sorrow for sins committed; but it is more. It is a resolution to forsake them; but it is more. It is actual 'ceasing to do evil, and learning to do well.' It is not merely, Be sorry for what you have done wrong; nor is it, Resolve to do better; nor even, Try to mend your ways; but it is actual amendment of life from the views and the motives which the Gospel of Christ exhibits. Gospel repentance is the offspring of Gospel light and Gospel motive, and therefore, it is the effect, and not the cause of belief of the testimony of God." [38] In speaking of Peter's Pentecostal sermon and his command to the conscience-stricken Jews to repent, Campbell says: "The profession of repentance without reformation or fruits worthy of it, they were clearly informed, would avail nothing. So evident is it that their contemporaries understood by the precept 'repent' what we associate with the word 'reform.'" [39] Because he did not believe in the emotional extravagances which were almost universally considered to be repentance, he was frequently accused of not believing in repentance at all. Against this accusation he defends himself: "It is not,

[36] In "The Living Oracles" which was universally referred to as "Campbell's Translation," Campbell translated the word μετανοέω, "to reform." This translation, as that of Βαπτίζω, by "immerse" was not widely popular although the work had a large influence, especially among the Disciples.

[37] "Christian Baptism," 77.

[38] "Christian System," 53, 54.

[39] "Christian Baptism," 79.

as often insinuated, because I have any objection to repentance, properly so-called; for, with me, repentance, or a
change of mind, or regret for the past, must always precede
reformation.   Reformation both presupposes or comprehends penitence in its biblical acceptation. I desire to see
the broken and contrite heart as the prelude of effectual
repentance; that is, reformation of behaviour." [40]

It is evident that he was influenced in his manifestly extreme definition of the nature of repentance, by the radical
emotionalism which was the prevalent concomitant of the
conversions of his time.   Such emotional manifestations
were considered as themselves constituting repentance. It
was against this distorted and dangerous view that he loosed
his thunders. In his eagerness to emphasize those things
which count most—the renewal of the life, and its conformity to the beautiful divine pattern, he went to the
lengths of including that which is the work of a lifetime,
sanctification itself, with the change which is but the beginning. When we remember, however, that, to him, conversion was one unbroken process, that "being saved" was all
that is comprehended in the life of faith, salvation could
be—indeed it must be, a life effort.

Genuine repentance means also restitution. The man
who truly turns away from his vain manner of life, will, so
far as possible, make good the wrong he has done. This
phase of repentance was much insisted upon by the earlier
Disciple preachers. Their sermons are full of exhortations
not only to turn from sin, but to repair the damage done, as
an evidence of good faith.

Opposing the current conception that God grants repentance and faith as a purely miraculous gift, Campbell shows
what is meant by the Scriptural phrase. "To 'grant repentance,' is, then, to make room for the advantage of a change
of views concerning Him—a change of feeling or heart to
Him—a change of conduct toward Him. It is to make possible a plenary remission of sins to all who are truly sorry

[40] "Campbell-Rice Debate," 495.

for their sins, and, forsaking them, turn to the Lord." [41]
To "grant repentance" is to provide those means which
evoke repentance. In the sacrifice of His Son on Calvary,
God has provided the greatest moral force in the world, to
bring man to a realization of his own sinfulness, to stir up
within him a desire to forsake it, for that righteousness
which is the life in Christ. It is not that God gives repentance as one might lodge a certain commodity in the soul. It
is not something infused. He grants it, in that he provides
all the means which bring it into being. [42]

In two eloquent passages, he sums up his exposition of the
meaning of "repentance unto life." "Thus we are led, step
by step, up to the apprehension of 'repentance unto life.'
Such a repentance implies, because it requires, an antecedent
faith in some proposition having life in it; for the life is not
in the repentance, but in that to which it leads. The life is
purposed as the end, while repentance is but the means to
attain it. Yet are they inseparably connected; for this life
is not without repentance, nor this repentance without life.
Views there are, in the faith, and motives inspired by it,
which, when perceived and possessed, work this mysterious
and sublime change. It is light that makes manifest everything. Yet light is very different from the things manifested by it. It is the truth developed in the great proposition that God is, by Christ, reconciling a world to Himself,
not imputing to men their trespasses, but beseeching them
to be reconciled to Him, because He has made His Son a
sin offering for us, that we might be made perfectly righteous
through Him. Now, all this is comprehended in that cardinal proposition, on the belief of which the Lord promised to
build His church, viz.;—that 'Jesus is the Messiah, the Son
of the living God.' It is this sublime proposition, apprehended and realized by faith, that works repentance unto
life; that subdues, softens, pacifies, and reconciles the heart
to God, and prepares it to be a temple of the Holy Spirit." [43]

[41] "Christian Baptism," 87, 88.
[42] Ibid., 82.
[43] "Christian Baptism," 85, 86.

In another passage closely related to this, he reaches the loftiest heights in his conception of faith and repentance as being a vitally personal thing, and not a mere reliance upon doctrinal propositions for acceptance with God. "This is the cardinal element in the Gospel which contains in it the principles of eternal life. Christ, indeed, is our life. 'Our life is hid with Christ in God.' But to us, Christ is first presented in the testimony concerning Him; then He is in the faith of him that believes that testimony; then in his heart He becomes the 'hope of glory,' and, finally, in His life of righteousness and holiness, He is manifested to the world. This, indeed, constitutes 'a reformation not to be repented of.' " [44]

In a discussion of the meaning of the death of Christ in its relation to our faith, he sets forth the influence of the sin-bearing love of the Master in its power to evoke faith and penitence in our hearts. With a liberal quotation from this passage, it would be well to conclude our consideration of his teaching on the subject of repentance. After speaking of the necessity for an understanding of the nature of the death of Christ as an atoning sacrifice, he says: "That is the radiating center of the whole remedial system. It is in that we discover all the divine excellencies. It is there, and only there, that inflexible justice, immaculate purity, inviolate truth, and infinite mercy, appear in perfect harmony with each other, combining all their effulgence and glory in opening for us a way into the holiest of all. Beholding there, as in a reflecting mirror, the purity of God and our own deformity; the majesty of His government and the dignity of His law; the malignity and hatefulness of sin, in contrast with the beauty and loveliness of holiness, righteousness, and truth, we are changed into the same image from glory to glory, by the Spirit of the Lord. Thus, contemplating Him whom our sins have pierced, we begin to mourn over them; we prostrate ourselves before His throne of mercy, and, with the humble and penitent publi-

[44] "Christian Baptism," 86.

can, we say: 'God be merciful to me a sinner.' Such is that repentance unto life which God, through Jesus Christ, has granted to the Jew and to the Greek." [45] A statement such as this is defense enough against the charge that Campbell was purely intellectual in his attitude toward the means through which the sinner appropriates forgiveness.

IV

In the Disciple conception of the way of salvation, faith and repentance are further objectified in a public confession. It has been, for more than a hundred years, the custom in each Church of Christ in America for a Gospel invitation to be extended at the close of every sermon. This is true of the morning as well as the evening service. While this custom is not followed in the morning service in Great Britian and Australasia, it is quite generally observed at the evening meetings. In this invitation men are urged to come forward and confess their faith in Christ as Lord. This confession is accepted as evidence of the fact that the one making it heartily believes Jesus to be the Christ, the Son of the living God, and that he has sincerely repented of his sins. Upon such a confession, the candidate for membership in the church is baptized. In a word, the confession of faith is considered evidence of conversion and readiness for entrance into Christ's Church. The confession is primarily a confession of faith. It has nothing to do with opinions, but it is an expression publicly made, of faith in the person who alone can save. It is only in a secondary sense, a confession of sin. The Disciples have taken the references which exhort to the confession of sins to each other, as having application essentially to the Church. In the confession of faith there is a confession of sinfulness, but this is not the fundamental reason for the confession being made.

[45] *Ibid.*, 86, 87.

While the Disciples have written largely, and have spoken much, upon the meaning and necessity of the confession of faith, Campbell did not say as much about it, as he did concerning the other so-called steps in the divine way. In his practice, he always demanded a confession from those who were to be baptized. He does refer to it in several instances. The confession respects the dignity of the person and office of the Messiah. Of these two ideas "the one asserts His divine relations, the other His official rank and glory." [46] The belief of the truth expressed in the words of the confession, and a cordial obedience to the one thus confessed, will make a man a Christian. This confession is also that upon which the Church was builded. It is an efficient bond of union. In it alone, can Christ's Church remain one. "When all societies build upon this one foundation, and on it only, then shall there be unity of faith, of affection and of cooperation; but never till then. Every other foundation is sand. Hence, they have all wasted away. Innumerable parties have perished from the earth; and so will all the present built on any other foundation than this rock." [47]

In the conversion process, faith still further objectifies itself in baptism. Campbell's teaching on the subject of baptism will be exhaustively considered in another connection. The only reason for attending to it here, is that he, and the Disciples universally, have ever considered it as one act on the way to salvation. There is no blinking the fact that the Disciples have emphasized the teaching, that in the New Testament no promise of remission of sins, or acceptance with God, is given, until after baptism. In nothing have they been more misunderstood than in this position. As a part of the "plan," then, it will be considered here.

Campbell speaks of the so-called steps in the way of salvation, and among them includes baptism. "It will again

[46] "Christian System," 58, 59.
[47] "Campbell-Rice Debate," 821.

fall in our path to hear and contemplate the connection between faith, repentance, baptism, and the remission of sins. Meantime it will suffice to say that all the links of that golden chain of grace which connects and binds our souls to the throne of God, are most intimately connected with one another." [48] The process of conversion is one process, and baptism is an act in it, through which the gracious forgiveness of the Father is appropriated. In his debate with Rice, the whole plan, as he conceived it, and as the Disciples from that day have proclaimed it, is rapidly reviewed. "We preach in the words of that book, the gospel, as promulgated by the apostles in· Jerusalem. We use in all important matters, the exact words of inspiration. We command all men to believe, repent and bring forth fruits worthy of reformation. We enjoin the same good works commanded by the Lord and His apostles. We receive men of all denominations under heaven, of all sects and parties, who will make the good confession of the faith, in the identical words of inspiration, so that they who avow it express a divine faith and build upon a consecrated foundation—a well-tried cornerstone. On a sincere confession of this faith, we immerse all persons, and then present them with God's own book of faith, piety and morality. This is our most obnoxious offense against the partyism of this age." [49] There is no other statement in Disciple literature, which better sets forth the Disciple procedure in receiving men into the church, than this one. There is no clearer résumé of what they have always considered the manward side of the conversion process.

As regards the place which baptism occupies in the divine scheme of forgiveness, it is an act of faith. It is not something which comes after man's acceptance by the Father, a plus, as it were; it is faith itself in action. As repentance is faith turning away from sin to God, so baptism is faith

[48] "Christian Baptism," 88.
[49] "Campbell-Rice Debate," 784, 785.

and repentance confessing before the world, in an act which at the same time pictures the grand saving facts of the Gospel—the death, burial and resurrection of Christ. It is not a work of the law, such as came under the fierce condemnation of Paul. No man can earn salvation simply by complying with an outward act. It derives all its significance from the relation which it holds to faith. "Baptism without faith is of no value whatever, for in truth, baptism is but the actual and symbolic profession of faith. It is its legitimate embodiment and consummation. And whatever virtue there is in it, or connected with it, is but the virtue of faith in the blood of Christ applied to the conscience and the heart." [50] It is doubtful if he could express his position more concisely or with greater clarity unless it be in another passage in the same discussion. "Baptism is, therefore, no work of law, no moral duty, no moral righteousness, but a simple putting on of Christ and placing ourselves wholly in His hand and under His guidance. It is an open, sensible, voluntary expression of our faith, to which, we being thus perfected, the promise of remission of sins is divinely annexed. In one word, it is faith perfected." [51]

The conception which he held regarding the so-called steps in the way of salvation in their inter-relations, may be summed up in a sentence. Faith is that belief in God through Jesus Christ, broad enough, deep enough, and high enough, to prompt one to do what the Father would have him do. It is that process in which belief is transmuted into action, into conduct, in conformity with the Christly pattern. "It was not Abel's faith in his head or heart, but Abel's faith at the altar, which obtained such reputation. It was not Enoch's faith in principle, but Enoch's faith in his walk with God, which translated him to heaven. It was not Noah's faith in God's promise and threatening, but his faith exhibited in building an ark, which saved himself and family

[50] "Christian Baptism," 285.
[51] *Ibid.*, 284.

from the deluge, and made him an heir of a new world, an heir of righteousness. It was not Abraham's faith in God's call, but his going out in obedience to that call, that first distinguished him as a pilgrim, and began his reputation. It was not faith in God's promise that Jericho should fall, but that faith carried out in the blowing of ram's horns, which laid its walls in ruin, etc. It is not our faith in God's promise of redemption, but our going down into the water, that obtains the remission of sins." [52]

V

Having considered the great principles in the way of salvation, as Campbell conceived them, we may proceed to a brief study of the illustration of these principles, under the various analogical terms employed in the New Testament. Religious truth must often be expressed in terms which reflect human relations. In such cases, "no good interpreter would think of considering truth, so defined, as precisely scientific." [53]   No one would reject such terms as false or misleading just because they are of this character. Frequently, they are more concrete and realistic than more abstract language would be. Such terms are often employed by Paul. The word "justification" is an illustration. It is a forensic term; about it there is the atmosphere of the law court. But into it, Paul pressed the Christian idea of forgiveness. His use of it was an effective instrument in his mighty battles with the Judaizers. Such terminology was native to their thinking. Under the form of this term, then, Paul brings the fundamental Christian idea of salvation.

To Alexander Campbell, such terms as justification, sanctification, adoption, etc., were analogical terms—terms into which as much as possible of the great Christian idea of salvation, might be compressed. Such expressions illustrated

[52] "Christian System," 232.
[53] "The Theology of the New Testament," Stevens, 421.

from different standpoints, the new state of foregiveness into which the justified or saved man had come. Since they are but different ways in which the happy results of the great salvation are analogically set forth, they are instantaneous and not successive acts. "Justification, santification, and adoption are instantaneous acts of Divine grace, and are simultaneous, not successive acts, as more than half our pulpits and presses in Christendom, preach and teach. They are, on the contrary, both instantaneous and concomitant, or contempory acts of Divine grace." [54] Of course, such teaching provoked immediate and indignant protest from the theologians of his day. The majority of them held to the theory that these illustrative terms represented successive acts, i.e., that a man was first converted, and then, after a wait, through prayer and agonizing, he was justified, and still later on, was sanctified. Their grave errors consisted in considering these terms as illustrative of states of character, whereas, they really represent a new religious state or condition. Confuting such contentions, Campbell says: "Regeneration, conversion, justification, sanctification, etc., are frequently represented as component parts of one process; whereas any one of these, independent of the others, gives full representation of the subject. Is a man regenerated? He is converted, justified and regenerated. With some system-builders, however, regeneration is an instantaneous act, between which and conversion there is a positive, substantive interval; next comes justification; and then in some still future time, sanctification." [55]

It must be borne in mind that, in speaking as he does in the foregoing passage, he refers to the religious change which comes with conversion. These analogical terms refer only indirectly to the ethical transformation which is one phase of sanctification. From this standpoint, we can appreciate his position, when he writes: "We are constrained to admit that

[54] "Millennial Harbinger," Volume XXIX for 1869, 62.
[55] "Millennial Harbinger," Volume XXIX for 1869, 83.

a change in any one of these states necessarily implies, because it involves, a change in all the others. Everyone who is pardoned is justified, sanctified, reconciled, adopted, and saved; and so everyone that is saved, is adopted, reconciled, sanctified, justified and pardoned." [56]

The distinction between state and character, in understanding the significance of the various terms which in the New Testament are used to illustrate the plan of salvation, was frequently and forcibly insisted upon. Childhood is a state, manhood is a state, marriage is a state. A person in a state of childhood may sometimes act like one in the state of manhood, or a person in the state of manhood may have the character of a child. A person in the state of a son may have the character of a servant. Parents and children, master and servants, husbands and wives, etc., are terms denoting relations or states. A person may enter into a state of matrimony, and yet act unworthly of it. There is a great difference between being in a state, and acting in accordance with that state or relation." [57]

A favorite Campbellian illustration of how a change of state in one regard implies a change in all the others, was found in the marriage relation. "A female changes her state. She enters into the state of matrimony. So soon as she has surrendered herself to the affectionate government and control of him who has become her husband, she has not only become a wife, but a daughter, a sister, an aunt, a niece, etc., and may stand in many other relations in which she before stood not. All these are connected with her becoming the wife of a person who stands in many relations. So when a person becomes Christ's, he is a son of Abraham, an heir, a brother, or is pardoned, justified, sanctified, reconciled, adopted, and saved." [58]

[56] Extra on "Remission of Sins," July 5, 1830, in "Millennial Harbinger Abridged," Smith, Volume I, 502.

[57] "Christian System," 187.

[58] "Christian System," 188.

VI

The way of salvation may be illustrated by a brief study of justification. It might just as well have been reconciliation, for under different figures, the same great process is analogically explained. Justification is defined as that state into which the forgiven man is received, in which, though he has offended, he is treated as if he were righteous. He is received back into the cordial favor of the Father. While the term is juridical, yet the state is personal. Treated as righteous, he is received back to the paternal heart and into the paternal home. God can justify the sinner, or treat him as though he were righteous and had never offended against the law, because of the sin-offering in the person of His own Son.[59]

The causes or means of justification illustrate both the Godward and the manward sides of the conversion process. In the New Testament, justification is ascribed to seven causes. "Paul affirms that man is justified by faith: Rom. V. 1; Gal. II. 16; III. 24. In the second place he states that 'we are justified freely by His grace'; Rom. II. 24; Titus II. 7. In the third place, on another occasion, he teaches that 'we are justified by Christ's blood'; Rom. V. 9. Again, in the fourth place, he says, that 'we are justified by the name of the Lord Jesus, and by the Spirit of our God'; 1 Cor. VI. 11. To the Galatians, in the fifth place, he declares, that 'we are justified by Christ'; Gal. II. 16. In the sixth place, Isaiah says, 'we are justified by knowledge'; Isa. LIII. 11. And James, in the seventh place, says, 'we are justified by works'; Chap. II. 21. Thus by divine authority faith is connected as an effect in some sense, with seven causes; viz., Faith, race, the Blood of Christ, the Name of the Lord, Knowledge, Christ, and Works. May it not,

[59] "Christian Baptism," 278.

then, be asked, Why do so many select one of these only, as essential to justification." [60]

The inadequacy of any one of these causes to explain the whole process of salvation, is insisted upon. The Protestant mysticism of his day frequently spoke of salvation by faith alone, meaning by this not that entire process of appropriation of the divine blessings, which is faith, but rather the initial act of belief. A sufficient reason why no one of these causes alone could be adequate, is found in the fact that the seven illustrate both the part of God and that of man, in salvation. God's love, and grace, and mercy; Christ's blood and His Name; this on the part of divinity has created the way of life. But through faith, and knowledge, and works, the sinner appropriates this wonderful gift made possible by divine love. Thus it is that justification illustrates the great principles in the divine salvation. [61]

While he considered justification and sanctification simultaneous acts, regarded from the religious standpoint, he was careful to distinguish between sanctification, so regarded, and that which was ethical—that which grew out of justification as a new religious state. It is in this distinction that he attacks the problem, "How does foregiveness make a bad man good?" From the modern standpoint, his handling of this problem is one of his most satisfactory contributions to theological thought. The relation between the formal acquittal of the sinner in the act of justification, and the new life resulting in that which is called sanctification, was indeed a battleground of the older Protestant theology. This battle continued in the time of Campbell, and on every side, he heard the rumbles of it. The weakness of the popular view consisted in its contention that justification was the formal act of pardon, in which the sinner was treated by the Father as though he had never sinned, and then after an interval, sometimes much prolonged, through another process altogether, he became sanctified.

[60] "Christian Baptism," 278, 279.
[61] Ibid., 279.

But when the formal verdict was given in favor of the sinner, he was not yet saved; sin remained with him, its tendencies were deeply rooted in body and spirit. Dr. Dale rightly expressed the problem presented by the current conception, when he said that "the remission of sins, if it stood alone, would leave us unsaved, is one of the commonplaces of Christian theology." [62] It is in his solution of this problem that Alexander Campbell, avoiding the dualistic error into which the majority of contemporary Christian thinkers had fallen, made a real contribution to the theological thinking of his own time. In his recognition of the indissoluble connection between justification and sanctification, he resolves the discordant conceptions into harmony. Foregiveness of sins is not merely a preliminary to sanctification; it is sanctification—a new religious state which we enter through faith and obedience: it is the beginning of the progress of the divine life in the soul, toward perfection.

Dr. Clarke says, "plainly sanctification is not an event, but a process." [63] But in opposing the view which obtained in Campbellian days, that it is totally an event, Dr. Clarke swings to the extreme and speaks a half truth. Campbell contended that it is both an event and a process, an event which results in, or makes possible, a process. The two senses in which he speaks of sanctification, are religious and ethical: as religious, it is an immediate act simultaneous with justification; as ethical, it is a life process resulting from the forgiven state. "Justification and sanctification, with me, are always associated. Paul associated them to the Corinthians; he said, 'you are washed; you are justified; you are sanctified, in the name of the Lord Jesus, and by the Spirit of our God.' Here then, justification precedes in position, if not in terms, sanctification." [64] "God cleanses the guilt of sin, before, or at least simultaneously with sanctification." "Justification and sanctification—although the

---

[62] "The Atonement," Dale, 336.
[63] "An Outline of Christian Theology," Clarke, 414.
[64] "Campbell-Rice Debate," 497, 498.

former is really no more than pardon, and the latter no more than separation to God, to his service, to his and our glory—cover a large space in the remedial economy." [65] It is clear that in these three statements, he refers to sanctification as a religious act, an immediate cleansing of the soul, a setting apart to the service of God, in the new relation or state. The ground of this new relation is the sacrifice of Christ; its appropriation for the pentient believer is assured in baptism.

It is of interest in this connection, to note a statement of Dr. Denney, appreciating this relation between justification and sanctification. In his discussion of the meaning of the word ἁγιάζειν, in the book of Hebrews, he says; "The people were sanctified—not when they were raised to moral perfection—a conception utterly strange to the New Testament, as to the Old—but when, through the annulling of their sin by sacrifice, they had been constituted into a people of God, and in the person of their representative, had access to his presence. The word ἁγιάζειν, in short, in the Epistle to the Hebrews, corresponds as nearly as possible, to the Pauline δικαιοῦν; the sanctification of the one writer, and the προσαγωγή or access to God, which Paul emphasizes as the primary blessing of justification (Rom. 5:2; Eph. 2:18; 3:12), appears everywhere in Hebrews, as the primary religious act of 'drawing near' to God, through the great High Priest (Heb. 4:16; 7: 19-25; 10:22). It seems fair, then, to argue that the immediate effect of Christ's death, is religious rather than ethical. In technical language, it alters their relation to God, or is conceived as doing so, rather than their character. Their character, too, alters eventually, but it is on the basis of that primary and religious act; the religious change is not a result of a moral one, nor an unreal abstraction from it." [66] The great Scottish theologian has stated the Campbellian position exactly, save that he does not here

---

[65] "Christian Baptism," 276.
[66] "The Death of Christ," 160.

mention (though he does in another connection) [67] that act through which the religious change is made possible. In the preface to his discussion of justification and sanctification, Campbell refers in the same sentence, both to the religious and the ethical sense of sanctification. "We shall, therefore, develop more at length justification and sanctification; the former of which changes our state, and the latter not only our state, but our character." [68]

In the majority of his references to sanctification, however, he refers, by the term, to both the religious and ethical sides of it, engrossing them into one process. The sanctified man is one who has been forgiven, and in the new state is in the process of developing the divine life toward perfection. State and character, then, are but other names for justification and sanctification ethically considered. State has immense influence upon character; they are not to be considered as distinct. "There is a relation between state and character, or an influence which state has upon character, which makes the state of immense importance in a moral and religious point of view." [69] In a word, to be forgiven is to be transferred into that condition in which the Christian life has opportunity to grow. The knowledge of the fact that the soul is forgiven, is, of itself, regenerative. "Reconciliation to God comes through God's forgiveness of that by which we have been estranged from Him; and of all the experiences in the religion of sinful men, it is the most deeply felt and far reaching. We do not here have to measure what is, or what is not, within its power; but everyone who knows what it is to be forgiven, knows, also, that forgiveness is the greatest regenerative force in the life of man." [70] From this consciousness of forgiveness, this realization of reception into a new religious relation with the Father, comes the most powerful urge to ethical and spiritual transformation. "In-

[67] *Ibid.*, 59, 60.
[68] "Christian Baptism," 276.
[69] "Christian System," 187.
[70] "Christian Doctrine of Reconciliation," Denney, 6.

deed, the strongest arguments which the Apostles use with the Christians, to urge them forward in the cultivation and display of all the moral and religious excellencies of character, are drawn from the meaning and value of the state in which they are placed. Because forgiven, they should forgive; because justified, they should live righteously; because sanctified, they should live holy and unblamably; because reconciled to God, they should cultivate peace with all men, and act benevolently toward all; because adopted, they should walk in the dignity and purity of sons of God; because saved, they should abound in thanksgiving, praises, and rejoicings, living soberly, righteously, and godly, looking forward to the blessed hope." [71] Sanctification and justification are not two processes; they are one. The Christian salvation is a complete salvation, or it is nothing. Forgiveness of sins does make a bad man good.

VII

In the best of the earlier philosophical treatments of the Campbellian theology, Longan, speaking of Alexander Campbell's conception of the priority of faith to regeneration, says, "It was the most fundamental conception of what may be called his theology." [72] Dean Garrison, while admitting that Longan is probably correct if the process of entering the kingdom of God is considered,[73] disagrees with him in the prominence which he accords it. He finds it rather in Campbell's conception of the kingdom itself.[74] If Garrison's position is sound, there can be no doubt but that the Disciples have gone far afield from the teachings of their great leader. It must seem clear that a principle which received much careful consideration from Campbell himself and all of the early leaders of the movement, today bulks more largely

[71] "Christian System," 187.
[72] "Origin of the Disciples of Christ," 73.
[73] "Alexander Campbell's Theology," 217.
[74] Ibid., 161.

than any of the others by which they were actuated. It
is so prominent that it deserves the designation as the fundamental principle of the Campbellian teaching. It is undeniable that the dominant passion in all the Campbells taught
and did, was the desire for Christian unity. This led them,
step by step, to the discovery of the only basis upon which
that unity might be consummated—the foundation upon
which the early Church was one,—Jesus Christ Himself.
After more than a hundred years of history, the realization
that faith is personal rather than doctrinal, stands out as
above all others the central principle of the Campbellian
theology.

It is interesting to note the concurrence of Dr. W. N.
Briney with this view. In summing up what he considered to
be the heart of the Disciple plea, he makes the following
arresting statement: "If we should be requested to name the
one prominent, conspicuous, outstanding thing for which the
Restoration movement stands, perhaps our answers would
differ somewhat in verbiage, but analysis would doubtless
show that the Disciples are agreed that loyalty to Jesus
Christ, to His person, to His spirit, to His program, and to
His word and gospel, is, and from the first has been, the
matter of greatest concern to those whose endeavor it is to
promote simple evangelical Christianity." [75]   Dr. Moore,
the recognized modern historian of the Disciples, himself a
student of Alexander Campbell at Bethany College, also
agrees substantially with this position. "The Disciples made
a splendid contribution to the faith of the nineteenth century by their insistence that the faith of the gospel is not
doctrinal but personal. It has already been seen that they
eliminated all doctrinal matters, that are purely philosophical, from their basis of fellowship. This at once compelled
them to find a basis that would be sufficient without the
divisive elements which had so long dominated the Chris-

[75] "The Watchword of the Restoration Vindicated," 20.

tian world. They found this basis in the personal Christ." [76]
The Doctor would have been a little more accurate had he
said that the discovery of faith as personal rather than doctrinal, led to the discarding of matters purely speculative
or philosophical. In another connection, he fully recognizes
this definition of faith as fundamental to all Disciple teaching and practice. "In this contention, the Disciples, as a
religious body, stood practically alone during the nineteenth
century. There were individual Christians who saw the folly
of philosophical statements, or even doctrinal statements, as
bonds of union or communion, but the Disciples were the
only religious body which, as a whole, made this contention
for faith in the personal Christ, as fundamental, both as
regards Christian life and Christian union." [77]

Out of Campbell's principle of faith as personal rather
than doctrinal, grew all the rest of his teaching. His under-

[76] "History of the Disciples of Christ," 793. Cf. Davidson: "It is certain, however, that if the true spirit of the Christian religion is to be rightly
displayed generation after generation, and its work rightly done in the
world, there must be a constant 'return to Christ' on the part of His
Church. The phrase, of course, must be adequately interpreted. Much
has been said concerning the 'recovery of the historical Christ' as characteristic of our time, and the expression represents an important truth.
Christ is seen more and more clearly to be the 'end of critical and historical
inquiry' and 'the starting place of constructive thought.' But it is the
whole Christ of the New Testament who is the norm in Christian theology,
the object of Christian worship, the guide of Christian practice. The
Christ of the Epistles cannot be separated from the Christ of the Gospels.
The modern attempt, fashionable in some quarters, to distinguish between
the Synoptic Gospels on the one hand as historic, and the fourth Gospel
and the Epistles on the other as dogmatic, cannot be consistently maintained, and does not adequately cover the facts in the case. The sermon
on the mount does not reveal to us the entire Christ, nor the first chapter
of St. John, nor the Epistle to the Romans; but there is no inconsistency
between these representations of the Christian's Lord. There is no contradiction between the Christ and the Synoptic Gospels and the Christ of
Apostolic experience and the Christ of historical Christianity except for
those who reject the element of the supernatural, which, as a matter of
fact pervades the whole. The Christ of the New Testament is the object
of Christian faith, as well as the Founder of the Christian religion in its
historical continuity." Article "Christianity," "Dictionary of Christ and
the Gospels," Hastings, I, 323, 324.

[77] "History of the Disciples of Christ," 794.

standing of faith as related to regeneration, was clearly an outgrowth of what was more foundational to his purpose, that principle through which alone the unity, so much the passion of his soul, could become actual. The same is true of what he believed to be the kingdom of God; his conception of it was created by his plea for unity, and the method through which he hoped to see it accomplished. It is only the same to say that his teaching regarding the restoration of New Testament Christianity was evolved from his desire for the reunion of the Church.

This history of the Disciples has demonstrated one thing: wherever this principle has been followed, unusually rapid growth has attended their teaching; wherever the uppermost idea has been the restoration of the Church of the New Testament to the very letter, stagnation has ensued. The foundational principle of unity in the faith once for all delivered, allowing the largest possible liberty of opinion in those things concerning which no clear revelation has been vouchsafed, leads to marvelous expansion, both numerically and spiritually. That attitude, however, which sees only the New Testament Church as it was—which fears to venture into new paths lest some mistake be made—eventuates in legalism and externalism, which can end only in spiritual decay and death. It must, therefore, be evident to the serious student of Disciple teaching and history, that every problem which confronts the great, virile communion at the present hour, must be solved in the light of this basic principle, or acknowledged insoluable.

VIII

From the very first, the Disciples have considered the conception of faith as personal rather than doctrinal, their noblest contribution to modern christian thought. The way of salvation is the way of faith—a faith in the personal Lord which objectifies itself in heart-felt repentance and in acts of loving obedience to Him. This is personal faith. It has been noted that Thomas Campbell first announced it in the "Declaration and Address." [78] His son and biographer relates the joy which came to him upon the discovery that Christ Himself as the Lord is the foundation of the Church. "His search ere long is crowned with success. A person, yes, a person, and not a theory or system of doctrine, is the one and only true foundation of that against which neither earth nor Hades shall prevail." [79] After almost half a century of active participation in the work of the new movement, Alexander acknowledges this as perhaps the finest contribution which he and his fellow-laborers had made to the Christianity of his day. "It is to the honor of the present Reformation, that it was the first to develop, in clearer terms than had ever been done before the primitive age, and to present, in a bold relief to the world, the grand and sublime truth, that the faith of the gospel is a faith in the personality of the Lord Jesus Christ, and that a union to him is the very life of the gospel; that He, and not doctrines, is the centre around whom all parts of the system revolve; that faith in him, and obedience to all he has commanded, is the sum and substance of the whole scheme. And this central and absorbing truth, which had lain so long entangled under the rubbish of ages, and smothered by the speculations of men—this effort to return to the primitive gospel, and to the Bible as our only source of religious knowledge, has most fully developed and demonstrated its transparency upon almost every page of the Sacred volume." [80] The distinction between Christ Himself as the object of faith, and doctrines about Him—a distinction decidely agreeable to modern minds—is here clearly made. Christ as the revelation of the Father's love, is the gospel; this gospel is mediated to us through the Scriptures.

Dr. Richardson, while admitting that individuals, notably

[78] "Overture," Kershner, 89.
[79] "History of the Disciples of Christ," 175.
[80] "Millennial Harbinger," Volume for 1854, 374.

Luther,[81] had realized the importance of faith as personal, contends that the Disciples have been distinguished in that, as a communion, they have emphasized it as central. In this he echoes the attitude of Campbell in the paragraph just quoted. Acknowledging the unity of all evangelical bodies, in making a distinction between "the faith" and a general belief of the Divine testimony in the Sacred writings, he continues: "But we differ from all parties here in one important particular, to which I wish to call your special attention. It is this: that while they suppose this Christian faith to be doctrinal, we regard it as personal. In other words, they suppose doctrines, or religious tenets, to be the subject matter of this faith; we, on the contrary, conceive it to terminate on a person—the Lord Jesus Christ himself. While they, accordingly, require an elaborate confession from each convert—a confession of a purely doctrinal and intellectual character, studiously elaborated into an extended formula—we demand only a simple confession of Christ—an heartfelt acknowledgment that He is the Messiah, the Son of God.

"The Christian faith, then, in our view, consists not in any theory or system of doctrine, but in a sincere belief in the person and mission of our Lord Jesus Christ. It is personal in its subject, as well as in its object; in regard to him who believes, as well as that which is believed. It con-

---

[81] "Millennial Harbinger Abridged," II, 335. Cf. Griffith-Jones: "The Jesus of history gives us an objective content and standard for faith; the Christ of experience gives us the spiritual quickening and atmosphere of faith. Without the history, faith would lose itself in a vague mysticism, a formless subjectivity; without the mystic presence, we should know only a Jesus according to the flesh, who might fill us with admiration and with longing for better things, but who could not save us from our sins and bring us to newness of life. In the fourth Gospel these two aspects of the Redeemer's activity are brought together into an idealized but valid picture; and while we depend less on it than on the Synoptics for the exact historical facts and words of Jesus (though there are solid additional facts and many authentic sayings of His given us in John) it brings home to us with far greater emphasis the spiritual significance for faith, and the immanent for living, of the person of our Lord in His redeeming activity." "Peake's Commentary on the Bible," 16.

sists of simple facts, directly connected with the personal history and character of Jesus Christ as the Messiah and promised Lamb of God who takes away the sins of the world. It is personal in its object, leading to personal regard and love for Christ, and a personal interest in his salvation. It consists not in definitions; neither does it embrace the litigated questions of sectarianism." [82]   Referring further to such a faith as that which is alone suitable for the whole world, he continues: "The gospel of salvation, indeed, were ill-fitted to be preached to every creature, illiterate or learned, if it consisted, as some imagine, of those ponderous bodies of divinity, and intricate systems of theology, which have oppressed the energies and entangled the movements of the Protestant world." [83]

Nothing is more characteristic of modern Christian thought than its insistance upon Christ Jesus as uniquely God's Son, and at the same time a manifest impatience with any contention that this faith or loyalty is bound up with an acceptance of inherited theologies about him. Dr. James Denney expresses the Campbellian idea of what faith is, when he discusses it as "the Christian attitude of the soul to Christ."   From the very beginning of the Christian age, to the present moment, Jesus has held a place in the affections of those who know Him, which in every sense is unique. They all accord to Him the same place, and it is one which no other could fill. Not only is it evident that there was through the New Testament age, this unity of the soul's attitude to Him, but in the self-consciousness of Jesus as we may enter into it in the Gospels, there is the indisputable evidence that He accepted this attitude; He assumes the place naturally and spontaneously as His own.[84] "When we open the New Testament we find ourselves in the presence of a glowing religious life. There is nothing in the world which offers any real parallel either to this life, or the

---

[82] "Millennial Harbinger Abridged," II, 334.

[83] *Ibid.*, 334.

[84] "Jesus and the Gospel," Denney, 330.

collection of books which attests it. The soul, which in contemporary literature is bound in shallows and miseries, is here raised as on a great tidal wave of spiritual blessing. Nothing that belongs to a complete religious life is wanting, neither convictions nor motives, neither penitence nor ideals, neither vocation nor the assurance of victory. And from beginning to end, in all its parts and aspects and elements, this religious life is determined by Christ. It owes its character at every point to Him. Its convictions are convictions about Him. Its hopes are hopes which He has inspired and which it is for Him to fulfill. Its ideals are born of His teaching and His life. Its strength is the strength of His spirit. If we sum it all up in the one word faith, it is faith in God through Him—a faith which owes to Him all that is characteristic in it, all that distinguishes it from what is elsewhere known among men by that name." [85] From the Disciple ranks, Dr. Richardson affirms that this is precisely what all who have understood the Campbellian plea, have considered faith in Christ to be. "Alas! it is a sad mistake to suppose that Christianity is a theory, or that it consists essentially in accuracy of intellectual conceptions. Christianity is not a theory. It is a life—an inner and an outer life. Christ came to implant this inner life in the soul that the outer life might be fruitful in good works. Hence, His teachings are not theological disputations. They address themselves to the conscience and the heart. They reveal, indeed, sublime truths but these are as simple as they are sublime, and as practical as they are simple." [86]

When faith is thus defined as personal, it follows logically that it is evoked by the facts of the gospel as they are set forth in the New Testament records. It was for this reason that Campbell and those associated with him, constantly insisted that faith has to do with facts and not with interpretations. Interpretations must differ endlessly, but there will ever be a unity in the attitude of the soul to Christ, as

[85] *Ibid.*, 1, 2.
[86] "Millennial Harbinger Abridged," II, 357.

evoked by the gospel story. Faith is the response of the soul to the good news. Dr. Richardson, who is by far the best of the first interpreters of Campbell, his co-worker and personal friend for almost half a century, sets forth the very heart of his doctrine in this important matter: "To believe in Christ, is to receive Him in all the glory of His character, personal and official; to trust in Him in all the relations which He sustains to us, as our Prophet, our Priest, and our King; to behold in Him our only hope and refuge; and renouncing ourselves, our own self-confidence, our righteousness, and every vain device, to lean on Him as our stay, and to look to Him as the 'Lord our righteousness,' as our salvation and our life. It is not merely to believe what is said of Him as the Son of God; as the Son of Man; as living, dying, rising, reigning, returning; but, believing this, to trust Him as OUR Saviour, to walk with him as OUR friend; to realize His gracious presence with us, and to discern his footsteps in the path we tread. It is to be brought into direct relation and fellowship with Him; to think of Him as of a person whom we know, and to whom we are known; to speak to Him as one who hears, and to listen to Him as to one who speaks. Such in our view, is the Christian faith; not a trust in definitions; in doctrines; in church order; in apostolic succession or official grace; in opinions or dogmas, true or false; but a sincere belief of the testimony concerning the facts of the personal history of the Lord Messiah, accompanied by a cordial reception of Him in His true character as thus revealed to us, and an entire personal reliance upon Him for our salvation." [87]   There has probably never been a clearer statement of the Disciple position regarding the nature of faith and its distinctness from the convictions which rise out of it, than this. Dr. Denney concurs, not only in what faith is, but in the manner of its production in the heart. "When we preach, we must certainly be able to tell men

[87] "Millennial Harbinger Abridged," II, 337, 338.

things about Christ which justify the Christian attitude to
Him. But these faith-producing things are not dogmatic
definitions of His person; they are not doctrinal propositions, such as those of the Nicene Creed; nor are they less
formal expressions of essentially the same character. They
are such things as we have been in contact with all through
our study of the gospels: they are the life, the mind, the
death, the resurrection of Jesus. If the exhibition of these
does not evoke the Christian attitude of the soul to Him,
the soundest metaphysical doctrine of His person is worthless." [88] The evil results of failing to recognize the personal
nature of faith, and the manner in which it comes to the
heart, were manifest, in Campbell's day, in the prevalent
idea that the doctrine of Christ was designed to make men
think right, when its evident intention was to make them do
right.[89]

IX

It is only in the light of the Campbellian definition of
faith as personal rather than doctrinal, that it is possible
to understand his unchanging aversion to human creeds and
confessions of faith. The way of salvation has nothing to
do with such documents—it is in no manner bound up with an
acceptance of them. Since faith terminates upon the person
of Jesus,—since it is that Christian attitude of the soul to
Him which is evoked by the facts of the gospel—it must
be distinguished from the historic creeds which are essentially bodies of divinity containing much theological and
philosophical speculation. In a word, since salvation does
not depend upon an acceptance of the creeds, since it was
enjoyed by thousands before creeds were composed, they
should not now be made terms of union and communion.
Campbell never objected to any man holding personally, a
body of doctrine—such a doctrine or theology he held him-

[88] "Jesus and the Gospel," 347; see also 14.
[89] "Millennial Harbinger Abridged," II, 358.

self, and much of it is written out in the works he gave to the
world; it was the making of any compendium of theological
ideas a test of fellowship in Christ's Church, which he de-
preciated. Dr. Denney has more clearly expressed the
Campbellian attitude on this point, than any modern scholar.
"What Christ claims and what is His due is a place in the
faith of men—in other words, it is an attitude of the soul to
Himself as He is presented to us in the gospel. We are
bound to Him, in that wonderful significance which He has
for the life of the soul, that unique and incommunicable
power which He has to determine all our relations to God
and man. To be true Christians, we are thus bound to Him;
but we are not bound to anything else. But for what He
is and for what He has done, and our sense of infinite obligation to Him as we realize the cost at which He has done it,
we could not tell what Christianity means. But we are not
bound to any man's or any Church's rendering of what He
is or has done. We are not bound to any Christology, or
any doctrine of the work of Christ. No intellectual construction of what Christ's presence and work in the world
mean, is to be imposed beforehand as a law upon faith, or a
condition of membership in the Church. It is faith which
makes a Christian; and when the Christian attitude of the
soul to Christ is found, it must be free to raise its own problems and to work out its own solutions. This is the point
at which 'broad' churchism is in the right against an evangelical Christianity which has learned to distinguish between
its faith—in which it is unassailable—and inherited forms
of doctrine which have been unreflectingly identified with
it." [90]

It is certain that Campbell would have but little interest
in the attempted solution of the creed problem as put forward by many earnest advocates of Christian unity at the
present time. It is but natural that the first steps of
churches holding to time-honored confessions, toward revision or abolishment, should be hesitant. The age of such

[90] "Jesus and the Gospel," 337.

documents, the authority which they have so long wielded, the reverence in which they have been held as expressions of the faith of great and glorious epochs in ecclesiastical history—these considerations, and others, deter all but the hardiest minds from tampering with them.

Nothing is more apparent, however, in modern Christian life, than that there is a changed attitude toward the ancient creeds. It is undeniable that the increasing realization on the part of the vast majority of evangelical Christians, of the independence of the mind in other realms of knowledge, has resulted in an almost universal indifference to the Christian confessions. It is not so much that there is an active disapproval, or even a deliberate dissent from them; there is simply no interest in them. There is a feeling that traditional theology is alien to the modern mind; it comes from another age, an age cabined by a much smaller view of the world, than that which is the proud possession of modern men. It is common experience that a vital Christian life depends not a whit upon those ancient documents. Christians in every communion are loyal to Jesus Christ as Lord and Saviour; their attitude is definitely in line with that of New Testament Christians; they are not concerned about many of the established intellectual constructions which are enshrined in the historic creeds. This certainly does not mean that modern men are destitute of any body of convictions about Christ; they do possess such, and there can be no doubt that they equal in depth and power, any that have been held by their fathers before them. However, it is being increasingly realized that such convictions must be held as private possessions, and not imposed as a law upon the faith of others. As the truth has become more widely understood, that men who are one with their brothers in other communions in their faith in the Master, are separated from them by different theological traditions which they have inherited and for which they have but slight regard, they look with unconcealed approbation upon any effort to make of no effect these speculative barriers, to which, they know in their souls, they are not bound as they are bound to Christ.

This attitude of the modern Christian, is well analyzed by Professor Curtis: "There can be no doubt that, whether the world is becoming anti-confessional or not, these documents are being given a greatly altered position in religious life. It is certain that in all the Churches, Roman Catholic and even Greek Orthodox included—an attitude of quiet personal independence, reverent but firm, towards them, is being adopted increasingly, alike by the clergy and by the people, in spite of every effort to arrest the movement. Particular confessions, among them the most time-honored, even the Œcumenical Creeds themselves, whose gradual evolution has become matter of common knowledge, are studied and appreciated in the light of our knowledge of their time, the controversies that led up to them, the vocabulary of current thought, and the limitations of the scholarship of their day and of the minds that framed them. And it is a feature of the change that those who are most dissatisfied with our inherited dogmas are also the least eager to provide substitutes for them." Whatever the reasons which may be assigned for this change, "it is not more certain that excommunications and anathemas have lost their terrors, than that the documents to which they were appended, have lost their interest and power." [91] One evident cause for this declension in interest in theological traditions, and one which is enthusiastically welcomed by Disciples, is the modern devotion to a critical study of the Bible. "Probably the most reasonable explanation is that Christian thinkers have been preoccupied with a fresh investigation and defense of the theistic foundations of the faith, and in particular with a fresh examination of the Bible, most of all the Gospels and their Central Figure, by means of an apparatus of textual and linguistic and historical information which no previous age possessed. If we are working at the sources with a solemn sense of the momentous issues that confront us, it

[91] "History of Creeds and Confessions of Faith," 427, 428.

need not be marveled that we forget these lower and lesser authorities. Till we have reached conviction on the questions raised by the new study of the Gospels, traditional systems once reared on older conceptions of their meaning, must needs seem hypothetical and provisional." [92]

Keenly appreciative of modern indifference to creedal inheritances, Disciples have not reacted with any enthusiasm to proposals for Christian unity through a modification of existing Confessions, or a return to earlier formulas of like kind. This is the possibility most frequently ventilated by commissions on Christian unity, and the latest writers on this ever-fascinating subject. It is but logical that those who are heirs of complex and elaborate systems of theology extant in the historic creeds, should think that reunion will be accomplished by a reduction or simplication of such confessional formulas, or by a return to much earlier ones of the same nature. This is the solution advanced by the Bishop of Gloucester, in his Bampton Lectures. "I think that experience has shown that a religious society requires a somewhat more definite standard of union than the Bible gives, that we require a doctrinal basis of Christian unity. That may, I believe, be found for us in that one Creed which has undoubted œcumenical authority, that which we call the Nicene." [93]

Such a solution of the Creed problem would have been unacceptable to Campbell, and would certainly be so to the millions who are today sympathetic with his attitude toward Creeds as bonds of union and communion. It is not a solution, in the Disciple view of the whole question, because it is based upon the old error that faith is doctrinal, while the supreme Disciple contention is that it is personal. What is wanted is not a creed of the same, but of an absolutely different kind. Dr. Denney has clearly set forth the failure of this suggestion to meet the exigencies of the situation. It is because he has given words to the position in this matter,

[92] "History of Creeds and Confessions of Faith," Curtis, 428.
[93] "The Doctrine of the Church and Christian Reunion," Headlam, 231.

precisely as the Disciples hold it, that he is quoted liberally here. "To simplify merely by going back from the seventeenth century to the fourth, is certainly an easy matter, but what contemptuous censure it passes on the Christian thought of the Centuries between. When a man speaks of giving up the Westminster Confession for the Nicene Creed, one can only think that he has no true appreciation of either. The Westminster Confession contains everything that is in the Nicene Creed, but the writer has no hesitation in saying that this is the least valuable part of what it contains, and that which has least prospect of permanence. The valuable parts of the Confession, those which still appeal to the Christian conscience and awaken a response to it, are the new parts—those which represent the gains of the Reformation revival and the insight into Christian truth acquired there; they are the parts which treat of the work of Christ and its consequences—of justification, adoption, and sanctification; of saving faith and repentance unto life; of Christian liberty and liberty of conscience; of Holy Scripture, or the Word of God, as the supreme means of grace. To simplify the creed by omitting everything which can be verified in experience, and then to expect men to unite in the purely metaphysical proposition—for whatever religious interest it is supposed to guard, it is a purely metaphysical proposition—that Christ is consubstantial with the Father, is only to show that one has not diagnosed the situation at all. Very few people can tell what Athanasius and the Nicene bishops meant by this term. No one knows whether all who use it now use it in precisely the same sense; or rather, it is as certain as anything can be, that they do not. Everyone feels that it is on something else than the understanding of such metaphysical propositions, that the life and union of Christians depend; and it is this something else, and not what anyone regards as its metaphysical basis or presupposition, which ought to find expression in the common Christian confession of faith." [94]

[94] "Jesus and the Gospel," 345, 346.

The confession which Christians make, must be a declaration of faith and not of opinions. It must be a confession of their soul's attitude to Christ, who determines everything in life for them. This can be expressed in the simple language of religion alone. The psychological and speculative implications of the experience of which such a confession is an expression, are proper material for theology, but they have no place in the confession itself. It must be a declaration which, while making vocal the universal faith of all who belong to the Master, at the same time leaves the individual making it free to think out its implications for himself. It must be, in Disciple language, a confession in which there shall be unity of faith with liberty of opinions.

For the theological Creeds the Campbells substituted the New Testament confession, couched in the simple language of religion, as the foundation of Christian union and communion [95] and as the only one necessary in the Christian way of salvation. The Disciples, for more than a hundred years, have contended that this confession commends itself, for three obvious reasons.

1. It is apostolic and catholic. It is certainly the first confession. There can be no dispute about its antiquity. While it does not always appear in the same phraseology as that employed by Peter, in its simplicity of form and as a declaration of the attitude of the soul to Christ, it is characteristic of the New Testament. It is catholic in that it was the confession made by everyone who became a follower of the Master. It antidates the creed of Nicea and the so-called Apostle's Creed. "Peter's Confession, which, after examination of the New Testament, Thomas Hobbes, the philosopher, found to be the only form it authorized, is the true and only Apostle's Creed in the strict sense of the expression, not simply apostolic in itself but on the Master's own view divinely inspired. Paul's Jesus is Lord, and John's Jesus is the Christ, are but variants of Peter's utterance already become current forms in the primitive Church. The

[95] "Christian Baptism," 18.

earliest Gentile name for believers, the term 'Christians' coined at Antioch, shows that from the first, it was recognized that the distinctive note of Christian profession was not simply following Jesus but owning Him Christ, being baptized literally into His name." [96]

2. It is the only confession which may lay claim to inspiration. While all other confessions are clearly human this one is as manifestly divine. The impetuous utterance which His life with the disciples evoked from Peter, was immediately approved by Jesus. The faith then declared—that faith upon which, like a mountain of rock, the Church was to be built—was, on Jesus' own word, divinely revealed. The Campbells, and the Disciples after them, have believed that it is always divinely revealed. Not that it is a gift of God in the sense that it is some intangible commodity miraculously lodged in the heart; it is inspired in that God, through Christ, has provided those divine acts which call it forth. It is the response of the soul to the grace of God, which is revealed with assurance through Christ. The spontaneous and oftentimes impetuous confession, is the loving declaration of that new attitude of the soul, toward God, evoked by the Master himself in his life and death and resurrection. Such faith was not begotten by the study of a speculative Creed, but by seeing Jesus as He is. Dr. Harry Fosdick has sensed the difference between the religion about Jesus and the religion of Jesus, which is the fundamental verity of Christianity. "Christ-likeness is the central criterion of Christianity. There is just one thing in Christianity, from which by no devices of thought can I escape, and that is Christ Himself." [97] Dr. Mackintosh, after discussing the speculative nature of the Creeds and the consequent difficulty which the beginner in the adventure of faith, experiences in dealing with them, concludes: "The New Testament, as usual, is wiser, when to the seeker's question, it returns the answer, 'Believe on

[96] "History of Creeds and Confessions of Faith," Curtis, 403.

[97] Notes of an Address at the Central Y. M. C. A., Cairo. From "The Egyptian Gazette," December 31st, 1925. "Christian World."

the Lord Jesus Christ and thou shalt be saved.' That is, it goes on the clear and sufficient principle that what alone can awaken and satisfy the faith of sinful man, is a Person. Instead of the creed it speaks of Jesus Christ." [98]

3. It is, above all others, the comprehensive confession. The Disciples have felt that it includes just what the Christian's declaration of faith should include, and no more. Robert Richardson well states the position which they have constantly maintained from the beginning. "It is the characteristic feature of the present reformation, to endeavor to disentangle the Christian faith from doctrinal controversy, and to restore it to its original character, as a simple reception of the facts concerning Christ—a heartfelt personal reliance upon Christ alone. Hence it is, that we plead so earnestly for the original formula of confession, by which the true nature of the faith is so clearly exhibited. We propose to the whole religious community, a return to the simple confession of faith, made by the converts under the apostolic ministry—a confession which, while it affords no legitimate ground of controversy, is yet sufficiently comprehensive to include all necessary truth, and sufficiently definite to exclude all fatal error." [99] Faith in Christ makes a man a child of God and a member of Christ's Church. The Disciples have ever firmly insisted that more than this has

[98] "The Divine Initiative," Mackintosh, 70. Cf. Griffith-Jones: "The importance of this problem is seen more clearly when we realize how entirely our religion stands or falls with faith in the person of the historical Jesus. Those writers who have recently been attempting to distinguish between the 'historical Jesus' and the 'eternal Christ' with a view to show that faith in the latter would survive the loss of the former, are really assuming a philosophical as opposed to a historical basis for the faith, and have the testimony of all past ages against them. Whatever kind of Christianity might survive a supposed proof that Jesus never lived, or that He is inseparable from the religion associated with His name, it would not be the Christianity that has been influencing men so profoundly for nineteen centuries. We know nothing of any Eternal Christ, or Christ-Principle except as the spirit of Jesus working out its influence in history and in the hearts of men; and 'what God hath joined, let no man put asunder.'" "Peake's Commentary on the Bible," 14.

[99] "Millennial Harbinger Abridged," II, 357.

no place in the confession. It must be a declaration of personal faith in the personal Lord, and that alone. It was always Campbell's teaching that cordial reception of the truth to which Peter's confession gave utterance, would make a man a Christian.[100] With him, to be a Christian meant, at the same time, to be a member of the Church. Richardson sets forth the Disciple position regarding the relation of the creed to Church membership—the position which we have found Thomas Campbell earnestly advocating in the "Declaration and Address."[101] But I need not multiply quotations, to show that a sincere belief in Jesus as the Christ, the Son of God, is emphatically and truly the Christian faith, and the only faith which can lawfully be demanded in order to admission to the Christian privileges and to church fellowship. This is the Christian's Creed, and the only creed to which anyone may be justly called upon to subscribe. And this being so, all other creeds and confessions are at once nullified and repudiated as without Divine authority, as mere inventions of men, leading the mind away from Christ, and a direct and personal reliance upon Him, to mere intellectual conceptions, abstract propositions, and human opinions; or, if not wholly to these, at least to subordinate truths, collateral questions, remote conclusions, which belong not immediately to what is properly called the Christian faith, but to the subsequent chapter of Christian knowledge. Hence even upon the hypothesis that the religious formularies of doctrines, now in vogue, contain nothing but truth, we deny the right of anyone to complicate the simplicity of the Christian faith in this manner, and to demand, in advance, a degree of knowledge and experience in the child, which, in the very nature of things, can be expected only in one who has attained to the stature of a man in Christ Jesus."[102]

The faith which was once for all delivered, the faith which

[100] "Campbell-Rice Debate," 822.
[101] "Overture," Kershner, 87, 89.
[102] "Millennial Harbinger Abridged," II, 340.

the self-disclosure of God in Christ evokes in the hearts of men and the experiences of communion with God which they have through Him, are one. Interpretations of that faith may differ endlessly but the faith itself continues unchanging through the years. Finally revealed in Christ in the New Testament it is finally kept. Professor Pringle-Pattison writes brilliantly of those unchanging things in faith which can never die. "One thing at least the sequel would teach us—the faithlessness and foolishness of despairing as to the future of the instincts and beliefs which constitute man's higher nature. These are indeed imperishable, the supreme example of that power of self maintenance and adaptation to changing circumstances which, science teaches us, is the characteristic of all that lives. Changes in our conception of nature may be fatal to one formulation after another; accidents of expression may drop away in deference to historical criticism, nay, much that seemed of the very essence of religious faith may have to be left behind. But each time that the earthly body of a belief is laid in the dust, it receives a more glorious spiritual body, in which it continues to function as of old in the heart of man. Timid theologians who tremble for the ark of God at every advance of scientific knowledge do but repeat the sacrilege of Uzzah in the sacred legend, smitten by the anger of heaven for his officious interference. Faith, which is an active belief in the reality of the ideal, is the very breath by which humanity lives, and it will reconstitute itself afresh as long as the race endures." [103] And this is the living faith which is but another name for which the New Testament calls "the way of salvation." To know Him, to love Him, to trustingly obey Him; this, and this alone is necessary to be received by Him to the salvation of our sinful souls.

[103] "The Idea of God," 81, 82.

CHAPTER VI

THE DOCTRINE OF BAPTISM

THE historical development of Campbell's doctrine of Baptism can be more easily and completely traced than any other portion of his teaching. As a lad he had experienced all the "state of conviction" and its resultant conversion, which was supposed to be essential to membership in the church. He was sprinkled in infancy, as were the infants of all the members of the Antiburgher branch of the Seceder section of the Presbyterian Church, of which his father was a minister. With more than usual fervor, Alexander enjoyed the religious experiences which were so common in Ireland in his day. But as far as the subject of baptism is concerned, there can be discovered no change whatever from the ordinary acceptation of the ordinance among the Seceders, during the days previous to Thomas Campbell's emigration to Pennsylvania.[1]

The sojourn in Scotland contributed nothing to the change which was afterwards so marked and influential in all his work. Through his association with the Independents of Rich-Hill—that devout band of "free and unconventional thinkers," he had received a letter of introduction to Mr. Grenville Ewing of Glasgow.[2] This acquaintance was of profound influence in his subsequent life, because, through it, he became quite closely connected with one of the most evangelistic and practical movements of the day, the religious movement under the Haldane brothers. Among these men and their coadjutors, the subject of baptism had come up for discussion shortly after Alexander's arrival in

[1] "Memoirs of Alexander Campbell," Richardson, I, 48, 49.
[2] Ibid., 59, 60.

Glasgow. Both the Haldane brothers were immersed; and while finally the baptisimal discussion precipitated a schism in the Haldane congregation in Glasgow, the close association of Campbell with Ewing, who held firmly to the old position and refused to follow the example of the Haldanes, probably kept him from considering the question carefully at this time. Although not hesitating occasionally to side in with the Haldanes against Ewing, in controversies concerning matters of administration which disturbed their friendly relations, he does not seem to have imbibed his friend's inveterate aversion to immersion.[3]

The reasons for Campbell's indifference to the whole vexing question of baptism during his sojourn in Scotland, are very clearly set forth by Dr. Richardson. "It may appear somewhat singular, at this period, that none of the questions connected with infant baptism and immersion, which had thus caused so many divisions in Scotland, and in regard to which Mr. Campbell became afterward so distinguished, engaged, at this time, his attention in the least. This may be accounted for, however, by the fact that immersion was not made a term of communion by the Haldanes, and was never urged upon any, being left as a matter of choice to private and individual consideration. In the next place, Mr. Ewing and his coadjutor, the amiable and accomplished Dr. Wardlaw, who had left the Burghers and was now an Independent minister, residing in Glasgow, and who was often at Mr. Ewing's, were both vehemently opposed to immersion, and earnest advocates of infant baptism, in favor of which they both subsequently wrote treatises, which were severely criticized and confuted by Mr. Ewing's former classmate at the University, Alexander Carson of Tubbermore. Under the circumstances, therefore, this particular subject was not likely to become a matter of discussion at Mr. Ewing's, in his family or among his guests, and Mr. Campbell's attention seems to have been

[3] "Memoirs of Alexander Campbell," I, 147, 194.

entirely confined to the main purposes of the reformation undertaken by the Haldanes, and to those principles of Independency and church order in which Mr. Ewing was particularly interested." [4]

Reference has already been made to the effect produced by Thomas Campbell's announcement of the underlying principle of the Restoration Movement, as expressed in the aphorism, "Where the Scriptures speak, we speak; where the Scriptures are silent, we are silent," and to the fact that it brought immediate attention to the subject of infant baptism.[5] The contention that the strict adherance to it, would result in the discarding of infant baptism, brought the reply from Thomas Campbell that he would willingly give it up if the Scripture did not sanction it: he was sure, however, that it could be clearly established by Scriptural authority. While he admitted that it would be difficult to frame a Scriptural argument for it, he urged the fact that long precedent was in its favor, that a mistake would be made if a hurried and precipitate abandonment of it were attempted, and that the attitude of all toward it, should be one of toleration. The form of baptism was not an essential matter, since baptism was not of fundamental importance like faith and repentance. His only positive argument was one which afterward the Reformers were to abandon and to contend against with success—the argument for infant baptism from the analogy with circumcision.[6]

I

Just after the beginnings of the discussion arising from the enunciation of the principles of the "Declaration and Address," Alexander Campbell arrived from Scotland. His first interest in the baptismal question was awakened by

[4] "Memoirs of Alexander Campbell," I, 186, 187.
[5] Ibid., 222, 246.
[6] Ibid., 238, 239.

reading the proof sheets of this document.[7] He tells so
vividly the story of what followed that the recital of the
experience is given here in its entirety. "The first proof
sheet that I ever read was a form of my father's 'Declaration
of Address,' in press in Washington, Pennsylvania, on my
arrival there in October, 1809. There was in it the following sentences: 'Nothing ought to be received into the faith
or worship of the Church, or be made a term of communion
among Christians, that is not as old as the New Testament.
Nor ought anything to be admitted as of Divine obligation,
in the church constitution and management, but what is
expressly enjoined by the authority of our Lord Jesus Christ
and his Apostles upon the New Testament church; either
in express terms or by approved precedent.' These last
words, 'express terms' and 'approved precedent,' made a
deep impression on my mind, then well furnished with the
doctrines of the Presbyterian church in all its branches.
While there was some ambiguity about this 'approved precedent,' there was none about 'express terms.' Still a
precedent, I alleged, might be in 'express terms,' and a good
precedent might not be clearly approved or expressly stated
by apostles or evangelists with approbation.

"While reasoning with myself and others, on these
matters, I accidently fell in with Doctor Riddle of the Presbyterian Union Church, and introduced the matter to him.
'Sir,' said he, 'these words, however plausible in appearance,
are not sound. For if you follow these out, you must become a Baptist.' 'Why Sir,' said I, 'is there, in the Scriptures, no express precept for, nor precedent of, infant
baptism?' 'Not one, Sir,' responded the Doctor. I was
startled and mortified that I could not produce one. Turning around to Mr. Andrew Munro, the principal bookseller
of Jefferson College, Canonsburg, Pa., who heard the conversation, I said:—'Send me, sir, if you please, forthwith,
all the treatises you have in favour of infant baptism.' He

[7] "Memoirs of Alexander Campbell," Richardson, I, 235.

did so. Disclaiming the Baptists as an 'ignorant and uneducated population,' as my notions were, I never inquired for any of their books or writings. I knew John Bunyan's 'Pilgrim's Progress,' and often read it; but I knew not at that time that he was a Baptist.

"All the members of the Washington Christian Association, whose 'Declaration and Address' my father had then written, were not only Pedobaptists, but the most leading and influential persons in it were hostile to the Baptist views and practice. So to work I went to maintain my position in favour of infant baptism. I read much during one year, on the subject.[8]

"I was better pleased with Presbyterianism than with anything else, and desired, if possible, to maintain it. But despite of my prejudices, partialities, and prospects, the impression deepened and strengthened that it was all a grand papal imposition. I threw away the Pedobaptist volumes with indignation at their assumptions and fallacious reasonings, and fled, with some faint hope of finding something more convincing, to my Greek New Testament. But still worse. I found no resting place there; and entering into conversation with my father on the subject, he admitted that there was neither express terms nor express precedent. But, strange to tell, he took the ground that once in the church, and a participant of the Lord's supper, we could not 'unchurch or paganize ourselves'; put off Christ and then make a new profession, and commence again as would a heathen man and a publican. Having the highest esteem for his learning, and the deepest conviction of his piety and devotion to the truth, his authority over me then was paramount and almost irresistible. We went into discussion.[9]

8 "Memoirs of Alexander Campbell," Richardson, I, 250, 252.

9 It is evident, although we are not told definitely, that the first discussion with his father began almost immediately after his reading of the proof sheets of the "Address" and his studies of the treatises on infant baptism. The discussion with his father to which he refers again, occurred after the birth of this first child and immediately preceded his baptism. Thus he was studying the whole question for three full years before his

He simply conceded that we ought not to teach or practice infant baptism without divine authority; but, on the contrary, preach and administer the apostolic baptism. Still, however, we ought not to unchristianize ourselves and put on Christ, having not only professed and preached the Christian faith, but also participated in its solemn rites. We discussed this question, and all that family of questions, at sundry interviews for many months. At length I told him that with great reluctance, I must dissent from all his reasonings on that subject and be baptized. I now fully and conscientiously believed that I had never been baptized, and consequently, I was then, in point of fact, an unbaptized person; and hence could not consistently preach baptism to others, of which I had never been a subject myself. His response was:—'I have then, no more to add. You must please yourself.' " [10]

On March 13th, 1812, Campbell's first child, a daughter, Jane, was born. The subject of infant baptism once more presented itself, and the whole baptismal question was again brought into discussion. The problem as to whether or not he should baptize his daughter, caused him to devote himself with greater assiduity than before, to the whole question.[11] Throwing aside all human treatises, he immersed himself in the New Testament alone, studying especially the meaning of the original terms, for a space of three months.[12] Convinced, finally, that these terms gave warrant

---

immersion. He engrosses all the experiences into the one narrative as though they had occurred in a short time. See Richardson's "Memoirs," I, 222, 247, 275, 405.

[10] "Millennial Harbinger," Volume for 1848, 280-283.

[11] "Memoirs of Alexander Campbell," Richardson, I, 391, 392.

[12] During the years 1810 and 1811, Campbell's attitude on the question is that of his first easy going tolerance. "On the third of February, 1810, and again on the 19th of May, 1811, as well as on the 5th of June following, Alexander had delivered a sermon on Christ's commission to the Apostles, Mark 16:15, 16, in which his position in regard to baptism, at those periods is distinctly stated, and in which he said in reference to it: 'As I am sure it is unscriptural to make this matter a term of communion, I let it slip. I wish to think and let think on these matters.' " "Memoirs of Alexander Campbell," Richardson, I, 392.

for the immersion of a penitent believer, as the only valid
Apostolic or Christian baptism, he resolved to be immersed
immediately.[13]   With Campbell, to make up his mind was
to act. He continues his narrative as to the experience
which followed. "On leaving in the morning, he (Thomas
Campbell) [14] asked me when, where, and by whom, I intended to be immersed. As to the place, I preferred to be
baptized near home, among those who were accustomed to
attend my preaching; as to the time, just as soon as I could
procure an acceptable Baptist minister. The nearest, and,
indeed, the only one known to me, was Elder Matthias Luse,
living some thirty miles from my residence. I promised to
let my father know the time and place, as soon as I had
obtained the consent of Elder Luse.

"Immediately I went in quest of an administrator, of one
who practiced what he preached. I spent the next evening
with Elder Luse. Having on a former occasion, heard him
preach, but not on that subject, I asked him into what
formula of faith he immersed. His answer was that 'the
Baptist church required candidates to appear before it, and
on a narration of their experience, approved by the church, a
time and place were appointed for the baptism.'

"To this I immediately demurred, saying:—That I knew
no scriptural authority for bringing a candidate for baptism
before the church to be examined, judged, and approved,
by it, as a prerequisite to his baptism. To which he simply
responded:—'It was the Baptist custom.' 'But was it,'
said I, 'the apostolic custom?' He did not contend that it
was, admitting freely that such was not the case from the
beginning. 'But,' said he, 'if I were to depart from my
usual custom, they might hold me to account before the
Association.' 'Sir,' I replied, 'there is but one confession

[13] "Memoirs of Alexander Campbell," Richardson, I, 394, 395.

[14] It is interesting to note the leadership of Alexander Campbell asserting
itself in this historic event. He was but twenty years of age when he thus
takes the lead over his father in the baptismal question. From this time
on, the movement is more and more definitely in his hands. See Richardson's "Memoirs," I, 401.

of faith that I can make, and into that alone can I consent to be baptized.' 'What is that?' said he. 'Into the belief that Jesus is the one Christ, the confession into which the first converts were immersed.[15] I have set out to follow the apostles of Christ and their master, and I will be baptized only into the primitive Christian faith.'

"After a short silence he replied saying:—'I believe you are right, and I will risk the consequences; I will get, if possible, one of our Redstone preachers to accompany me. Where do you desire to be baptized?' 'In Buffalo Creek, on which I live, and on which I am accustomed to preach. My Presbyterian wife,' I added, 'and, perhaps, some others will accompany me.'

"On the appointed day, Elder Henry Spears, from the Monongahela, and Matthias Luse, according to promise, met us at the place appointed. It was the 12th of June, 1812, a beautiful day; a large and attentive concourse was present, with Elder David Jones of Eastern Pennsylvania. My father [16] made an elaborate address on the occasion. I followed him with a statement of the reasons of my change of views, and vindicated the primitive institution of baptism, and the necessity of personal obedience.

"To my satisfaction, my father, mother, and eldest sister, my wife,[17] and three other persons beside myself, were that same day immersed into the faith of that great proposition on which the Lord himself said that he would build his church. The next Lord's day, some twenty others made a

[15] The Disciple custom of baptizing converts upon a simple confession of faith in Christ, to which allusion has already been made in these pages, had its origin in this conversation between Alexander Campbell and Elder Luse and the historic events which immediately followed.

[16] Thomas Campbell and his wife made no reference to their decision to be immersed, until the morning on which the ordinance was performed. They, then, simply related their decision and accompanied the baptismal party to the place of immersion. See Richardson, I, 395, 396.

[17] Dr. Richardson gives a very eloquent and comprehensive account of the baptismal scene and relates the fact that the whole meeting continued seven hours. "Memoirs," I, 396, 398.

similar confession, and so the work progressed, until in a short time almost an hundred persons were immersed. This company, as far as I am informed, was the first community in this country that was immersed into that primitive, simple, and most significant confession of faith in the divine person and mission of the Lord Jesus Christ, without being brought before a church to answer certain doctrinal questions, or to give a history of all their feelings and emotions, in those days falsely called 'Christian experience,' as if a man could have Christian experience before he was a Christian." [18]

The action of baptism now being decided, it was apparent that from this time onward, the Reformers would be an immersionist body.[19] And yet, in it all there was but little, if any, influence from the Baptists. The influence was rather the other way, in the action of Elder Luse, in surrendering to the Campbellian position regarding the primitive confession of faith, in the case of the baptism of the Campbells and their companions. It was, however, but natural that this congregation, holding now indentical views with the Baptists as regards the action of the ordinance, and rejecting infant baptism as a human invention, should seek association with them. The points yet to be worked out were those of the prerequisites, and the design of baptism.[20] It was at these points that differences from the orthodox Baptist position were developed, which eventually caused the separation from that body.

[18] "Millennial Harbinger," Volume for 1848, 280, 283.

[19] "Upon the whole, then, it will be seen that a very great progress had now been made, and that a very great change had been effected, at least in the external aspect of this little community of reformers. Immersion had been unanimously adopted as the only true scriptural baptism; infant baptism had been finally and absolutely rejected as a human invention, and the simple confession of Christ, made by the early converts to Christ, was acknowledged as the only requirement which could be scripturally demanded of those who desired to become members of the church." "Memoirs," I, 404.

[20] "Memoirs of Alexander Campbell," Richardson, I, 405.

II

With increasing clearness of explanation concerning the phrase, "the remission of sins," the doctrine of the design of baptism was worked out in three great periods. In addition to this explanation of the phrase "baptism for the remission of sins," the place of the ordinance in the whole Christian scheme of things, was increasingly emphasized and clarified. The two public discussions in which the new doctrine was beaten out through the sweat of conflict, were that with Walker in 1820, and that with McCalla in 1823. The third period, following immediately the McCalla debate, saw his doctrine clarified in the publication of the "Christian Baptist." This development will be noted as prefatory to an explanation of his matured doctrine.

1. In the debate with Walker, Campbell appears as "a regular Baptist minister," [21] being at this time still a member of the Redstone association.[22] The sole argument of Walker, for infant baptism, was that it had come in the room of circumcision,[23] assuming, thus, the identity of the covenants upon which the Jewish institution and the Church of Christ, had been built. Relying upon his Covenant Theology, Campbell endeavored to overthrow the argument by destroying its basis.[24] He showed that the covenants are not identical; they are contrasted. He tried to establish the utter impossibility of the carnal, temporal, and national covenant of the Jewish institution being the same as the

[21] See Title Page of "Campbell-Walker Debate."

[22] In refutation of the current accusation that Campbell sought public discussion, Dr. Richardson says, "When Alexander Campbell was urged, in the spring of 1820, to engage in a public oral debate with Mr. Walker, on the question of baptism, he at first declined to consent, 'not regarding,' as he said, 'public debates' to be the proper method of proceeding in contending for the faith once delivered to the saints. He adopted this conclusion, however, more from deference to his father's feelings on the subject, than from his own matured convictions of expediency or from his natural temperament." "Memoirs," II, 14.

[23] "Campbell-Walker Debate," 9.

[24] Ibid., 9, 14, 15, 21,

new, spiritual and universal covenant ratified in Christ and under the economy of the Holy Spirit.[25]   In reply to the argument drawn from the household conversions recorded in the book of Acts, he particularized the facts that "All the house of Cornelius feared God and received the Holy Spirit: Lydia's household were comforted as brethren. The word of the Lord was spoken to all in the jailer's house and they all rejoiced believing in God. All the house of Crispus believed on the Lord, and all the house of Stephanus are said to have addicted themselves to the ministry of the saints." Now, "if these things affirmed of all the baptized, will not apply to infants, then it is plain there were no infants baptized in those houses." [26]   In reply to Walker's argument from the antiquity of the practice, he at once admitted both the antiquity of infant baptism, and sprinkling and pouring, but objected to this as an argument, on the ground that many evils were introduced into the church at a very early day, such, for instance, as the divine right of episcopacy, the observance of Easter, the doctrine of purgatory, the celibacy of the clergy, etc.[27]

It was in this debate that he first gave utterance to the peculiar office of baptism which he was to develop to its final position, in the future years. "Baptism," said he, "is connected with the promise of the remission of sins and the gift of the Holy Spirit." [28]   This was but a general statement of the design of the ordinance, and was not further developed in the discussion. "While, however, he thus, in 1820, distinctly perceived and asserted a scriptural connection between baptism and the remission of sins, he seems at this time to have viewed it only in the light of an argument, and to have had but faint appreciation of its great practical importance. A momentary and passing glance only seems as yet to have been directed to the great purpose of baptism,

[25] Ibid., 25, 36, 39, 51, 53, 64.
[26] "Campbell-Walker Debate," 72.
[27] Ibid., 100, 124.
[28] Ibid., 13.

which subsequently assumed so conspicuous a position in the restoration of the primitive gospel." [29]

2. The debate with McCalla, differed from that with Walker only in the clearness with which the arguments were formulated, since the second debate dealt with the same matters as those discussed in the first one. Its interest in this connection, is in the fact that the doctrine of baptism for the remission of sins, is for the first time, definitely stated, and an exposition of it given. There is also a distinction made between "real" and "formal" remission of sins. He says: "I know it will be said that I have affirmed that baptism 'saves us,' that it 'washes away sins.' Well, Peter and Paul have said so before me. If it was not criminal in them to say so, it is not criminal in me." [30] "The blood of Christ, then, really cleanses us who believe from all sin. Behold the goodness of God in giving us a formal proof and token of it, by ordaining a baptism expressly 'for the remission of sins.' The water of baptism, then, formally washes away our sins. The blood of Christ really washes away our sins. Paul's sins really were pardoned when he believed, yet he had no solemn pledge of the fact, no formal acquittal, no formal purgation of his sins, until he washes them away in the water of baptism. To every believer, therefore, baptism is a formal and personal remission, or purgation of sins. The believer never has his sins formally washed away or remitted until he is baptized." [31]

He insisted, however, that the washing away of sins applied to the personal sins of the believer, and, therefore, could not be applied to infants to cleanse them from so-called original sin. "Our argument from this topic is, that baptism being ordained to be to a believer a formal and personal remission of all his sins, cannot be administered to an infant without the greatest perversion and abuse of the nature and import of this ordinance. Indeed, why should an

[29] "Memoirs of Alexander Campbell," Richardson, II, 20.
[30] "Campbell-McCalla Debate," 134.
[31] *Ibid.*, 135.

infant that never sinned—as Calvinists say is guilty only of
'original sin,' which is an unit—be baptized for the remission of sins?" [32]   Progress of a very definite kind had been
made in the time intervening between the debate with
Walker and that with McCalla. He had often discussed the
design of baptism with his father, during these three years,
as well as with Walter Scott, who was later to have such influence on the whole question.[33]   Thomas Campbell had,
indeed, in the September number of the "Christian Baptist," asserted that "the primary intention of the Gospel
was the complete reconciliation of the sinner to God,
through the atonement of Christ, and the effect of this was
a belief of a full and free pardon of all his sins, received in
baptism." [34]   While the design of baptism was thus stated
in this polemic battle, there yet remained many things to
be cleared up before Alexander came to his matured view
of the real purpose of the ordinance. The debate is, however, epochal, in that the most distinguishing and original [35]
Campbellian doctrine in relation to the whole subject of
baptism, was announced. Campbell himself so counted this
discussion. To him it was, in a sense, a real beginning of
his understanding of the design of the rite.[36]

[32] "Campbell-McCalla Debate," 136.

[33] "Memoirs of Alexander Campbell," Richardson, II, 83.

[34] "Christian Baptist," 11, 13.

[35] Dr. Longan, one of the most eminent of Disciple critics, says: "Campbell's view of the design of baptism, was the product of honest and patient
study of the New Testament. He borrowed it from no one, nor is it identical with that held by any party since the days of the apostles, and their
immediate successors." "Origin of the Disciples of Christ," 67.

[36] In speaking of the difficulties of those who, for the first time, began
to appreciate the design of baptism, and, referring to the evidence of the
authorities on the question, Campbell says: "Though we had, many years
ago, read most of these documents, we read them as many of our readers
read the Bible; without attending to what they read, or feeling the import
of it. We can sympathize with those who have this doctrine in their own
creeds unregarded and unheeded in its import and utility; for we exhibited
it fully in our debate with McCalla, in 1823, without feeling its great importance, and without beginning to practice upon its tendencies, for some
time afterwards. But since it has been fully preached and practiced upon,
it has proved itself to be all divine." "Millennial Harbinger Abridged,"
Smith, I, 567.

3. The period of the publication of the "Christian Baptist," which followed mainly the McCalla debate, witnessed a further and much clearer working out of Campbell's ideas concerning the design of baptism.[37]   The final result was to give greater prominence to those embryonic conceptions which had appeared in the Walker debate, and which had been more definitely stated in that with McCalla.   The influence of Walter Scott, to which allusion has already been made, was perhaps just at this time, the most powerful force in the finalizing of the Campbellian idea of baptismal design. His proclamation of the *ordo salutis* in 1827, as that of faith, repentance, and baptism, and the "relation in which these factors stand to one another," [38] not only gave more powerful emphasis to the doctrine of baptism for the remission of sins, but assisted also in defining just what that doctrine meant.

III

An understanding of Campbell's matured view of the whole subject of the doctrine of the ordinance, may be gathered from a study of the "Christian System" (1835), the debate with Rice [39] (1843), and "Christian Baptism" (1852).   So lucidly does he state his positions in these works that numerous and liberal quotations will be made from them, in an attempted estimate of his final doctrine.

A prefatory summary of his teaching will first be given.

[37] "Christian Baptist," 415, 421, 436, 438, 445, 454.

[38] "Alexander Campbell's Theology," Dean Garrison, 242, 243.

[39] The debate with Dr. N. L. Rice, a Presbyterian minister of Paris, Ky., was the greatest discussion in which Campbell engaged.   Dr. J. J. Haley calls it "the greatest of the world's religious debates."   See "Debates that made History," 175.   It was held in Lexington, Ky., and continued for seventeen days.   In its published form, it contains 912 pages, averaging 900 words to the page, or about the size of seven ordinary volumes.   As to the position which this published debate still holds, especially in regard to its treatment of the subject of baptism, Dr. Haley writes, "All the material is here, nothing has been added since, little has been altered, nothing has been better said, the seal of historic finality is still unbroken."   "Debates that made History," 202.

1. The antecedants of baptism [40] may be divided into two classes, objective and subjective. The objective antecedent is the Bible in which we know of baptism as a command of Christ. Since, under the new institution, He is the supreme lawgiver, He has the right to make remission of sins conditional upon obedience in baptism. The subjective antecedents have to do with the attitude of the soul of the sinner toward God. He must turn to the Lord in faith and repentance before he can rightfully be a subject of the ordinance.[41]

2. The action [42] is immersion in water in the name of the Father, Son, and Holy Spirit. The arguments, both in the Rice debate and in "Christian Baptism," are mostly philological, and are worked out with a degree of exactness and comprehensiveness which quite fully exhausts the subject.

3. The subjects[43] of baptism are penitent believers, those who are subjectively prepared to confess Christ publicly in this ordinance. The fullest discussion of this phase of the question is given in the Rice debate, in which Campbell denied the proposition defended by Rice, that "the infant of a believing parent is a scriptural subject of baptism."

4. The design [44] of the ordinance or the change which it is intended to effect, is "the remission of past sins." The clear meaning of this scriptural phrase which has caused so much contention in connection with the whole baptismal controversy, in its Campbellian [45] significance, will become

[40] "Christian Baptism," 23, 63.

[41] *Ibid.*, 63, 115.

[42] "Campbell-Rice Debate," 49, 272. "Christian Baptism," 117, 204. "Christian System," 55.

[43] "Campbell-Rice Debate," 273, 430. "Christian Baptism," 205, 246. "Christian System," 56, 57.

[44] "Christian Baptism," 247, 273. "Campbell-Rice Debate," 431, 566. "Christian System," 57.

[45] Dean Garrison says, "He is saved (from baptismal regeneration as it was taught by the Catholic church), by making a distinction between the state of a man and the character of a man, and between real and formal remission of sins." "Alexander Campbell's Theology," 246. The first part of the statement is undeniable; the last is open to criticism. In his matured view, Campbell did not insist upon the distinction between real and formal remission.

apparent as the numerous passages from his works on the
subject, are critically studied.

IV

1. In regard to its action, baptism is a monumental act in
which the great facts of the Gospel are sensuously set forth.
It is an act most powerfully commemorative of what God
has done in Christ. It is firmly founded upon the atonement
and derives all its meaning from what Jesus accomplished
in His death. Had there never been any death, burial and
resurrection, there never would have been any baptism.
Baptism is thus connected with what Jesus did as a finished
work on the cross, as effect is with cause. "It is a sort of
embodiment of the gospel: a solemn expression of it all in
a single act. Hence the space and place assigned to it in
the commission. It is a monumental and commemorative
institution, bodying forth to all ages, the great facts of man's
redemption as developed and consummated in the death,
burial, and resurrection of the Lord Jesus Christ." [46] All
that the death of Jesus was for, in relation to sin, baptism
is for, because all its meaning is derived from that sin-
annulling death. No act with such a foundation can be of
small moment.

Both ordinances of Christ are monumental of the great
facts of the Gospel. "Being" thus "monumental of the
Christian facts—Christ's death, burial, and resurrection—
and containing in them the grace of God," they should be
diligently observed in the Christian assemblies.[47] The act
is monumental because it is symbolic. The going down into
the water, of one who has died to sin in his repentance, his
burial, and his resurrection out of the watery grave, is itself
a veritable picture of the foundational procuring facts of
our salvation. It is thus a living memorial, a constant witness to the fact that Christ "died for our sins and was raised

[46] "Christain Baptism," 257.
[47] "Christian Baptism," 19.

of our justification." "Baptism as administered by the primitive church, was a monumental evidence of the three great facts of man's redemption from sin, death, and the grave, by the death, burial and resurrection of Christ. On presenting himself, the candidate confessed judgement against himself by admitting his desert of death for sin, and promising to die unto it; while confessing that Jesus died for our sins, was buried, and rose again for our justification. His immersion in water, and immersion out of it, was a beautiful commemorative institution indicative of the burial and resurrection of the Messiah. All the world comprehends this definition of βαπίζω.[48] There is in such an act, not only a symbolic representation of the facts of the Gospel of Christ, but there is also a symbolic declaration of the soul's experience in coming to Christ. As Christ died upon the cross, so the soul must die to sin. As Christ was buried in the new tomb, so the soul in picture is buried in a grave of water. As Christ was raised up, so in the likeness of that resurrection, the penitent believer is raised from the baptismal waters. Every baptism is, therefore, a recapitulation of the wondrous saving facts upon which we rest our hope. Baptism, as such an act, "declared and enacted the whole Gospel, and not merely an initiatory stage of it." [49] It is truly "a solemn expression of it all in a single act." [50]

A faint evidence of his Lockianism, is once more seen in his insistence on the monumental significance of the baptismal ordinance. It is something which strikes the eye as well as the heart. It is a means through which the Gospel message in its mighty saving facts, is sensuously portrayed. "But this ordinance is monumental also. It is always a monument and an attestation of the burial and resurrection of

[48] "Campbell-Rice Debate," 234. Cf. with this position the words of Dr. Gore: "The rite viewed externally is symbolical. The going down into the water and being immersed in it and rising out of it is an acted representation of life through death, the dying of an old life and being buried and rising again to the new life." "The Holy Spirit and the Church," 125.

[49] "The Church and the Sacraments," Forsythe, 179.

[50] "Christian Baptism," 257.

the Lord. No one can sensibly contemplate one exhibition of it without remembering the burial of the Messiah, and his glorious resurrection by the power of the Father; for it is the administrator that raises from the watery grave, the buried saint. With the vividness of a sensible demonstration, it strikes not only the eye, but the heart of an intelligent spectator." [51]

2. Baptism, as regards its action, is also an act prospective of our future resurrection with Christ. It looks forward to a heavenly experience. This is a position upon which Campbell loved to dwell. When life is completed, we die, and are buried in the grave. But as Christian men, we are not as those who perish without hope. There will come a day on which we will be resurrected with Christ. This future resurrection with Him, is prospectively pictured when we rise from the waters of baptism. "It is not only a commemorative institution, but also it is prospective of our future destiny in the new relation; that when we die, and are buried in the earth—when the Administrator of the new and everlasting institution, revisits our earth, he will raise from their graves, all his dear brethren, and glorify them with his own immortal beauty and loveliness. How appropriate the symbol of the new birth, this washing of regeneration! How kind that the precept, on which man's enjoyment of salvation, rests, should commemorate the Lord's burial and resurrection, should prospectively anticipate our own, while it inducts us into Christ and invests us with all the privileges of citizenship in his kingdom!" [52] The ordinance, therefore, is not only symbolic of our entrance into the Christian life; it is likewise anticipatory of our resurrection into the eternal life with the Lord.

Believing thus, as he did, in the symbolic nature of baptism, he found no justification for a form which could not "body forth" or symbolize what he considered to be the foundational Gospel facts. In opposition to the current

[51] "Campbell-Rice Debate," 442.
[52] "Campbell-Rice Debate," 442. See also 121.

view, which held that baptism was symbolic of the cleansing of the soul from sin, and that only, he maintained that the symbolism was one which constantly pictured the procuring facts. Since sprinkling and pouring could not in any sense represent a burial or resurrection; since they were, thus, totally lacking in the sensuous value, which in the light of his conception of the Gospel facts, they should have, he rejected them. While, as has already been noted, his main arguments for the action of baptism, were philological, yet this conception of the commemorative, symbolic, and prospective nature of the act, powerfully influenced his argument for immersion "as the one, only apostolic or Christian baptism." [53] Following his lead, the Disciples generally have emphasized this phase of it, far more than they have the somewhat tedious arguments from the meanings of the original terms. His position on the symbolic meaning of baptism, was really one of the distinctive points in his teaching.

V

1. As regards its subjects, baptism is an act confessional of faith, to which is attached the solemn assurance of the forgiveness of sins. It is, therefore, something which comes from the heart of the believer. It has already been noted that he considered baptism one of the steps in the way of salvation, an act in which the faith of the heart is publicly expressed. It is not a mere meaningless performance, separate and distinct from faith; it is faith itself enacted in symbol of those very facts upon which it rests for forgiveness of sins. It is, as a modern scholar exactly expresses the Campbellian idea, that "baptism and faith are but the outside and the inside of the same thing." [54] The faith of which baptism is a public confession, is not a belief in Jesus as simply a unique Galilean-peasant teacher. It is not that

[53] *Ibid.*, 47.
[54] "The Death of Christ," Denney, 133.

the believer rests his hope of present salvation and future reception, on some etherial Gospel divorced from historical association, and in some manner above it; it is faith in the historical Christ and preëminently in what He accomplished when He died upon the cross, was buried in the grave in the garden, and was raised from the dead by the power of His heavenly Father. It is faith in God through Christ who works out in history the salvation of man. To Campbell, Christianity is a religion based upon facts,[55] upon something which actually happened in Palestine and upon that Gospel interpretation of facts which he believed the Holy Spirit revealed to the apostles. These men have left, in the New Testament, their testimony;[56] that testimony produces faith and penitence in the heart, and this is confessed in baptism. "Such being the true philosophy of justification by faith, and of justification sought and supposed to be obtained by works of law, we need not marvel that the God of all grace, after having sent his Son into the world to become a sacrifice for us—to die for our sins, and to rise again for our justification—should have instituted faith in him, in his death, burial, and resurrection, as a means of a perfect reconciliation to himself, commanding us not only to cherish this faith in our hearts, but to exhibit it by a visible death to sin; and a rising again to walk in a new life, expressed and symbolized by an immersion in water, into the name of the Father, of the Son, and of the Holy Spirit, not as a work of righteousness, but as a mere confession of our faith in what he did for us, and of our fixed purpose to walk in him. Hence, it is the only suitable institution to such an indication, as being, not a moral work of righteousness, but a mere passive surrendering ourselves to die, to be buried, and to be raised again by the merit and aid of another." [57] To this "visible

[55] "Christian System," 110.

[56] "Christian Baptism," 63.

[57] "Christian Baptism," 285. In regard to Paul's position on baptism Dr. Rahsdall writes: "At the same time he probably could not have understood the sort of disparagement of the sacraments which is characteristic of a certain type of Protestantism. If anyone had raised the question

embodiment of faith," a faith confessed in act and "thus perfected," the promise of remission of sins is "divinely annexed." It is also a solemn pledge and solemn assurance on the part of our Father, that he has forgiven all our offenses—a positive, sensible, solemn seal and pledge, that, through faith in the blood of the slain Lamb of God, and through repentance, or a heart-felt sorrow for the past, and a firm purpose of reformation of life, by the virtues of the great Mediator, we are thus publicly declared forgiven, and formally obtain the assurance of our acceptance and pardon, with the promised aid of the Holy Spirit to strengthen and furnish us for every good thought, and word, and work." [58] In a similar vein, he writes in another connection, and progresses to an affirmation that in the reception of this assurance there is the only sense in which we are saved by baptism. "Baptism, according to the apostolic church, is both 'a sign' and 'a seal' of the remission of all former sins. In this sense only, does 'baptism now save us.' Not in a putting away of the filth of the flesh, but in obtaining a good conscience through the death and resurrection of the Lord Jesus. This faith in our hearts is expressed in the sign of baptism, our burial and resurrection with him, indicated by an immersion in water, and an immersion out of it." [59]

2. A consideration of the proper subjects of baptism— and this is what he does when he discusses baptism as an act of the believer—necessarily involves attention to the design of it. In the light of the ordinance as a seal and

---

whether it was not possible to be saved without the sacraments, he would doubtless have asked how anyone could expect to be saved who neglected what he regarded as an express command of Christ. He would perhaps have denied that the faith of any such man could be a real faith. Any interpretation which makes of them more than obligatory and divinely appointed signs or symbols, or aids to moral and spiritual processes, would be inconsistent with his fundamental doctrine: on the other hand to speak of 'mere' symbols would equally fail to express his mind." "The Idea of Atonement in Christian Theology," 486.

[58] "Christian Baptism," 284.

[59] *Ibid.*, 272.

sign or a pledge to the penitent believer, he exhibits the true relation which it sustains to the remission of sins. No where does he make more lucid statements on this position about which he was so misunderstood, than in the two which are here quoted. "We have now before us the special design of baptism, as the assurance of remission; a pledge of pardon, of our burial with Christ, and our resurrection to a new life. This 'is baptism for the remission of sins.' That baptism was designed for the remission of sins, for a pledge and assurance of pardon, through the Messiah, our Lord and Saviour Jesus Christ, we shall now proceed to prove." [60] While in the obedience to Christ in this act, the believer receives his certificate of remission, the act itself has no power to secure this coveted blessing. He firmly objects to the implication that by some form of magic, the mere physical act of baptism itself can make pardon possible. "While, then, baptism is ordained for the remission of sins, and for no other specific purpose, it is not as a procuring cause, but as an instrumental cause, in which faith and repentance are developed and made fruitful and effectual in changing our state and spiritual relations to the Divine Persons whose names are put upon us in the very act." [61]

Baptism is the means through which faith and repentance appropriates foregiveness; more than this it can never be. In the light of such a statement as this, it is manifestly inaccurate to accuse Campbell of teaching baptismal regeneration.

[60] *Ibid.*, 260. Cf. Dr. Rashdall's statement in his Bampton lectures. "Immense importance was attached to communion with the visible Church, but still more to the initiatory rite of baptism. It was certainly believed that baptism carried with it an immediate and plenary remission of past sins. But this does not imply so unethical an attitude as it might seem to do at first. For baptism did not mean to them mere immersion in the baptismal waters. It included public confession of sin, the profession of faith, the solemn turning away from evil and the resolution to obey the very exacting and practical demands which the Christian society made upon them. . . . The most mechanical view of baptism was hardly possible so long as infant baptism was either altogether unknown or a rare exception." "The Idea of Atonement in Christian Theology," 203, 204.
[61] "Christian Baptism," 256.

3. Since baptism is an act of faith, one in which faith is publicly and sensuously confessed, it is evident that it can have nothing to do with infants who must necessarily be unconscious in the whole transaction. To Campbell, when the reason for baptism is removed, it becomes worthless and meaningless. It is only in its connection with faith and the remission of sins, that it can be of interest. Since an infant cannot believe and since he has no sins of which he must repent, even were repentance possible in him, he cannot be in any sense a candidate for baptism. "Faith, then, being in any case, required in order for baptism, not only according to a fair construction of the commission, as reported by all the evangelists, but also in particular cases—as in the case of the eunuch—positively inhibits infants and untaught persons from christian baptism." [62]

VI

1. In respect to its design, baptism is a translational act through which the penitent believer is transfered from the unforgiven state into that "where the saving power of Christ operates." [63]

---

[62] "Campbell-Rice Debate," 429, 431. It is interesting to note the concurrence of modern scholars with Campbell's contention that New Testament baptism was always an act of faith and that therefore infant baptism cannot be substantiated from its pages. Thus Principal Clow says: "When we make an appeal to the New Testament we find abundant references to the rite of Baptism, but no express sanction for its administration to infant children." "The Church and the Sacraments," 139. With this Dr. Vernon Bartlett agrees: "Infant Baptism is not an Apostolic usage. It is not only that there is no trace of it in the first century: but the very idea of baptism then universal, namely as a rite of faith's self-consecration (often outwardly ratified by manifestations of the Spirit), is inconsistent therewith." "Apostolic Age," 472. Professor Andrews joins the chorus in his almost blunt phrase: "There is no shred of real proof that baptism was ever administered to infants in the Apostolic Age." See Dr. Forsyth's work "The Church and the Sacraments," 150. Professor Gwatkin writes: "We have good evidence that infant baptism is no direct institution either of the Lord himself or of His apostles. There is no trace of it in the New Testament." "Early Church History,' 431, 440.

[63] "The Atonement, the Heart of the Gospel," McLeod Campbell, 190.

A study of what he conceived to be the design of baptism, takes one into the very heart of his baptismal doctrine. Nothing is more distinctive or novel in his theology, than his doctrine of baptism for the remission of sins.   The phase had often been used, previously, but the meaning which Campbell puts into it, had hardly been appreciated before.   From his standpoint, the whole subject of baptism must be considered in the light of its purpose.   In his comprehensive work on the subject, he says: "But the design of this institution has long been thrown into the shade because of the wordy and impassioned controversy about what the action is, and who may be the proper subject of it.   Now it must be confessed that, whatever importance there may be in settling these questions, that importance is wholly to be appreciated by the design of the institution.   This is the only value of it.   The question concerning the value of any action is incomparably superior to the question, What is the act itself? or to the questions, Who may perform it? or, Upon whom may it be performed?   We are, therefore, induced to believe that the question now before us, is the all interesting important question—indeed the transcendent question in this discussion." [64]   This vigorous statement so forcefully sets forth his own appreciation of the importance of his doctrine of design, that it needs no comment.   Every phase of the question, in his own thinking, must be settled by the design of the ordinance.   The paramount issue is, What is it for?

2. As translational, then, baptism is an initiatory act, one in which the believer is inducted into all the rights of the kingdom of God.[65]   It is a real act, one in which something is done to and for the candidate for admission into Christ's body.   There is always a danger of baptism degenerating into one or other of two extreme positions.   It may become a mere act of magic, or, in the other direction, it may fade

[64] "Christian Baptism," 248.
[65] Ibid., 250.

away into a meaningless symbol.[66] The teaching that it is
an act through which we come formally into all the blessings of children of God, an experience in which we are
actually initiated into the sphere where His gracious power
is effectual to our salvation, avoids, in the view of Campbell,
these two extremes, and conserves the truth of the New
Testament position.[67]   In a comment on the language of
the commission, he strikingly deposes, " 'Baptizing them
into the name of the Father, and of the Son, and of the
Holy Spirit.'   No language could more clearly indicate a
change of state than the phrase just now read.   The prominent design of baptism is thus fully expressed by the transition spoken of in the words 'baptizing into the name.'   The
subject is here represented as in some way, entering into
the name, or into the persons represented by the Father,
Son, and Holy Spirit.   This may be supposed to resemble
the act of naturalization, in the fact that a person in that
process is inducted into the possession of the rights of
citizenship under a political institution.   So Christ commanded the candidates to be immersed into the name of
the whole Divinity; that is, into the privileges and immunities of the new kingdom over which the Messiah now
presides, by the authority of the Father through the Holy
Spirit.   It is, then, a solemn enfranchisement of a believer,
with all the rights and privileges of Christ's kingdom." [68]
It is thus a tremendously solemn and dignified act, for it
"is designed to introduce the subjects of it into the participation of the blessings of the death and resurrection of
Christ." [69]

[66] "Campbell-Rice Debate," 431, 440.
[67] "Christian Baptism," 246.
[68] "Campbell-Rice Debate," 441.
[69] "Christian System," 193.   What Campbell called "a change of
state" Dr. Gore denominates "a new sphere" or a "new spiritual status"
and agrees with Campbell that baptism introduces one into it.   While the
act is symbolical it is more in that "it effects what it symbolizes.   It is the
transference of a man into a new spiritual sphere.   It is a baptism 'into
Christ' or 'into the one body'—the church."   "Incorporation into Christ
or His body, the being invested in a new spiritual nature which is Christ,

3. As initiatory, it is evident that baptism is an act of faith, which changes the believer's state or religions condition toward God. Faith of itself, in the sense of belief, can never change any state or condition. Faith could never make a foreigner an American citizen; it would be only an act to which faith leads. Faith alone could never bring about the marriage relation; it is an act inspired by it, which makes two people husband and wife. Thus it is, that religiously, "it is not faith, but an act resulting from faith, which changes our state." [70] This act, as has been repeatedly stated, is baptism. "All feel the difference between 'in the name of the Lord,' and 'into Christ.' The former denotes authority, alone—the latter intimates union and relation." [71]

4. Carrying this fundamental idea of the change of state in an act, over into his exposition of the meaning of regeneration, he taught that baptism is itself the act of regeneration or "New Birth." It regenerates or is related to the spiritual life, in exactly the same manner as birth is related to the physical life. No Campbellian position brought forth such vehement protest from the theologians of his time, as did this. In a true understanding of it, however, lies the very marrow of his whole position on baptism as related to the forgiveness of sins. "Regeneration and immersion are, therefore, two names of the same thing." "If immersion

---

'cleansing' from defilement and mediated by washing, a new birth into a new spiritual status—all these phrases convey the same idea, and the process thus variously described is assigned to the same agent, the Holy Spirit, with the same external rite as its instrument. There is then in baptism an outward and visible sign and an inward and spiritual gift, and the two appear to be inseparably connected." "In the Acts also baptism is regarded as effecting the great transition from the world of sin to the world of righteousness." "The Holy Spirit and the Church," 125, 126, 127. With this view agrees Professor Underwood, "The merely symbolic view of baptism does not do justice to the Apostle's phrases about 'putting on Christ,' 'dying to sin,' and being raised to 'newness of life,' in baptism. For Paul, baptism means an experimental union with Christ in His redeeming acts." "Conversion: Christian and Non-Christian," 110.

[70] "Christian System," 188, 192.
[71] "Campbell-Rice Debate," 441.

be equivalent to regeneration, and regeneration be of the same import with being born again, then being born again and being immersed are the same thing; for this plain reason, that things equal to the same thing, are equal to one another." [72] Such statements as these aroused astonishment and indignation. Were they isolated and without explanation of what Campbell meant by them, it is not to be wondered at that they could cause the charge to be current that the "Sage of Bethany" believed in baptismal regeneration as it had been held by the early Church Fathers.

The whole misunderstanding rests upon a misapprehension of Campbell's definition of regeneration.[73] The current view was that regeneration is entirely an act of God. Not by argument or persuasion, but by a mighty act of divine power, is the soul regenerated. God gives faith and repentance in a miraculous manner. The soul, therefore, is passive in the whole process. It is not in any sense, an act performed by us, but one wrought in us by the mighty power of the Father. The sinner is as dead in sins as was Lazarus in the grave. The act by which he was quickened was the act of God; so it is with the newly-quickened soul. The sinner is, therefore, passive, "for the Holy Spirit is the sole agent in regeneration, and the sinner has no more efficient agency in accomplishing it, than had Lazarus in becoming alive from the dead." [74]

In direct antithesis to this popular conception, Campbell contended that the sinner is active in his own regeneration. While gratefully acknowledging the part which the Father

[72] "Christian System," 200. From the modern standpoint Dr. Gore's statement regarding the position of baptism in the primitive church is significant. "Thus they believed that baptism was their new birth—that by the action of the Holy Spirit in that sacrament they passed into a new spiritual status 'in Christ' and their old sins were washed away. Baptism was both 'their grave and their mother.'" "The Holy Spirit and the Church," 297.

[73] "History of the Disciples of Christ," Moore, 193.

[74] "Christian Baptist Journal," July 26, 1833; quoted by Campbell, "Millennial Harbinger Abridged," Smith, 465.

plays in the whole process, he yet believed that without the
active cooperation of the sinner, there can be no regeneration at all. Baptism, since it is the consummating act in
that whole process by which the unregenerate becomes a
new being, is called regeneration. Through faith and repentance, the sinner has experienced an intellectual and
moral change; in baptism, he is to be born into a new state
or relation—he is to experience a religious change. "We
have already seen that the consummation of the process of
generation or creation, is in the birth of the creature formed.
So it is in the moral generation, or in the great process of
regeneration. There is a state of existence from which he
that is born passes; and there is a state of existence into
which he enters after birth. This is true of the whole
animal creation, whether oviparous or viviparous. Now
the manner of existence, or mode of life, is wholly changed;
and he is, in reference to the former state, dead, and to
the new state alive. So in moral regeneration. The subject
of this great change, before his new birth, existed in one
state; but after it, he exists in another. He stands in a
new relation to God, angels, and men. He is now born of
God, and has the privilege of being a son of God, and
is consequently pardoned, justified, sanctified, adopted,
saved." [75] In another connection, he emphasizes the sense
in which he usually employs the term regeneration. Conversion may consist of several distinct acts in the one
process through which the soul comes to God, but "it is in
accordance to give to the beginning, or consummating act,
the name of the whole process. For the most part, however,
the name of the whole process is given to the consummating
act, because the process is always supposed to be incomplete until that act is performed." [76] "In the same sense
it is that most Christians call regeneration, the New Birth;
though being born is only the last act in natural generation,

[75] "Christian System," 266.
[76] Ibid., 263.

and the last act in regeneration." [77] "By 'the bath of regeneration' is not meant the first, second, or third act; but
the last act of regeneration which completes the whole, and
is, therefore, used to denote the new birth. This is the
reason why our Lord and his Apostles unite this act with
water. Being born of water, in the Saviour's style, and
the bath of regeneration, in the Apostle's style, in the judgement of all writers and critics of eminence, refer to one and
the same act—*viz.*: Christian baptism." [78] "Baptism being
the last of the series of truth, faith, repentance, love, and
profession, it is properly styled, in figure, 'being born again,'
or being 'born of water and of the Spirit.' And faith being
an active, operative principle, containing in it all that is in
the gospel of Christ's blood, it is the vitalizing principle of
Christian activity and all Christian excellence and enjoyment." [79] The liberal number of quotations are given here,
because in nothing has Campbell been so inaccurately represented, as in his views concerning the relation of baptism to
regeneration. It is but fair to allow him emphatically to
speak for himself.

In a somewhat caustic refutation, he replies to his critics,
in a summation so comprehensive and pithy, that it is here
given in its entirety. "It may again be necessary in this fas-
tidious age to remark, that in this essay, in order to disabuse
the public mind on our use and acceptation of the term
regeneration, we have taken the widest range which a supreme regard for the apostolic style could, in our judgement,
allow. While we argue that the phrase, bath of regeneration
(Titus 3:5), is equivalent to immersion, as already explained, and as contradistinguished from the renewing of
the Holy Spirit, of which the immersed believer is a proper
subject; we have spoken of the whole process of renovation,
not in the strict application of the phrase (Titus 3:5), but
rather in whole latitude employed by the Apostle. It is

[77] *Ibid.*, 263.
[78] "Christian System," 263.
[79] "Christian Baptism," 276.

not the first act of begetting, nor the last act of being born, but the whole process of conversion alluded to in the figure of generation, to which we have directed the attention of our readers. For, as often stated before, our opponents deceive themselves and their hearers by representing us as ascribing to the word immersion and the act of immersion ALL THEY CALL REGENERATION. While, therefore, we contend that 'being born again,' and being immersed, are, in the Apostle's style, two names for the same action, we are far from supposing or teaching that in forming the new man there is nothing necessary but to be born." [80]

He then proceeds to a brief but vitrolic statement of the position of those who so often opposed him, even to the point of bitterness, and in it, as he states, gives this as his reason for the essay on the subject. "Our opponents contend for a regeneration begun and perfected before faith or baptism—a spiritual change of mind by the Holy Spirit, antecedent to either knowledge, faith, or repentance, of which infants are as susceptible as adults; and, therefore, as we contend, make the gospel of no effect. By way of reprisals they would have their converts to think that we go for nothing but water, and sarcastically call us advocates of 'water regeneration.' They think there is something more sublime and divine in 'spirit regeneration,' and therefore claim the title of orthodox. This calumny has been one occasion of the present essay, and has occasioned that part of it which gives the fullest latitude to the terms regeneration, which analogy gives to the figure used by the Apostle." [81]   In this statement, there is evidence of the

[80] "Millennial Harbinger," Volume for 1832, "Extra Defended," 24, 36. Quoted in "Millennial Harbinger Abridged," Smith, I, 446.

[81] "Millennial Harbinger Abridged," 446. In view of the unmistakable evidence here adduced the statement of Principal Robinson that the Campbellian doctrine of baptism is the Catholic doctrine of baptismal regeneration is indeed astonishing. "Of course this doctrine of Baptism for which the Churches of Christ plead, is essentially the Catholic doctrine, as is of course that of the Protestant Confessions; though Protestantism has generally rejected it, regarding Baptism as a bodily act which signifies something already accomplished, rather than an act which effects something.

prevalency of the Hervian conception of regeneration. There was hardly anywhere, exception to this as the universally accepted orthodox ground.

What Campbell believed concerning the new birth, may be gathered by following him through the analogy [82] as it pictures the whole process of conversion. Before there can be a birth, there must of necessity be a begetting. There are three agents in this begetting process; the heart in which the new life is to begin, the seed from which it is to come, and the Father from whom we are begotten. The Father begets a new life in the heart, through the Holy Spirit, for "the Spirit of God is the begetter." The Spirit brings the new life into being through the Gospel which is the seed. Life begins before birth; spiritual life begins before the birth of water. "A child is alive before it is born, and the act of being born only changes its state, not its life." And, thus, also, is it in the spiritual birth. "Persons are begotten by the Spirit of God, impregnated by the Word, and born of the water." The reason why water is always placed before Spirit in the order of birth, is that one cannot be said to be born of the father until he is first born of the mother. When he is born of the mother, then it may be said, also, that he has been born of the father. Strictly, we are never born of God, but begotten of Him by the Spirit through the Word.

But if life has begun through the divine begetting, why be born? Unless that which is begotten is born, it will die, —it will be still-born. Unless resolution becomes action,

---

Churches of Christ differ from Catholics in general as to the subjects of Baptism, and from Western Catholics as to the administration of Baptism, regarding as Eastern Catholics do, immersion as the valid form; but as to doctrine they hold essentially the Catholic doctrine, because it is also the doctrine of the Apostolic Church, and moreover it is psychologically sound." "What Churches of Christ Stand For," Footnote, 61. This is exactly the thing Campbell did not teach and it is certain that here the Principal has missed the whole point of the Disciple position. According to the Catholic position Baptism changes the nature; according to that of Campbell it changes the state.

[82] "Christian System," 201.

unless faith is transmuted into conduct, it will cease to be. Without birth, therefore, that which is begotten will never enjoy the delights of the kingdom of God. "All means of salvation are means of enjoyment, not of procurement. Birth itself is not for procuring, but for enjoying the life possessed before birth. So in the analogy—no one is to be baptized, or to be buried with Christ; no one is to be put under the water of regeneration for the purpose of procuring life, but for the purpose of enjoying the life of which he is possessed." [83]

As the act of the new birth, then, baptism is no unmeaning ceremony, but a solemn moral and spiritual ordinance of the Lord, by which, through a change of state, we come into a change of character. It does not give life; it translates life into that sphere in which the character becomes conformed to the image of the divine. It is no mere act of magic in the Romish acceptation of it, which works *ex opere operato,* but the most sublime moral and spiritual ordinance. "Not, indeed, that there is anything in the mere element of water, or in the form of placing the subject in it, or in the person that administers it, or in the formula used upon the occasion, though both good taste and piety have something to do in these particulars, but all its virtue and efficacy is in the faith and intelligence of him that receives it." [84] Realizing that his position might be construed, even by friends and followers, as being an advocacy of the rite as but a bodily act, he takes care frequently to emphasize its spiritual meaning. "Views of baptism as mere external and bodily acts, exert a very injurious influence on the understanding and practice of men. Hence many ascribe to it so little importance in the Christian economy. 'Bodily exercise,' says Paul, 'profits little.' We have been taught to regard immersion in water, into the name of the Father, the Son, and the Holy Spirit, as an act of the whole man—body, soul, and spirit. The soul of the intelligent subject is immersed into the Lord

[83] "Christian System," 266.
[84] "Christian Baptism," 273.

Jesus, as his body is immersed in the water. His soul rises with the Lord Jesus, as the body rises out of the water; and into one spirit with all the family of God, is he immersed." [85] It is upon this lofty plane that Campbell always stands, opposing any view of the sacred rite as being but an external or bodily act destitute of spiritual reality and power. He enforces this position with one more statement, the meaning of which is unmistakable. Baptism "has no abstract efficacy. Without previous faith in the blood of Christ, and deep unfeigned repentance before God, neither immersion in water, nor any other action, can secure to us the blessings of peace and pardon. It can merit nothing. Still to the believing penitent it is the means of receiving a formal, distinct, and specific absolution, or releases from guilt." [86]

It is evident that the sinner is not only born out of the old sinful relation; he is also born into the new one, and that one which is conducive to his life and growth. He is born into the family. Such a change is no little thing: it is the most glorious and sublime translation to be imagined. "Baptism, my fellow-citizens, is no mere rite, no unmeaning ceremony, I assure you. It is a most intellectual, spiritual, and sublime transition out of a sinful and condemned state, into a spiritual and holy state. It is a change of relation, not as respects flesh, but the spirit. It is an introduction into the mystical body of Christ, by which one necessarily obtains the remission of sins." [87] Such an experience is spiritually sublime, because it is an induction into the most wonderful spiritual relation in the universe, that of the family of God. "No one can understand or enjoy the sublime and awful import of a burial with Christ; of a baptism into death, who does not feel that he is passing through a most solemn initiation into a new family; high and holy relations to the Father, as his Father and his God—to the Son, as his Lord and his Messiah—to the Holy Spirit, as his

[85] "Christian System," 246, 247.
[86] "Christian System," 58.
[87] "Campbell-Rice Debate," 442.

sanctifier and comforter. He puts off his old relations, to the world, the flesh, and Satan. Consequently, that moment he is adopted into the family of God, and is personally invested with all the rights of a citizen of the kingdom of heaven." [88]

Contemplating the glory of a spiritual [89] change, which results from a devout and intelligent obedience in baptism, in a passage classic among the Disciples, Campbell rises eloquently into almost a mystical view. "With me, union with Christ is not mere union with a creed and a party built upon it. The kingdom of God is no party, no one party on earth. It is a spiritual kingdom, and is in the hearts of men: consisting not in meats, drinks, creeds, and covenants, 'but in righteousness, peace, and joy in the Holy Spirit.' Into this no one can enter without faith, and the Spirit of God. Baptism into Christ, the effect of faith, is a sensible introduction into this spiritual state, and outwardly unites us with the public profession; but when properly understood, spiritually, sometimes called mystically, or under the symbol, inducts us into an intimate, near, and holy union with the Saviour of the world, by his spirit. The outward act, then, is but the symbol of the transition, inward and spiritual, by which our souls are bathed in that ocean of love, which purifies our persons, and makes them one with the Lord. Without this, being born of water, or being connected with a church, is nothing—worse than nothing. Hence without previous knowledge, a faith, and repentance, immersion into the name, etc., is a mere outward and unprofitable ceremony. Hence my opposition to infant baptism; and hence my opposition to adult baptism, without a previous knowledge of the gospel." [90]

[88] "Campbell-Rice Debate," 442.
[89] "Millennial Harbinger Abridged," Smith, I, 459.
[90] "Campbell-Rice Debate," 493. Cf. the statement by Dr. Gore: "There is no subject on which the early teaching is richer and more spiritual than on the subject of baptism; and no part of the expressive ritual of the Church was more full of meaning than the rite of baptism. Nor during all the early period, when to become a Christian was a dangerous adventure, was there much peril of a mechanical or magical idea of baptism." "The Holy Spirit and the Church," 297.

The relation between justification and sanctification, in Campbell's theology, has already been considered. A summary may be made in a sentence, of the part which baptism plays in the process of making a bad man good. In relation to regeneration, it is the act of birth—the act through which the newly-begotten soul enters formally into the Christian family or Church, an environment in which the new life may be nurtured to Christian maturity. In relation to justification and sanctification, it is that act in which the certificate of pardon or forgiveness is formally given, and the new state entered, in which the desired ethical transformation may be ultimately attained.

One objection which is often urged against the whole Disciple position in regard to baptism is that it really invalidates the catholicity of the plea for Christian unity. In order, therefore, to make the plea truly catholic it is contended that the open membership plan must be adopted. This suggested alternative will be considered exhaustively in the next chapter and Campbell's attitude toward it evaluated. It should be observed here, however, that the basic reason which has accuated the Disciples in adopting their baptismal position—apart from the fact that they firmly believe it to have the undisputed weight of Scriptural authority behind it—is its undenied catholicity. In a word, they believe it to be universally admitted that the baptism of the New Testament was usually if not exclusively the immersion of a penitent believer and that the purpose of such baptism as set forth in the New Testament writings and the ancient creeds was "the remission of sins." The baptismal controversy has not been over the question as to whether or not this baptism is scriptural—this is universally acknowledged—its incontestibility has never been challenged: it has sought rather to establish the validity of sprinkling and pouring. The Disciple conviction that Jesus Himself was immersed has further confirmed them in the continuation of the practice. Since also baptism, as set forth in the New Testament, is always an act of faith—an act in which personal loyalty to Jesus is confessed—they believe it should be practiced as consecrated by His example and command. The conviction, and it is almost universal among them, that baptism is sacramental—that it does have vitally to do with the foundational things in the way of salvation, makes them react with determination against any effort to which would accord to it any significance less than that which it admittedly holds in the New Testament. The objection too is unsound in its assumption that an acknowledgment of the Pedobaptist position is necessary to catholicity. This is exactly the thing to be proved; the immersionist case, as we have seen, is acknowledged.

Dr. Moore advances an interesting solution to the whole baptismal controversy. "We need not concern ourselves with any special theory of either regeneration or baptism but simply insist upon all that the Lord has commanded, without formulating anything whatever." [91] Practically this is what the Disciples have been doing throughout their history. While holding to the position that the New Testament does teach baptism for the remission of sins they have never made an acceptance of this essential to fellowship in their churches. In the union between the Disciples and Christians in Lexington, Kentucky, in 1832 the design of baptism was not even discussed although it was well known that there was no unanimity on the question. It was determined to insist upon the immersion of a penitent of believer as alone obedience to the Lord's command and upon such obedience to receive converts into their communion. But is this, after all, a solution of the baptismal problem? Is it not rather merely a postponement of a troublesome enigma? I have elsewhere argued that the difficulty will some day be resolved only as a proper understanding of the design of the ordinance is attained. In a word, to ignore the purpose of baptism and to insist upon its observance purely as an arbitrary command of Christ is but to play with the problem.[92]

[91] "Comprehensive History of the Disciples of Christ," 200.
[92] "Studies in the Forgiveness of Sins," Chapter IV.

Campbell was on indisputable ground when he contended
that the most important thing about the ordinance is its
design. The whole difficulty has been the reluctance of
many in the Christian world to accept the Apostolic explanation of what baptism is for. Once that is acknowledged the
discordant notes die away and the divergent views are resolved into harmony. If baptism is all the Apostles claimed
for it, if it does all they contended it can do, then every
modern difficulty regarding its administration is cleared
away. If it is for the remission of sins there is no sense in
which it can be administered to infants. If it is—as Paul
undoubtedly conceived it to be—a symbol of a burial and a
resurrection into a newness of life it can only be properly
observed in an act which is itself a burial and resurrection.
It is becoming increasingly apparent also, as I have contended in another connection and I see no reason to modify
the position in any regard—that modern men must accept
the New Testament position or courageously cast the rite
into the theological discard. The attempt of some of the
Critics to account for the rise of baptism out of the rites of
the Mystery religions shows the tendency of modern
thought. From the purely pragmatic standpoint it is significant that where the wholeness of the Disciple witness is
faithfully proclaimed, including the position on baptism as
we have been in contact with it throughout the present
study, their communion continues to enlarge amazingly, and
their work to go forward with unprecedented vigour. On
the other hand stagnation and decay has been the inevitible
concomitant, of the attempt to water down their plea to
square with an unfounded theory that it is somehow out of
joint with modern thought and life. If it should ever be
unquestionably established that there is clear New Testament evidence for sprinkling and pouring, the Disciples will
be among the first enthusiastically to accept it; but at the
present time there is wide-spread certainty among them that
such evidence is non-existent.

The contention that the Disciple position on baptism un-

Christianizes the members of all other communions, is certainly a misapprehension of their whole plea and program and an evidence of a lack of knowledge of their literature. They could not very effectively plead for Christian unity did they not honestly believe there are Christians to unite. Campbell vigorously repudiates any such implication in his famous Luxenburg letter. "But who is a Christian? I answer, Everyone that believes in his heart that Jesus of Nazareth is the Messiah, the Son of God; repents of his sins, and obeys him in all things according to the measure of knowledge of his will." [93] "Should I find a Pedobaptist more intelligent in the Christian Scriptures, more spiritually minded and more devoted to the Lord than a Baptist, or one immersed on a profession of the ancient faith, I could not hesitate a moment in giving the preference of my heart to him that loveth most. Did I act otherwise, I would be a pure sectarian, a Pharisee among Christians. Still I will be asked, How do I know that anyone loves my Master but by obedience to His commandments? I answer, in no other way. But mark, I do not substitute obedience to one commandment, for universal or even general obedience. And should I see a sectarian Baptist or Pedobaptist more spiritually minded, more generally conformed to the requisitions of the Messiah, than one who precisely acquiesces with me in the theory or practice of immersion as I teach, doubtless the former, rather than the latter, would have my cordial approbation as a Christian. So I judge, and so I feel. It is the image of Christ, the Christian looks for and loves; and this does not consist in being exact in a few items, but in general devotion to the whole truth as far as known." "With me mistakes of the understanding and errors of the affections are not to be confounded." [94]

While cordially recognizing Christians of every other communion, and working hand in hand with them in the

[93] "Millennial Harbinger," 1847, 411.
[94] *Ibid.*, Volume for 1837, 411, 412.

extension of the kingdom of God, the majority of the Disciples are convinced that were they to relax their conception of immersion as the ideal so far as the form of baptism is concerned, they would, at the same time, destroy the ideality of their plea.

CHAPTER VII

THE LORD'S SUPPER

FOR more than a hundred years it has been the custom of Churches of Christ around the world to assemble each Lord's day for the purpose of breaking the bread. The position accorded the supper in the worship of the church is unique. It is not observed as an after thought—it is the very center of the worship, the purpose for which the Church comes together. The same emphasis which the Disciples have placed upon baptism is given to the Lord's Supper. The beautiful new buildings which are being erected by this communion in America give prominence in their interior architecture to these two ordinances of Christ. Two articles of furniture stand out above all others, and in central positions, the baptistry and the Lord's table. Campbell himself wrote voluminously upon this subject and since it has been so powerfully emphasized in all the practice of the Disciples this study of the distinctive Campbellian teaching which resulted in the organization of the Churches of Christ will be incomplete unless some attention be devoted to it.[1]

[1] Campbell does not discuss the institution of the Supper. He considered the records of its inauguration genuine. Dr. Percy Gardner represents those critics who deny that the Supper owes its origin to the Lord. "There is no proof that Jesus intended to institute a Lord's Supper." "The Christian sacrament as we know it, represents the early Christian custom of the common meal mixed with an infusion of sacramental mysticism, probably due to Paul." "Exploratio Evangelica," 461. Rashdall agrees with this view. "Whatever exactly happened at the Last Supper, the idea of perpetually commemorating that supper or of investing with a new significance the Jewish offering of cup and bread at the table was the work of the Church, not of its Founder." "The Idea of the Atonement in Christian Theology," 59. Principal Clow states the matured position of the more sober criticism: "There is no event in the life of Jesus which has surer historical verification than the record of the night on which he

285

While all of its phases have been considered two aspects of the subject have claimed more attention than others, the time of its observance, and the question as to who shall partake. In his famous series on "The Restoration of the Ancient Order of Things" which appeared in the "Christian Baptist." Campbell devotes four essays to the "Breaking of the Loaf." This is probably his best work on the subject. In 1830 he issued an "Extra" in the "Harbinger" on the same theme in which he restated the arguments advanced in the Baptist with some additional matter pertaining to the question. In the "Christian Messenger," the periodical in which his works appeared in the British Isles he discusses at some length the question of "close communion" and the relation of the Bishop's office to the proper observance of the feast.

I

In respect to the significance of the Supper all metaphysical explanations were rigidly excluded. For this reason Transubstantiation of Catholicism and Consubstantiation of Lutheranism were reprobated as being philosophical explanations destined only to confuse the worshiper and lead him away from the fundamental thing which was in the mind of the Master in its institution. While such metaphysical attempts were frowned upon the Disciples have never advocated the exclusively memorial view. This was

---

was betrayed." "The Church and the Sacraments," 160. Dr. Denney accords with this view: "There is nothing in Christianity more primitive than the Sacraments." "The Death of Christ," 60. Weizsäcker agrees with Denney "This festival was based, according to Paul (I Cor. 11:23) as well as the Synoptic Gospels, on a command made by Jesus Himself at the close of a common meal taken on the last evening of His life. Every assumption of its having arisen in the Church from the recollection of intercourse with Him at table, and the necessity felt for recalling His death, is precluded. The celebration must rather have been generally observed from the beginning." "Apostolic Age," II, 279. Harnack follows Weizsäcker as against Spitta's position (that the Supper was celebrated but not instituted by Jesus) because of the fact that the words of Paul as to his reception of it from the Lord "are too strong for me." "History of Dogma," I, 66, footnote.

certainly true of Campbell himself and those who followed him as the moulders of the movement which he had so successfully launched.[2] While most of his writing on the subject has to do with the time of its observance, in certain passages of his work he deals definitely with the problem of the presence of the Lord in the bread and wine and puts his seal to the view that there is a sense in which Jesus may be truly known in the emblems of His broken body and shed blood.

1. The supper, then, is an act of worship in which the Church as a priestly body partakes of Christ's sacrifice. The fourth proposition of his "Extra" affirmed the great doctrine that under the New Testament, Christians are a royal priesthood. "All Christians are members of the house or family of God, are called and constituted a holy and royal priesthood, and may, therefore, bless God for the Lord's table, its loaf, and cup—approach it without fear and partake of it with joy, as often as they please in remembrance of their Lord and Saviour."[3] As a priestly body we are to offer spiritual sacrifices to God. This is done in our worship, our hymns of praise, the prayers of our hearts, the gifts which we lay upon the altar for the extension of the Kingdom of Christ. But as the priests of the earthly house

[2] In 1849 W. K. Pendleton writes: "What is the meaning of the ceremony? Is it not the Christian's passover?" "Millennial Harbinger Abridged," II, 222. Dr. Robert Milligan says, "But to say that it is commemorative is not enough. It has reference to more than the mere recollection of a fact. It is also the medium of spiritual food to the hungry and thirsty soul." . . . "Every ordinance of God is a medium of food to the hungry soul. But no other institution is so well and so directly adapted to this end as the Lord's Supper. In it we are therefore commanded to eat of the Lord's broken body, and drink of his shed blood." "We must, therefore, simultaneously eat of the commemoration loaf and of the bread of life; and while we literally drink of the symbolic cup, we must also, at the same time, drink spiritually of that blood, which alone can supply the wants of the thirsty soul. Unless we do this, the bread that we eat can in no sense be to us the body of the Son of God; nor can the wine that we drink be in any sense the blood of the New Covenant, which was shed for the remission of the sins of many." "Millennial Harbinger," 1859, 601 ff.

[3] "Millennial Harbinger Abridged," II, 192.

were nourished by the sacrifices so the priest of the royal line is fed upon what was accomplished for him by the great High Priest in the sacrifice of Himself once for all upon the cross. "We have said that the loaf must be broken before the saints partake of it. Jesus took a loaf from the pascal table and broke it before He gave it to His Disciples. They received a broken loaf, emblematic of His body once whole, but by His own consent, broken for His Disciples. In eating it we then remember that the Lord's body was by His own consent broken or wounded for us. Therefore, he that gives thanks for the loaf should break it, not as the representative of the Lord, but after his example; and after the Disciples have partaken of the loaf, handing it to one another, or while they are partaking of it the disciple who break it partakes with them of the broken loaf. And thus they as priests feast upon his sacrifice. For the priests ate of the sacrifices and were thus partakers of the altar." [4]

2. The Supper is not only a communion in which the death of Jesus is commemorated and the nourishing power of His sacrifice made our own, it is commemorative of the love of God through which our reconciliation to the Fatherly

[4] *Ibid.*, II, 194, 195. In his comment on Hebrews 13:10, Dr. Milligan gives further proof that the Disciples have not considered the Supper to be a memorial feast only. "To eat of the altar is therefore manifestly to eat of the sacrifice which is offered on the altar. And that the sacrifice in this case was the sacrifice of Christ, is evident from the context, as well as from many parallel passages." "The New Testament Commentary," IX, 377, 378. In the same work he sets forth the view that the ordinances are but channels through which the true inwardness of God's grace is made known to the soul. There are those who "glory in the so-called 'sacraments' of the Christian religion, and talk much about 'baptismal regeneration,' 'the real presence,' and many other hallucinations that are equally vain and chimerical. But though intent upon ordinances they have never tasted of the bread and water of life. The ordinances of God are of course not to be despised or neglected. They are all divinely appointed means to the attainment of a divinely appointed end. They are the media through which God pours into our hearts the rich treasures of his grace, which alone can satisfy the soul. The Lord's Supper, for example, is most admirably adapted to bring the soul into communion with Christ; but unless it really does so, and in this way makes us partakers of the bread of life, what does it profit?" p. 387.

heart was made possible. "This institution commemorates the love which reconciled us to God and always furnishes us with a new argument to live to Him who died for us. He who feels not the eloquence and power of this argument, all other arguments assail in vain. God's goodness developed in creation and in His providence, is well designed to lead men to reformation. But the heart on which these fail, and to which Calvary appeals in vain, is past feeling, obdurate, and irreclaimable, beyond the operation of any moral power known to mortal man." [5]

3. An incentive to crucify the lusts of the flesh, to turn in sorrow from our sins is presented to us in the weekly observance of the memorial feast. Nothing is so potent in unmasking sin—in making it stand forth just as it is, as to face it with Calvary. In the presence of the cross we see sin in all its sinfulness, in all its damning power. In the supper each week we stand with contrite hearts before the cross. It is here we feel its power to evoke within us cleansing repentance. "Every time the disciples assemble around the Lord's table they are furnished with a new argument also against sin, as well as with a new proof of the love of God. It is as well intended to crucify the world in our hearts and to crucify our hearts to the world, as to quicken us to God, and to diffuse His love within us." [6] Such passages as these certainly demonstrate the fact that Campbell and his fellow-Disciples did not hold the Zwinglian view. The Lord's Supper is memorial—its is beautifully commemorative but it is more. [7]

---

[5] "Millennial Harbinger Abridged," II, 196.

[6] *Ibid.*, II, 197. For an exhaustive study of the modern Disciple view of the sacramental nature of the Supper see my book "Studies in the Forgiveness of Sins," 185, 224.

[7] An interesting view of the doctrine of the Supper is advanced by M. Goguel, "L'Euchariste," 100, 101. "Ce que Jésus donne aux siens, c'est lui-même, c'est-à-dire l'essence même de sa pensée, de sa foi, de son coeur, il se dépense sans compter pour illumer en eux la flamme qui le dévore, pour faire naître et pour entretenir en eux et chacun d'eux les aspirations, les energies, les certitudes qui l'animent." "That which Jesus gives to His own is Himself, that is to say the essence itself of his thought, of His faith, of

II

The Campbellian doctrine of the Supper is further inextricably bound up with his discussion of the time of its celebration. As his arguments for the observance of this divine institution each week and by all the house of God are expounded his conception of its glorious purpose will be brought more clearly into relief.

1. The proper time for the celebration of the memorial feast can be determined with exactitude only as we consider the fact that "there is a divinely instituted order of Christian worship in Christian assemblies" and "that this order of worship is uniformly the same." [8] One essay is devoted to an attempted proof of this position. Either there was such an instituted order of worship in the New Testament Church or there was not. If no such order was instituted by divine authority then a door is open to all manner of imposition and anything which the human mind can devise may be

---

His heart, He spends Himself without cost to kindle in them the flame which consumes Him, to make to be born and to nourish in them and in each of them the aspirations, the energies, the certitudes which animated Him." In his late book Goguel, as he sets forth the theology of Paul acknowledges that the apostle saw in the Supper a closer connection with the Master's death. The Supper "c'est, pour Paul, un acte institué par Jésus incommémoration de son sacrifice et comme moyen d'entrer en relation avec lui dans sa mort. Dans cet acte auquel s'associe le'Eglise entière, les fidèles sont invités à asseoir à la table du Seigneur et à recevoir sa coupe. Le pain et le vin qui leur sont distribués sont le corps et le sang du Christ, ils mettent ceux qui les consomment en relation directe avec Christ dans sa mort." "The Supper is, for Paul, an act instituted by Jesus in commemoration of His sacrifice and as means of entering into relation with Him in His death. In this act the whole church associated, the faithful are invited to seat themselves at the table of the Lord and to receive His cup. The bread and wine which are distributed to them are the body and blood of Christ, they introduce those who consume them into direct relation with Christ in His death." "Jésus de Nazareth," 163. See also the splendid discussion of the true sacramental significance of the Supper by Forsythe. "The Church and the Sacraments," 214, 262.

[8] "Christian Baptist," 165. Cf. Weizsächer's discussion of church order, "Apostolic Age," II, 246, 290.

practiced in the name of worship.[9] This is unthinkable. While Jesus Himself gave no direct instructions recorded in the Gospels, yet, He promised unto His Disciples that Holy Spirit who should "guide them into all truth." Under the leading of the Spirit we are informed that the first disciples in the Church in Jerusalem "continued steadfastly in the apostles teaching and fellowship, in the breaking of bread and prayers." There were then four characteristics of a divinely ordered service as organized by the apostolic leadership under the inspiration of the Holy Spirit; it was a teaching or doctrine, it was a fellowship, it was a communion and it was a service of prayer.[10] Four things must always be done in every assembly of Christians meeting for worship; the doctrine of the apostles must be taught, the fellowship of giving must be observed, the breaking of the bread or the communion supper must be celebrated and the prayers of the Church must be offered. While many modern disciples would not go all the way with Campbell in his contention that every item of practice in the Church has been divinely appointed there is universal agreement that these four things ought to be observed in every true service in which the Church as a body meets for the worship of our Lord.[11]

In regard to the time of the celebration of the Supper it should be noted that it was a part, and a central part, of the worship of the Church. "The breaking of the loaf and, the joint participation of the cup of the Lord, in commemoration of the Lord's Supper," is an instituted part of the worship and edification of all Christian congregations in all their stated meetings. "The Apostles taught the churches to do

[9] "Millennial Harbinger Abridged," II, 197, 198.

[10] Cf. Clow, "The Church and the Sacraments," 170, 171.

[11] Dr. Gates is in error when he says: "He took the appeal to the precept and precedent of Holy Scripture with an extract and faithful literalness, requiring a 'Thus sayeth the Lord' for every item of faith or practice in the church. Nothing seemed to him to be left to the sanctified common sense of the church in after ages by Christ and the Apostles." This statement ignores altogether Campbell's conception of the province of the "Law of Expediency." See "The Early Relation and Separation of Baptists and Disciples," 53.

all the Lord commanded. Whatever then, the churches did by the appointment or concurrence of the Apostles, they did by the commandment of Jesus Christ. Whatever acts of religious worship the Apostles taught or sanctioned in one Christian congregation, they taught and sanctioned in all Christian congregations, because all are under the same government of one and the same King." [12]

Luke tells us that the Church in Troas followed the custom of that in Jerusalem in its steadfast continuation in the breaking of the bread. The language employed is very explicit. "And upon the first day of the week, when we were gathered together to break bread, Paul discoursed with them, intending to depart on the morrow." [13]   From this verse two things are apparent, (1) that it was a custom or rule of the brethren in Troas to meet on the first day of the week, and, (2) that the primary reason which brought them together was that they might break the bread. The objection that Luke does not say they met every first day is unsound.[14] Why then should we contend against the Sabbatarians that we ought to observe every first day as a memorial to His resurrection? There is but one first day of the week and it comes every week. The same arguments which prove that the Lord's day is the day for the Christian assembly apply with equal force to the observance of the Supper on that day. "From the second of Acts, then, we learn that the breaking of the loaf was a stated part of the worship of the disciples in their meetings; and from the twentieth we learn that first day of the week was the stated time for those meetings; and above all we ought to notice that the most prominent object of their meetings was to break the loaf." [15]

[12] "Millennial Harbinger Abridged," II, 197.
[13] Acts 20:7.
[14] "Millennial Harbinger Abridged," II, 198.
[15] *Ibid.*, II, 199. Cf. the statement of Harnack: "The common worship, with its center in the celebration of the Supper, is the cardinal point." "Expansion of Christianity," II, 53, footnote. With this view Duchesne agrees. "The Eucharist was always the chief act of worship. In the beginning it was celebrated at the end of a corporate meal." "The Early History of the Church," I, 385.

That the Churches met upon the first day of the week is admittedly set forth in Paul's charge to the congregations in Galatia and the church in Corinth. "Now concerning the collection for the saints, as I gave order to the churches of Galatia, so also do ye. Upon the first day of the week let each one of you lay by him in store, as he may prosper, that no collections be made when I come." [16]

In the eleventh chapter of the same letter Paul throws much light upon the whole communion service as it was observed in the churches of his day. In the severe rebuke which he administers to the Corinthians we learn not only how much the Supper had degenerated but a further attestation is given to the fact that they met on this day for the primary purpose of breaking bread. "When therefore, ye assemble yourselves together, it is not possible to eat the Lord's Supper: for in your eating each one taketh before other his own supper; and one is hungry and another is drunken." [17] The rich brought with them their delicacies and in the common meal which then preceded the Supper they ate and drank, often rudely passing by the poorer brother whose contribution to the common meal had been more meager. Thus they had made of the Supper a drunken feast. Paul's meaning is "when you come together in this spirit, when you thus prositute the Memorial feast you do not come together to observe the Lord's Supper." [18] But to do that very thing had been the purpose for which they came together. It is as though a teacher should reprove his pupils for wasting time saying "When you act like this you have not assembled to learn.[19] "We have seen, then, that the saints met every first day in Corinth; and when they assembled in one place it was to eat the Lord's Supper, a declaration of the practice of the primitive congregations as explicit as could incidentally be given, differing only from

[16] I Cor. 16:1, 2.

[17] I Cor. 11:20, 21.

[18] See a fine discussion of this passage, "The Church and the Sacraments," Principal Clow, 173, 174.

[19] "Millennial Harbinger Abridged," II, 200, 201.

a direct command in the form in which it is expressed. But it is agreed on all hands that whatsoever the congregations did with the approbation of the Apostles, they did by their authority. For the Apostles gave them all the Christian institutions. Now as the Apostle Paul approbated their meeting every week, and their coming together into one place to show forth the Lord's death; and only censured their departure from the meaning of the institution, it is as high authority as we could require for the weekly meeting of the disciples." [20]

But there are other reasons advanced for the weekly celebration of the memorial feast. Not only is it evident that "among the acts of worship, or institutions of the Lord, to which the disciples attended in these meetings, the breaking of the bread was so conspicuous and important, that the churches are said to meet on the first day of the week for this purpose," [21] but it is also certain that "no example can be adduced from the New Testament of any Christian congregation assembling on the first day of the week unless for the breaking of the bread." The burden of proof is upon those who contend that the Supper is not a constituted part of the regular worship. The same arguments which will prove that the Church ought to assemble monthly or quarterly or semi-annually will establish the obligation to meet on every first day. What are such arguments? Where in the New Testament is there even a hint of such procedure? As physical health requires regular food so the health of the spiritual man is dependent upon a regular spiritual diet and this is afforded him in the divinely instituted plan of worship in which the Supper holds a centrally important place. It is also manifest that there is not a memorial institution in all the Bible which does not have a stated time for its observance. This applies to every social institution and to almost everyone of individual character. How often should baptism be observed? Was the feast of

[20] "Millennial Harbinger Abridged," II, 200.
[21] *Ibid.*, II, 197.

the passover celebrated indiscriminately? If the Lord's Supper has not a stated time for its observation "then it is an anomaly—a thing *sui generis*—an institution like no other of divine origin." [22]

He argues for this position of the Lord's Supper from another angle; this time it is analogical in character. "There is a house on earth, called the house of God." [23] This house is the Church, the Christian community. Paul so teaches the Corinthians, "Ye are God's building." [24] This temple of the Lord is "built upon the foundation of the apostles and prophets, Christ Jesus himself being the chief cornerstone; in whom each several buildings, fitly framed together groweth into a holy temple in the Lord; in whom ye also are builded together for a habitation of God in the Spirit." [25] In this analogy the Church of Christ occupies the middle place between the outer court and the holiest of all. The common priests went always into the holy place but once a year the high priest entered the holiest of holies. "Thus our Great High Priest went once for all into the true 'holiest of all,' into the real presence of God, and has permitted us Christians as a royal priesthood, as a chosen race, to enter always into the only holy place now on earth, the Christian Church." [26] Thus, also, "we as living stones, are built up a spiritual house, to be a holy priesthood, to offer up spiritual sacrifices, acceptable to God through Jesus Christ." [27] There is not only a perfect analogy between the Jewish holy place and the Christian Church but the furniture in the one is also analogous to the other. As in the Jewish holy place there are certain emblematic articles of furniture, the candlestick from which came the light, the table of shewbread with its twelve loaves "of the presence" which were changed each Sabbath after having been exhibited there for a week, so in

[22] *Ibid.*, II, 201.
[23] "Millennial Harbinger Abridged," II, 189.
[24] I Cor. 3:9.
[25] Eph. 2:20, 22.
[26] "Millennial Harbinger Abridged," II, 189.
[27] I Pet. 2:5.

the spiritual house of God, the Church, there is the word of God from which comes light and the table of the Lord upon which are the loaf and cup. As the priests ate of the twelve loaves which were taken from the golden table so the new community of royal and holy priests may come with holy boldness and joy to the table far more precious than that of gold.[28] If it is then apparent that in the house of the Lord there is thus a table as a part of the furniture and upon it the one loaf emblematic of the unity of the people purchased by His sacrifice, it is also evident that "it must always be there when the disciples meet, unless it can be shown that only some occasions require its presence and others its absence; or that the Lord is poorer or more churlish at one time than at another, that he is not able always to keep a table, or too parsimonious to furnish it for his friends." [29]

One fundamental mistake has been made by the whole Christian world in regard to this institution of the Lord. "While Romanists, Episcopalians, Presbyterians of every grade, Independents, Methodists, Baptists, etc., acknowledge the breaking of bread to be a divine institution, an act of religious worship in Christian assemblies, they all differ in their views of the import of the institution, the manner and times in which it is to be observed, and the appendages thereunto belonging. In one idea they all agree, that it is an extraordinary and not an ordinary act of Christian worship; and consequently, does not belong to the ordinary worship of the Christian church." [30] Because of this fact they have held the wrong attitude toward the Supper making it a terrible pennance instead of seeing in it the feast of solemn joy as it was so clearly in the experience of the first disciples. The time of the observance of the feast, therefore, has a vital bearing upon what we conceive the significance of Supper to be. "Much darkness and superstition are found in the

[28] "Millennial Harbinger Abridged," II, 189, 191.
[29] "Millennial Harbinger Abridged," II, 191.
[30] "Christian Baptist," 175.

minds and exhibited in the practice of the devout annual, semi-annual and quarterly observers of the breaking of the bread. They generally make a Jewish passover of it.[31] Some of them indeed make a Mount Sinai convocation of it. With all the bitterness of sorrow, and gloominess of superstition, they convert it into a religious pennance, accompanied by a morose piety and an awful affliction of soul and body, expressed in fastings, long prayers, and sad countenances on sundry days of humiliation, fasting and preparation. And the only joy exhibited on the occasion, is, that all is over; for which some of them appoint a day of thanksgiving. They rejoice that they have approached the very base of Mount Sinai unhurt by stone or dart. In the opposite degrees to their assent to, and their descent from this preternatural solemnity, their piety is equal. In other words, they are as pious one week or ten weeks after, as they were one week or ten weeks before. If there be anything fitly called superstition in this day and country, this preëminently deserves the name." [32] This attitude toward the Supper has direct bearing upon the time of its observance. If it is analogous to a Passover feast the more infrequently it is observed the better.

The Lord's Supper to the Christian is a feast, a feast of

[31] While Campbell undoubtedly believed that the Supper was instituted on the passover night his view of the significance of the feast would seem to accord with the position of those who hold that it was not at the passover supper but at a common meal. Professor Bacon holds this view of it. "At the evening meal—not the passover supper, which would have presented the closer symbol of the slain lamb—Jesus assumed His usual part as dispenser of the food." "The Beginnings of the Gospel Story," 204. For detailed statement of this view cf. R. H. Kennet, "The Lord's Supper," 30, 38. Weizsäcker agrees with Campbell, "The failure of the Fourth Gospel to narrate the institution of the Supper cannot, from the character of the book, surprise us. Nor is it astonishing that in it Jesus' last meal is not a Pascal Supper. That it actually was this there is no doubt. It was on account of the Passover that Jesus went to Jerusalem that evening. It was the Pascal feast which was actually held that caused His death to be compared with the killing of the Pascal Lamb (I Cor. V:7)." "Apostolic Age," II, 279.

[32] "Christian Baptist," 175.

solemn joy. In opposition to the position so generally held "the intelligent Christian views it in quite another light. It is to him as sacred and solemn as prayer to God, and as joyful as the hope of immortality and eternal life. His hope before God, springing from the death of his Son, is gratefully exhibited and expressed by him in the observance of this institution." [33] It is, therefore, "a religious feast; a feast of joy and gladness; the happiest occasion, and the sweetest antepast on earth of the society and entertainment of heaven, that mortals meet with on their way to the true Canaan." If such be its true import then how should it be considered, as a privilege or a pain? If its institution is any proof of the goodness and kindness of the Saviour at all, then it would be far better to observe it often. "But reverse the case and convert it into an awful and grevious pennance, and then grace is exhibited in not enforcing it but seldom." Thus it is that "as we understand its nature and design, will its frequency appear a favour or a frown." [34]

III

The question "who should partake of the Lord's Supper," has been frequently discussed in Disciple history. It deserves exhaustive treatment because of the unique and unassailable ground which was finally occupied. In 1826 Campbell appears to be very much disturbed about the whole problem of communion with the unimmersed. Although a Baptist he did not at this time hold with the Baptists that the unimmersed should be excluded from the Lord's table. While differing from them in this important matter he yet considered himself in communion with them and rather proudly proclaims this fact in the "Christian Baptist." [35] For this declaration he was quite severely taken to task by a correspondent signing himself, "An Independent Baptist."

[33] *Ibid.*, 175.
[34] *Ibid.*, 175.
[35] "Christian Baptist," III, 47.

A somewhat lengthy discussion ensued in which Campbell defends himself against the charge of inconsistency and defines most exactly his conception of the nature of communion. It is in this discussion that his mixed mind regarding the proper relationship which should obtain between the Baptists and the unimmersed appears. "I have thought and thought and vacillated very much on the question whether Baptists and Pedobaptists ought, could, would, or should, irrespective of their peculiarities, sit down at the same Lord's table. And one thing I do know that either they should cease to have communion in prayer, praise, and other religious observances or they should go the whole length. Of this point I am certain. And I do know that as much can be said and with as much reason and scripture on its side to prove that immersion is as necessary prior to social prayer, praise, etc., as it is to eating the Lord's Supper." [36] His critic, assuming that he had openly advocated mixed communion, replied in vitriolic language: "Your very charitable recognition of Pedobaptists, etc., as brethren serves to neutralize the distinction between truth and error—between allegiance and rebellion. As for the societies of sprinkled 'new creatures' with whom you could wish (if they would let you) to have full communion, equal to what you have with the whole Baptist society, they resemble what a synagogue of Jews would be who rejected circumcision." [37] Campbell hastened to clear himself of this charge: "Permit me to remark that you have taken for granted what has not been asserted yet; that Baptists and Pedobaptists should, irrespective of their differences on the subject of baptism, break bread together. Whether they ought, or ought not, has not been asserted by me. This question is yet with me *sub judice*." [38] From these statements there can be no doubt but that his mind at this time was not made up on the question as to policy of allowing those who had not been baptized to

[36] *Ibid.*, III, 68.
[37] *Ibid.*, III, 87.
[38] "Christian Baptist," III, 86.

come to the table of the Lord. While he did not agree with the close communion position of the Baptists he had come to no clear position of his own.

Three years later, however, there is evident a much stronger attitude toward this problem. While he has not as yet arrived on the ground which he was afterwards to hold with such success the underlying principle which should make his own position unique asserts itself. In answer to a correspondent who had presented him with a constitution for a local church requesting his opinion of the same, he engages in a very vigorous discussion of the whole question of the unimmersed and the Lord's Supper.[39] In this spirited rejoinder he makes known his determined opposition, not to an occasional observance of the Supper with Baptists by a Pedobaptist, but to making such action a practice—a settled policy.

He found the hypothetical constitution objectionable "because it admits an unimmersed person to all the ordinances of the Christian community or congregation as an occasional member; and yet refuses to receive such as regular and constant members. I know of no scriptural authority for such a discrimination. It is arbitrary and unreasonable. If I can admit an unimmersed person once a month for a year to all social ordinances, I can for life for good behaviour. When I say, I can do so, I mean that all precepts, and scriptural reasons, authorize such a course." It is significant in the light of his future position to note the statement with which he prefaces his five objections to making a regular practice of admitting unbaptized people to the privileges of the Lord's table. "But I object to making it a RULE, in any case, to receive unimmersed persons to church ordinances." He particularizes his reasons for such vigorous

---

[39] Professor Gates is in error in his contention that Campbell in this reply "defends essentially the Baptist position of close communion." While there has been a change of attitude in the direction of the Baptist position he does not go all the way with them. See, "The Early Relation and Separation of Baptists and Disciples," 59.

objection. It is nowhere commanded nor is there precedent for it in the New Testament. It is also suspect because it "corrupts the simplicity and uniformity of the whole genius of the new institution." To make a habit of inviting unimmersed people to communicate is also objectionable because it makes of a positive command of the Lord a mere opinion. "It necessarily makes immersion of non-effect. For, with what consistency or propriety can a congregation hold up to the world either the authority or utility of an institution which they are in the habit of making as little of, as any human opinion?" [40] The last objection reflects the fear which has ever haunted Disciples—the fear of an assumption of authority which would lead to apostasy. Those who would make it a rule to invite unimmersed persons to regular celebration of the Supper are in danger of this very thing, for, "they who do so, assume the very same dispensing power, which issued in that tremendous apostacy which we and all Christians are laboring to destroy." [41] If this right to dispense with an undoubted command of the King is once assumed who can tell where the whole matter will terminate?

To the question "But do you not expect to sit down in heaven with all the Christians of all sects, and why not sit down at the same table with them on earth?" he replies, "It is time enough to behave as they do in heaven when we meet there. I expect to meet with those whom we call Patriarchs, Jews, and Pagans, in heaven. But this is no reason why I should offer sacrifice like Abel or Abimelech; circumcise my children like Reuben or Gad; or pray to the Great Spirit, as an Indian; because some of these sort of people may be fellow-citizens in heaven. Perhaps I am too charitable now, for some? Be this as it may. I do expect to meet with some of 'all nations, tribes, and tongues,' in the heavenly country. But while on earth I must live and behave according to the order of things under which I am

[40] "Christian Baptist," VI, 67, 68.
[41] "Christian Baptist," VI, 67, 68.

placed. If we are now to be governed by the manners and customs in heaven, why was any other than the heavenly order of society instituted on earth? There will be neither bread, wine, nor water, in heaven. Why, then, use them on earth? But if those who propose this query would reflect, that all the parts of the Christian institution are necessary to its present state, and only preparatory to the heavenly, by giving us a taste for the purity and joys of that state, they could not propose such a question." [42]

The problem of communion with the unimmersed figured largely in the discussions which preceded the historic union between the "Disciples" and "Christians" in 1832. Stone and his fellow Christians followed the custom of freely admitting to the table all who professed faith in the Lordship of Jesus without question regarding their baptism. The Disciples objected to this and the discussion between Campbell and Stone cleared the atmosphere and helped to pave the way for the union for which both of them were striving. The discussion turned on the relation between faith and opinion and once more demonstrated the fact that a clear apprehension of this relationship is the true philosophy of Christian unity. Stone falls into the error of confusing that which is clearly an item of the faith—that which is unquestionably a matter of divine revelation, with opinions which have not to do with facts but with speculations. "Christians cannot be blamed for their different opinions when they have honestly searched for the truth. My opinion is that immersion is only baptism; but shall I, therefore, make my opinion a term of Christian fellowship? If, in this case, I thus act, where shall I cease from making my opinions terms of fellowship? I confess I see no end. But one may say that immersion is so plainly the meaning of Christian baptism that he knows not how any honest man can be ignorant of it. This is the very language of all opinionists. . . . One may say my idea of baptism, as meaning

42 *Ibid.*, VI, 68.

immersion, is not an opinion, but a fact. So say the orthodox respecting many of their unscriptural opinions, and they
are as firmly persuaded of them as you can be respecting
immersion not being an opinion of baptism." [43]

In answer to the objection "I cannot have communion
with an unimmersed person, because he is not a member of
the Church of Christ however holy and pious he may be,"
he exclaims, "Shall we say all are enemies of Christ who
are not immersed? We dare not. If they are not enemies,
or if they are not against Him, they are for Him and with
Him. Shall we reject those who are with Jesus from us?
Shall we refuse communion with those with whom the Lord
communes? Shall we reject those who follow not with us
in opinion? Shall we make immersion the test of religion?
Shall we centre all religion in this one point?"

In his reply Campbell places his finger squarely upon
the difficulty and settles the question in such manner as
to preclude successful refutation by his esteemed and distinguished editorial friend. Until it is proved that we do
not know what New Testament baptism was and that we
can, therefore, never be sure about it, we cannot relegate it
to the realm of opinion, for "opinions are always, in strict
propriety of speech, doubtful matters, because speculative.
If ever the word be applied to matters of testimony, to
laws, institutions, or religious worship, we must be confounded in our faith and practice. If opinion applies
equally to immersion and the doctrine of the Trinity, then
it will apply equally to the Messiahship of Jesus, the resurrection of the dead, eternal life, and every item of Christian
faith and hope. . . . I know that baptism means immersion
as certainly as I know that *manus* means a hand, and *penna*,
a pen; or as certainly as I know that sprinkling is not pouring, and pouring is not dipping. . . .

"We are represented as refusing communion with him
with whom God communes, if we do not recognize as a

43 "Christian Messenger," 1831, V, 19.

fellow-citizen everyone whom God regards as one of His people. Has God anywhere commanded us to sit down at the Lord's table with a person who refuses to be immersed because he was sprinkled? Or has He enjoined upon me to treat any person as a brother in the Lord, because He has recognized him as such, when he fails to keep the ordinances of the Lord? It is only in obedience to the Lord, not on the principle of expediency, but because the Lord has enjoined it, that we are to associated with any person as a brother in the Lord. Nor do I say that none are Christians but those who walk orderly: we only say that we are commanded to associate with those who walk orderly. If we can dispense with the neglect or disobedience of one Christian, we may with another; and so on, till we have in the Church all the vices of the world." [44]

Answering the question which had frequently been put to him "Why do not the Disciples and Christians unite seeing they are agreed in purpose?" Stone sets for the differences seemingly barring the way to the unity which all were desirous to see become actual. One of the chief obstacles in the way is "that we have fellowship and communion with unimmersed persons. They contend—so we understand them—that, according to the New Institution, none but the immersed have their sins remitted, and, therefore, they cannot commune with the unimmersed. On this point we cannot agree with them; and the reason for our disagreement is, that this sentiment, in our view, will exclude millions of the fairest characters, for many centuries back, from heaven. . . . I know our brethren say: 'We do not declare that they are excluded from heaven, but only from the kingdom on earth. We leave them in the hand of God.' But does not this sentiment lead to that conclusion? We believe and acknowledge that baptism is ordained by the King a means for the remission of sins to penitent believers, but we cannot say that immersion is the *sine qua non*, with-

[44] "Millennial Harbinger," II, 103.

out maintaining the awful consequences above, and without contradicting our own experiences. We, therefore, teach the doctrine, 'Believe, repent, and be immersed for the remission of sins,' and we endeavour to convince our hearers of its truth, but we exercise patience and forebearance towards such pious persons as cannot be convinced." [45] This is, of course, the argument which is advanced today for so-called open membership. It is, however, certainly a misapprehension of the position of the Disciples as first expressed by Campbell. He did not unchristianize the Pedobaptist world as the whole tenor of his writings testify. He could never have made a plea for Christian unity had he not devoutly believed that among all the sects and divisions of Christendom there were Christians to unite. He closes the discussion with an unanswerable reaffirmation of his objection, not to the occasional admission of some unimmersed brother to the table, but to the practice of inviting such. We must follow the plan divinely given to us or acknowledge union impossible. "But that God's rule or principle of rewarding men hereafter, is to be, as near as we can guess at it, the rule of our conduct to them in receiving them into his kingdom on earth, and in treating them as members of it, is inadmissable. The question is, Are we authorized to make the sincerity and honesty of a person's mind our rule of conduct? It is God alone who is judge of this; and surely he would not require us to act by a rule which we can never apply to the case. Neither, perhaps, is it a fair position to assume that a man's sincerity in opinion or belief will have any weight in the final judgement; but whether it will or not, it cannot be a rule of our proceeding in any case. We judge from actions; God judges the heart, and, therefore, we look for visible obedience, and, when we are assured that the Lord has commanded every man to confess Him or to profess the faith, and be immersed into His name, we can never justify ourselves before God

[45] "Life of John Smith," Williams, 443, 444.

or man in presuming in our judgement of charity to set aside His commandment, and in accepting for it a human substitute." [46]

The publication of the Campbell-Rice debate provoked a great outcry among the British Churches of Christ. It was charged that Campbell, reversing his position, had become an advocate of open communion as the term was understood among the English Baptists. Influenced strongly by the Scottish Baptists the British Churches from the very beginning had been firm protagonists of close communion. They did not restrict the Supper to their own members but rather to the immersed. A critical study of the passages in the great debate which caused such offense fails to disclose any change in the attitude which Campbell had held from the beginning. These provocative excerpts are given here not only because they most effectively refute the accusation against him but because they further illustrate the broad ground which he held unswervingly to the end. "The English Baptists very generally practice open communion, as they call it. They invite persons unbaptized to participate with them at the Lord's table. Now the difference between them and our brethren, in cases where such persons occasionally commune with them, is this: They do not invite them, as such, to commune in the Supper, but some of them sometimes say, that 'the table is the Lord's,' and not theirs, and that though they cannot invite anyone to partake of it but those visibly and ostensibly, by their own baptism, the Lord's people, still, not presuming to say that those only are the Lord's people, in this day of division, we debar no consistent professor of the faith of any party, who, upon his own responsibility, chooses to partake with us. Thus we throw the responsibility upon him, while the English Baptists, in many instances, take it upon themselves." [47] In a further passage he flatly denies that the American Churches of Christ have ever practiced open communion in

[46] "Life of John Smith," Williams, 445.
[47] "Campbell-Rice Debate," 798.

the only true sense in which open communion may be defined. Rice had quoted a statement in Campbell's correspondence with the venerable Elder Jones of London and to this he replies: "I repeat it, also, that there is not now, and certainly there was not when that was written, anything amongst us, strictly and literally construed, like that which Mr. Jones had in his eye in England, when that was strictly and literally construed. We have NO OPEN COMMUNION WITH US, and in England they have. That principle is not at all recognized amongst us. In England there are large communities of free communion Baptists, who admit Pedobaptists as freely as they do the baptized. We have no such custom amongst us. There may be ten or one hundred congregations amongst us that have made that matter a question; the great majority, as far as I know, have not." [48] D. S. Burnet, one of the best known of Campbell's contemporaries refutes the charge of open communion in caustic language: "Let me say to you, and the brethren, that this charge of mixed communion, is a vile slander as regards myself, and I must say the same of Alexander Campbell. As to Brother Scott, I do not recollect that I have ever heard anything from him on the subject, but I am apprehensive that he never 'publicly advocated it.' " [49]

In 1845 Campbell very clearly places his position before the British Churches in his answer to the accusations arising from the reception of the Rice debate in Great Britain. The "Christian Magazine" of London in its issue for December, 1844, exults in what its editor was pleased to term "A Campbell's change of views." In reply Campbell sums up the whole matter in a statement which sets forth the view of the overwhelming majority of the American Churches of Christ and those in South Africa to the present hour. "If I were asked the question in the year of Christ, 1845, 'Do any of your churches admit unbaptized persons to communion?' I would still answer, 'Not one, so far as known

[48] "Campbell-Rice Debate," 808.
[49] "Christian Messenger," IX, 290, 291.

to me,' if it were added as Elder Jones added to the above question—'a practice that is becoming very prevalent in this country.' We have no such PRACTICE. Professors of unblemished reputation, of Pedobaptist churches, are sometimes informed at our large meetings, that we do not suppose all unimmersed persons to be absolute aliens from the family of God, nor are they absolutely excluded from any participation with us in prayer or in the Lord's Supper; on the contrary, if any of them takes upon himself the responsibility, being satisfied in himself of his own baptism, to participate with us at a table which is not ours, but the Lord's, we have no power to forbid him, and would not withhold from him the symbolic loaf and cup. But to make it a PRACTICE to receive such persons as members of our churches into regular communion, is a practice unknown to me in any one church in the Reformation. There is not, indeed, in the extracts furnished from the Rice discussion, nor in any passage of my writings, as far as remembered by me, a single sentence indicative of such a 'PRACTICE.'

"I am still pleased, indeed, 'to see Pedobaptists of good Christian character occasionally take upon themselves the responsibility to break the loaf in commendation of their love to their Saviour, and to us, because such persons, on a more intimate acquaintance, generally become disciples of Christ, or withdraw from such intimacy. Cannot the editor of the 'Christian Magazine' distinguished between an act of hospitality to a stranger, and the PRACTICE of inviting all strangers to become members of the family—between Paul's circumcising Timothy and circumcising every half-bred Jew who embraced the Christian faith—between taking upon himself once a Jewish vow, and assuming the whole code of Levitical and Jewish rites—between saying AMEN to a Christian prayer, and acquiescing in all the ceremonies of the Church of England?

"I am also of opinion, that I have more good reasons and scriptural authority for refusing communion with many immersed persons than for refusing Christian communion with some unimmersed but very exemplary followers of the Lamb. Still, should anyone persist in treating immersion as a human tradition, with whom I might have communed on several occasions, after that he had opportunity of better instruction, and indicated an uncandid temper, I would say to him, that I could not, in good conscience, invite him to participate with me in any Christian institution." [50]

As late as 1861 the question as to the reception of the unimmersed at the Lord's table agitated the leaders among the Disciples but after the discussion which then took place in the "Millennial Harbinger" the problem seems to have been solved. In answer to the query as to the exact position of the Disciples on the question Isaac Errett says; "We are pleading for further reformation; our plea proceeds on the integrity of previous pleas—it is a plea for the reunion of the scattered people of God. It does not recognize sects, on human bases, as divine; but it recognizes a people of God among these sects, and seeks to call them out. We are compelled, therefore, to recognize as Christians many who have been in error on baptism, but who in the spirit of obedience are Christians indeed. . . . I confess, for my own part, did I understand the position of the brethren to deny this, I would recoil from my position among them with utter disgust. It will never do to unchristianize those on whose shoulders we are standing, and because of whose previous labours we are enabled to see some truths more clearly, than they. Yet while fully according to them the piety and Christian standing which they deserve, it is clear that they are in great error on the question of baptism—and we must be careful not to compromise the truth. Our practice, therefore, is neither to invite nor reject particular classes of persons, but to spread the table in the name of the Lord, for the Lord's people, and allow all to come who will, each on his own responsibility." [51]

In discussion of the same theme Robert Richardson up-

[50] "Christian Messenger," (enlarged series) I, 40, 41.
[51] "Millennial Harbinger," 1861, 711, 712.

holds the view taken by the overwhelming majority of the leaders among the Disciples. Repudiating the assumption that the Disciples invite the unimmersed to communion he says: "Our position is quite different; we neither discuss nor determine this question. We simply leave it to each member to determine for himself." [52] Those who advocated exclusion of the unimmersed while acknowledging the whole matter to be an "untaught question" still attempted to answer it by their rigid exclusionist policy. Dr. Richardson directs their attention to this inconsistency: "If they would reflect a moment, they might see that on their own premises, if it is an 'untaught question,' they can have no right to decide it against those concerned. And further, that in so deciding, they presume to decide two questions, 1st, that no unimmersed persons are Christians; 2nd, that all immersed persons are Christians—neither of which propositions can be proved." Since these questions cannot be decided the only policy which can possibly be followed is to "neither invite nor prohibit." [53]

Commenting upon the correspondence on this question W. K. Pendleton expresses his approbation of the position taken. "We have ever most cordially approved the general, I may say almost universal custom of our Churches, in disclaiming all authority to exclude from the Lord's Supper any who, by their walk and conversation, and in their own hearts, approve themselves as the Lord's people. . . . To plead for union, and at the same time exclude the really pious from the communion of the body and blood of the Saviour, is, in the very nature of things, to destroy the practical power of our plea." [54] In further substantiation of his contention that such exclusivism would negate the historic plea which the Disciples have made he recalls his brethren to the great purpose to which they have resolutely set themselves. "It is important to keep clearly and always before the mind

---

[52] *Ibid.*, 1861, 712.
[53] "Millennial Harbinger Abridged," II, 240.
[54] *Ibid.*, 241.

the great principle of our movement in reformation. We must remember that we are laboring, not to introduce a totally new church, but to restore the things which are wanting in one already existing; not to overthrow what is good, but to teach the way of the Lord more perfectly. Error as to ordinances may exist where there is genuine faith. Error is always injurious but not necessarily fatal." [55] It must sadly be acknowledged that all the Disciples have not always held such a lofty ideal of the plea which their fathers have made. One cannot but believe that had this same Christian attitude been characteristic of all who became enthusiastic for the movement the plea for Christian unity would have wielded far greater influence in the Christian world.

In a most eloquent reply to further articles from Brethren Elley and Benjamin Franklin which appeared in the "American Christian Review," Isaac Errett sets forth the great principle by which the whole problem must be solved or acknowledged insoluable. The basic mistake, apparent in all their writings on the subject, is their assumption that the unimmersed are of the world. The objection, therefore, is founded upon the certainly grevious assumption that so-called open communion is communion between the Church and the world. It was also charged that those who defended the historic Disciple position were inviting such to commune. Errett, after most vigorously denying this, announces the only principle which can be followed in this case. "They are discussing the question of communion as, between the Church and the world. Brother Elley's questions would be pertinent in such a controversy; but this is a question arising out of the apostacy, and relates to parties not known in the Scriptures. It relates to a condition of things known only in prophecy, in the Scriptures—in which the people of God should be found scattered, bewildered, and erring, but still fearing God and working righteousness; loving Christ, and as far as known to them, earnestly and

[55] *Ibid.*, 241.

joyfully walking in His ways. There are myriads of godly people, who are in error on baptism, of whom, nevertheless, we are compelled to say, 'They are not of the world.' To urge against these a strict and literal application of passages which were meant to mark the distinction between the Church and the world, and thus to attempt to thrust them out from our Christian love among heathens and reprobates, is, in our view a grievous wrong. As it is a question growing out of the time—a question not directly known in form in the Scriptures, it must be settled in the light of well-established Christian principles, and not by a severely literal construction of Scripture language, spoken with reference to certain classes of persons, and another condition of things." [56]

Since the question is one which admittedly is not dealt with directly in the Scriptures there is but one course which the Disciples may follow—they must follow the spirit of Scriptural teaching. There are "facts and principles in the Bible which can be fairly applied to the existing condition of things, and out of which we may elaborate conclusions safe and certain." [57] Restriction of "the communion" to the immersed involves those who do it in great difficulties. A Baptist would be received without question and yet he believes in baptism only on the narration of a religious experience, that sins are pardoned before baptism is administered and that a creedal statement is necessary to Christian union and communion. For those, who in the present day adopt this exclusionist attitude the difficulty is even more involved. A Mormon would be admitted yet he holds to all the vagaries of the Book of Mormon. An Adventist would not be refused though he holds a position identical with the ancient Judaizers. "It has now become a question, growing out of the peculiar logic of these brethren, whether we shall have any religious fellowship whatever with any outside our own churches? Whether we shall not outvie the old Landmark

[56] "Millennial Harbinger Abridged," II, 245, 246.
[57] "Millennial Harbinger Abridged," II, 246.

Baptists themselves in exclusiveness and make ourselves ridiculous before the whole religious world by the monstrous extravagance of our assumptions?" [58]

One of the noblest passages in Disciple literature is that in which he further humbly acknowledges the debt of his people to all the thousands of Christians whose labours have made possible the very plea which he and his fellow-Reformers were making to the world. Because it so beautifully expresses the sentiments of ninety-nine percent of the Disciples as regards their relationship to all the true children of God it is given in its entirety here. "The saints were carried into Babylon, and remained there a long time. The Church lost her primitive purity and excellency. The truth was in chains. Yet God had a people in Babylon—for when the time came for reformation, the proclamation was to be, 'Come out of her, my people.' . . . Now our good brethren may be able to prove to their own satisfaction that all the people of God in Babylon were immersed believers; and they may point, here and there, to bands of religionists, who kept up a protest against the corruptions of Rome. But it strikes us that a people could not come out of Babylon who were not in Babylon; and immersed believers walking in the light, would have been hard to find within Babylon's limits! But there was a people of God in Babylon. We incline to the opinion that most of them were unimmersed. They were in many respects an erring people—in regard to baptism they certainly were in great error; but they 'feared God and wrought righteousness'; and—what seems as great a stumbling-block to many good men now as it was to Peter until the trammels of sectarianism were knocked off—'in every nation, he that feareth God and worketh righteousness is accepted with him.' At one and another trumpet call of reformation, multitudes came forth from Babylon. They did not reach Jerusalem. But they wrought great deeds for God and for His word. They talked much and suffered

[58] *Ibid.*, 248.

much for the name of Christ. We inherit the blessed fruits of their labours. We follow them through the scenes of their superhuman toil, to the dungeons where they suffered, and to the stakes where they won the glories of their martyrdom, and whence they ascended in chariots of fire to the heavens; and as we embrace the chains they wore, and take up the ashes from the altar-fires of spiritual freedom, we ask not whether these lofty heroes of the Church militant, to whom we owe our heritage of spiritual freedom, may commune with us—but rather, if we are at all worthy to commune with them! We feel honored in being permitted to call them brethren. Our reformation movement is the legitimate offspring of theirs. Neither in Pennsylvania, where the Campbells and Scott began, nor in Kentucky, where Stone and others led the van of reformation, did this movement spring from Baptist, but from Pedobaptist influences. It is the legitimate result of Pedobaptist learning, piety and devotion. Unless we can recognize a people of God among these heroical, struggling, sacrificing hosts of Protestants, from whom we have legitimately sprung, then the promise of Christ in regard to His church has failed: —since if we insist on the rigid test of the letter of Gospel conditions, no such people as the Disciples can be found for many centuries. But of this people of God of whom we speak, we affirm that they loved the Lord Jesus Christ in sincerity. They loved and magnified His word. They possessed his spirit—manifesting it in very precious fruits of righteousness and holiness. The spirit of obedience dwelt not less in them than in us. They erred in regard to the letter of baptism, even as it may yet be found that we have erred in regard to the letter of other requirements. We felt the necessity of further reformation. We have seen the mischievous and wicked tendencies of the sect-spirit and life. We have eschewed it. We invite all who love the Saviour to a Scriptural basis of union. We do not, meanwhile, deny nor refuse their prayers, their songs, their exhortations, nor their sympathy with truth and goodness. Whilst we cannot endorse their position nor their practice, as lacking immersion, and as practicing infant rantism, but lift up loud and constant voice against it—we must still deal with them as Christians in error, and seek to right them. To ignore their faith and obedience, and to deal with them as heathen men and publicans, will be indeed to weaken the hands of the pleaders for reformation, and to expose ourselves, by a judgement of extreme narrowness and harshness, to the pity, if not the scorn, of good men everywhere." [59]

The question as to who should commune remains today among the Churches of Christ throughout the world in practically the same position as it occupied in Campbell's time. The Churches in Great Britain cling to the close communion position, those in America hold the view which must now be admitted to be that of the great leaders among the Disciples. The Churches in Africa, recently organized under American leadership and by American money, hold to the position as advocated by Campbell and his great coadjutors. The Australian Churches while theoretically close communionists are not so in reality. Were an unbaptized person to attend a communion service he would not be refused the loaf and cup. The churches in New Zealand, however, lean more to the distinctively British position.

The British view has been very succintly stated in Principal Robinson's recent work. "The Churches in this country have ever been 'close communionists,' but not in the sense of restricting communion to their own members, but to the baptized. They have never intended by this any reflection on the honesty of purpose, or sincerity of heart of those, the validity of whose Baptism they could not accept, nor have they in any way wished to place any limits on the operation of God's grace; but they have recognized the inconsistency of pleading for a valid Baptism and then ignoring such a plea when it came to the administration of Holy

[59] "Millennial Harbinger Abridged," II, 246, 247.

Communion. In America the case has been somewhat different. From the very early days the difficulty was overcome by adopting a policy of 'neither inviting nor debarring' from the Lord's table." [60] It is to be regretted that the Principal dismisses this whole matter with such a brief and unsatisfactory footnote. One feels that he should have devoted an entire chapter to this question. It should be borne in mind that the reference in two short sentences to the "policy" of the Churches in America refers to the position of ninety-seven percent of the members of the world communion and of ninety-nine percent of its leaders.

IV

One question which to the present time agitates the minds of some Disciples is this: "If unimmersed people are admitted to the Lord's table, should they not also to be admitted to membership in the Church?" In a word, the disciple position on the communion logically eventuates in open membership. It has been intimated that Campbell himself was not very sure about this matter.[61] A careful study of his writings, however, reveal the fact that the question was settled in his own mind. Since the Churches of Christ had no practice of inviting the unimmersed to the table they made no decisions as regards their relation to the Lord.

The whole problem, in the thinking of Campbell, was bound up with the question of the meaning of communion. It is clear that he could have communion with various denominations, Baptist and Pedobaptist, without belonging to them as a member of their Church organizations. Com-

---

[60] "What Churches of Christ Stand For," footnote, 88. In fairness, however, it should be stated that this little book is only intended as a popular manual and not as an exhaustive treatment of the subject.

[61] Dr. Gates is evidently in error in his contention that "it is not clear whether or not Campbell would have admitted the unimmersed to church fellowship." See "Early Relation and Separation of Baptists and Disciples," 56.

munion did not mean membership. Nor does it now. If we accept his definition of what it means to be in communion with others we need have no difficulty whatever about such communion and church membership. In his reply to the "Independent Baptist," before alluded to, he explains what he means by being in communion with the Baptist denomination throughout the United States. The bond of union and communion which has ever been that set forth by the "Christian Baptist" is that "a sincere and hearty conviction, expressed or confessed by the lips, that Jesus is the Christ: and this belief, exhibited by an overt act of obedience which implies that the subject has put on Christ, prepares him, or qualifies him, if you please, to be saluted as a brother." [62] "Full communion" did not mean that he approbated everything taught by the Baptists. "When I unite in prayer with a society of disciples, I have full communion with them in certain petitions, confessions and thanksgivings; but requests may be presented, confessions made, and thanksgivings offered, in which I have not full communion." "There is, I confess, a great inconsistency somewhere; yes, everywhere, on the subject of communion. Baptists and Pedobaptists generally confine communion to the Lord's table, and, indeed, call it, by way of distinction, the communion. Hence full communion, with the majority, means no more than breaking the bread together, or sitting down at the same 'communion table.' Here originates all error . . . on the subject of intercommunity with the Christian world." [63] According to this definition of communion—that it is far more than breaking the bread together, it is impossible to associate with members of other communions at all without having intercommunion. As far as any people were in line with the truth Campbell was willing to go with them, so long as he could have the right to dissent from them in anything he believed contrary to the will of His Master. This did not and could not mean that he would hold member-

[62] "Christian Baptist."
[63] "Christian Baptist," 238.

ship with every religious society with whose religious views he found himself substantially in accord.

An interesting confession of a change of attitude is made in his reply to the "Independent Baptist." "I have tried the pharisaic plan, and the monastic. I was once so straight, that, like the Indian's tree, I leaned a little the other way. And however much I may be slandered now as seeking 'popularity' or a popular course, I have to rejoice, that to my own satisfaction, as well as to others, I proved that truth, and not popularity, was my object; for I was once so strict a separatist that I would neither pray nor sing praises with anyone who was not as perfect as I supposed myself. In this most unpopular course I persisted until I discovered the mistake, and saw that on the principles embraced in my conduct, there never could be a congregation or church upon earth." [64] The exclusionist policy does not square with a noble plea for Christian unity. It negates the plea by its bland assumption that there are no Christians to unite. The largest possible communion, is, therefore, vitally essential if the desire for a real and permanent unity is sincere. It was a realization of this which worked such a change in Campbell's attitude toward others who loved his Lord. It was this that inspired him to write; "I frankly own, that my full conviction is, that there are many Pedobaptists congregations, of whose Christianity, or of whose profession of Christianity, I think as highly, as of most Baptist congregations, and with whom I could wish to be on the very same terms of Christian communion on which I stand with the whole Baptist society." [65] The profound disgust which eventually filled his soul as he contemplated attempts at union which degenerated only into a purblind separatism expressed itself in a stinging paragraph. "Dear sir, this plan of making our own nest, and fluttering over our own brood; of building our own tent, and of confining all goodness and grace to our noble selves and the 'elect few' who

[64] *Ibid.*, 238.
[65] "Christian Baptist," 238.

are like us, is the quintessence of sublimated pharisaism.
The old Pharisees were but babes in comparison with the
modern: and the longer I live, and the more I reflect upon
God and man—heaven and hell—the Bible and the world—
the Redeemer and His Church—the more I am assured that
all sectarianism is the offspring of hell; and that all differences about words, and names, and opinions, hatched in
Egypt, or Rome, or Edinburgh, are like the frolics of
drunken men; and that where there is a new creature, or a
society of them, with all their imperfections, and frailities,
and errors in sentiment, in views, in opinions, they ought to
receive one another, and the strong to support the weak, and
not to please themselves. To lock ourselves up in the
bandbox of our own little circle; to associate with a few
units, tens, or hundreds, as the pure church, as the elect, is
real Protestant monkery, it is evangelical pharisaism." [66]

It was because he had become convinced that the vast
majority of unimmersed Christians were devoutly honest—
that they were in the way of obedience and that their mistakes were of the head and not of the heart that he most
vigorously advocated the largest possible intercommunity
with them that Christian unity might become more than a
beautiful dream. In regard to these "there is no rejection
of the ordinance of baptism but a mistake of what it is." [67]
A mistake of such nature, pardonable because they are
in the way of obedience, should not exclude such from our
fullest communion and Christian love, for, "If there is any
position laid down with unusual plainness, and supported
with more than ordinary demonstration, in the epistolary
part of the New Testament, it is this: that Christians should
receive one another as Christ received them, with all their
intellectual weaknesses." [68]

But while the fullest intercommunion ought to be exercised, communion in song, in prayer, in giving, in assembling

[66] *Ibid.*, 238.
[67] "Christian Baptist," 257.
[68] *Ibid.*, 257.

at the Lord's table, this does not at all mean that unimmersed
people should be received into the membership of the Church.
The fundamental error in approaching this whole question
of open membership has been the assumption that communion means Church membership. This does not necessarily follow. In a discussion of the history of various reform-
ing churches whose communications had come to him, and
which he had published in the "Christian Baptist," Campbell discusses the whole question of the admission of the
unimmersed into membership. He confesses that the problem is no easy one: On this subject I write with great cau-
tion, for I know this question of forbearance has in it some
perplexities of no easy solution, and is at least of as difficult
solution as that concerning the amalgamation of the Jews
and Gentiles in the Christian Church decided by the apostles
and elders in the city of Jerusalem. On the scriptural propriety of receiving unnaturalized or unimmersed into the
kingdom into which the Saviour said that none can enter
but by being born of water and the Spirit, little can be said
either from precept or example. For it is exceedingly plain,
that from the day on which Peter opened the reign of the
Messiah, on that ever memorable Pentecost, no man entered
the realm but by being born of water." [69]

The new situation in which the Church finds herself, due
to the apostacy from the faith once for all delivered, makes
him slow to speak harshly. "But the question of the greatest difficulty to decide, is, whether there should be any laws
or rules adopted by the churches relating to the practice of
receiving persons unimmersed in the assemblies of the saints.
Whether on the ground of forbearance, as it is called, such
persons as have once been sprinkled, or not at all, but who
are satisfied with their sprinkling, or without any, are, on
their solicitation, to be received into any particular congregation, and to be treated in all respects as those who have,
by their own voluntary act and deed, been naturalized and

[69] "Christian Baptist," 457.

constitutionally admitted into the kingdom." [70] The dilemma is clearly set forth in the following paragraph. It is exactly the same as confronts some devout Disciples at the present day. "To make a law that such should be received, appears to me, after long and close deliberation, a usurpation of the legislative authority vested in the holy apostles, and of dangerous tendency in the administration of the Reign of Heaven. Again, to say that no weak brother, however honest in his professions, excellent in his deportment and amiable in his character, who cannot be convinced that his infant sprinkling is infant baptism, and who solicits a participation with us in the festivities of Zion: I say, to say by a stern decree that none such shall on any account be received, appears to be illiberal, unkind, censorious, and opposite to that benevolence which is one of the primary virtues of Christianity."

There is in Disciple literature no clearer statement of what the overwhelming consensus of sober Disciple thought has conceived to be the solution of the problem than the one with which he closes his discussion of this perplexing question. "Now, although I could feel myself at perfect liberty, in full accordance with requirements of the Great King, to receive into the most cordial fellowship everyone which I have reason to recognize as a disciple of Jesus Christ, with all his weaknesses, as I would call them; yet I could not, and dare not, say to all members of a Christian congregation, that they must do so too; and as I have no right to dispense with any of the institutions of Jesus Christ, I could not approve the adoption of a rule to receive such persons, which, in its direct tendency, aims at the abolition of one of the fundamental laws of the empire. Again, if we are to fritter down the Christian institution to suit the prejudices and weaknesses of disciples, it would soon be divested of every prominent feature characteristic of its grand original. There are, indeed, many matters on which there is full scope given

[70] *Ibid.*, 457.

for the display of moderation, condescension, and forbearance, without infringing upon the constitutional provisions of the kingdom. We may show all courtesy, kindness, and hospitality to strangers, but to invest them with the rights and immunities of citizens, without their voluntary submission to the constitutional requirements in order to naturalization, would neither be beneficial to them, nor safe to the empire." [71]

A number of cogent considerations inforce the impression that the Disciples are not going to become greatly interested in the present acknowledged attempt to establish the open membership plan as a universal practice among them. It it not a new thing. From the time of the union of 1832 there have been some in each generation who have contended that the Disciple plea would be more consistent and far more effective were the so-called immersion dogma discarded. One section of the followers of Stone refused to unite with the Christians and Disciples because immersion was adopted as the only valid Christian baptism. To this section we will advert later. The whole question has become acute in recent years through the deliberate efforts of a powerful journal to propagate the position. Two observations should be made regarding the plan as at present ventilated and in substantiation of the statement that it is improbable that the Disciples will in large numbers react favorably to the supposedly new position.

(1) It should be noted in the first place that it is definitely a repudiation of the history and practice of the Disciples from the days of the fathers of the movement to the present time. We have found Alexander Campbell to be determinedly opposed to it. This was true of every one of the primitive leaders—Richardson, Burnett, Errett, Pendleton, Lard and the host of others whose courage and faith brought the great work into being. The reason for this opposition is to be found in the theory which they held concerning the

[71] "Christian Baptist," 457.

Church as we have found Thomas Campbell expressing it in the "Declaration and Address." Their rebellion was against the whole denominational or branch theory of the Church. Of course, if that theory be correct, if the denominations are alike Churches of Christ it is the worst form of religious bigotry and intolerance to refuse the fullest fellowship to their members. But if the position of the Campbells be correct then the denominational idea is wrong. They never refused to recognize members of other communions as Christians nor to cease their contentions that the system of which they were members were unauthorized in the Scriptures. To return then to the position which the leaders in the Restoration plea discarded is to repudiate the plea which they advocated and to write the word folly across the hundred years of Disciple history. It is pleasing to Disciples around the world to note the growing interest in Christian unity among Christians of every dye. There can be no gainsaying the fact that this is due in large measure to the message of those hardy pioneers whose hearts were set on fire for the healing of the divisions in the riven body of Christ. It is commendable too that many plans are being confidently set forward for the accomplishment of this noble purpose. But the present denominational plans for unity based upon an acceptance of the validity of the denominational order are hopeless. It is the solemn conviction of those who best know the history of the Restoration plea that unity can never, through a process of patching up of the old denominational organizations but only through a courageous discarding of them all and a return to the plan for Christian cooperation and unity which is indubitably enshrined in the pages of the New Testament. Dr. Kershner's clear cut statement places the issue squarely before the Disciples. "If we accept the denominational theory of union, we must undoubtedly be willing to accept open membership and a host of other things. When we do this, however, we give up the whole substance of the Restoration ideal of unity, and acknowledge that the plea which has furnished the only excuse for our existence for over a century is, and always has been, a mere will-o'-the wisp. Are we ready to do this? If we are not ready, then this particular argument for open membership has no meaning for us." [72] Surely this is sound. It is really a matter of ideals. The Disciples have something eminently worth while for the religious world or they have not. If the plan for union which has been preached for a century and more is right then they are under an unescapable constraint to preach and practice it on every possible occasion. For the compromise on the matter of baptism is not the end. Once recognize the denominational theory and all the rest goes aglimmering as well. If they can recklessly smash the ideality of the plea here they can as wholehearted subscribed to a written creed, submissively bow to the mandates of Popes and Bishops and adorn themselves with the human names which their fathers so joyously cast off in the years agone.

(2) The present advocacy of open membership also rests upon a glaringly erroneous interpretation of Disciples history. The serious student of that history finds himself amazed and affronted by the gross assumptions, the fallacious reasonings and the unpardonable mistatements of this propaganda. One is reluctant to relax that reserve which should characterize a study of this nature but such a threat to Disciple progress as the open membership plan constitutes is deserving of heroic treatment. If appeal is made to history surely the authorities in that realm ought to be consulted. Briefly, then, the so-called historical arguement for open membership is as follows. From the days of Alexander Campbell until the present the Disciples have been following the wrong plan. Thomas Campbell, who was the real founder of the movement heroically endeavoured to direct the movement into its proper channels which was Christian unity upon the basis of open membership and a number of other things which do not enter into

[72] "Watchword of the Restoration Vindicated," chapter on "Open Membership."

our present study. But the elder Campbell was over-influenced and even theologically brow beaten by his headstrong and impetuous son into an abject surrender of the fundamental principle which he had at first espoused. Falling under "Baptistic" influences he accepted the immersionist dogma and willed it to the people who had blindly followed his leadership. Scott, Errett, Pendelton, and Milligan, therefore, followed a false lead and the movement for the Restoration of New Testament Christianity was wrecked. The way out of the difficulties into which the leadership of Alexander Campbell has plunged the movement is a return to the primitive teaching of Thomas Campbell and this means open membership.

This position not only repudiates the whole plea as we have been in contact with it in our present pilgrimage but it blandly ignores the plain facts of Disciple history as well. What are these facts? In Dr. Richardson's great work which we have used so often in this study we have a very complete record of the lives of Thomas and Alexander Campbell with a most intimate description of the mental and spiritual experiences through which they passed in their journey to the "haven of New Testament and Christianity." His life long intimacy with these two men gave him every opportunity to know the facts. His work has therefore been accepted as the standard authority in regard to the beginnings of Disciple history. Quoting him copiously Dr. Kershner trenchantly disposes of the so-called historical argument of the small but influential group of open membership protagonists. I shall follow him closely on this point. In the first place, then, there is not extant one shred of evidence of any clash between the Campbells as to the fundamentals of the plea which they advocated. Such widely divergent views of the purpose of their movement assuredly would have left its trace in their writings. It is further absolutely certain that both of them stood adamant upon the basic principle announced by the elder Campbell at the meeting in the home of Abraham Altars. We have found that

Alexander came to his position only after years of the most intensive examination of all the facts in the field. Neither was the action of his father precipitate but only after very mature reflection did he accept the new position and to it he held unswervingly to the end. It is certainly uncritical to treat the facts of Disciple history in the manner which would twist the whole plea as made by the early leaders. We may think them wrong but that they were agreed and that they clung to their position until the close of their lives there can be no doubt.

Open membership will not solve the baptismal question. It is significant that its adoption does not bring the unity which its advocates claim as one of its most beneficient fruits. Instead it has divided practically every congregation which has adopted it. There is no half way ground between the New Testament position and that of the Quakers. It is either the baptism of Christ and the Apostles or a repudiation of water baptism entirely and an acknowledgment that the only baptism now to be expected is that of the Spirit. The emphasis of the Disciples has been distinctive and where they have stoutly contended for it unusual progress has been made. Alive to the dangers which lurk in the proposed position an increasing indifference to the new propaganda is manifesting itself among the Churches of Christ around the world. The Churches abroad have never been seriously interested in it and those in America who adopt it frequently return to the historic position. It is probable that there may always be a few churches which will experiment with the plan but that it will have any great vogue is improbable.

CHAPTER VIII

THE WORK OF THE HOLY SPIRIT

NOTHING is more fundamental in Campbell's religious thinking than his determined opposition to the hurtful Protestant mysticism of his time. The Calvinian manifestation of the doctrine of hereditary total depravity, inherited from Augustine, and perpetuated by the Protestant world, bore the brunt of his vigorous attacks from the very beginning of his editorial work. To Campbell, the doctrine that man was incapable of receiving the truth of God as it is enshrined in the Scriptures, that he could not believe or repent until the Holy Spirit, by direct and irresistable agency, performed a miracle upon his heart, was abhorrent for three reasons. (1) It was a menace to religion itself, in that it made it impossible for a man to become a Christian of his own will; (2) it was contrary to the teaching of Scripture; and, (3) it was philosophically unsound according to the principles of John Locke. He, therefore, sought to develop a doctrine of the Spirit which should be free from these objections—one which would make it possible for a man to become a Christian by following a plain and definite plan—one which should be in harmony with what he believed to be the clear teaching of the Scriptures, and which should square with the Lockian psychology which he so firmly held. The student of Campbellian thought can understand the time devoted to the work of the Holy Spirit, only by realizing the prevalence of the Protestant mysticism against which he so constantly waged war.[1]

[1] The affinity of Ritschl with Campbell on this point is striking. They not only share in their almost extreme aversion to mysticism but also in the reasons which they held for the incessant war which both raged against it. The Protestant mysticism of America was paralleled in Germany by

I

The work of the Holy Spirit came up for consideration in the first volume of the "Christian Baptist." Following the negative method characteristic of his work at this period, he states four positions to which he is opposed. (1) That "there is some invisible, indescribable, energy exerted upon the minds of men in order to make them Christians; and that, too, independent of, or prior to, the word believed." [2] The Spirit thus considered is like some fluid poured into the soul, and through this direct energy the elect are regenerated before they believe. Regeneration, therefore, precedes faith and is miraculously accomplished. Revolting against the absurdity of this position, he instances the case of a devout friend who claimed that he was regenerated for three years before he believed in Christ, and that during all this time he was a saved man. (2) That all men are as spiritually dead as a stone, and that their becoming alive is purely a matter of the will of the Holy Spirit, he objects to with all his soul. The belief that man, thus dead, is utterly incapable of taking a step toward God until the Spirit performs a miracle upon him, is a doctrine wholly without foundation in reason or in Scripture. There is here a challenge to the whole Augustinian and Calvinian anthropology with its insistence upon the fall of man and the blighting and damning effects of

---

Pietism which evoked from Ritschl some of his most vitriolic criticisms. "Justification and Reconciliation," 112, 113. When, for instance, he denounces it because it makes of none effect justification, he but echoes Campbell in his contention that the mystical theories of the Spirit's working nullifies the Gospel and renders unnecessary the saving work of Christ. "Justification and Reconciliation," 113.

[2] "Christian Baptist," 49. Cf. Ritchl, "Justification and Reconciliation," when he speaks of the Spirit as the attribute of the community of believers, (472), that it dwells in the thus regenerated community which Christ has formed (605); when he objects to the belief that the Spirit is a "hyperphysical natural force" or a "resistless natural force" which regenerates immediately. In such positions he is employing almost Campbellian language. See, 534, 603, 604.

original sin.[3] In almost sarcastic vein, describing an imaginary address of a Calvinistic divine to a sinner, he says, "fellow-sinner, you are in a miserable condition, mired from head to foot. Believe me, you are both cold and hungry; and I can assure you that you are unable to help yourself out of this calamity. You could as easily carry one of these hills upon your shoulders, as extricate yourself from your present circumstances. Perish with cold and hunger you must; it is vain for you to attempt an escape. Every effort you make to get out only sinks you deeper in distress. Your Creator could, if he pleased, bring you out; but whether he lists or not, is uncertain." [4] (3) In the third place, he objects to "the popular belief of a regeneration previous to faith, or a knowledge of the gospel," because it "is replete with mischief," in that it makes the sinner go through an awful period of sorrow and despair as "through the pious Bunyan's slough of Despond, before he can believe the gospel." In a word, "it is all equivalent to this; that a man must become a desponding, trembling, infidel, before he can become a believer." [5] The Campbellian reason for objection to this, is found in the fact that "the gospel makes no provision for despondency, inasmuch as it assures all who believe and obey it, upon the veracity of God, that they are forgiven and accepted in the Beloved." [6] (4) That physical manifestations are to be accepted as evidences of pardon, or that emotional experiences are to be made the criterion by which one may know that he has been accepted by the Father, are also unwarranted by the facts of revelation and reason. The teaching of such things tends to make the people "lay themselves out for operations and new revelations." Such an attitude conduces to bring the gospel into contempt, and is the fruitful source of unbelief.

In the second volume of the "Christian Baptist," he pub-

[3] "Christian Baptist," 48, 50.
[4] "Christian Baptist," 49.
[5] *Ibid.*, 49.
[6] *Ibid.*, 82.

lished a series of articles on "The Work of the Holy Spirit in Salvation," in which his position on the whole question is positively stated. The following résumé of the nine essays in this volume, will show the position which he here maintained, as compared with that denied in the first volume.

The Holy Spirit is the revealer of God. All we know of the Father, we know because of the Spirit through whose agency we have the Scriptural testimony about Him. Knowledge of the will of God is the first step in salvation; therefore, the reading of the divine testimony in the Scriptures, is necessary to becoming a Christian.[7]

The Holy Spirit makes possible the acceptance of the testimony which is given in the divine record, not by a miracle through which a creative act is performed in the individual, but by authenticating a series of evidences which he has given in the facts of the Gospel. God, through the life, the death, and resurrection of His Son, has done wonderful things in the world. The record of these acts is ours, enshrined in the New Testament which has been "dictated from heaven." Now according to the constitution of man, it is as natural for him to believe the testimony, as to see light, or to hear sound. It is not necessary that there be "enabling grace" to give a man new faculties that he may believe, but evidence which he can grasp with those faculties which he already possesses.[8]

The Holy Spirit has given testimony concerning God, but he has given more—he has given evidence of the truth of that testimony. Some of these evidences which the Spirit gives in attestation of the truth of his testimony are (1) miracles, or the "suspension of the known laws of nature," which are proof of a power which is superior to the law itself.[9] "Miracles were wrought by the influence of the Holy Spirit, in confirmation of the apostolic testimony—that is, signs or proofs of a supernatural character followed their

7 "Christian Baptist," 83.

8 *Ibid.*, 83.

9 *Ibid.*, 89, 91.

testimony." [10]   From the premises that the Spirit of God is
the great Revealer, and that he attests his revelation by
incontrovertable evidence, Campbell deduces two conclusions. "The first is that the truth to be believed could never
have been known but by the revelation of the Spirit; and
secondly, that though it had been pronounced in the most
explicit language, yet it could not have been believed with
certainty, but by the miracles which were offered in attestation of it." [11]   The moral character of the miracle-worker is
known in his works. The moral character of the works
wrought by Jesus, is evidence that the signs attributed to
him, were not done by the Prince of Demons. The benevolent character of these miracles is sufficient evidence of the
exalted nature of their author.[12]   (2) Spiritual gifts are also
an evidence of the truth of the Spirit's testimony. These
special gifts of the Holy Spirit, were of a miraculous character and were given for purposes of confirmation until the
church of Christ was firmly established, they then ceased
by limitation.[13]   (3) Prophecy, a kind of spiritual gift, is
also considered as a type of miracle which has power to
evidence the truth of the divine testimony. This term includes all the Old Testament prophecies concerning the
coming Messiah, which are applied to Jesus of Nazareth, and
also those made by Jesus Himself, concerning His suffering,
His death and His resurrection, the destruction of the Temple, and the fall of the City of David.[14]

Since the Bible has been dictated from heaven, the words
in which the miracles, the spiritual gifts, and the prophecies
are described, are the work of the Holy Spirit as much as
the signs themselves. The work of the Holy Spirit, therefore,
is final. It has made permanently possible, man's acceptance of the truth which God has revealed in Christ, and

[10] *Ibid.,* 83.
[11] "Christian Baptist," 83, 84.
[12] *Ibid.,* 89.
[13] *Ibid.,* 102, 104.
[14] *Ibid.,* 108, 111.

which has been preserved for us in the Spirit-dictated word. The inspired records are so trustworthy that the reading of them now, gives us as clear evidence as though we had seen the events as they transpired. The work of the Holy Spirit may, then, be divided into two parts: he reveals the nature and will of God as the Spirit of Wisdom, the Great Revealer; as the Spirit of Power, he gives indisputable evidence of the truth of the testimony.[15] The natural man which Paul describes in I Corinthians, is not the Calvinistic natural man who has the revelation and the evidence for its authenticity but lacks the "enabling grace" to accept it; he is the natural man with human reason and ability to comprehend the truth and obey it, but without the revelation of the Holy Spirit or the divine evidences of its truth.[16]

In the ninth article of the series, he sums up his position as developed up to this period. In an eloquent passage which contains the germ of all his future teaching, he closes his argument in the "Christian Baptist." "Thus we see that the whole work of the Spirit of God in the salvation of men, as the Spirit of wisdom, the Spirit of power, and the Spirit of grace or goodness, is inseparably connected with, and altogether subservient to, the gospel or glad tidings of great joy to all people, of the love of God exhibited in the humiliation to death of His only begotten Son. Detached from this view we know nothing of it, because nothing more is revealed. And to indulge in metaphysical speculations, or to form abstract theories of our own, is not only the climax of religious folly; but has ever proved the bane of Christianity."[17] As though he had an intuition of the stream of innuendo to which he would be subjected because of his position, he thus early defends himself against any accusation that he denies the providential works of God or His Spirit. "I am not to be understood as asserting that there is no divine influence over the minds and bodies of men. This

15 "Christian Baptist," 139.
16 *Ibid.*, 137, 138.
17 *Ibid.*, 139.

would be to assert in contradiction to a thousand facts and declarations in the volume of revelation; this would be to destroy the idea of any divine relevation; this would be to destroy the idea of any divine government exercised over the human race; this would be to make prayer a useless and irrational exercise; this would be to deprive Christians of all the consolations derived from a sense of the superintending care, guidance and protection of the Most High. But to resolve everything into a 'divine influence' is the other extreme. This divests man of every attribute which renders him accountable to his Maker, and assimilates all his actions to the bending of the trees or the tumults of the ocean, occasioned by the tempests." [18]

II

The matured Campbellian doctrine of the work of the Holy Spirit in conversion and sanctification, is developed in the "Christian System" (1835), and the "Campbell-Rice Debate" (1843). In his "Christian Baptism" (1852), the arguments advanced in the debate with Rice were revamped and published as his final pronouncements upon the whole subject. The method of considering the question as presented in the Rice debate, will be followed here, with occasional references to the "Christian System." In his discussion with Rice, he defended the proposition, "In Conversion and Sanctification the Spirit of God operates on Persons only through the Word." [19] This statement may be

[18] "Christian Baptist," 138, 139. See also, Richardson's "Memoirs of Alexander Campbell," II, 123, 128.

[19] "Memoirs of Alexander Campbell," Richardson, II, 513. In the same connection, Dr. Richardson speaks of the effect of this address upon the famous American statesman, Henry Clay, who was the moderator of the debate. "It was remarked that Henry Clay, who had been very careful to avoid, previously, the slightest appearance of favoring either disputant, was so captivated by it as for a time, to forget himself. A gentleman well acquainted with him, noticed that, soon after Mr. Campbell began, he became unusually attentive, and that as the subject became unfolded and successive arguments were presented, he leaned forward, and began to bow

considered as embodying his last word on the interminable question of converting and sanctifying power.

In his first address, which "has been greatly and deservedly admired for its beauty of diction, its clearness of statement, and its power of argument," he takes care to define the terms of the proposition. In these definitions he forestalls the objections which Rice later repeats so frequently. Many objections, even of Disciple writers, would never have had foundation, had his position in these definitions been more clearly scrutinized. It is observable in the voluminous correspondence which precedes the debate, that both parties desired to commit him to the proposition that all the operations of the Spirit are through the Word of Truth.[20] He was not altogether pleased with the wording of the proposition, not because he considered it too sweeping or inclusive, but because it seems to indicate that conversion and sanctification are different processes. It has been noted in these pages, that he did not so consider them. At the seeming risk of repetition, it will be necessary to state again his conception of the relations subsisting between these terms, which he considered analogical thought forms expressing different views of the same process. The foundational difference between himself and Rice is to be discovered in diametrically opposed views of the nature of conversion, regeneration, and sanctification. Understanding this to be the issue, he is at great pains in the opening address, to clear up the whole matter by a critical definition of the terms. Decrying the divisions and party systems which have arisen because of inadequate conceptions of terms used in

---

assent, waving his hand at the same time in that graceful, approving manner peculiar to him." p. 514. Dr. Haley, who may be taken as a representative type of scholarly Disciple teacher, refers to this first address as "a club of Hercules entwined with flowers." "Debates that made History," 211. An eminent Episcopal divine, writing in the "Protestant Churchman" soon after the debate, refers to this opening argument as "one of the most splendid specimens of eloquent reasoning I ever remember to have read." "Memoirs of Alexander Campbell," Richardson, II, 514.

20 "Campbell-Rice Debate," 21, 48.

the Word, to express the divine revelation, he deposes that such divisions might be resolved into harmony were it but possible accurately to define the terms used. He then adds, "to this class (of terms) belong the words regeneration, sanctification, and conversion." [21]

There are two conditions in which all men may be classed; those who are in Adam the first, and those who are in Adam the second. These conditions are manifestly two very different and opposed religious states. It is evident that such metaphors as "dead, lost, destroyed, alien, enemy, going astray, condemned in law, debtor, unclean, sold to sin," etc., are terms descriptive of the state of those who are in Adam the first. It is also clear that any one of the terms, as well as all of them together, may adequately describe this condition. They are not expressive of component parts in the process of coming to this condition, but analogical terms illustrative of the state from various points of view.[22] This is precisely true, likewise, as regards the opposite metaphors which set forth the condition of those who are in Adam the second, and the manner by which they were brought into that condition. "These metaphors, just now quoted, give rise to a corresponding class, indicative of this new condition in Adam the second, such as—quickened, made alive, born again, new created, saved, reconciled, friend, converted, illuminated, pardoned, redeemed, etc. The changing of these states is also set forth in suitable imagery; such as—regeneration, conversion, reconciliation, new creation, illumination, remission, adoption, redemption, salvation, etc. Now the error to which I allude, primarily consists in not uniformly regarding each one of these as a complete view of man, in some one condition, or, in his whole condition in Adam the first, or in Adam the second; but in sometimes contemplating them as parts of one view, as fractions of one great whole, and consequently, to be all added up to make out a full scriptural view of man, in Adam

[21] "Campbell-Rice Debate," 611.
[22] *Ibid.*, 612.

and in Christ, and of the transition from one state to the other." [23] In the "Christian System," this same manner of considering the terms as expressive either individually, or collectively, of one great process, is set forth. "We are not to suppose that regeneration is something which must be added to the faith, the feeling, and the action of the believer, which are the effects of the testimony of God understood and embraced. It is only another name for the same process in all its parts." [24] Again, "conversion is a term denoting the whole moral or spiritual change, which is sometimes called sanctification, sometimes regeneration. These are not three changes, but one change indicated by these three terms, regeneration, conversion, sanctification." The use of these expressions must depend upon what metaphor we have in mind in contemplating man as connected with the first Adam. Is he dead in sin? then, he is now born again, and made alive in the second Adam. Is he, in the first, lost? he is, in the second, saved. "Is he destroyed and ruined in the first?—he is created anew in the second Adam, the Lord from heaven." [25]

While all of the analogical terms used are descriptive of the new state into which the Christian man enters, yet they are not synonymous. Certain words are expressive of the legal and external change, and others deal with that which is inner and spiritual. He was careful to make clear that he had to do with that change which is moral and spiritual in nature. "I therefore now, most distinctly and emphatically state, that with me, and in reference to this discussion, these terms, severally and collectively indicate a moral, a spiritual, and not a physical or legal change. A physical change has to to with the essence or form of the subject. A legal change is a change as respects a legal sentence, or enactment. Hence pardon, remission, justification, have respect to law. But a moral or spiritual change, is a change of the moral state of

23 "Campbell-Rice Debate," 612.
24 "Christian System," 276.
25 "Campbell-Rice Debate," 613.

the feelings, and of the soul. In contrast with a merely intellectual change—a change of view, it is called a change of the affections—a change of the heart. It is in this acceptation of the subject of my proposition, that I predicate of it, 'The Spirit operates only through the Word.' " [26] This statement of his conception of the whole question, as decidedly spiritual and moral in nature, is of interest to the student of Campbellian thought, since it was the constant effort of his detractors to make it appear that his whole system tended to legalism.

In further definition of the terms used, he states that in reality the term "only" is unnecessary. "The term only, indeed, is redundant; because a moral change is effected only by motives, and motives by arguments; and all arguments ever used by the Holy Spirit, are found in the book called the 'Word of Truth.' " [27]

III

The terms of the discussion having been defined, the Campbellian position may be stated, and the arguments which he advanced for it presented. With clarity, he examines in vigorous language, the position of the three schools, on the work of the Holy Spirit in conversion and sanctification. "On the subject of spiritual influence, there are two extremes of doctrine. There is the Word alone system, and there is the Spirit alone system. The former is the parent of a cold, lifeless rationalism and formality." [28] In this statement, there is an interesting echo of his experience in publishing in 1831, his "Dialogue on the Holy Spirit." [29]

[26] *Ibid.*, 613.
[27] "Campbell-Rice Debate," 613.
[28] *Ibid.*, 614.
[29] Dr. Richardson speaks of this incident and of those who had so misunderstood Campbell as to advocate this "word alone" theory. "These persons were found chiefly among those who had been previously sceptical, and who were habitually disposed to rely upon reason rather than to walk by faith; and their crude and erroneous doctrines were well calculated to bring reproach upon the Reformation. They were disposed to resolve

Abandoning his usual adherance to the Scriptures, he employed abstractions and distinctions in regard to "moral and physical power," which, instead of making himself more clear to the Baptist people, for whose understanding he had undertaken the exposition, resulted in new and greater misunderstandings. Because of the speculative nature of the work, and because the distinctions were unknown to the Scriptures, Thomas Campbell openly disapproved, feeling that it was not a just and fair exposition of the subject. Deferring to his judgement, Alexander subsequently omitted it from his "Christianity Restored." The two-fold result of this "Dialogue" which had appeared in the first edition of "Christianity Restored" along with several extras from the "Harbinger," was, first, to cause his enemies to raise a tremendous outcry against him, claiming that he did not in reality, believe in the operation of the Holy Spirit, and, second, to cause some of his co-laborers to construct the "Word alone" theory, which really dispensed with the gift of the Holy Spirit to believers. It was to counteract the influence of this earlier mistake of trying, by philosophical speculations, to set forth his position, that he so frequently emphasizes his aversion to the "Word alone" theory. About this time, Walter Scott brought forth his "Discourse on the Holy Spirit," [30] for the purpose of further counteracting the spread of the error which Campbell denominated "cold and formal." The speculations of this school were wholly inconsistent with the principles of the Campbellian movement, and Scott's

---

religion entirely into a system of moral motivity; to disbelieve the actual indwelling of the Holy Spirit in believers; to deny special providences and guidings, and, by consequence, the efficacy of prayer. Taking Locke's philosophy as the basis of their system, and carrying his 'Essay on the Human Understanding' along with the Bible, in their saddle-bags, they denied even to its Creator, any access to the human soul except by 'words and arguments,' while they conceded to the author of evil, a direct approach, and had more to say in their discourses about 'the laws of human nature' than about the gospel of Christ." "Memoirs of Alexander Campbell," II, 356, 358.

[30] "Memoirs of Alexander Campbell," Richardson, II, 356, 357.

work, just at this time, was particularly opportune.[31] He showed that Christianity, as it is revealed in the New Testament, is sustained by three missions—that of the Lord Jesus Christ, that of the Apostles, and that of the Holy Spirit. The mission of Christ while on earth, was to the Jews; that of the Apostles, to the world; while that of the Holy Spirit, was to the Church. The work of each agent terminated upon its proper subjects—Christ confining his ministry to His own people, the Apostles going out into the world to bring salvation to all the nations, and the Holy Spirit dwelling in the Church as the spirit dwells in the body, strengthening and comforting the saints and through them bringing conviction to the hearts of sinners. The popular impression that the Spirit was sent to the world, came in for vigorous consideration. Scott contended that the world could not receive him, and quoted the words of Jesus to his disciples, in John 16:7-9, as conclusive proof of his contention. The union of the people of God, and their production of the fruits of the Spirit, depended solely upon the indwelling of that Spirit, actually and really, in the heart of every Christian. In closing his argument, he affirmed that while the mission of Christ to the Jews, and that of the Apostles to the world, was temporary in nature, that of the Holy Spirit in the heart of the Christian and through the Christian upon the world, is permanent. The Holy Spirit is to abide in the Church forever. One striking statement from this work, so influential in the Disciple movement of the period, sets forth the position in unmistakable language, and is a refutation of the unfounded charge that the Disciples as a body, ever espoused the "Word alone" theory. "There is no member of the body of Christ, in whom the Holy Spirit dwelleth not;

[31] "Concerning the effect of this timely work of Scott, Dr. Richardson writes, 'This discourse, being widely circulated in pamphlet form, had a powerful effect in imparting clearness and definiteness to the views of the Reformers upon this important subject. It was the first time it had been brought forward in so particular a manner, and the clear scriptural evidence presented in the discourse was generally received as decisive of the questions involved.'" "Memoirs," II, 357.

for it will hold good at the end of the world and in eternity as it does now, and it holds as good now as it did on the day of Pentecost and afterward—that 'if any man have not the Spirit of Christ, he is none of His.' " [32]

Campbell's enthusiastic commendation of this work, immediately made known to those who in their zeal for Lockian philosophy had strayed into the maze of speculation, his own position on the mooted question. "Brother Scott, who in the fall of 1827, arranged the several items of faith, repentance, baptism, remission of sins, the Holy Spirit and eternal life, and restored them in this order to the Church, under the title of the Ancient Gospel, and successfully preached it for the conversion of the world—has written a discourse on the fifth point (viz., the Holy Spirit), which presents the subject in such an attitude as cannot fail to make all who read it understand the views entertained by us, and as we think, taught by the apostles in their writings. We can commend to all the Disciples this discourse as most worthy of a place in their families, because it perspicuously, forcibly, and with brevity favorable to an easy apprehension of its meaning, presents the subject to the mind of the reader. Our opponents, too, who are continually misrepresenting, and many of them no doubt misconceiving, our views on this subject, if they would be advised by us, we would request to furnish themselves with a copy, that they may be better informed on this topic, and, if they should still be conscientiously opposed, that they may oppose what we teach, and not a phantom of their own creation." [33] These words must absolve Campbell of any hesitency in affirming that the Holy Spirit actually dwells in the heart of the believer. His faith in the divine indwelling, is as clear and definite as that of his most determined opponent— as that of the most pronounced Protestant mystic of his day. He differed from them on the manner of the Holy Spirit's working, but not in this.

[32] "Memoirs of Alexander Campbell," Richardson, II, 357.
[33] "Memoirs of Alexander Campbell," Richardson, II, 357.

Resuming his exposition of the positions of the schools concerning the operation of the Spirit, as they existed in his own time, it should be noted that he not only condemned the attitude of those who believed in the impossible theory of the Word alone, but that he was as determinedly opposed to that which advocated the theory of the Spirit alone. In reference to the results of this theory, he says that in some temperaments "it is the cause of a wild, irrepressible enthusiasm; and, in other cases, of a dark, melancholy despondency." [34] With some, there is a sort of compound system, claiming both the Spirit and the Word—representing the naked Spirit of God operating upon the naked soul of man, without any argument, or motive, interposed in some mysterious and inexplicable way—incubating the soul, quickening, or making it spiritually alive, by a direct and immediate contact, without the intervention of one moral idea, or impression. But after this creating act, there is the bringing to bear upon it the gospel revelation, called conversion. Hence, in this school, regeneration is the cause; and conversion, at some future time, the result of that abstract operation." [35]

In the teaching of this school, and in its influence in America at the time, we find the whole reason for the "Campbell-Rice Debate." The Protestant mysticism of the day has already been frequently considered in these pages. Reference must be made to it again, to understand the reason for the time and energy spent on the subject of how the Spirit works in conversion and sanctification. The issue is to be found in the prevalent Calvinism which affirmed the doctrine of hereditary total depravity—that man is wholly incapable to think a good thought or do a good deed; that he cannot believe the Gospel of Christ, or repent of his sins, until an abstract and miraculous operation of the Spirit of the living God makes it possible for him to accept the divine conditions. To Campbell, this dogma of the current Calvinism,

[34] "Campbell-Rice Debate," 614.
[35] *Ibid.*, 614.

hung like a pall over the country. Believing as he did, that man is responsible for the manner in which he receives the Gospel; believing, also, that he can receive it without a miracle on the part of God; this doctrine which made men indifferent to their own salvation, and that of others, until the Divine Spirit by direct impact regenerated them, was, to him, the greatest hindrance to the progress of the truth of God. It was for this reason that he was willing to debate the subject, and also that he placed the little qualifying adverb "only" in the proposition. In reality, it is the biggest word in the entire debate; in it is the issue of the whole discussion.

IV

The lengths to which the theology of the day was willing to go, may be illustrated by the position of Rice. The doctrine that it is necessary for the Spirit to regenerate a man before he can believe and repent, was the very crux of his position. "Why, then, will it be asked, is it necessary that there should be an influence of the Spirit, in addition to that of the Word, and distinct from it? The necessity arises simply from the depravity of the human heart—its pride, its love of sin, and its deep-rooted aversion to the character of God, to His pure law, to His soul-humbling gospel." [36] This depravity of human nature is so inveterate that the Gospel cannot change it; it is necessary for a miracle to be performed on the part of God, in order that this nature be subdued and a new heart created. God can present motives to angels and they will obey, for they are holy. Motives, however, will not move the sinful nature of man. "It is, then, perfectly clear, that every individual must experience a radical change in his moral character, before he will ever love God or embrace the gospel of Christ. But are the truths of revelation sufficient to effect this

[36] "Campbell-Rice Debate," 630.

change? They are not." [37] "Through the light of revelation
we have presented to our minds the character of God, his
law, his gospel, heaven and hell. This revelation presents
these objects in their true character; but men, because of
their depravity, feel a strong aversion to them. They are
not averse to the gospel of Christ through mistake, but they
dislike these glorious objects in their real character. Now
when a man whose heart is enmity to God in his true character, has that character presented to his mind by the light
of divine truth; will the light cause him to admire it and
love it? Or will he whose proud heart rises in rebellion
against the pure and soul-humbling gospel, be induced to
love and embrace it by having it very clearly presented to
his view? Surely not. It is clear, then, that man must
experience a radical moral renovation—must be greatly
changed, or he will never love God or obey the gospel of
Christ." [38]

Holding to such a doctrine of regeneration, it would be
necessary for Rice to affirm the Hervian position that regeneration precedes faith. This he unhesitatingly does.
"Regeneration is the cause of which faith is an effect." [39]
"Faith is certainly the act of a being who is spiritually alive,
and he must be quickened before he exercises faith." "The
faith that works by love and overcomes the world, is consequent upon regeneration." Man is really converted without
the Word of God at all; after his conversion, saving faith
comes through the Gospel. "We believe and teach that the
Word is ordinarily employed in conversion and sanctification. Yet there must be, and there is, an influence of the
Spirit on the heart, in addition to the Word, and distinct
from it; and by this influence, especially, man is converted
and sanctified." [40]

A second result of this doctrine of the Spirit's working,

[37] "Campbell-Rice Debate," 633.
[38] *Ibid.*, 634.
[39] *Ibid.*, 704.
[40] *Ibid.*, 669. See also, 756.

Rice accepted with equal alacrity; that infants are regenerated by the Spirit without faith. Since the whole race is totally depraved, infants who die in infancy, unless regenerated, must go to hell. This no man can believe. The only conclusion, therefore, is that since they are in the grip of hereditary, total depravity, they must be made new by direct impact of the Spirit of God. John the Baptist was thus regenerated while he was yet in his mother's womb. Since, without salvation, infants will be forever lost, it is evident that "they are sanctified by the Spirit without the Word. This is our doctrine; and it is the doctrine of the Bible." [41]

✓ It was in opposition to this current doctrine, so well represented by Rice, that Campbell developed his position of the method of the Spirit's working to convert man from his sins and to sanctify the Christian. To him, the most deadly obstacle to the evangelization of his generation, was this theory which attributed to the Spirit the work of making the soul new by overwhelming and irresistable power. Men's minds were directed "not to the evidences and assurances furnished by the word of God, but to the varying moods of the mind and the fitful feelings of the heart." [42] On such feelings and moods, when judged by some mystical standard to be genuine, men were taught to rely, and the place which baptism had held in the early church, as the seal and assurance of pardon, was usurped by this so-called "religious experience." [43] To the average man, this experience was the very essence of the Christian religion. In a very pointed statement, Campbell tells why he objects so determinedly to this teaching. "The doctrine which I oppose, so far as it is really believed and acted upon, neutralizes preaching, annuls the Bible, and perfectly annihilates human responsibility. I know of no doctrine more fatal. For if God, by some mysterious power, without light,

[41] "Campbell-Rice Debate," 755.
[42] "Memoirs of Alexander Campbell," Richardson, II, 105.
[43] "Debates that Made History," Haley, 215, 216.

knowledge, a new idea, view or reflection, touch the soul of A, B, or C, and make it holy by 'infusion of a holy principle,' if he does this without any thought, motive, or argument, instantaneously and immediately, what becomes of the doctrine of human responsibility? Of what use is preaching, or the name of the Lord Jesus, or any instrumentality whatever? While, then, I believe and teach, and rejoice in the presence and power, and positive influence of God's Spirit in the work of conversion and sanctification; I do repudiate a doctrine full of desolation—which makes man a mere machine, annihilates all rational liberty, destroys human responsibility, and makes the Word of God a mere superfluity, of no essential importance, of no salutary instrumentality in the great work of regeneration." [44]

In another vitriolic passage, the deep-seated aversion which he felt toward the doctrine defended by Rice, is set forth. "I will insist that Mr. Rice explain to us why preach the Word; why print the Bible; why send missionaries to foreign lands; why set on foot any human instrumentalities whatever, on the assumption that God makes men and infants holy as he did Adam? I never objected to a spiritual religion. Nay, I love it—I preach it—I contend for it. I never would have jeopardized my reputation in questioning the popular notions of spiritual influence, but to aim a blow at the root of all fanaticism, and of a wild irrepressible enthusiasm. I believe not only in the Holy Spirit, but in a religion in which this Divine agent is both the substance, orgin, cause, and reason. But, sir, in my humble opinion this metaphysical abstraction, this theological speculation, this electric, immedial operation, that makes an infant or a pagan holy in a moment has been the most soul ruining dogma ever invented, preached, or propagated. It has slain its tens of thousands. It has made sceptics, fanatics, despondents, and visionaries without number, and without limit." [45] The reason for the Campbellian doctrine's de-

[44] "Campbell-Rice Debate," 644.
[45] "Campbell-Rice Debate," 644.

velopment and the absolute horror with which its author objected to the popular view of the Spirit's working, is summed up in one other scorching paragraph. "These elect infants, elect pagans, elect idiots, on whom God acts when, where, and how he pleases, but makes them holy in a moment, without light, knowledge, faith, or love (for though these may be called by them, the effects of regeneration, the thing, the work, the operation itself, is anterior to them, above and independent of them, without any human agency whatever), are figments of distempered brains, the creatures of religious romance, the offspring of a metaphysical delusion, for which there is no cure, except in the rational reading and study of the 'Book of God.' " [46]

The position of Campbell himself, on the whole vexed question of the work of the Spirit in conversion and sanctification, is stated with such vigor and clarity that nothing is necessary to understand it, save to quote the classic passages in which an exposition of it is given. After defining the position of the school of Word alone, and that of Spirit alone, or Spirit followed by Word, he says: "There yet remains another school, which never speculatively separates the Spirit and the Word; which, in every case of conversion, contemplates them as cooperating; or, which is the same thing, conceives of the Spirit of God as clothed with the gospel motives and arguments—enlightening, convincing, persuading sinners, and thus enabling them to flee from the wrath to come. In this school, conversion and regeneration are terms indicative of a moral and spiritual change—a change accomplished through the arguments, the light, the love, the grace of God, expressed and revealed, as well as approved by the supernatural attestations of the Holy Spirit. They believe, and teach, that it is the Spirit that quickens, and that the Word of God—the Living Word —is that incorruptible seed, which, when planted in the

[46] *Ibid.*, 654.

heart, vegetates, and germinates, and grows, and fruitifies
unto eternal life. They hold it to be unscriptural, irrational,
unphilosophic, to discriminate between spiritual agency and
instrumentality—between what the Word, *per se,* or the
Spirit, *per se,* severally does; as though they were two independent, and wholly distinct powers, or influences. They
object not to the cooperation of secondary causes; of various
subordinate instrumentalities; the ministry of men; the
ministry of angels; the doctrine of special providences; but,
however, whenever the Word gets into the heart—the spiritual seed into the moral nature of man; it as naturally, as
spontaneously grows there, as the sound, good corn, when
deposited in the genial earth. It has life in it; and is,
sublimely and divinely called 'The Living and Effectual
Word.' " [47]

The view thus taken of the method of the Spirit's working
is itself a deeply spiritual conception. Its disagreement with
the current mysticism, does not mean that it is cold and
materialistic. This was frequently charged against him, and
it is in the refutation of such implications that he constantly
emphasizes his faith in Christianity as preëminently the religion of the Spirit. "I would not, sir, value at the price of
a single mill, the religion of any man as respects the grand
affair of eternal life, whose religion is not begun, carried on,
and completed by the personal agency of the Holy Spirit.
Nay, sir, I esteem it the peculiar excellence and glory of
our religion, that it is spiritual; that the soul of man is
quickened, enlightened, sanctified, and consoled by the indwelling presence of the Spirit of the eternal God. But,
while avowing these my convictions, I have no more fellowship with those false and pernicious theories that confound
the peculiar work of the Father with that of the Son, or
with that of the Holy Spirit, or the work of any of these
awful names with that of another; or which represents, il-

[47] "Campbell-Rice Debate," 614.

lumination, conversion and sanctification as the work of the Spirit without the knowledge, belief and obedience of the gospel, as written by the holy apostles and evangelists, than I have with the author and finisher of the book of Mormon." [48]   The exposition of the place of the Spirit in the work of the Godhead, presented by Walter Scott, and already considered in this study, was frequently employed. It is one of the many illustrations which might be given of the influence of those who labored with him, upon his own teaching.   In the debate with Rice, after very definitely drawing the lines of demarkation between the work of the Father, and of the Son, and of the Holy Spirit, he says: "The Father originates all, the Son executes all, the Spirit consummates all.   Eternal volition, design and mission belong to the Father; reconciliation to the Son; sanctification to the Spirit." [49]   One may not agree with Campbell's conclusions as to the manner in which the Holy Spirit brings men to conversion, and sanctifies the Christian, but that he was thoroughly a believer in the spirituality of all that may be called the religion of Christ, no one who has made an exhaustive study of his writings, can deny.   The passages already quoted abundantly establish this fact, but one more may be noted, a classic in Disciple literature, for its beauty and spiritual power.   "I do, sir, most sincerely regard the Spirit of God as the author of every spiritual and noble desire in the human heart; the author of every pious affection, of every holy aspiration of our souls.   His mysterious but certain power, is in, and with the gospel, and he makes it the power of God to salvation to every man that believes it.   He sanctifies us through the truth.   He works in us to will and to do his good pleasure.   He is the Spirit of grace, because he is the Spirit of truth." [50]

[48] "Campbell-Rice Debate," 616.
[49] *Ibid.*, 615, 616.
[50] "Campbell-Rice Debate," 701.

V

Because of the adverb "only" in the proposition which Campbell defended, he was frequently accused of denying any influence of the Spirit in any manner whatsoever, other than that exercised directly through the Word. It was easy for his opponents to jump to the conclusion that he denied all providential influences; that God had the power so to move on conditions that a man could be brought under the influences which are ordained for the purpose of conversion, or, that God ever had used that power. Many of the Disciples, themselves, have fallen into error here concerning his true views. In numerous strong statements, he not only vigorously defends himself against this accusation, but very positively states just what he means when he contends that "in conversion and sanctification the Holy Spirit operates only through the Word of God." In reply to Rice's oft-repeated implication that he does not believe in providential influence, he says: "The question is not about total depravity. I believe man is depraved. I believe that God presides over the work of His hands. But that is not the point of debate; nor is the question about what God can or cannot do—whether or not He turns the hearts of kings and mortals, as the channels of the rivers or seas are turned. Whether he disposes the hearts of men, without words, is not the question; for were it proved that He can move kings and princes, and men of all ranks and degrees, as I believe, without the Bible, and without words, that reaches not this issue at all. The question before us is about sanctification, and conversion." [51] "The question is whether God converts men to Christ, or sanctifies Christians without the truth of the Bible." Many of the objections to the Campbellian doctrine of the Holy Spirit, would manifestly be abandoned, were the real issue which he defended, kept in mind. In another brief statement, he calls attention to the limits of

[51] "Campbell-Rice Debate," 641.

the word "only" in his proposition. Whether or not God may work in mysterious ways, is not the question; "whether the ever-living and ever-present Spirit of our God may not through the truth, in ways unknown to mortals, affect the soul of man, by fixing the attention upon it, or removing, providentially, obstructions, etc., is neither affirmed or denied." [52] That God could, and that He does, do these things, Campbell held as an opinion; as a fact which he could unhesitatingly affirm, he would not state it. In a very pointed paragraph, he sums up the issue. "The legitimate point of discussion in this proposition, is not whether the Spirit operates, but whether the instrumentality of the Word be necessary, according to the words, 'only through the Word.' I never said, nor wrote, that the Word was the original cause of man's salvation, nor even the efficient cause. All that has been offered by Mr. Rice upon the subject, in any other view of the matter, is gratuitous and irrelevant. It is to change the proposition, and hide the point in this system, which I repudiate. The proposition is, in its own language, a refutation of all these insinuations. It affirms that the Spirit of God operates. The question is not upon operation, but upon instrumentality—'only through the Word.'" "What the Spirit of God does, is not the question; but by what means the Spirit of God operates in conversion and sanctification." [53]

From the numerous passages already quoted, it is obvious that he believed firmly, in an actual indwelling of the Spirit in the heart, and that the special work of the Spirit thus indwelling, is that of sanctification. While it was a peculiarity of his thought to make sweeping definitions, it is yet clear that he often considered sanctification as a continuation of that process of which conversion is the beginning. "We know very well, and so teach, that conversion but ends the sinner's life and state, and introduces or begins the Christian's; that, from that time forth, he is to feed upon

[52] *Ibid.*, 712.
[53] "Campbell-Rice Debate," 673.

the bread of life, until he grows to the fullness of the stature of a perfect man in Christ Jesus, and to go on to perfection and sanctification of the Christian life; which is an absolutely essential prerequisite to his eternal happiness in the heavens. This truth it is necessary to have constantly impressed upon the mind, and that, without this living character, our conversion will avail us nothing in the great day of reckoning. It must be confessed, and also corrected, that a vague impression exists on the minds of some, who have not grown so rapidly in knowledge as the Scriptures and their necessities require, that the great object was secured in their conversion, and that nothing more was to be done. Such persons need to be taught the very rudiments of Christianity—principles that lie upon the very surface, cognizable to all who will open their eyes." [54] While the terms conversion and sanctification, each comprehend all that the new state means when considered simply as a change from that of the old man of sin, they are not in his thought, synonymous. The misapprehension of this fact has been a fruitful cause of much misunderstanding on the part of Disciple writers, on the real Campbellian position. "It is a truth very clear that it scarcely requires repetition, that the work of sanctification commences with our spiritual birth— the sanctification of our Christian life with the beginning of that life. As in nature, so in grace, we enter into life by a birth, and the growth and development of the man and Christian begin there. These truths, being so self-evident to the independent thinker and careful student of the Bible, the apprehension and comprehension of all their harmonies, are facile in the extreme; and no question can arise, involving either the conversion of the sinner or the sanctification and perfection of the saints, but what is capable of ready and easy solution." [55]

[54] "Millennial Harbinger," Volume for 1854, 373. It is significant that these words were written in the last years of Campbell's life. They show how clearly the relation of conversion and sanctification had become fixed in his thinking.

[55] "Millennial Harbinger," Volume for 1854, 373.

That the Holy Spirit is shed abroad in our hearts as the means of sanctification, but that his power is exerted in doing that work through the Word of God, is undoubtedly the Campbellian teaching. In a much debated passage in the "Christian System," he says: [56] "Being born of water and the renewing of the Holy Spirit are not works of merit or righteousness, but only the means of enjoyment. But this pouring out of the influences, this renewing of the Holy Spirit, is as necessary as the bath of regeneration to the salvation of the soul, and to the enjoyment of the hope of Heaven, of which the Apostle speaks. In the kingdom into which we are born of water, the Holy Spirit is as the atmosphere in the kingdom of nature; we mean that the influences of the Holy Spirit are as necessary to the new life, as the atmosphere is to our animal life in the kingdom of nature. All that is done to us before regeneration, God our Father effects by the word, or gospel as dictated and confirmed by the Holy Spirit. But after we are thus begotten and born by the Spirit of God—after our new birth—the Holy Spirit is shed on us richly, through Jesus Christ our Saviour; of which the peace of mind, the love, the joy, the hope of the regenerate is full proof; for these are among the fruits of that Holy Spirit of promise of which we read." [57]

As to the manner of spiritual operation, save that it is exerted through the Word of truth, he did not claim to know. He could believe that the Spirit actually accompanies the Word, that it is always present with the Word, even though he could not understand the nature of spiritual operations.

---

[56] The contention of Dean Garrison that in this passage, we have evidence of the fact that Campbell acknowledged an influence of the Spirit on the heart of Christians, which could not be accounted for on strictly Lockian principles, is open to question. If it were isolated from all that he has elsewhere taught on the subject, it might imply that he did believe in an influence in sanctification, apart from means. Nothing is affirmed in the statement, however, more than that the Spirit does actually dwell in the heart. It makes no affirmation as to the method of his working. See "Alexander Campbell's Theology," 272.

[57] "Christian System," 267.

"I believe the Spirit accompanies the Word, is always present with the Word, and actually and personally works through it upon the moral nature of man, but not without it. I presume not to speculate upon the nature of this power, nor the mode of operation. I believe the Holy Spirit sheds abroad in our hearts, the love of God, and dwells in all the faithful; that it sanctifies them through the truth; that 'it works in them to will and to do,' and that it comforts them in all their afflictions." [58]   In another lucid paragraph, he declares his unswerving faith in the operation of the Holy Spirit through means, though he does not understand the nature of the power put forth. "There is no debate upon spiritual operations. They are of an abstract nature and quality. It is not possible for man to conceive of spiritual operations. Who can grasp the idea of a Spirit? Who can apprehend the idea of its nature, its identity, its form, its person, its modes of living, moving, and operating? We can neither have a consistent idea of a spirit nor of any of its operations. That the Spirit of God operates on the human understanding and heart, is just as certain as that a man has an understanding and affections. Our spirit is allied to the spiritual system, to the Great Spirit. God can commune, and does commune with man, and man with God." [59]   As far as the Scriptures speak on the subject of the manner of the Spirit's working, Campbell is willing to speak. Where they are silent—where revelation ends, he is content to be silent. In this position, he is absolutely consistent with the ground occupied in the Rule of Faith. This really is the key to his position. That the Spirit operates in conversion and sanctification, and that its operations are confined to the Word of Truth, is a matter of revelation. Beyond this he would not venture, for beyond this assured truth were the realms of speculation. He believed that God can and does work to "dispose the hearts of Kings and Princes to hear the truth," but this belonged

[58] "Campbell-Rice Debate," 745.
[59] "Campbell-Rice Debate," 708.

to the realm of his own opinions, and was not a part of his teaching on those things that were to him, matters of faith. "That the Spirit operates through the instrumentality of the Word, I doubt not; but if asked to explain the *modus operandi*, I confess my inability. The fact of the power, I admit; but how it works, I presume not to comprehend." [60] It was the wild and fanatical speculations which he abhorred, and against which he battled so untiringly. Because he would not affirm with finality, where the Scriptures made no affirmations, he was often accused of entirely rejecting the Holy Spirit. In a letter to Mr. Lynd, he defends himself in no uncertain words, against such accusations. "In rejecting these speculative traditions of the elders, I am very far from rejecting the Spirit himself as necessary to our sanctification and salvation. God our Father gave his Son for us, and He gave His Spirit to us. The promise of His Son was the peculiar glory of the Old Testament, while the promise of His Spirit is the distinguishing excellency of the New. By the sacrifice of His Son, the guilt of sin is taken from us; by the power and grace of the Holy Spirit, the power of sin is subdued in us.[61] It is not necessary that we should speculate upon the manner in which the Spirit exerts his converting and sanctifying power. Especially does this hold good of the Christian, in whom the Spirit dwells, and for whom the blessings which He has for him, originates. We do not need to know all about Him to enjoy Him as an indwelling guest. "Nor do we think it necessary to inquire how, or in what manner, the Spirit operates through the truth, on our spiritual nature, before we confidently ask for His presence, power, and comfort. It is enough to know that the Holy Spirit has been promised, and that we have been commanded to ask for it. We have a command to ask, to seek, to knock, and the promise of receiving, finding, and obtaining all that we ask in faith, and

[60] *Ibid.*, 641.
[61] "Campbell-Rice Debate," 719.

all that we could wish on the subject. Our duty is plain, however mysterious our philosophy; our privileges are clear, however dark our metaphysics may be." [62] While this passage anticipates what shall later be developed concerning Campbell's doctrine of prayer, it is quoted here to illustrate his position, that the fact of the Spirit's indwelling, and his work in sanctification through the truth, may be apprehended without speculation on the manner in which he does that work. It also directly states his belief in the necessity of prayer, for the Spirit's work in the Christian.

VI

1. The first argument by which Campbell attempted to establish his position is from the constitution of the human mind. The Holy Spirit, in conversion and sanctification, has respect to the mind as constituted. This constitution is never violated on the part of the Creator. Ideas are received only through sensation and reflection. Thus, in doing his work, the Spirit makes no changes in man as he has been created by the Father. "No new faculties are imparted— no old faculty destroyed. They are neither more nor less in number; they are neither better nor worse in kind. Paul the Apostle, and Saul of Tarsus, are the same person, so far as all the animal, intellectual, and moral powers are concerned. His mental and physical temperament were just the same after, as before, he became a Christian. The Spirit of God, in effecting this great change, does not violate, metamorphose, or annihilate any power or faculty of the man, in making the saint. He merely receives new ideas and new impressions, and undergoes a great moral, or spiritual change

62 In 1838, Campbell conducted a written discussion with a Mr. S. W. Lynd, a very talented Baptist minister of Cincinnati, on the subject of converting power. In this discussion, he opposed "the popular doctrine of regeneration before faith, or the necessity of special spiritual operations to enable sinners to believe the gospel." "Memoirs of Alexander Campbell," Richardson, II, 434, 435.

—so that he becomes alive wherein he was dead, and dead wherein he was formerly alive." [63]

Campbell's Lockianism is, in this argument, clearly to the fore. It is based directly upon the Lockian position that "all knowledge comes through sensation and reflection. Again, it embodies a purely intellectual view of the nature of faith. There is also an implied protest, elsewhere pointedly and vigorously stated, against what he calls "metaphysical regeneration." In this objection there is an echo of Locke's turning away from the realm of metaphysics, and limiting philosophy to a consideration of the powers of the human mind, with special reference to the problem of knowledge. With this general position basic in his own thinking, Campbell, in this argument, defined salvation, not in terms of mysterious changes made in the soul of man as the current Protestant mysticism defined it, but in terms of knowledge which the Holy Spirit brings to man through the Word of truth. It has been shown elsewhere that this one view cannot adequately set forth the whole of the Campbellian attitude on the question. Were these the only terms in which his foundational beliefs are stated, he must be convicted of being a strict Lockian. It is probable that this philosophical argument, and others, which he at times made from this starting point, is the least consistent with the general position which he had adopted in his conception of the Rule of Faith, "Where the Scriptures speak, we speak; where the Scriptures are silent, we are silent." That he did rise above his Lockian foundation when the religious necessity demanded, has been abundantly established. [64]

2. The second argument "is deduced from the fact, that no living man has ever been hear of, and none can be found, possessed of a single conception of Christianity, or of one spiritual thought, feeling, or emotion, where the Bible,

[63] "Campbell-Rice Debate," 617, 620. See also, "Christian Baptism," 291, 295.

[64] "Alexander Campbell's Theology," Dean Garrison, 267, 271.

or some tradition from it, has not been before him." [65]   The first part of this contention, that which refers to Christianity, is obviously true; the second is manifestly so sweeping that it is impossible of proof. Its Lockianism is also apparent, for it is really but a further development of the one which precedes. Man receives his material for ideas through sensation. No sensations furnished from the purely natural world, could produce spiritual ideas. The conclusion, then, is that such sensations must come audibly or visibly through revelation.[66]   This argument is open to the same general criticism as the first one. It partakes of the speculative, and this very thing he was most determined in condemning.

The remaining arguments may be summarized in a paragraph. 3. It is impossible for anyone to express a correct idea of the Christian Religion without the Word of God, though they may profess to have been converted by direct agency of the Spirit, without the Word. All such so-called knowledge, turns out to be, in reality, no knowledge at all. In each case, the cause of the conversion may be traced to the Word itself.[67]   4. Whatever is essential to conversion or regeneration in one case, is essential in all cases. If it is necessary for the Word of God to be preached to convert one man, it is essential in the conversion of every other man.[68]   5. The Holy Spirit's method, as illustrated in the Scriptures, in addressing the minds of men through all the ages, has been that of using intelligible "signs addressed to the sense, and words to the understanding and affections." [69]   6. The name which Jesus gives to the Holy Spirit, Paraclete or Comforter and Advocate, is indicative of the method which He will use in doing the blessed work which He has been sent to do.[70]   7. The gift of tongues, through which the Advocate commenced his work in the new age, is signi-

[65] "Campbell-Rice Debate," 619, 620.
[66] "Christian Baptism," 294, 295.
[67] "Campbell-Rice Debate," 620.
[68] *Ibid.*, 620, 621.
[69] *Ibid.*, 621, 622.
[70] *Ibid.*, 622, 623.

ficant. Nothing was more essential than that men should be able to understand in the language in which they were born. Through the apostles on Pentecost the Holy Spirit spake to the multitude in words, the words they had known all their lives.[71] 8. Peter contends that we are born again, "not of corruptible seed, but of incorruptible seed, the Word of God which liveth and abideth forever (I Peter 1:23)." The means employed by the Spirit in conversion and sanctification are, in these words explicitly stated, as in several passages which are here quoted (James 1:18; I Cor. 4:15; etc.).[72] Arguments nine to fourteen are chiefly scriptural declarations of the fact that the Spirit works through the Word.[73] The fourteenth deals with all the cases of conversion in the book of Acts, and shows that the Spirit's work in each instance was done through instruments—men speaking the words of the Gospel.[74]

VII

Two objections only, of the many first offered against Campbell's doctrine that in conversion and sanctification, the Holy Spirit operates only through the Truth, may be considered, because of their influence in modern discussions of the question. These objections were forestalled by his careful definitions in the first address of the Rice Debate. A superficial reading of the argument has made many, even among Disciple writers,[75] do his thought an injustice, where

[71] "Campbell-Rice Debate," 623, 625.

[72] *Ibid.*, 664, 668.

[73] *Ibid.*, 699, 701, 720, 725.

[74] *Ibid.*, 746, 748. See also, "Christian Baptism," 295, 312.

[75] Dr. J. J. Haley, one of the most distinguished of Disciple scholars, according to his own confession, considered these objections of greater force than a later critical study of the whole question, proved them to be. In his "Makers and Moulders of the Reformation," referring to the debate with Rice, on the work of the Holy Spirit, he says: "The argument in support of this thesis is perhaps the most eloquent to be found in the literature of the Spirit's relation to saint and sinner, but it fails to carry conviction to the religious mind of today. Mr. Rice agreed with Mr.

a more careful study of his first principles, so painstakingly laid down in his introductory speech, would have resulted in a less critical attitude being taken.

1. The first objection is that the position limits the power of God. Rice urged this repeatedly. "I can never subscribe to the doctrine that God can exert over the human mind no more power than I, except that He may employ stronger arguments; that the Creator can influence men morally, only as they may be pleased to listen to His arguments. I can never consent to place the Holy Spirit on a perfect equality with man, except that He is a better preacher. This doctrine, which thus limits the power of the Spirit, is most unreasonable as well as most unscriptural." [76] It has already been noted that Campbell did not teach any such doctrine. He believed that God presides over the work of His hands. That He may, through providentially arranged circumstances, influence men toward right, was a matter of firm conviction with him. In a pointed statement, he acknowledges such influences and sets forth the issue in unmistakable manner. "I said in the commencement of this discussion, that I did not affirm nor deny as to other operations of the Spirit, save in conversion and sanctification.

Campbell, that the Spirit operated through the truth, but denied that it operated through the truth only. He said, in criticism of the adverb in the proposition, 'If the Holy Spirit operates through the truth only, why does Mr. Campbell pray for the conversion of sinners?' Why not preach the Word and leave the truth to do its work without the invocation of an influence outside of both? If this affirmation is true, said the Presbyterian divine, that the Spirit is shut up in the Word of Truth, the devil is more resourceful and powerful than God, for he reaches the minds of men without the intervention of words. Mr. Campbell did not answer these objections, but the Disciples, for more than a generation, have answered them by the elimination of the word 'only.'" In his last book, he confesses that this conclusion was "hasty and not sustained by the facts." He continues: "A careful and critical re-reading of the discussion has convinced me that Mr. Campbell made no mistake in the use of the word 'only.' The two points about praying for the conversion of sinners, and the devil's abstract and mystical operations in carrying on his work, needed no answer, because all such objections had been forestalled by the definitions and qualifications of Mr. Campbell's first address." "Debates that Made History," 213, 214.

[76] "Campbell-Rice Debate," 634, 635.

What He may do in the way of suggestions or impressions, by direct communication of original ideas, or in bringing things to remembrance long since forgotten, I presume not to discuss. I believe He has exerted, and can exert, such influences. Nor do I say what influence He may exert, or cause to be exerted, in bringing men's minds to consider these matters; but I confine my reasonings and proofs to conversion and sanctification." [77] Here is evident a clean break with the extreme Lockianism, which characterized his first two arguments.[78] It has been noted before, that he did this when the religious necessity demanded.

In direct reply to the objection that his position limits the power of God, he says: "He argues against my views, because they 'limit the power of God.' That is, of course, in confining the operation to the instrumentality of the Word. It limits, but it does not deny the operation. He is right here. This is the issue, and the objection was made in a just view of it. Well, now, I meet the objection as a legitimate one. We shall try its merits. The Universalian says, the Unitarian, the Calvinist, and especially the Presbyterian, limits the power of God, because he makes salvation depend upon faith and a holy life. When Mr. Rice defends himself from that charge, his defense shall be mine from his charge of limitation. The Unitarian, too, talks about limiting the great God, in extending salvation beyond the precincts of Bible influence. But all this is idle talk. I do limit the power of God, only because He Himself has limited it. God can only do by his power, what His wisdom and benevolence approve. He has no power beyond that, though almighty to do what these two perfections approbate. Therefore, 'He cannot lie'; he cannot deny Himself. Therefore, He cannot make a wicked man happy; and, therefore, He can convert men only through the gospel. There are physical as well as moral impossibilities. God cannot make two mountains without a valley. He cannot make light and

77 "Campbell-Rice Debate," 641.
78 Ibid., 722.

darkness co-habit the same place at the same time. He cannot lie. This is another *ad captandum* argument. God can do many things He will not do. I say again, He can only do what is in harmony with all His perfections. There are, also, moral impossibilities. A virtuous and kind father could not kill all his children, and yet he could. He has physical but not moral power. His arm could, but his heart could not; and, therefore, the moral sometimes triumphs over the physical. God can only save through the means His wisdom, justice, and benevolence dictate." [79] This statement is so clear that comment upon it is needless. Refuting the implications which were drawn without warrant from his ground position, he acknowledges that he does limit the power of God, but only as God Himself has limited it, in using intelligible means through which to speak to man.

2. The second objection was urged with seemingly greater force than the first. It has doubtless had more influence, especially upon the modern mind, than the one just considered. If the Holy Spirit converts sinners and sanctifies saints only through the Word of Truth, then, of what value are prayers offered for the salvation of the non-christian world? Rice offered this objection with apparent effect. "This doctrine makes it both useless and improper to pray for the conversion of men. I know, he will not deny, that it is the duty and privilege of Christians to pray, that God would convert sinners; for we have both precept and example authorizing and requiring it. But whilst the duty is perfectly clear, if we regard precept or precedent, or both, that doctrine of Mr. Campbell makes it wholly unnecessary, if not improper." [80] Strictly speaking, there is, in the Lockian philosophy, no places for prayer for help in time of temptation and trouble. Since the Spirit can influence men only through the senses, there is no need to pray for influence other than this. But in this regard, Campbell was not a rigid Lockian. A thinker always reaches the highest alti-

[79] "Campbell-Rice Debate," 674.
[80] "Campbell-Rice Debate," 729.

tudes when he finds his system cramped and too small to contain him. Realizing that God, through the Spirit, does influence men providentially, and knowing the spiritual necessity for prayer, he promptly forsook his Lockian foundation, and stated religious truth simply as religious truth. He did not understand it always, but if the Scriptures affirmed it, he unhesitatingly ranged himself with the Word and against the philosophy. This is exactly his situation in regard to prayer. Answering Rice's objection, he says: "The best philosophy of prayer is, that God has granted the privilege, enjoined the duty, and given a promise. We, therefore, violate no decree, and sin against no revelation in praying for all men. I believe, practice, and preach the necessity and propriety of praying for the salvation of our children, families, friends, etc., as much as I believe, preach or practice any point of domestic and social duties and privileges." [81] Though he claimed not to understand all that prayer signifies, he was yet happy to follow the divine leading, to pray both as a duty and a privilege. Whatever the Word teaches concerning prayer, he is willing to teach; whatever has been definitely revealed, he without hesitation will proclaim; beyond this he could not go and be consistent with the great principles he had adopted. In another connection, he deposes; "With regards to the operation of the Spirit through the Word, on sinners and on saints, while we strongly affirm the fact of His sanctifying, reviving, cheering, and saving efficacy through the word of prophets and apostles, we ought to teach no new terms, phrases or dogmata—preach good news to sinners and teach holiness to the converted—teach the Christians to pray for the Spirit in all his holy influences, and to lift up their voices to the Lord for all his promised aids. Thus the love of God will be poured out into their souls by his Holy Spirit that dwelleth in them, and they will learn to love His children and to rejoice in hope of the coming glory." [82] Here are dis-

---

[81] *Ibid.*, 745.

[82] Letter to Elder J. M. Peck, 1841, quoted by Richardson in "Memoirs of Alexander Campbell," II, 488, 489.

tinct expressions of faith in the indwelling of the Holy Spirit; that he exerts upon the Christian, in sanctification, "holy influences," and that Christians should be taught to pray for such aids.

Instead of the legalist, which he was painted by those who misunderstood him, there are passages in which Campbell almost approaches the position of the mystic. By this it is not meant that he had any love for the absurd mysticism of his own day. It is not only Christian to pray for the indwelling of the Spirit, and for his holy influence in us, but we must also pray according to His promptings. "We must be led by the Spirit; for we know not what we should ask without his teachings. In other words, we must pray according to the suggestion of the Holy Spirit, or its promptings in us. For example, we cannot pray for worldly riches and honor in faith, in repentance, in the Holy Spirit: not because we have no promise of these things, but because such requests are not compatible with repentance, nor with the teachings of the Holy Spirit. We may, indeed, pray for competence, for wisdom, for influence, for the salvation of our families, etc., because such desires are prompted by the Holy Spirit." [83] In his discussion of the Gift of the Holy Spirit, in the "Christian System," he forever settles the question about his faith in the Spirit as actually dwelling in the heart of the Christian, to sanctify him through the Word; that Christians should pray for his work and in him. Our sanctification, which begins with a religious setting apart when we obey the Gospel, is a continuous process through life. "Sanctification in one point of view, is unquestionably a progressive work. To sanctify is to set apart; this may be done in a moment, and so far as mere state or relation is concerned, it is as instantaneous as baptism. But there is the foundation of a holy character as well as a holy state. The formation of such a character is the work of means." [84] That means, as has already been shown in the

[83] "Millennial Harbinger Abridged," Smith, II, 60.
[84] "Christian System," 65.

present study, is the Holy Spirit of God working through the truth. But He actually dwells in the heart of the child of God, and is to be prayed for in all His power of helpfulness. "Assistance is to be prayed for; and it is promised. Now as the Spirit of God, under the administration of Christ, is the author of all holiness in us—he is called the 'Holy Spirit,' the 'Spirit of holiness.' [85] The Holy Spirit is, then, the author of all our holiness; and in the struggle after victory over sin and temptation, 'it helps our infirmities,' and comforts us by seasonably bringing to our remembrance the promises of Christ, and 'strengthens us with might, in the new or inner man.' And thus God works in us to will and to do his own benevolence, 'while we are working out our own salvation with fear and trembling.' Christians are, therefore, clearly and unequivocally temples of the Holy Spirit; and they are quickened, animated, encouraged, and sanctified by the power and influence of the Spirit of God, working in them through the truth." [86]

If, after such statements, there could be any further doubts as to Campbell's faith in the actual indwelling of the Spirit, two other utterances should forever allay them. "God gives His Holy Spirit to them that ask him, according to his revealed will; and without this gift no one could be saved or ultimately triumph over all opposition. He knows but little of the deceitfulness of sin, of the combating of temptation, who thinks himself competent to wrestle against the allied forces of the world, the flesh, and the devil. Hence, the necessity of 'supplications, deprecations, intercessions, and thanksgiving,' of praying always with all prayer and supplication in the Holy Spirit." [87] "To those, then, who believe, repent, and obey the gospel, he actually communicates his Good Spirit. The fruits of the Spirit in them are 'love, joy, peace, longsuffering, gentleness, goodness, fidelity, meekness, temperance.' The attributes of character which distinguish

[85] *Ibid.*, 66.
[86] "Christian System," 66.
[87] *Ibid.*, 66.

the new man are each of them communications of the Holy Spirit, and thus we are sons of God in fact, as well as in title, under the dispensation of the Holy Spirit." [88]

In the light of such teaching two closely-related objections to the Campbellian theology are answered. The first one, and it is urged frequently and with force, is that it is in-tellectualistic—it does not give adequate place to the mystical elements in religion. It must be frankly acknowledged that the Disciples have not tended much to mysticism: as a matter of fact they have generally been afraid of it, believing that it leads in one direction to fanaticism, and in the other to spiritual inactivity.

While it must be confessed that the Disciples have not been inclined toward mysticism, there is nothing in their plea which precludes an appreciation of those deeper things in religious experience, which the mystics have sometimes thought to be peculiarly their own. The conception of faith as personal rather than doctrinal, of itself opens the door to a realization of all the experiences one ought to have, who feels that Christ is personally his Saviour and Lord. It will be pointed out that there are passages in Campbell and Richardson, which equal in spiritual insight and power, anything which the mystics have produced.

The second objection, allied closely to the one just considered, is that the emphasis which the Disciples have placed upon the Church and the way of salvation, especially baptism as related to the plan, eventuates in legalism and externalism. It must be confessed that were this emphasis the whole of the Disciple plea, the validity of the objection might be acknowledged. It is undoubtedly true that in the hands of ignorant men, or those who have not penetrated to the very heart of its meaning, it has often degenerated into a legalistic and externalistic presentation. That the Campbells themselves so conceived it, must be denied. Their fundamental conception of the meaning of faith in Christ,

[88] *Ibid.*, 66.

led them to thing of their plan for Christian union through a restoration of primitive, evangelical Christianity, as thoroughly ethical and deeply spiritual. It was not only the form of the New Testament Church, which they wished to produce, but its life and spirit, as well. In one of his finest paragraphs, Alexander Campbell shows his appreciation of the significance of the restoration which all through the years, he had desired to see realized. While deploring defeats, and keenly sensitive to the dangers which his plan provoked, he yet believed in its basic soundness and its ultimate success. "The attempt to restore to the world the primitive order of things, involves something more than a revival of the faith of the New Testament disciples. The effort is to restore Original Christianity; and this is something more than to have a correct view of its theory and practice. While correct views are essential to a full, and rational, and spiritual enjoyment of what God has so graciously given us in his holy word, yet this is not all; nay, it is not the vital part. While a correct theory leads us to a lucid intellectual appreciation of the beauty and grandeur of the scheme, and of our relations to, and dependence on God, as our Creator, Redeemer, and bountiful Benefactor; still, something more is requisite to place us in a proper relation to God—to place us in a state of union and communion with him, as the Source and Author of our spiritual life. If we fail in this effort for a restoration of Original Christianity—to revive primitive life, devotion and zeal— it is problematical whether or not we may do more than heighten our own condemnation, and that of the world, also, by increasing our light, and knowledge, and opportunities. The enlightenment of the mind must be followed by a corresponding vitality of the heart. It must be known, and must not be forgotten, that Christianity is more than intellectual enlightenment; that the conviction of the mind is but the means to the great end, object, and design of the mission of the Messiah—the regeneration of the entire man —the renewing of the life and character to an assimilation of

the great type and model presented to us in the life of the
Son of God. And this assimilation is, itself, but a means to
the grand and ultimate conception of God in the introduction of the remedial system—namely, the restoration of man
to the society of God in the heavens. This being the grand
and ultimate object of the remedial plan, all its provisions
are subordinate to, and in harmony with, this design. In
all our efforts in teaching and preaching, this design must
be continually kept before the mind; and anyone who builds
upon any other foundation, or with reference to any other
design, is building upon the 'baseless fabric of a vision.'
Christianity having for its object, first and last, the improvement and sanctification of the life of man, with a special reference to the glories and honors which shall be revealed to
him as his own hereafter, it is evident that if this purpose
be not kept in view, both of the teacher and taught, the very
object to which all that God has said and done is antecedent
—is ignored.[89]

In a final paragraph, he confesses that the accusation
against his message, that it tends to legalism, has often had
just foundation, and reminds his people that only as life is
consistent with teaching, will their reformation come to
victory. "In our effort to restore primitive faith and measures, we seem, in some instances, to have overlooked, for
the time being, when assailed and pressed on all sides by the
incumbents of an effete and perverted Protestantism, the
necessity of insisting upon all things our Lord has commanded, and impressing upon all minds that conversion is
but the first step in the divine life." [90] The sudden breaking
in of the new light which came with the teachings of the
restoration movement, caused men to seize upon the cardinal
points of the Gospel with avidity. The first days were, therefore, characterized by a great zeal for holiness of life, as well
as correctness in doctrine. Then came the period of warfare, in which the new principles had to be defended, with a

[89] "Millennial Harbinger," Volume for 1854, 373.
[90] *Ibid.,* 373, 374.

consequent stressing of the externals of the faith. "Now that the battle is won," and "the enemies' batteries are all silenced," it is time to turn our guns upon our own hearts. "When this warfare is begun in earnest and prosecuted to a successful issue, then will Original Christianity once more appear among men, revived in faith and life—then will every phase of religious apostacy and corruption be driven from the earth, and 'righteousness, and peace, and joy in the Holy Spirit,' pervade and fill every heart, and unite every soul, and mankind realize the mighty truth, 'Thou in me, I in thee, and they in us.' " [91] The Campbellian theology is practical, but this does not mean that it lacks ethical content, or that it is, therefore, legalistic, concerned only with externals. When its true purpose and aim is realized, it is seen to be ethical and spiritual, through and through.

[91] "Millennial Harbinger," Volume for 1854, 373, 374.

CHAPTER IX

THE CHRISTIAN ORGANIZATION

THERE can be no appreciation of the position of Alexander Campbell in the theological world, without an understanding of his teaching concerning the Kingdom of God. This idea holds a central place in his theology, and around it group the other doctrines which, in the aggregate, form his systematized view of the Christian institution. Since the reunion of the scattered forces of God is to be accomplished by a restoration of primitive Christianity, it is essential to know just what he considered primitive Christianty to be. Since, also, the real basis for this unity is to be found in those terms, which in the New Testament are laid down as conditions of membership in Christ's church, it is necessary that the significance, in the Campbellian thinking, of citizenship in the kingdom of Heaven, should be clearly set forth. The ordinances of Christ, to which he devoted so much time in all his writings, derive their meaning, in his theology, from their relationship to the Christian organization from a purely modern standpoint, the fact that the right wing of Disciple thought tends to emphasize the restoration of New Testament Christianity even more than the plea for unity, makes imperative a restudy of his position as regards the nature of the Christian organization.

The influence of the Covenant Theologians in the formulation of the doctrine of the Kingdom, is most strikingly apparent. While these men influenced practically the whole of his thinking, yet that influence is most powerfully exerted through his final positions regarding the Kingdom of God. Dean Garrison points out [1] the two implications which

[1] "Alexander Campbell's Theology," 161, 162.

necessarily accompany the doctrine of the Covenants: (1) the idea of successive dispensations, as being stages in the history of the salvation which God has granted—a sharp distinction being made between the Christian dispensation and the Covenant of the Law which has been transcended; —and, (2) the conception of the relationship between man and God, as that of a Covenant or agreement into which man enters voluntarily by the acceptance of certain specified conditions on the basis of definite promises. This influence of the Dutch Theologians has been noted before; it is referred to here because of its fundamental importance in the formation of the Campbellian conceptions regarding the nature of the Kingdom. In two articles "The Kingdom of Heaven" and "The Nature of the Christian Organization" is this conception developed.

I

Where shall we find the true nature of the Christian organization? Did Christ have clearly in His mind the plan of His future kingdom on earth? "Did he unfold it in writing? Did he give plenary power and instructions to his apostles on this subject; or did he leave the scheme to be unfolded by the course of events and the seasonable teachings of the Holy Spirit?" [2] These questions from one of Campbell's most cultured and far-seeing correspondents elicited from him his clearest discussion of what he conceived New Testament Christianity in its organization to be. The gentleman, signing himself AC—n., who carried on this discussion with him was a member of the Episcopal Church and advocated with a grace and dignity seldom equaled in Campbell's forensic experience the position of the communion to which he belonged. The insufficiency of the New Testament documents to give us the nature of the Christian organization is manifest. They are confessedly fragmentary. The allusion to the nature of the organiza-

[2] "Christian Messenger," I, 147.

tion of Christ's kingdom to be found in them are usually
"strictly casual and incidental." [3]   While it is probable that
before the last of the apostles had finished his course a
clearly defined plan of the Christian organization, "either
by providential intimation or special illumination" had been
made known to them yet no complete outline of that scheme
was ever reduced to writing.   "So far from it, that the
notices of it in the apostolic writings are purely incidental
and exceedingly incomplete." [4]   Where then is the model of
that organization to be sought?   "I answer in the matter-of-
fact impress of it, left upon the church institutions of that
age."   Although there may be numerous seemingly insuper-
able objections to this principle it is nevertheless sound.
It is not to be contended that whatever may by such a
principle be discovered is true but "whatsoever of the
scriptural germ is found, thus unfolded, is true; whatever
of the teaching detail is thus supplied, is worthy of all acceptation; whatever is thus highly primitive, and confessedly
universal, having its germs in the New Testament, must be
apostolic." [5]   It is not to be thought that the opinions of
the apostolic fathers are of any value more than are the
opinions of men of like goodness and intellectual acumen
today.   "They were mere, erring, fallible men, and many
of them very narrow-minded and superstitious, however self-
sacrificing and sincere; and their opinions are of just the
same value with those of men similarly situated in our own
times; if sound and scriptural, they are worthy of reverence;
if corrupt and visionary, they are deposited along with other
useless, antiquated lumber." [6]   Neither is the authority of
these men of any weight.   They have no divine authentica-
tion that they may speak to us an assured message.   But
the facts which they universally attest are of just as much
value in an induction of the nature of the Christian organi-

[3] *Ibid.*, 403.
[4] "Christian Messenger," VII, 147.
[5] *Ibid.*, 148.
[6] *Ibid.*, VIII, 263.

zation as those which we may infer in the New Testament. "The facts of Scripture furnish the germs—the facts of the most highly primitive antiquity, exhibit the development of those germs." [7] The modern statement, sometimes heard from dispirited Disciples themselves, "It is impossible to restore New Testament Christianity because no one knows what New Testament Christianity was" is but an echo, although not so elegantly phrased, of the position of Campbell's talented and broad-minded correspondent.

To this well-stated view of the authority from which the Christian organization may be inferred Campbell brings the vigorous rejoinder "Christianity is all found in the New Testament." [8] If the Christian organization was incomplete in the New Testament age and if, therefore, its wholeness is discoverable only by an excurison into the mists and fogs of the centuries immediately succeeding, why is there not harmony among the various Christian bodies which appeal with such confidence to this authority? Those who are in favor of "both the presbyterial and congregational forms, with equal confidence appeal to what they call ancient and primitive fathers, in proof of their respective theories of government and organization." If the canon of a logical development from New Testament germs is allowed, a way is opened for all manner of fraud and apostacy. "The germs, or what may very plausibly be called the germs of monastic life, of celibacy, and a hundred of the most evident fooleries of Popery, are by some alleged to be found in the New Testament; and the primitive fathers are summoned to demonstrate the matured development of these germs." [9] The absurd result of the application of such a canon is that "the New Testament is a volume of germs, and the primitive fathers a greenhouse of developments, which in a short time exhibit them like the mustard seed developed in a considerable tree, under whose wide-spread branches, not merely the

[7] "Christian Messenger," VIII, 264.

[8] *Ibid.*, 301.

[9] *Ibid.*, VII, 149.

sweet songster of the garden, but sometimes the birds of prey take shelter." [10]   And what magnificent distances separate the New Testament writers from the so-called apostolic fathers.   "The Barnabases, the Polycarps, the Clements, and the Ignati of the schools of successors consecrated with the titles of 'apostolic men' and 'fathers of the church,' were children in their minority, compared with that masculine energy of style, force of thought, elevation of sentiment, and commanding authority which characterize and adorn every period of the inspired teachers.   At best they are but imperfect copyists of the style, and feeble imitators of the manners of Christ's ambassadors, without the living fire, the vivid light, and the kindling devotion of their eloquence. Their views are so cloudy, and their responses so ambiguous, and their authority so questionable, that a church founded in whole or in part upon them, much more resembles a pyramid erected on a quagmire, than a city founded upon a rock." [11]

That there is progress in the Christian organization is not to be denied, but that such progress lies in the realm of expediency is manifest.   With his correspondent, therefore, Campbell agreed "that we have 'a distinct and comprehensive idea,' of the ancient order of things in the New Testament so far as it is essential to the perfection of church organization; and whatever is wanting to the mere rearing of the tabernacle is to be supplied, not by the traditions of the fathers—their opinions, their authority, or their facts; but to be supplied by, and regarded as, the dictates of human prudence, varying its arrangements according to the ever varying circumstances of society." [12]   A more exhaustive exposition of just what is meant by this type of progress will be attempted in a consideration of his view of the law of expediency.   The New Testament alone contains the plan

[10] *Ibid.*, VII, 151.
[11] "Christian Messenger," VIII, 21.
[12] *Ibid.*, VIII, 272.

for the Christian organization—that organization is adequate to the task which Jesus imposed upon His people; this is unqualifiedly the Campbellian position.

II

In opposition to what he considered erroneous positions, Campbell developed his definition of the church or Kingdom of Heaven. In the main, it agrees with that adopted by the older Protestant theologians, that the church is an assembly of persons united by the profession of the same Christian faith, and the participation of the same ordinances.

1. It may be defined from the nature of its membership, or the "materials for its construction." "The materials for a church or congregation of Christians, must, in the necessity of things, exist before a church can be formed. We have the stones quarried before we can put them together in the house. The Lord's house is built of living stones, closely laid together and well cemented. Figure apart; the materials for a church are regenerated men and women—disciples of Christ. By regenerated persons, we mean those born of water and the Spirit—those who, believing that Jesus is the son of God on the proper evidence, according to the witness of the Spirit, penitent for their sins, understanding his blood as the only procuring cause of remission, and determined to obey the Lord in all things according to His Word; such persons having confessed the Lord by being immersed into the name of the Father, and of the Son, and of the Holy Spirit, according to His commandment, are the proper materials for the congregation of the Lord." [13] He clearly differentiates between the church, and a church. In answer to the question, "What is the church of Christ?" he replies, "the congregation of saints on earth and in heaven." [14] The church, thus, is composed of all living and dead, who

[13] "Millennial Harbinger," 1835, Extra on Order, quoted by Ben L. Smith in "Millennial Harbinger Abridged," II, 110.

[14] *Ibid.*, 106.

in faith have obeyed the Christ, and to the best of their
ability have tried to serve Him. Though he does not use
the phrase, it is evident that he believed in the church militant and the church triumphant. In defining "a church of
Christ," he affirms that it is "an assembly of persons meeting
stately in one place; built upon the foundation of the
Apostles and Prophets, Jesus Himself the chief cornerstone." [15]

An assembly of regenerated persons, however, is not an
accidental coming together. He very clearly sets forth the
fact that a church is an organization, the members of which
have come together upon a solemn pledge to each other.
"The simple existence of such persons, or their being thrown
together by accident, does not make them a church or house
of God. There is some form of coming together as a church.
There must be an agreement expressed in some way. They
pledge themselves to one another in the name of the Lord,
that they will walk together as becometh saints in the relation of a Christian congregation. How this is to be done, or
in what form, is not prescribed in the way of a positive
statute, or by special formalities. It is enough that they give
themselves to one another by some token or pledge—'the
right hand of fellowship,' or some significant action, the un-
equivocal token of accord." [16]

2. The church is also defined as a divine creation. Jesus
Christ, through His Holy Spirit, is the author and finisher of
it. By providing the facts through which faith, repentance,
and obedience are evoked; by the choosing and training of
the apostles through whose efforts its establishment was
made possible, Christ is the author of His church. In an
eloquent passage, he says, "so Jesus, in the new creation,
by His Spirit sent down from heaven after his glorification,
did, by a positive, direct, and immediate agency, create one
congregation, one mystical, or spiritual body; and, according
to the constitution or system of the kingdom of heaven, did

15 *Ibid.*, 106.
16 "Millennial Harbinger Abridged," Smith, II, III.

give to that mystical body created in Jerusalem, out of the more ancient earthly kingdom of God, the power of reproducing and multiplying to an indefinite extent. But still this new and spiritual life, is transmitted, diffused, and sustained by the Spirit of God, operating through the constitution, or system of grace ordained in the kingdom of heaven." [17]

This divine creation of the kingdom of heaven, or church, produced an organization in which the Holy Spirit of God should dwell as long as time lasts, and through which His power for the conversion of the world should be exerted. Campbell glories in the fact, also, that this establishment of the kingdom was a wonderful display of divine power. "In setting up the kingdom of heaven, as in setting up the kingdom of nature, there was a display of divinity, compared with everything subsequent, properly supernatural. Hence the array of apostles, prophets extraordinary, teachers, gifts, powers, miracles, etc., etc., etc." [18] It is thus clear that the Church of Christ is a body—the mystical body of Christ on earth, the dwelling place of the Holy Spirit, and the medium through which the work of God in the world is to be accomplished. Its first and greatest purpose is to reproduce other churches of Christ, and for this work it is spiritually prepared, because it is the abiding place of the Spirit of God. "But after this new mystical body of Christ was created and made, it had, and yet has, according to the system of grace under the present administration of the kingdom of heaven, the power of multiplying and replenishing the whole earth, and will do it; for as God breathed into the nostrils of Adam the spirit of life after he had raised him out of the dust; and as he bestowed on His beloved Son Jesus, after he rose out of the water, His Holy Spirit, without measure; so on the formation of the first congregation, figuratively called the body of Christ, Jesus did breathe into it the Holy Spirit to animate and inhabit it till He come again. The only temple and habitation of God on earth, since Jesus

[17] *Ibid.*, I, 263, 264.
[18] "Millennial Harbinger Abridged," Smith, I, 264.

pronounced desolation on that in Jerusalem, is this body of Christ." [19]

There are many by-products of the gospel, but to Campbell the church has done its work in the world, when it reproduces other churches. Everything else beneficent for mankind, is implicit in the establishment of the kingdom of heaven. "Now this first congregation of Christ, thus filled with the Spirit of God, had the power of raising other congregations of Christ; or, what is the same thing, of causing the body of Christ to grow and increase. Thus we see that other congregations were soon raised up in Judea and Samaria, by the members of the Jerusalem body. Many were begotten to God by the Spirit of God, through the members of the first congregation. And since the Spirit himself, ceased to operate in all those splendid displays of supernatural grandeur, by still keeping the disciples of Christ always in remembrance of the things spoken by the holy Apostles, and by all the arguments derived from the antecedent blessings bestowed, working in them both to will and to do according to the benevolence of God, He is still causing the body of Christ to grow and increase in stature, as well as in knowledge and the favor of God. Thus the church of Christ, inspired with His spirit, and having the oracles and ordinances of the reign of heaven, is fully adequate to the conversion of the whole world if she prove not recreant to her Lord." [20]

3. Campbell also defines the church in relation to the kingdom of God. The old kingdom of God was to be found in the Jewish institution. It was a temporal, earthly, kingdom—a theocracy. In this old kingdom, the new kingdom of heaven was implicit. He did not believe, as did some of his followers later, that the term "Church of God" and "Kingdom of God" are synonymous. Neither did he believe that the terms "Kingdom of God" and "Kingdom of Heaven" refer to the same government. The kingdom of God had

[19] *Ibid.*, 264.
[20] "Millennial Harbinger Abridged," Smith, I, 264.

long been the possession of the Jews; the kingdom of heaven was not to be, in any sense of the term, an earthly reign of Christ, but rather a wonderful new spiritual institution, His own divine creation. "When compared with the earthly kingdom of God among the Jews, it is certainly the kingdom of heaven; for Jesus alleges that His kingdom is not of this world; and Daniel affirmed that in the days of the last worldly empire, the God of heaven would set up a kingdom unlike all others than on earth; in which, as Paul teaches, men are blessed with every spiritual blessing in heavenly places in Christ (Eph. 1:3); for he has raised the Jews and Gentiles, and 'has set us down together in the heavenly places in Christ Jesus (Eph. 2.6).' " [21]

There are many elements in a kingdom, such as the territory, the King, the Constitution, subjects, and laws. It is evident that the church and the kingdom cannot, therefore, be exactly the same. "The communities collected and set in order by the Apostles, were called the congregations of Christ, and all these taken together, are sometimes called the kingdom of God. But the phrases 'Church of God' or 'Congregation of Christ,' and the phrases 'Kingdom of Heaven' or 'Kingdom of God,' do not always nor exactly represent the same thing. The elements of the kingdom of heaven, it will be remembered, are not simply its subjects, and, therefore, not simply the congregations of the disciples of Christ, but as these communities possess the oracles of God, are under the laws and institutions of the King, and therefore enjoy the blessings of the present salvation, they are, in the records of the kingdom, regarded as the only constitutional citizens of the kingdom of heaven; and to them exclusively belongs all the present salvation. Their King is now in heaven, but present with them by His Spirit in their hearts, and in all the institutions of His kingdom." [22]

Membership in the church of God is equivalent to that in the kingdom. He believed the church to be but a part of

[21] "Millennial Harbinger Abridged," Smith, I, 241.
[22] *Ibid.*, 260.

the kingdom. In a word, the term "kingdom," has a wider meaning than the term "church." "Every immersed believer, of good behavior, is, by the constitution, a free and full citizen of the kingdom of heaven, and entitled to all the social privileges and honors of that kingdom. Such as these as meet together statedly in one place, in obedience to the King, or his ambassadors, the Apostles, for the observance of all the institutions of the King, compose a family, or house, or congregation of Christ; and all these families or congregations, thus organized, constitute the present kingdom of God in this world. So far, the phrases kingdom of heaven, and the congregation or body of Christ, are equivalent in signification. (Rom. 12:4-8; I Cor. 12:27; Heb. 3:6)." [23]

III

1. As regards the government of the church, Campbell always considered it an absolute monarchy. It is a kingdom of which Christ is the King. To the hypothetical American objection that the realm of God in the world, should be called a republic, he replies that "Monarchy is the only form of government which nature recognizes. It was the first, and it will be the last." [24] (1) A monarchy would always be the best government, the most efficient, the cheapest, and the most dignified, provided only that the crown could be placed upon the "wisest head, and the sceptre wielded by the purest hands." [25] The obvious conclusion which he leaves for the reader to draw from this, is that since Jesus Christ is the wisest and purest of the universe, the government can be safely left in His hands. (2) A second reason for the monarchial form of government, is that it is the best suited for war; the church is an army; a war to the death is on. The kingdom of Christ is, however, but temporary.

[23] "Millennial Harbinger Abridged," I, 260.
[24] "Christian System," 158.
[25] *Ibid.*, 157.

It had a beginning, and it will have an end. He must reign only until he has put all enemies under His feet.[26] "But the transition of the sceptre into the hands of Emmanuel, has not changed the nature of the government. He is now the hereditary monarch of the universe, as well as the proper King of his own kingdom. He now reigns as absolutely over all principalities, hierarchs, and powers, celestial and terrestial, as did the great God and Father of the universe, before He was invested with the regal authority."[27] Jesus, therefore, is King now. He needs not to wait until some future time when His kingdom shall be established. It has already been founded and He has been crowned.

2. The present administration of the Kingdom of Heaven or Church is next considered. Before the ascension of the Lord, he, to whom the Father had given all authority in heaven and on earth (Matt. 28:18), delegated that authority to his apostles. Thus, "the Apostles were plenipotentaries and ambassadors for Jesus, and had all authority delegated to them from the King. Hence, everything was first taught and enjoined by them. They were the first preachers, pastors, overseers, and ministers in the kingdom, and had the direction and management of all its affairs (II Cor. 3:6; 5: 18-20)."[28] Next in rank to those whom the King has left in charge of affairs of the kingdom during his personal absence, are "prophets; next, teachers; then, assistants, or helpers; then directors or presidents, all furnished with gifts, knowledge and character, suited to their respective functions. Besides these, many persons possessed of miraculous powers—gifts of healing and speaking foreign [29] languages,

[26] "Millennial Harbinger Abridged," I, 236.
[27] "Millennial Harbinger Abridged," Smith, I, 238.
[28] *Ibid.*, 259.
[29] Professor C. Anderson Scott's discussion of the "Tongues at Pentecost" is of interest as representative of the modern view. "Ecstatic utterance, requiring, but on the occasion of Pentecost lacking, interpretation to make it comprehensible to the hearers, but utterance which at the same time quickened in those who had some religious feeling in common with the speakers a sympathetic response, an excitation of religious emotion and insight—such appears to have been the phenomenon of glossolalia as mani-

were employed in setting up and putting in order the communities composing the kingdom of Heaven. Angels were also employed, and the still employed, under the great King, in ministering to them that are heirs of salvation. For Jesus now, as Lord of all, has the Holy Spirit at his disposal, and all the angels of God; and these are employed by Him in the affairs of His kingdom (I Cor. 12:28; Eph. 4:11; Heb. 1:14)." [30]

In gathering together the communities, which in the aggregate compose the divine kingdom, the Apostles appointed Bishops or Elders in each congregation or church. The authority which Christ had delegated to them, they still retain. They held it personally during their lifetime, and still hold it in the documents which they wrote, and which are now held by the church as the containers of the precious deposit of divine revelation. It is not according to human nature, nor is it so contemplated by the will of Christ, that his people should be governed by a written document alone. For this reason, the Apostles in each community, appointed

---

fested at Pentecost and after." "What Happened at Pentecost?" in "The Spirit," 129. Professor Vernon Bartlett, while admitting that "there can be little doubt that the former view (the use of foreign languages before unknown to the speakers) of what Acts here intends is correct" ("Acts," 137), yet explains the phenomenon as a gradual coloring of the original facts through successive stages of the tradition until the author describes what was originally but ecstatic praise as actual languages of the multitude then present. ("Acts" 384, 385.) See also his "Apostolic Age," 13, 14. Professor Foakes-Jackson dismisses the whole difficulty in a sentence: "The story is symbolical rather than literal." "Peter, Prince of Apostles," 76. The frank statement of Alford is probably nearer the truth: "There can be no question in any unprejudiced mind that the fact which this narrative sets before us is that the disciples began to speak in various languages, viz.: the languages of the nations below enumerated, and perhaps others. All attempts to evade this are connected with some forcing of the text, or some far-fetched and indefensible explanation." Quoted by McGarvey, "Acts," 22, 23. Meyer admits that the author's meaning is evident but brings to the whole problem the peculiar type of mind which finds no room whatever for the miraculous. "The sudden communication of a facility of speaking foreign languages is neither logically possible nor psychologically and morally conceivable." Quoted by McGarvey, "Acts," 23.

[30] "Millennial Harbinger Abridged," I, 259.

Bishops or Elders to labor in the word of the Lord, and to oversee the affairs of the new spiritual organization. In addition, also, were appointed the Deacons, who were the ministers or stewards of the congregation.

In opposition to the widely held view, that the Bishops are the successors of the Apostles, and that there is, therefore, in the church, an elect order of priests—an order in succession from the Apostles, Campbell developed his doctrine of the nature of the true apostolic succession. "The right to ordain, is then, in popular esteem, a right invested in an order of men, now of eighteen hundred year's continuance, transmitted through many hands; and is, therefore, to us, indirect from Jesus Christ. We, however, for many reasons, are constrained to reject the idea of an elect order in succession in the Christian Church, possessing vested rights, derived not from the community as such, but from Jesus Christ, through a distinct class in the community, as essentially papistical in its tendency, and contrary to the letter and spirit of the Christian institution." [31]

One of the reasons for rejecting the position held by those who believe in such an elect body of rulers within the church, is the fact, that were their claims true, and could the succession be traced back in an unbroken line to the Apostles, and through them to the Master himself, it must be traced through hands that have often been stained with the blood of the saints of Jesus. If this is true, then the Lord has left the Church to seek for her authority to preach, teach, and administer the ordinances, from the hands of her worst enemies. "Or has the grace of ordination descended to us, pure and uncorrupt, through hearts and hands stained with Christian blood? It cannot be. We must look for authority from the Lord more direct and less liable to deterioration than that of which many Catholics and Protestants make their boast." [32] Ordination, or the setting apart of the Bishops or Elders to their holy office, is not thus conferred; it is an

[31] "Millennial Harbinger Abridged," Smith, II, 115, 116.
[32] *Ibid.*, 116.

appointment from those who are to be governed. In answer to the question, "What is ordination as respects the Christian Church?" he replies: "It is the solemn election and appointment of persons to the oversight and service of a christian community. To ordain is to appoint; and all appointments, from that of a successor of Judas as a witness of the resurrection, from an apostle to the messenger of a church, or an almoner, was in the beginning, by election of the whole community (Acts 1:23; 6:3, 5; II Cor. 8:19)." [33]

While it is true that ordination is a setting apart by the whole community, in reality, it is the work of the apostles themselves, in that they, through the Holy Spirit, have set forth those qualifications which must ever be the possessions of all true Bishops of the flock of Christ. Since the citizens of the kingdom are all free men in Christ, "they all have a voice in the selection of the persons whom the Apostles appoint to these offices. The Apostles still appoint all persons so elected, possessing the qualifications which they, by the Holy Spirit, prescribed." [34] Thus it is "the Holy Spirit, and not the congregations, which creates Bishops and Deacons. The Spirit gives the qualifications, both natural and acquired, and, speaking to the congregations in the written oracles, commands their ordination or appointment to the work." [35] The Holy Spirit, through the laying on of hands of the whole community, or its chosen representative, sets apart the Overseer to his ministry. [36]

The true apostolic succession, is that a church shall be in the way of the apostolic churches. In his debate with Rice, he plainly states this as his own conception of the whole mooted question. "When ever then, a christian community legitimately arises out of such circumstances, as already described, sanctioned by the New Testament—that is, holding the same doctrines and ordinances, customs and

[33] *Ibid.*, 116.
[34] "Millennial Harbinger Abridged," I, 261.
[35] *Ibid.*, 261.
[36] *Ibid.*, II, 117, 119. See also, 284, 285.

usages, when it appoints officers, and when they dispense ordinances, they are as divine and authoritative as any other officers and ordinances in any christian community on earth." [37] Authority received through the imposition of the hands of the whole community of saints in any given place, is authority direct from Heaven itself. "It may not be out of order to observe, that if any particular congregation thus elect and ordain its officers by the authority of the Lord, and according to the suggestions of the Holy Spirit, then, in that case, the right and authority of such officers to administer the affairs of the church, is directly derived, not by succession, through ignorant and blood-stained hands, but directly from Heaven. To such Elders, it may in truth be said, 'Take heed to yourselves and to the whole flock over which the Holy Spirit hath constituted you bishops (Acts 20:28).' " [38]

He acknowledges that there is neither a specific command for the ordination of bishops by the whole congregation, nor is there a direct example in the New Testament, of where this was done. He is positive, however, that it may be proven by analogy. The general principle of popular election, can be fully sustained without any such command or example. The deacons were chosen by all the disciples. Other representatives of the church were also appointed in this manner (Acts 15:22; I Cor. 16:3; II Cor. 8:19; 8:23). [39]

In the New Testament, the highest office in a local church, is described by two designations, $\epsilon\eta\grave{\iota}\sigma\kappa\circ\eta\circs$ —bishop and $\eta\rho\epsilon\sigma\beta\acute{\nu}\tau\epsilon\rho\circs$ —elder. The same persons who in Acts 20:17, are denominated elders, are in the twenty-eighth verse of the same chapter, called overseers— $\epsilon\eta\iota\sigma\kappa\acute{\circ}\eta\circus$. Paul left Titus in Crete to ordain elders in every city; but in describing their qualifications, he called them bishops or overseers. The reason for the use of these various terms is obvious. "No

[37] "Campbell-Rice Debate," 583.
[38] "Millennial Harbinger Abridged," II, 120.
[39] *Ibid.*, 291.

one of them expresses all the attributes, properties, and accidents of the other. Elder simply signifies an old man. An overseer is a superintendent—one who has the care and oversight of something. The word bishop is a mere Anglo-Saxon corruption of ἐπίσκοπος; the same that is commonly and correctly rendered overseer. Hence, when contemplated with reference to their age, they are called elders, because they are selected from among the old men. But when regarded with respect to their official relation, they are called overseers or bishops, because their duty was to watch over the flock.[40]

In every properly organized New Testament congregation, there was a plurality of elders.[41] Paul and Barnabas ordained elders in every church. In the debate between Jewish and Gentile converts, the subject was considered by the apostles and elders in Jerusalem. The elders or bishops were all officially equal. Each one, legally ordained, had the right to participate in all the duties and privileges which his office comprehended. There is no record that one bishop was ever appointed over two or more churches. We read of the elders or bishops of the church in Ephesus; of the church in Jerusalem—"of elders ordained in every church, but never of one bishop over two churches." [42]

The distinction between the terms bishop and elder, began early after the death of the apostles,[43] and had its rise in the appointment of one from among the number, to the position of presiding officer in the deliberations of the body, and his gradual exaltation into a separate office. Thus by "translating this influence and presidency to mean church authority, and not distinguishing between moral influence an ecclesiastic power, before the end of the second century, they called the president bishop, 'the bishop,' and others were commonly regarded only as the eldership; and

40 "Millennial Harbinger Abridged," Smith, II, 291.
41 Ibid., 287.
42 Ibid., 122.
43 Ibid., 124.

finally the bishop became the only bishop, and his jurisdiction was extended, first over the city—then, over the suburbs—then, over its vicinity—then, over the province—then, over the world, until it ended in 'His Holiness, the Father universal,' or 'the Pope.' " [44]

IV

Following strictly the statements of the New Testament, Campbell considered the duties of the bishops to be three in number. Law giving is no function of theirs, because no legislative power was given unto them by Christ or the Apostles. "The Messiah was careful to repeat that He taught only what he had heard and learned from the Father. The Apostles were peculiarly attentive to inculcate that they had received from the Lord whatever they taught the disciples; and the primitive elders and bishops gave all attention to inculcate only the commandments of the Apostles of the Lord and Saviour; and James says there is but one law giver, who is able to save and destroy." [45] (1) The first duty of a bishop is that he must be able to teach "the whole counsel of God." [46] In doing this, he must consider the congregation as composed of children, young men, and fathers —he must take into consideration the fact that all are not of the same mental or spiritual capacity; that there are degrees and conditions imposed by birth.[47] Regarding the manner of his teaching, it is the duty of the Bishop to direct the minds of the flock to the faithful study of the divine word, to see that it is read constantly in the assembly of the Church, and that it is applied in every contingency. As teachers, the elders are, also, to see that all the talents of the congregation are developed, that all may serve the Lord effectively. It is not presumed that they are to be the only

[44] *Ibid.*, 125.
[45] "Millennial Harbinger Abridged," Smith, II, 125.
[46] *Ibid.*, 125.
[47] *Ibid.*, 287.

teachers, exhorters, singers, or intercessors in the church. Others there are who are able to do these things, and they must, under the direction and by the permission of the bishops, be encouraged to engage in them. But no one should, for a moment, presume to undertake such service without the permission of the bishops, or under the guidance of the bishop who presides for the day.[48]

(2) The bishop must also "rule well." [49] The work of presiding and that of ruling, while akin, are not exactly the same. Presidency may have regard simply to the work of presiding over a worship meeting of the church or an assembly met to transact business. To "rule well," has respect more immediately to those disorders and divisions of opinion which necessarily arise in every congregation—for even the Church of Christ, since it is a human organization as well as divine, has never been fully exempt from such disturbances. The doctrine of the church is not more important than its discipline for no congregation can be prosperous and happy, no matter how zealous it may be for the great doctrines of the gospel, if it be remiss in its discipline, and allow flagrant transgressions of the law of Christ, to pass by without rebuke.[50] "To rule well, is one of the most difficult attainments. It calls for meekness, candor, firmness, patience, and indefatigible attention to the first indications of remissness or delinquency. So peculiar is the assemblage of attributes requisite to ruling well, that they are more rarely to be met with than the gifts of eloquence and highest didactic powers." [51]

He wisely deposes that one of the finest qualifications in the bishop who rules well, is that he shall have the ability to anticipate and prevent transgression, delinquency, or actual apostacy. This is far better than sternly to rebuke such, when it has actually occurred. That one who best rules his

---

[48] "Millennial Harbinger," Volume for 1838, 127.
[49] "Millennial Harbinger Abridged," Smith, II, 126.
[50] *Ibid.*, 287.
[51] *Ibid.*, 125, 126.

own household according to this method, is more fully qualified to occupy the exalted position of overseer in the flock of God.[52]

(3) Besides the duties of teaching and ruling well, there is a third class comprehended in pastoral visitation for the purpose of edification, good order, and the growth of a congregation.[53] The sick should be visited, the erring should be exhorted—and private teaching and exhortation in such cases, is always perferable to that delivered in public—personal exhortation for sinners to become members of the body of Christ; all these are duties of the true elder or bishop in the church. How far short modern Christianity has fallen of this ideal, is evidenced by the fact, that in reality, all these duties have been imposed upon the one teaching the elder, the preacher or minister of the local church.[54]

The office of deacon is sparingly discussed in Campbell's writings. He defines the office in one brief sentence; "the deacon, as the name imports, is the minister or servant of the congregation. He is the steward, the treasurer, the almoner of the church. The seven, chosen and ordained in the congregation at Jerusalem, were set over the business of supplying the tables of the poor saints and widows. They are a standing institution in the Christian House of God." [55] Very clearly, it was the custom to commit the care of the Lord's table, the bishop's table, and the tables of the poor, to the diaconate. The teaching regarding their office as it is set forth in the Epistles, and the qualifications demanded of them, makes it clear that they must be regarded as were the deacons in the synagogues—"the public servants of the church in all things pertaining to its internal and external relations—in all matters of temporal concern (Acts 6:1-3; Phil. 1:1; I Tim. 3:8-12; Rom. 16:1)." [56] It is apparent

52 *Ibid.*, 126.
53 "Millennial Harbinger Abridged," Smith, II, 127.
54 *Ibid.*, 287.
55 "Millennial Harbinger," Volume for 1838, 127.
56 "Millennial Harbinger Abridged," Smith, II, 127.

from two of these passages, also, that there were deaconesses in the primitive church, as well as deacons. There are many duties to women, in the membership, which demand this. As in the office of bishop, so also in that of deacon, there should be a plurality in every congregation.[57]

3. The church is not only a monarchy: there is a sense in which it is a democracy. In an exposition of order, as respects voting in the church, Campbell interestingly differentiates between those things which are the legitimate subjects upon which a congregation itself may have a decision, and those over which it has no authority. Every thing which is a matter of unquestioned revelation, is entirely out of the sphere in which the church may make any decision concerning it. These things have to do with faith and morality—in a word, with the divine salvation. As regards those items concerning which no clear revelation has been vouchsafed, the church may make her own decisions—she is a democracy. In answer to the question, "on what occasion and for what purposes, are Christians authorized to vote?" he says: "they are not to vote on questions of faith, piety or morality. Truth is not to be settled by a vote, nor is any divine institution, respecting the worship or morality of the Christian church, to be decided by a majority. These are matters of revelation, of divine authority, and to be regulated by a 'thus saith the Lord,' and not by a 'thus saith the majority.' But in all matters not of faith, piety or morality; in all matters of expediency, and sometimes in questions of fact pertaining to cases of discipline, there is no other way of deciding but by vote of the brotherhood." [58]

No principle in his religious thinking is more important than the differentiation which he constantly makes between the moral law and the law of expediency. Moral laws, indeed, are immutable, because the center and heart of them is love, and this can never cease to be the only rational way to human happiness. "Positive precepts, however, prescrib-

[57] "Millennial Harbinger Abridged," Smith, II, 127, 128.
[58] *Ibid.*, 132.

ing the forms of religious and moral action, emanating from God himself, have been changed, and may again be changed, while all the elements of piety and morality are immutable." [59]   Further defining the sphere in which the law of expediency operates, he says: "Still, there are many things left to the law of expediency, concerning which no precepts are found in the apostolic writings.   They are then, in one sentence, those things, or forms of action, which it was impossible or unnecessary to reduce to special precepts; consequently they are not of faith, piety, nor morality; because whatever is of faith, of the worship, or of the morality of Christianity, was both possible and necessary to be promulgated; and is expressly and fully propounded in the sacred scriptures.   The law of expediency, then, has no place in determining the articles of faith, acts of worship, nor principles of morality.   All these require a 'thus sayeth the Lord' in express statements, and the sacred writings have clearly defined and decided them.   But in other matters that may be called the circumstantials of the gospel and of the church of Christ, the people of God are left to their own discretion and to facilities and exigencies of society." [60]

Many things of vital importance to the progress of the kingdom, are left to the law of expediency.   He illustrates this by reference to the manner in which the sacred writings have been preserved, the various translations made, the grinding toil of those, who through the years, have copied and edited the manuscripts which are now ours.   The message is ever the same, the manner in which it comes down to us is regulated by the law of expediency.   The Lord's Supper also furnishes an illustration for his definition.   There is no divine rule, nor even an undisputed precedent, for the observance of the Lord's Supper—how much bread each communicant shall eat, how much wine shall be consumed, who shall partake first, or how the cup shall be conveyed from

[59] "Christian System," 90.
[60] *Ibid.*, 91.

one to the other.[61] "These are all discretionary matters, and left to the prudence and good sense of the Christian communities—in other words, to the law of expediency." [62] In further illustration of those matters which properly belong to this law, he says: "Next to these are meeting houses, baptisteries, Lord's tables, the emblamatic loaf and cup, times of convocation, arrangements for the day, etc. Acts of parliament, decrees of synods and councils, but no apostolic enactments, statutes or laws, are found for any of these important items. There is neither precept nor precedent in the New Testament for building, hiring, buying, or possessing a meeting house; for erecting a baptismal basin, font, or bath; for chancel, altar, table, leavened or unleavened bread, chalace, cup, or tankard, and many other things of equal value." [63]

Nothing has more frequently caused dissention, in one case even to the point of division among the Disciples, than a failure to understand this Campbellian principle. The schism which arose over the position of instrumental music in the worship of the church, resulted from a failure to realize that the whole question belonged to the realm of expediency, and not to that of divine revelation. The opposition of many of the best leaders of the Disciple movement, to the tightening of organizational lines in the furtherance of missionary endeavor, has arisen largely as a result of a misunderstanding regarding the sphere to which the whole question belongs. Since the Master and his Apostles have not left explicit directions as to the manner in which missionary funds may be assembled, it is the consensus of the best Disciple opinion, that the entire matter belongs to the law of expediency, and has, therefore, been left to the enlightened common sense of the people of God. The law of expediency which deals with opinions and methods of procedure, must never be made to apply to those things, which

[61] "Christian System," 92.
[62] *Ibid.*, 92, 93.
[63] *Ibid.*, 93.

because they are clearly matters of divine revelation, belong to "the faith."

In answer to the inquiry—one which in modern times is agitating Disciple ranks—"Who shall ascertain and who shall interpret this law of expediency?" Campbell falls back upon a principle which is uniquely his own, his unswerving faith in the correct judgements of the enlightened common mind. In a word, the majority of those who love the Lord, must always decide such questions, and the minority, as in all social compacts, must quietly bow to its will. There is no other "principle of cooperation, no other law of expediency, which can secure the interests, the union, harmony, and strength of any people, but that of the few submitting to the many." [64] The very nature of the law, and of those matters with which it deals, makes such decisions imperative. "The law of expediency is the law of adopting the best present means of attaining any given end. But this is a matter which the wisdom and good sense of individuals and communities must decide. This is not, this cannot be, a matter of standing revelation." [65] The church has never been unanimous in matters of opinion, as in matters of faith, and the time will never come when it can be. The only rule, then, which may be followed without dissension, is that those who constitute the enlightened majority, shall prevail. Campbell means by enlightened majority, that this shall be composed of those who are seniors in Christ—seniors in the sense that they are not immature spiritually. "The law of expediency enacts that a majority of the seniors shall decide in all cases, what is most expedient to be done in attaining any of the ends commanded in the Christian Institution, the means to which, are not divinely ordained in the written laws of that institution; and that the minority shall cheerfully and conscientiously acquiese in such decisions." [66] Love must be the very heart of the law of expediency, as it is the

[64] "Christian System," 93.
[65] *Ibid.*, 93.
[66] "Christian System," 93, 94.

heart and soul of the whole Christian Institution. When
the members of the church love each other, methods of procedure will be settled according to the law of love, through
the will of the enlightened majority. Without this, there can
be no church of Christ in any sense of the term.

4. In discussing the "Body of Christ," he emphasizes the
necessity for cooperation. Such necessity grows out of the
nature of the kingdom. "This institution, called the congregation of God, is a great community of communities—
not a community representative of communities, but a community composed of many particular communities, each of
which is built on the same foundation, walks according to the
same rules, enjoys the same character, and is under the
jurisdiction of no other community of Christians, but is to
all other communities as an individual disciple is to every
other individual disciple in any one particular community
meeting in a given place." [67] While one congregation has no
authority over another—while all are equal, yet in the aggregate, they form one kingdom of God or Church, and
should cooperate with one another "in all measures promo-
tive of the great ends of Christ's death and resurrection." [68]
To the end that this cooperation shall be actual, frequent
meetings of churches should be held, in order that the members of the various congregations may know each other.[69]
While they may thus cooperate in the promotion of the
kingdom, they have no more authority to legislate on matters of faith or morality, as a cooperative body, than have
the elders or bishops of a local congregation, for "whatever
is a part of the Christian faith or Christian hope—whatever
constitutes ordinances or precepts of worship, or statutes of
moral right and wrong, like the ark of the covenant, is not
to be touched with uninspired and uncommissioned hands."[70]
Thus, as regards matters of faith, worship, righteousness, or

[67] *Ibid.*, 93.
[68] "Christian System," 73.
[69] *Ibid.*, 74.
[70] *Ibid.*, 73.

the doctrine, the piety, and the morality of the gospel, the church may not legislate, for these matters are not legitimate subjects of human legislation, alteration, or arrangement.[71]

Cooperation is one thing—it is Christian and necessary, and belongs to the very nature of the Christian institution —the manner of cooperation is quite another.[72] As to the districts into which churches may be grouped, as to the manner of their collecting and dispensing missionary funds —these things are circumstances of Christ's kingdom, and are the legitimate subjects of legislation and arrangement, on the part of the churches acting as one great body.[73] In this distinction between the Christian necessity for cooperation, and the method of cooperation, he harks back to the difference between faith and opinion, or between matters of revelation and the law of expediency. This is a principle which many of the Disciples in the latter years of their history, have failed utterly to observe. An understanding of it, would have gone far to eliminate some of the unhappy discussions which have occurred regarding their organized missionary program.

V

1. Campbell recognizes two classes of ministers [74] in the history of the Kingdom: those extraordinary, whose business it was to establish the church, and to whom, in order that this work might be completed, extraordinary gifts were vouchsafed; and the ordinary ministry which serves after the kingdom has been founded. The Apostles and Prophets belonged to the first class. When their work of establishment was completed, the miraculous gifts with which they had been endowed, ceased by limitation. The ordinary ministry, that which is standing and immutable, is composed of Bishops, Deacons, and Evangelists. The duties of

[71] *Ibid.*, 74.
[72] *Ibid.*, 73.
[73] *Ibid.*, 75.
[74] "Christian System," 77.

Bishops and Deacons have already been considered. Campbell thought of them, always, as officers or ministers of the local church. The teaching and exhortation was done by the Bishops, and the temporal forms of service were executed by the Deacons. These ministers of the church "all belong to one order, though possessing great diversity of gifts." [75] The idea that because the miraculous gifts, frequently possessed by Bishops and Deacons and generally by Evangelists, have passed away, the offices themselves have lapsed, is erroneous. As long as there are officers, or services to be performed, there must be officers.

2. Evangelists do not belong to a local church as such, but are sent to all the churches. Their work, as the term itself implies, is to devote themselves to preaching the Word, to the making of converts, and the planting of churches. No office in the ancient church required such a variety of gifts. Often the gift of tongues was conferred, although this qualification was not immutably fixed. The gifts bestowed, depended upon the field in which the Evangelist might be called to labor. "His work is to proclaim the word, intelligibly and persuasively—to immerse all the believers, or converts to his ministry—and to plant and organize churches wherever he may have occasion; and then to teach them to keep the commands and ordinances of the Lord." [76] Concerning the origin of the name by which this minister was called in the early church, he says, "Evident, then, it is, that he obtained the title of Evangelist, from his itinerant labors in the gospel, and in the converting of men." [77]

The Evangelist is not only to gather his converts into communities, but he must superintend such infant congregations until they are able to care for themselves. He must "set in order the churches," and see to it that a local ministry is appointed and trained, before he leaves for another field of labor. While every Christian has the right to teach

[75] *Ibid.*, 77.
[76] "Christian System," 78, 79.
[77] *Ibid.*, 80.

and baptize on certain occasions, it is far better that this be done by the regular ministry of the church. "A Christian is, by profession, a preacher of truth and righteousness, both by precept and example. He may, of right, preach, baptize, and dispense the Supper, as well as pray for all men, when circumstances demand it. This concession does not, however, either dispense with the necessity of having evangelists, bishops, and deacons; nor, having them, does it authorize any individual to assume to do what has been given in charge to them. Liberty without licentiousness, and government without tyranny, is the true genius of the Christian Institution." [78]

Evangelists, as well as the other members of the ministry of the church, are to be solemnly set apart to their sacred office, by the imposition of the hands of the presbytery or eldership. "The whole community chooses—the seniors ordain. This is the apostolic tradition (Acts 6:2-6)." [79] This law is unchangeable. "The qualifications for any office are always found in the nature of the office." "When one possesses these qualifications, and has been thoroughly proved, then, and not until then, should he be set aside to the labors of this office." "We say the seniors or elders always ordain. Popery says, 'none but those on whom the apostolic hands have been laid, can of right ordain.' Such an idea is not in the 'Christian System.' The seniors always lay on hands, whether hands have been laid on them or not. This is true Protestantism. Better still, it is true Biblism. Nay, it is the 'Christian System.'" [80] As regards the meaning of "holy hands," he repudiates the notion that they are officially so by a jure divine. He admits that "they are sometimes, but not always." [81] Hands become holy when they have long served the Lord in his holy cause. "Christian elders (for I do not mean mere old men) who have long

[78] "Christian System," 81.
[79] *Ibid.*, 82.
[80] *Ibid.*, 83.
[81] *Ibid.*, 83.

walked in the ways of the Lord, have holy hands, and much more power with and from the Lord, than ever dwelt in any pontiff or pretended vicar of Christ." [82]   Such men, elected or appointed to their office, by the whole community of the faithful, can lay their hands on any person, for any office to which the church elects them, for the "community, the church, the multitude of the faithful, are the fountains of official power. The power descends from the body itself— not from its servants." [83]   In a somewhat caustic statement, he sums up his whole position on the authority through which the ministry of the church, received its office. "But the body of Christ, under Him as its head and animated by His Spirit, is the fountain and spring of all official power and privilege. How much surer and purer is the ecclesiastic authority thus derived from Christ the head, immediately through His body, than when derived through a long, doubt- ful, corrupt, dynasty of bishops and pontiffs!   The church is the mother of all the sons and priests of God; and to look for authority to her servants or creatures, as do all sorts of Papists, whether Catholic or Protestant, is to worship and serve the creature more than the Creator—a species of idolatry worthy only of the darkest night or the darkest day of the dark ages." [84]

Many abuses had grown up in the rapidly growing Disci- ple movement incident to the somewhat haphazard method of appointing ministers. Campbell flames forth again and again against these slipshod methods because of their lack of appreciation of the dignity of the position to which young and frequently blatantly egotistical boys were too often thoughtlessly ordained. The results were slow in coming but eventually there came about a very much higher realiza- tion of the necessity of a well-trained and solemnly set apart ministry of the word. In one passage he sums up his posi- tion as regards the ministry and their place in the Church.

[82] *Ibid.*, 83.
[83] "Christian System," 83.
[84] *Ibid.*, 84.

"We have since the day of our renunciation of human creeds till now, renounced and abjured the application of the law of the Aaronic priesthood as the law of the Christian ministry. The laws of priesthood ended in Christ. He is the end of that law for sacerdotal righteousness to every Christian Church under heaven, as much as he is the end of all legal observances 'for righteousness to everyone that believes.' Still I believe in ordination by the imposition of hands, fasting, and prayer, because it was so done in the church when all its plenipotentiaries were on earth; because, in the judgement of Christ, and in that of His apostles, it was expedient and necessary to the good order of the Christian communities. Even so is it now. Still the idea of hereditary official grace is not found on the pages of the New Testament. Elders or seniors, indeed are the proper persons to ordain, by and with the consent of the church. But elders as a distinct class in the church, and independent of it, belong to the church of Rome, the church of England, the church of John Wesley; and, perhaps, in a somewhat qualified sense, to the church of John Calvin. But to the apostolic church the idea of a sacerdotal line, a priestly lineage, or a classic and hereditary priesthood, is a foreign and barbarian appendage." [85]

VI

A summary of Campbell's position in regard to the nature of the Christian organization reveals the fact that he takes ground about half way between Presbyterianism and Congregationalism. It is clear from the whole tenor of his writings that he did not believe in what he termed "Mere Independency"—indeed he abhorred it—on every occasion he fiercely assailed it. He would not be in sympathy at all with what some modern Disciples mean when they speak feelingly of "the autonomy of the local congregation." He notes the rise of the ultra-congregational theory. "Soon as

[85] "Christian Messenger," VII, 22.

disrespect for hereditary office, or, what is the same thing in effect, under another name, for Bishops from succession from the apostles, the partiality for what we have called lay bishops, or those chosen without regard to such sacerdotal and hereditary ordination, gradually increased, and Independency was born. This among many protestants became a popular theory, and they undertook to reform the church by making every congregation a sort of kingdom of Christ within itself." [86]   The fondness of the Baptists for this type of polity receives passing consideration and while commending them for their evident improvements upon the system he makes the spirited observation that because of the "fierce democracy of their congregational movements and disciplinary proceedings, they have been the most disputatious, feeble, and factionable people on earth." [87]   He again raps the ultra-Congregational theory. "There must, then, be some great mistake in the minds of those who imagine that Christ's kingdom is a collection of ten thousand particular communities, each one being wholly absolved from any respect, cooperation, inspection or subordination in reference to any work or purpose necessary to the carrying out and perfecting that grand system of sanctification and conversion which began in Jerusalem under the rich effusion of the Holy Spirit." [88]   In another connection he warns against extremes: "We have not yet to learn that the two extremes of all sorts of governments are absolute tyranny and fierce democracy." [89]   He did not believe in independency which eventuated in anarchy and revolt against all order. Those who would so accuse him have misunderstood or perverted his message.

In "The Nature of the Christian Organization" he summarizes in brilliant manner his conception of just what that organization was in New Testament times, and what, there-

[86] *Ibid.*, VI, 159.
[87] *Ibid.*, VI, 159, 160.
[88] "Christian Messenger," VI, 160.
[89] *Ibid.*, VII, 22.

fore, it ought now to be. He assumes a hypothetical missionary tour of two evangelists to the island of Guernsey whose evangelistic efforts result in the establishment of five churches. These congregations in the aggregate constitute "the whole church in the island of Guernsey." [90] The oneness of the church is emphasized again and again. They are not independent entities having no interest in the other congregations of like faith and order but a body—the body of Christ in that locality, and they bear to one another the same relation as all of them bear to the church throughout the world. While this is the New Testament theory basic to their foundation they do not act as a body or one church until a meeting of "all the elders and deacons of all the churches" is convened at the oldest and most exemplary of the congregations to consider the most approved plan under which they may act as a unit. This assembly draws up eight resolutions in which the rights of the churches as individual congregations and their duties as constituents of the whole Church of God are carefully defined.[91] As setting forth the Campbellian conception of the true Christian organization the eighth is peculiarly interesting. It deposes that "as all moral and religious duties are the result of direct and positive enactments, so all economical and prudential duties, not directly and positively enjoined because circumstantial and contingent on the unstable and mutable forms of political society and human revolutions, are in their nature and design conventional, and must be enacted by the authority of the whole community; and then, like the by-laws of all other corporations, when agreed to, are to be conscientiously respected and obeyed by all the good and orderly constituents or members of that community." [92] The limits of congregational authority are here clearly set forth. In matters which have been revealed—in things of faith the whole church may not legislate; in those things which

[90] *Ibid.*, IX, 368.
[91] *Ibid.*, IX, 369, 370.
[92] "Christian Messenger," IX, 370.

are rather circumstantials, or, as we have already considered, those which rightfully belong to the realm of expediency the whole body of Christ through its messengers or elders and deacons may speak, and their findings are to be conscientiously respected and obeyed by all the members of the community of Christ. The private rights, privileges, and duties of the individual congregations are to be respected and not interfered with by the body as a whole. Among these may be enumerated "the election and appointment of their congregational officers. That each church should have its own eldership and diaconate, and at least one president-elder, whose whole time should be sacred to the calls and supervision of the church; for which services he shall be supported by the brethren so far as his needs require, and their abilities allow." [93] There can be no doubt but that in this statement we have a swing away from the rigid conception of the ministry which characterized his first writings. This has already been considered but he should be noted here as definitely tending in the direction of the so-called "one man ministry."

Where occasion arises for the appointment of general officers, or those representative of the whole body of Christ —such as evangelists—"a concurrence of a plurality of churches by their officers (shall) be regarded necessary, if not to empower them to discharge official duties in a single congregation, at least necessary to give them general acceptance, and to constitute them public and responsible agents of the whole body." [94] While he does not here explicitly affirm it, there can be no doubt but that on this principle missionary directors, and missionaries themselves, should be elected by a meeting or assembly of the whole church, and sent out by them, and, as such, to be responsible to the body sending them forth. In his plan there is provision for such meetings and their nature is stated: "that whenever any great question of finance, or the means of

93 *Ibid.*, IX, 370, 371.
94 *Ibid.*, IX, 371.

successfully prosecuting any great public object, or any other event of great public interest shall require it, a special, general meeting of messengers from all the congregations shall be called by the person who presided at the last general meeting; and that the eldership and diaconates of all the congregations, or so many of them as can attend, shall always be at least a portion of the messengers who shall attend on such occasions." [95]   Here he takes high ground in his conception of the organization of the Christian community.   It avoids the crying dangers of ultra-Congregationalism; it does not go as far as rigid Presbyterianism.   It leaves the individual churches free in matters of private concern to exercise their own will while making possible a strong organization for the vigorous prosecution of the Gospel ends.   The largest measure of congregational liberty consistent with that virile unity essential to a world proclamation of the truth of God, is allowed.

It is illuminating to note the concurrence of two great modern authorities with this Campbellian position regarding the Christian organization and their contention that it is essentially that which the New Testament describes to us. Harnack writes: "Designed to be essentially a brotherhood, and springing out of the synagogue, the Christian society developed a local organization which was of double strength, superior to anything achieved by the societies of Judaism. One extremely advantageous feature of these local organizations in their significance for Christianity fails to be added.   It was this: every community was at once a unit, complete in itself; but it was also a reproduction of the collective church of God, and it had to recognize and manifest itself as such."   In a footnote on this paragraph he continues: "We do not know how this remarkable conviction arose, but it lies perfectly plain upon the surface of the apostolic and post-apostolic ages.   It did not originate in Judaism—since to my knowledge—the individual Jewish

[95] "Christian Messenger," IX, 371.

synagogue did not look upon itself in this light. Nor did
the conception spring up at a single stroke. Even in Paul
two contradictory conceptions still lie unexplained together;
for while on the one hand he regards each community, so
to speak, as a 'Church of God,' sovereign, independent, and
responsible for itself, on the other hand his churches are
at the same time his own creations, which consequently remain under his control and training, and are in fact even
threatened by him with the rod. He is their father and
their schoolmaster. Here the apostolic authority, and, what
is more, the general and special authority, of the apostle as
the founder of the church, invade and delimit the authority
of the individual community, since the latter has to respect
and follow the rules laid down and enforced by the Apostle
throughout all his churches. This he had the right to expect. But, as we see him from the epistles to the Corinthians, and especially from the second, conflicts were
inevitable. Then again in 3 John we have an important
source of information, for here the head of the local church
is openly rebelling and asserting his independence against
the control of an apostle who attempts to rule the church
by means of messengers. When Ignatius reached Asia not
long afterwards, the idea of the sovereignty of the individual
church had triumphed." [96]

Weizäcker points out the foundation upon which the
primitive Church found an enduring unity in all matters
pertaining to the good of the whole community with liberty
in regard to those of individual concern. "The essential
foundations on which were based the existence of the individual Church and the regulation of the intercourse of its
members were furnished by the ministry of the word,
through which the Church was instituted and supported, and
by the possession of the Holy Scripture and of the sayings
of Jesus. These two sets of conditions taken together gave
a concrete form to the inner power of the religion, a form

[96] "Expansion of Christianity," II, 47, 48.

that rested by means of the Apostolate wholly on the person and mission of Jesus Himself, and that warranted the Church and believers, united spontaneously on this foundation, being represented as the body and members of Christ.

This explains the indisputable fact that each community governed itself, and in all important affairs framed its own decrees, and that accordingly the decrees were passed by the exercise of an equal right on the part of all the members.

That such a state of affairs prevailed in the Primitive Church is sufficiently evident from the Acts. The Church elected and appointed to offices and missions: thus the vice-Apostle Matthias (1:25), the seven deacons (VI:5), Barnabas to be its representative at Antioch (XI:22). It passed judgement on Peter's procedure at Caesarea (XI:1, 4), and on Paul's principles (XV. 12, 22 f., XXI. 22). Paul's narrative of the course of his case in Jerusalem (Gal. 11:1 ff.) could only verify this state of matters. And it existed side by side with the active ministry of the Apostles." [97] In another connection, after instancing all the cases in which the Church made her own decisions, he concludes: "In all these respects the community was fully empowered to exercise the most important right, choosing representatives, holding courts, and making collections among its adherents for definite purposes. An ecclesiastical office endowed with independent authority could not subsist along with this self-government. It could only take the form of a ministry whose warrant rested from day to day on the voluntary approval of the members, just as it began with a free offer of self, and was therefore included by Paul among the charismata (I Cor. 12:28; Rom. 22:7 f.)." [98]

Agreeing with Campbell that all authority comes originally from Christ Himself, through the word which is the precious deposit committed to His Church, it would be evident that even that of Paul was moral and not ecclesiastical.

[97] "Apostolic Age," II, 309.
[98] Ibid., 314.

The local community through her elected and ordained representatives decides on matters of expediency as regards individual matters, and as a body on those things which concern the whole community in its world program for the Master.

And now we have come to the end of our long study. In the light of the Campbellian discussion of the Christian Organization we are enabled to see what he meant by his ever-recurring phrase "The Restoration of the ancient order of things" and what modern Disciples mean when they talk and write about the restoration of Primitive Christianity. Christian unity by a return to New Testament Christianity —this is the heart of the Campbellian plea. It is probable that there exists at the present time, more misunderstanding in regard to this phase of Disciple advocacy—the so-called Restoration movement—than any other position which they have preached. There is manifestly a modern indifference to the plea for a restoration of primitive Christianity, if a restoration of the New Testament Church exactly as it was, is contemplated. The fact of the matter is that the modern man does no want to reproduce the Church just as it was in the beginning. If this is what the Disciples have meant, it is certain that they have been committed to the static conception of the Church,—that it is an unchangeable organization, the plan of which was ordained by the Lord, executed by the Apostles, and thus, being divinely constituted, an institution to be forever the same. It does not seem to admit of reasonable doubt that this was the position at first held by both the Campbells. That a restoration of the organization and the forms of worship which obtained in the first Church, would bring about Christian unity, seems to be the solemn conviction of that Declaration and Address." It soon became apparent that a return to these original forms would not accomplish the results so confidently expected. It is significant that, at the present time, those churches which have contended for this as the essence of the Campbellian plea, have failed, not only to bring about

Christian unity, but also to make any appreciable progress. That this, however, was not the true genius of the plea, is evidenced by the example of Campbell himself. The evolution in his own positions is well established. His bitter opposition to missionary organizatons in the early numbers of the "Christian Baptist," and his eventful advocacy of a missionary organization and acceptance of the presidency of it, is an illustration in point. The position which he took, also, regarding the character of the ministry, underwent a marked change. In his early preaching he was definitely opposed to the one-man ministry; before his death he writes of the work of the pastor of the local church, contrasting it with that of the evangelist.[99] His vigorous insistence upon the law of expediency, in the "Christian System," in contrast to his father's almost timid handling of it, in the "Declaration and Address," and his own first views of it, evidences this evolution.

It is in this very law of expediency, that the Disciples have found their escape from the inevitable stagnation and death to which a purely static conception of the New Testament Church, would have consigned them. The gospel is clear; we must preach it; we must be united upon it; the manner of our taking it to the world, is left to the good sense of the people of God. Methods belong to the realm of expediency, and must be decided by the majority of the congregation. Thus it is that the dictum of Thomas Campbell, so solemnly pronounced at the meeting in the home of Abraham Altars, "Where the Scriptures speak, we speak; and where the Scriptures are silent, we are silent," has been, in practice, absolutely reversed, as with increasing clarity, the law of expediency has been understood. The modern Disciple recites it in other words: "Where the Scriptures speak, we are silent (it is ours to obey); (where the common mind has spoken as to the indisputable truth of revelation, we accept it, and follow it) where the Scriptures are

[99] "Millennial Harbinger Abridged," II, 323.

silent, we may speak." This view of it, alone, has made vital the principle "in faith unity, and in opinions liberty." It is significant that the only division which the Discples have ever experienced, was occasioned by a failure to understand the difference between faith and expediency. A small band of "Antis" or "Non-Progressives," as they are called in the United States, seceded from the Disciples because they were opposed to the introduction of instrumental music into the worship of the Church, and because they did not believe Missionary Societies to be Scriptural. These two things, belonging to the realm of expediency, should have been treated as such, and division averted. The "Antis," however, refused so to consider them, and, making the whole issue a question of faith, withdrew from the main body. Their gradual disappearance as a communion, is evidence that a misapplication of the Campbellian principles, eventuates in stagnation and decay.

It is a long road from the small country churches of Campbell's day, to the great congregations, with sometimes two to five thousand members, of which the Disciples are now so proud. With the development of organizational life, new offices in the Church have been created, such as that of "Director of Religious Education" or "Secretary of the Board of Church Erection." The changing age demands a change in methods. It has been in these, that the Disciples have departed farthest from the platform of Campbell's day. The main contentions for which he battled, are still held to be valid, by the majority of those who have accepted his teachings.

The true meaning of the plea for a restoration of New Testament Christianity, must be found in the Campbellian emphasis upon the inerrancy of the devout common mind, and the consistency with which this underlying philosophical principle was applied to the problems of the Church. Motivated by the passion for Christian unity, the conviction was borne in upon the minds of the Campbells, that it could be accomplished only as a ground common to all followers of the Master, could be discovered. It was soon clear that this universally acknowledged common ground was that which had been plainly revealed in the New Testament. In a word, it was found that the great fundamental things— those which all Christians acknowledged to be fundamental —were the glorious Christian facts which had created the New Testament Church. This courageous acceptance of the pronouncements of the common mind, resulted in a very definite body of convictions regarding primitive Christianity. This method through which they came to their present accepted doctrinal basis, may be illustrated. The Campbellian position on baptism, was reached through a conviction, after years of study, that the overwhelming consensus of scholarship was on the side of the immersion of a penitent believer, as the undoubted form of baptism which the New Testament sanctions. The universal reason had spoken on the subject, and the only thing they could do, committed as they were to this principle, was unhesitatingly to accept its conclusions. It was not because he had come to this position himself, that Alexander was immersed, but because he was convinced that this was what the common mind of the Church believed the New Testament to teach on the subject. The same thing may be illustrated by the acceptance of congregational government, by the Disciples. They did not stress this as absolutely authoriative, but followed it as preferable to others, and as most probably having the weight of New Testament authority behind it. They observed the Lord's Supper weekly, because they believed the New Testament precedent was in favor of it. Since the common mind had not spoken with the same unanimity, upon this ordinance, as it had on the question of baptism, they did not lay the same stress upon it as upon other points of their advocacy. The opposition to human creeds and confessions, and their insistance upon the New Testament baptismal confession as sufficient, was dictated by the belief that the overwhelming consensus of scholarship had agreed that the simple confession of Christ as Lord, was the only form known in the New Testament era. The names they wear, "Disciple," "Christian," etc., are worn because they are common to all who love the Lord Jesus, and are the undoubted names which were worn by His followers in the New Testament Church.

It is manifest that what the Disciples mean by a restoration of New Testament Christianity, has its roots in their great basis conception, that faith is personal rather than doctrinal. There can be no gainsaying the fact, that for a hundred years and more, there has been the increasing realization that what the Campbells were striving for, was a return to the position which would best express the mind and spirit of Jesus. In name, in confession, in baptism, in all they plead for, there is the ever growing conviction that all the honor and glory should be given to Him. They would restore the New Testament Church, because they have believed that it best expresses the will of Christ. But, as we have been trying to say, it is not to be the Church as the Apostles left it, in the sense that no progress is to be made, with the shifting years. It is to be a restoration of the Church of the New Testament, in its faith, in its zeal, but free to proclaim its never changing message, through ever changing methods, to the swiftly changing years.

the New Testament era. The names they wear "Disciple," "Christian," etc., are worn because they are common to all who love the Lord Jesus, and are the undoubted names which were worn by His followers in the New Testament Church.

It is manifest that what the Disciples mean by a restoration of New Testament Christianity has its roots in their great basis conception, that faith is personal rather than doctrinal. There can be no gainsaying the fact that for a hundred years and more there has been the increasing realization that what the Campbells were striving for, was a return to the position which would best express the mind and spirit of Jesus. In name, in confession, in baptism, in all they plead for, there is the ever growing conviction that all the honor and glory should be given to Him. They would restore the New Testament Church, because they have believed that it best expresses the will of Christ. But, as we have been trying to say, it is not to be the Church as the Apostles left it, in the sense that no progress is to be made with the shifting years. It is to be a restoration of the Church of the New Testament, in its faith, in its zeal, but free to proclaim its never changing message through ever changing methods to the swiftly changing years.